A Guide to
The Norton Reader
TENTH EDITION

A Guide to

The Norton Reader

TENTH EDITION

Linda H. Peterson
Yale University

John C. Brereton
University of Massachusetts, Boston

Joan E. Hartman
College of Staten Island, City University of New York

W. W. NORTON & COMPANY
New York • London

Cover illustration: Barbara Zaring, *Aspen Procession*, 1997 (detail).
Collection of Wallace Lankford. Photo courtesy of the artist.

ISBN 0-393-97554-1 (pbk.)

W. W. Norton & Company, Inc., 500 Fifth Avenue, New York, N.Y. 10110
    www.wwnorton.com
W. W. Norton & Company Ltd., 10 Coptic Street, London WC1A 1PU

1 2 3 4 5 6 7 8 9 0

Contents

* Indicates selections included in the *Shorter Edition*.

HUMAN NATURE

CULTURAL CRITIQUE

Index of Rhetorical Modes

NARRATION

Dorothy Allison: *Gun Crazy* (NR 275, SE 149, G 65)
Maya Angelou: *Graduation* (NR 1, SE 1, G 1)
Margaret Atwood: *True North* (NR 162, SE 91, G 40)
Lord Chesterfield: *Letter to His Son* (NR 670, G 177)
Judith Ortiz Cofer: *More Room* (NR 158, SE 83, G 39)
Annie Dillard: *Terwilliger Bunts One* (NR 149, SE 74, G 37)
Frederick Douglass: *Learning to Read* (NR 428, SE 224, G 110)
Loren Eiseley: *The Brown Wasps* (NR 66, SE 45, G 15)
Robert Finch: *Very Like a Whale* (NR 618, SE 336, G 164)
Amitav Ghosh: *The Ghosts of Mrs. Gandhi* (NR 805, SE 454, G 208)
Dagoberto Gilb: *Northeast Direct* (NR 1009, G 253)
Langston Hughes: *Salvation* (NR 1094, SE 616, G 270)
N. Scott Momaday: *The Way to Rainy Mountain* (NR 177, SE 87, G 44)
Sherwin B. Nuland: *The Strangled Heart* (NR 297, G 72)
Edward Rivera: *First Communion* (NR 1096, SE 618, G 271)
Scott Russell Sanders: *Under the Influence* (NR 138, SE 63, G 35)
William J. Scheick: *Books Oft Have Such a Charm* (NR 432, G 111)
Gary Soto: *The Guardian Angel* (NR 72, SE 51, G 16)
Fred Strebeigh: *The Wheels of Freedom: Bicycles in China*
 (NR 198, G 48)
James Thurber: *University Days* (NR 471, SE 236, G 119)
Sallie Tisdale: *We Do Abortions Here: A Nurse's Story*
 (NR 720, SE 391, G 190)
Barbara Tuchman: *"This Is the End of the World": The Black Death*
 (NR 765, SE 417, G 200)
Alice Walker: *Beauty: When the Other Dancer Is the Self*
 (NR 44, SE 34, G 10)
E. B. White: *Once More to the Lake* (NR 74, SE 53, G 17)
Walt Whitman: *Abraham Lincoln* (NR 92, G 23)
Patricia J. Williams: *The Death of the Profane: A Commentary on the*
 Genre of Legal Writing (NR 556, G 143)
Terry Tempest Williams: *The Clan of One-Breasted Women*
 (NR 663, SE 356, G 175)

DESCRIPTION

Edward Abbey: *The Serpents of Paradise* (NR 613, SE 331, G 163)
Michael J. Arlen: *The Tyranny of the Visual* (NR 1067, G 266)
Arthur C. Clarke: *The Light of Common Day* (NR 955, G 241)
Richard Conniff: *Spineless Wonders: Leapers* (NR 622, G 165)
Joan Didion: *On Going Home* (NR 50, G 11)

EXPOSITION

Essays That Classify and Divide

Essays That Define

PERSUASION/ARGUMENT

Thematic Table of Contents

GENDER AND SEXUALITY

Judith Ortiz Cofer: *More Room* (NR 158, SE 83, G 39)
Herb Goldberg: *In Harness: The Male Condition* (NR 349, SE 198, G 85)
Charles Lamb: *A Bachelor's Complaint of the Behaviour of Married People* (NR 270, G 64)
Dorothy Guies McGuigan: *To Be a Woman and a Scholar* (NR 488, SE 264, G 125)
Casey Miller and Kate Swift: *Who's in Charge of the English Language?* (NR 550, SE 289, G 141)
Anna Quindlen: *Between the Sexes, A Great Divide* (NR 263, SE 142, G 61)
Adrienne Rich: *Taking Women Students Seriously* (NR 482, SE 258, G 123)
Betty Rollin: *Motherhood: Who Needs It?* (NR 354, SE 203, G 86)
Scott Russell Sanders: *Looking at Women* (NR 253, SE 132, G 59)
Andrew Sullivan: *What Is a Homosexual?* (NR 266, SE 145, G 63)
Paul Theroux: *Being a Man* (NR 251, G 58)

RACE, CLASS, AND ETHNICITY

Gloria Anzaldúa: *How to Tame a Wild Tongue* (NR 537, SE 283, G 136)
James Baldwin: *Stranger in the Village* (NR 375, G 90)
Judith Ortiz Cofer: *More Room* (NR 158, SE 83, G 39)
Malcolm Gladwell: *The Sports Taboo* (NR 278, SE 152, G 67)
Zora Neale Hurston: *How It Feels to Be Colored Me* (NR 10, G 2)
June Jordan: *For My American Family: A Belated Tribute to a Legacy of Gifted Intelligence and Guts* (NR 154, SE 79, G 38)
Maxine Hong Kingston: *Tongue-Tied* (NR 527, SE 273, G 133)
Gloria Naylor: *"Mommy: What Does 'Nigger' Mean?"* (NR 525, SE 271, G 132)
Vanessa Ochs: *Not in My Backyard* (NR 368, G 89)
Jonathan Rauch: *In Defense of Prejudice* (NR 677, SE 365, G 181)
Richard Rodriguez: *Aria* (NR 531, SE 277, G 134)
Brent Staples: *Black Men and Public Space* (NR 384, SE 217, G 91)
Shelby Steele: *The Recoloring of Campus Life* (NR 387, G 92)
Marianna De Marco Torgovnick: *On Being White, Female, and Born in Bensonhurst* (NR 52, G 12)
Patricia J. Williams: *The Death of the Profane: A Commentary on the Genre of Legal Writing* (NR 556, G 143)

CRIME AND VIOLENCE

Dorothy Allison: *Gun Crazy* (NR 275, SE 149, G 65)
Debra Dickerson: *Who Shot Johnny?* (NR 398, SE 220, G 94)
Amitav Ghosh: *The Ghosts of Mrs. Gandhi* (NR 805, SE 454, G 208)

Gary Soto: *The Guardian Angel* (NR 72, SE 51, G 16)
Paul Tillich: *The Riddle of Inequality* (NR 1132, SE 647, G 280)
Zen Parables (NR 1088, G 269)

HOME AND FAMILY

Judith Ortiz Cofer: *More Room* (NR 158, SE 83, G 39)
Joan Didion: *On Going Home* (NR 50, G 11)
Annie Dillard: *Terwilliger Bunts One* (NR 149, SE 74, G 37)
Henry Louis Gates, Jr.: *In the Kitchen* (NE 334, G 80)
June Jordan: *For My American Family: A Belated Tribute to a Legacy of
    Gifted Intelligence and Guts* (NR 154, SE 79, G 38)
N. Scott Momaday: *The Way to Rainy Mountain* (NR 177, SE 87, G 44)
Edward Rivera: *First Communion* (NR 1096, SE 618, G 272)
Richard Rodriguez: *Aria* (NR 531, SE 277, G 134)
Scott Russell Sanders: *Under the Influence* (NR 138, SE 63, G 35)
Gary Soto: *The Guardian Angel* (NR 72, SE 51, G 16)
Marianna De Marco Torgovnick: *On Being White, Female, and
    Born in Bensonhurst* (NR 52, G 12)
Virginia Woolf: *My Father: Leslie Stephen* (NR 134, SE 59, G 33)

FOREIGN PLACES AND OTHER CULTURES

James Baldwin: *Stranger in the Village* (NR 375, G 90)
Cathy Davidson: *From the Best of Japanese Families* (NR 444, G 115)
Charlotte Gray: *The Temple of Hygiene* (NR 193, G 47)
Pico Iyer: *The Contagion of Innocence* (NR 310, G 75)
Jamaica Kincaid: *The Ugly Tourist* (NR 595, SE 320, G 159)
George Orwell: *Shooting an Elephant* (NR 842, SE 471, G 216)
Fred Strebeigh: *The Wheels of Freedom: Bicycles in China* (NR198, G 48)

EDUCATION AND SCHOOLS

Maya Angelou: *Graduation* (NR 1, SE 1, G 1)
Benjamin R. Barber: *America Skips School* (NR 453, G 116)
Caroline Bird: *College Is a Waste of Time and Money* (NR 463, G 118)
Cathy Davidson: *From the Best of Japanese Families* (NR 444, G 115)
Frederick Douglass: *Learning to Read* (NR 428, SE 224, G 110)
John Holt: *How Teachers Make Children Hate Reading*
    (NR 436, SE 228, G 113)
William J. Scheick: *Books Oft Have Such a Charm* (NR 432, G 111)
Brent Staples: *Why Colleges Shower Their Students with A's* (NR 405, G 97)
Shelby Steele: *The Recoloring of Campus Life* (NR 387, G 92)
James Thurber: *University Days* (NR 471, SE 236, G 119)
William Zinsser: *College Pressures* (NR 475, SE 241, G 121)

Preface: To the Instructor

We have prepared this *Guide* in order to offer collegial advice about using *The Norton Reader*. Occasionally we have drawn on materials from earlier *Guides*, retaining entries we found imaginative and practicable but substituting our own ideas when we thought them likely to produce better classroom discussion. More often we have written completely new entries, drawing on our combined experiences as writing teachers and our enthusiasm for the essays new to the tenth edition. Not every suggestion will work for every instructor, nor will every writing assignment work for every student. But we have tried hard to be helpful—even when that has meant including more suggestions than any single instructor can use in any single class.

In conceiving the *Guide*, we have kept in mind the various kinds of writing courses for which *The Norton Reader* is well suited. One model for freshman composition calls essentially for serious, solid essays that first-year college students will enjoy reading and writing about. Textbooks for such courses are often labeled "liberal arts readers" or just "college readers," suggesting that they introduce students to the college curriculum even as they improve critical thinking and writing. Whether or not you use this label, we think *The Norton Reader* ideal for such a course, and we have tried to suggest discussion questions and writing assignments that will engage students seriously in significant issues, in and out of the academy. You will find a syllabus for a version of this course, "Great Ideas and Enduring Questions," at the end of this *Guide*.

The Norton Reader works well in other kinds of writing courses, too, including those that focus on writing in the disciplines, those that address contemporary debates in North American culture, and those that focus on the essay form itself. Writing across the curriculum, one of the major pedagogical movements of the last decade, has reshaped the thinking of many of us who teach composition; it has reminded us not only of the importance of writing to learn but also of the discipline-specific nature of academic discourse. For instructors who use a writing-across-the-curriculum approach, the second half of *The Norton Reader* will prove especially valuable—as will, we hope, our suggestions in the *Guide*. We have tried to send students back to sources, for example, to see how a professional historian works or to compare the prose of a scholar writing for a lay audience versus for fellow academics. For units representing a range of discourse, we have tried to include questions that get at discourse conventions within disciplines, as well as at rhetorical options that individual writers may—or may not—choose to exercise.

If you prefer to focus your reading and writing on contemporary cultural debates, we urge you to consider a syllabus based on the "Cultural Critique" section, with additional essays from "Human Nature," "Education," "Nature and the Environment," and "Philosophy and Religion." We have labeled the section "Cultural Critique" to acknowledge that a major tradition of the essay focuses on analyzing and reforming culture, but in fact *The Norton Reader* includes essays of contemporary relevance in every section—whether on ethnicity in "People, Places" and "Language and Communication," on gender in "Human

Nature," on race in "Cultural Critique," or on American religion in "Philosophy and Religion." If you choose, you can build an entire course on issues of race, ethnicity, class, and gender—as we have done in another sample syllabus in the last pages of the *Guide*.

If you plan to teach a course that emphasizes argument and persuasion, we encourage you to start with a new section in this edition: "Op-Eds." The short pieces we've included were published in major newspapers or magazines and represent what is often called "civic discourse." Each writer has taken an issue of public debate and clearly argued a position within that debate, whether on gun control (Ivins), assisted suicide (Huttman, Sandel, Walzer), grade inflation (Staples), or the abuse of the English language (Baker). For more extended arguments, the "Ethics" section is particularly useful in that it contains longer essays, but as the syllabus on "Persuasion and Argument" shows, there are examples of argument in virtually every section of the *Reader*.

Finally, *The Norton Reader* offers a superb resource for courses that focus on the essay as a literary and social genre. The early sections of the *Reader*—"Personal Report," "People, Places," "Prose Forms: Journals," "Cultural Critique"—reproduce some of the best essays and essayists of the last half-century, whereas the later sections include many fine examples of what is often called "the literature of fact." In writing the *Guide*, we have retained questions with a literary slant—questions about style, tone, persona, and rhetorical techniques—and we have suggested assignments that give students the opportunity to experiment with various forms of the essay genre. But we have also added questions that explore the personal, social, and political uses of the essay—so that classes can, if their instructors feel so inclined, think about how an essay situates itself at a historical moment for a specific rhetorical purpose.

The *Guide* follows the contents of *The Norton Reader*, Tenth Edition, and provides suggestions for teaching every selection. It can, of course, be used with the Shorter Edition, and our entries give page numbers for both editions. The Index of Rhetorical Modes (pp. xi–xvi) and the Thematic Table of Contents (pp. xvii–xix) also cite page references for both editions (NR = Regular Edition, SE = Shorter Edition, G = *Guide*). The rhetorical index, intended to help instructors who prefer to organize their courses by rhetorical modes, lists most of the essays included in the *Reader*.

We hope the *Guide* will serve as a springboard for questions you may ask and observations students may make. Entries consist of three or four parts:

1. An introduction to the essay and the author, which may be supplemented with the biographical sketches in the appendix of the *Reader*.
2. Questions reprinted from the *Reader*, when available.
3. "Analytical Considerations," which take up matters of form and content, rhetoric and style, and which are meant to help instructors plan their syllabus and class discussion.
4. "Suggested Writing Assignments," which supplement assignments in the *Reader* itself and draw on key concepts from the work, other essays related in theme or style, topics that touch students' lives, and enduring issues central

to a liberal education—all with the aim of giving students provocative, wide-ranging possibilities for writing.

We hope you will find most—if not all—our suggestions in the *Guide* useful. They represent the collective wisdom of former authors of the *Guide*, most notably Craig Bradford Snow, Wayne E. Blankenship, and Robert E. Hosmer; the editors emeritii, most notably Arthur Eastman; the coeditors of *The Norton Reader* itself; our editors at Norton, Julia Reidhead, Carol Hollar-Zwick, and Jennifer Bartlett; and our colleagues at our home institutions and in the profession at large.

Linda H. Peterson, *Yale University*

John C. Brereton, *The University of Massachusetts, Boston*

Joan E. Hartman, *College of Staten Island, City University of New York*

To Students: Reading and Writing with *The Norton Reader*

The Norton Reader includes essays on a range of subjects, some familiar, others more specialized, some personal, others more public. You'll find the first kind in sections like "Personal Report" and "People, Places," the second in sections like "History" and "Science." "Personal Report" goes back to the earliest edition; "Cultural Critique" was added to the previous edition, "Op-Eds" to this one. Some essays—E. B. White's "Once More to the Lake," for example, and Jonathan Swift's "A Modest Proposal"—are constant favorites. Other essays—about one-quarter—are new to this edition.

The editors read widely in order to include a variety of authors writing on a variety of topics in a variety of ways. We include male and female voices; American, British, and Canadian voices; African American, Asian American, American Indian, Caribbean, and Hispanic American voices. Some essays are calculatedly challenging, others relatively simple. Some are long, others short. Although most are contemporary, some are not; although most are written in English, a few are translated from other languages. What they have in common is excellence: three editors, without actually defining good writing to ourselves or for each other, have agreed on the inclusion of each. We find their authors, sometimes well known, sometimes less well known, speaking with authority and, often, seeing with a distinctive angle of vision. We find their subjects important, timely, timeless, engaging. We find their writing convincing and clear, their style lean when elaboration is not required and adequate to complexity.

Both the Regular and the Shorter editions contain a large number of essays, more than any instructor will assign during a semester: in the Tenth, the Regular Edition contains 212 essays, the Shorter Edition 119. We know that there are many kinds of college writing courses; we know that instructors link reading and writing in a variety of ways. Our aim in *The Norton Reader* is to accommodate all or most of them. We leave it to your instructors to direct you through the essays, to decide which ones to assign and how to use them.

Reading

Most of the essays in *The Norton Reader* originally appeared in publications read by informed and educated general readers. They were written for and read by people who wanted to know—or know more—about their subjects, who knew—or knew of—their authors, or who were tempted to launch into unfamiliar subjects written about by authors they had never heard of, because they encountered these essays in publications they ordinarily read. Outside the classroom, readers bring their own interests and motives to essays. Putting them in a textbook of necessity makes reading essays artificial.

As editors, we've tried to make available to you some of the things the original readers of these essays knew. Information about their publication and authorship appears in two places, in footnotes at the beginning of each essay and in the section called "Authors" at the end of the volume. The footnotes provide information about when and where the essays first appeared and, if they began as talks, when and where they were delivered and to whom. Maya

Angelou's "Graduation," for example, is a chapter from her autobiography, *I Know Why the Caged Bird Sings*, published in 1969; Francis Bacon's "Of Youth and Age" was published in collections called *Essays*, first in 1612, revised in 1625; Frances FitzGerald's "Rewriting American History" comes from her *America Revised*, published in the *New Yorker* and then as a book in 1979; Scott Russell Sanders's "Looking at Women" was published in a journal called the *Georgia Review* in 1989; the "Cherokee Memorials," along with a dozen supporting documents, were presented to the United States Congress in 1830. We don't, however, explain the differences between the *New Yorker* and the *Georgia Review*; the former, a large-circulation commercial weekly magazine, the latter, a small-circulation journal published three times a year by the University of Georgia. If more information than we provide about context helps situate you in relation to what you are reading, we urge you to ask your instructors. As editors, we could swamp a smaller number of essays with additional information about publication and authorship, but we prefer to include more essays and keep contextual information brief.

The entries in the section called "Authors" provide information about who wrote the essays. Putting this information at the end provides you with choices. You may know something about their authors already. If you don't, you may prefer to know something about them before you read their essays or you may prefer to encounter them as unknowns, letting them identify themselves. Sometimes knowing who authors are and where their voices come from helps readers hear them and grasp what they say—and sometimes it doesn't.

We also provide explanatory footnotes—a sure sign of a textbook. When the authors themselves provide footnotes we mark them, in square brackets, "author's note." But most of the footnotes are ours. Our guide for them goes something like this. (1) *Don't* define words that appear in standard collegiate dictionaries unless they are foreign. You can go to your dictionary or guess from context. If an unfamiliar word is central to the meaning of an essay, the author is likely to define it. (2) *Do* provide information about people, places, works, theories, unfamiliar things. For example, for Maya Angelou's "Graduation" we explain Gabriel Prosser, Nat Turner, and Harriet Tubman but not Abraham Lincoln and Christopher Columbus; Stamps (it's an Arkansas town); and "Invictus" (it's a poem). For Frances FitzGerald's "Rewriting American History" we explain socialist realism and American nuclear bomb tests in the Pacific.

Our last rule is the trickiest. (3) Explain, don't interpret; that is, provide information but leave readers to interpret essays by deciding how authors frame and engage information and how it contributes to their meanings. Francis Bacon's "Of Youth and Age" requires extensive annotation. It is possible to figure out from the essay itself that Julius Caesar and Septimus Severus succeeded later in life, after stormy youths; our note, in addition to translating the Latin quotation about Severus, confirms their late success by giving dates and explains that Severus, like Caesar, ruled Rome. Another note identifies three figures, one perhaps familiar and two certainly unfamiliar—Augustus Caesar; Cosmus, Duke of Florence; and Gaston de Foix—and confirms that their success was early. Our notes measure the distance between Bacon's original readers and you: Bacon assumed that his readers read Latin, were familiar with ancient and what to them was contemporary European history, and were willing to take as illustrative examples of "youth" and "age," generally, particular male rulers and public figures. We give dates and facts but leave you to work out the meanings engaged by Bacon's examples.

The editors' experience in the classroom helps us to make guesses about what you know, what you don't know, and what you may need to know. But you can be sure that we'll fail you in some places by not explaining enough and annoy you in others by explaining what you find clear. When we fail, ask your instructors for help; when we annoy, take our efforts as well-intentioned. Again, rather than swamping a smaller number of essays with notes, we keep them brief.

Annotation, then, while it facilitates the making of meaning in reading, never takes its place. Reading is an active process. Inexperienced readers may move their eyes over the words on the page and expect meaning to overtake them; experienced readers take responsibility for making it. They have a repertory of strategies for reading and use them appropriately according to what they read and their purposes in reading it. They monitor themselves, noticing when they drift off or become distracted. They make predictions and revise them, ask questions and answer them. They connect words, phrases, sentences, and paragraphs, generalizations and particulars; what they know from prior experience and what they now read. They create sensory as well as visual images; they voice, using intonation and phrasing, silently most of the time but, when they are stuck, out loud. They take the time reading requires or, when their time is limited, use the time they have to advantage. They expect partial understandings on a first reading, fuller understandings when they reread.

Many of the suggestions for reading that follow (many but not all of) the essays in *The Norton Reader* are directions to *do* something. They ask you to locate, mark, or identify because we want you to notice the essays' structural features, the patterns that undergird and make manifest their meanings. Narrative, description, exposition, persuasion, and argument take conventional shapes—or distort them—and recognizing these shapes enhances comprehension. Other suggestions ask you to paraphrase meanings—that is, to express them in your own words; to extend meanings by providing additional examples; and to reframe meanings by connecting them with meanings in other essays. Still others ask you to notice rhetorical features that contribute to meanings: authors' voices (or *personae*); authors' authority (and how they earn it); authors' assumptions about audience (and the evidence for them); authors' choices of styles and forms of expression. We also ask you to consider the effects of these rhetorical choices.

At least one of our suggestions, usually the last, asks you to write something. Ordinarily we ask you to demonstrate comprehension by an informed assent—that is, by bringing in something from your experience or reading that extends an essay—or by an informed dissent—that is, by bringing in something from your experience or reading that qualifies it or calls it into question.

Or we ask you to adapt one or more of an essay's rhetorical strategies to a topic of your own choosing.

Although making meaning is a rather private and somewhat mysterious activity, writing about reading helps to demystify it. Keep a reading journal. Watch yourself as you read. Mark up essays. Write queries and comments in their margins and in your journal. Make notes about what you read and your responses to it. Stop reading to look back over you're journal entries or look ahead to make predictions and ask questions. Write a preliminary summary after your first reading of an essay; expand your summary after rereading the essay. Reread what you've written about an essay and respond to your own writing. Notice what happens when you succeed in making meaning and when you fail, for failure can be as instructive as success. Ordinarily you are the sole judge of both. Sentence to sentence, paragraph to paragraph, your comprehension is manifest only to you.

Sharing reading journals in class also helps to demystify reading. Discussion, in class as a whole or in smaller groups, can elucidate features of our own and others' reading. What interests and motives do we bring to particular essays? Do some interests and motives yield better readings than others? Can we borrow or adapt others' interests, motives, and readings? What strategies do we employ when we read? Are there other, more useful ones? What meanings do we agree about, what meanings do we disagree about? Can we account for our differences? Can we persuade each other to agree about meanings? Should we try? What are responsive and responsible readings? What are irresponsible readings, and how do we decide? Can writers protect themselves against irresponsible readings?

Readers write, writers read, and these questions concern them both, for making meaning by writing is the flip side of making it by reading. In neither enterprise are meanings passed from hand to hand like nickels, dimes, and quarters.

Writing

The process of making meaning by writing is less mysterious than the process of making it by reading and so too is its product, a text. Nowadays most instructors, however they choose to link reading and writing, emphasize process and multiple products—that is, the first drafts and revisions that precede final drafts. As students you will seldom have time for as many drafts as professional and experienced writers produce. But learning to distribute the time you have over several drafts rather than one will turn out to be the most efficient use of it.

Experienced writers know they can't do everything at once: find or invent material, assess its usefulness, arrange it in paragraphs, and write it out in well-formed sentences. Student writers, however, often expect to do all these things in a single draft. If that's what you expect of yourself, then a writing course is a good place to change your expectations and cultivate more profitable practices. When you try to produce a single draft, you are likely to thin out your material; lock yourself into arrangements you don't have time to change even if, in the course of writing, you make discoveries that suggest other arrangements; and write jumbled paragraphs and clumsy sentences that need to be reworked. In addition, writing a single draft—when you're hoping to produce something reasonably thoughtful and deserving of a respectable grade—is harder than writing several drafts and rarely quicker, especially when you write with a computer.

The process experienced writers go through when they write is something like this. They start with brainstorming, note-taking, listing, freewriting, or whatever heuristic devices—that is, means of discovering what to write—they have learned work for them. They try out what they have to say in rough drafts. As they shape their material, they find what it means and what they want it to mean; as they find what it means and what they want it to mean, they figure out how to shape it—shape and meaning are reciprocal. At any point in this process, with a computer, they can print out a clean, readable version of their text, read it, and add, subtract, rearrange, and revise parts of it without the burden of recopying.

Large and small elements are also reciprocal: they work back and forth among wholes and parts, sections and paragraphs in longer drafts, paragraphs in shorter. As shape and meaning come together, they refine smaller elements: sentences, phrases, even words. They qualify their assertions, complicate their generalizations, and tease out the implications of their examples. At some point they stop, not because there isn't more to be done but because they have other things to do.

This is the rough sequence of tasks experienced writers perform in overlapping stages. They revise at all stages and their revisions are substantial. What inexperienced writers call revision—tinkering with surface features by rewording, pruning, and correcting—experienced writers call editing and proofreading. These things they do at the end, when they are ready to stop revising and prepare what they call a final draft; when larger elements of a text need repair, it's too soon to work on smaller ones. Spell-checks help with editing and proofreading but do not substitute for sharp eyes and attentive ears.

Experienced writers also need readers: though they compose and revise by themselves, they need to try out the meanings they think they have made on responsive and responsible readers. At their best, writing classes enable students to put less-than-final drafts into circulation and receive responses to them through group work and peer editing. Experienced writers often know what they want to ask their readers. The questions below are all-purpose. They should probably be asked in the order they appear, since they go from larger elements to smaller ones.

Take introductions as promises and ask: "Does this essay keep the promises the introduction makes?" If it doesn't, either the introduction or the essay needs to be revised. Experienced writers ordinarily write rough introductions and revise them after their drafts take shape. But you may discover that you've wandered off topic and need to pull yourself back to the task assigned through substantial revision of content and organization.

Then ask, "Does this essay include enough material, and is it interpreted adequately?" Experienced writers ordinarily include more material than student writers. You may find the essays in *The Norton Reader* dense and overspecific; your instructors, on the other hand, may find your essays skimpy and underspecific. Experienced writers thicken their writing with particulars to transmit their meanings and engage readers' recognition, understanding, and imagination. Because they are more in control of their writing than student writers, they are able to be more inclusive, to sustain multiple illustrative examples.

Experienced writers ordinarily specify the meanings they derive from their examples. Student writers are more likely to hope that examples speak for themselves; they seldom do. A case in point is the use of quotations. How many are there? Experienced writers ordinarily use fewer than student writers. How necessary are they? Experienced writers paraphrase more than they quote. How well are they integrated? Experienced writers introduce quotations by explaining who is speaking, where the voice is coming from, and what to listen for; they finish off quotations by making connections.

All writers need to try out their interpretations before they produce a final draft. Slanted interpretations are the stock-in-trade of advertisers and hucksters. But, because the world itself is complex and open to multiple interpretations, examples that seem to one person clearcut illustrations may seem to another forced or exaggerated. Experienced writers know how to qualify and limit their examples. Student writers may overstate, and responsive readers will point out to them interpretations that need qualification.

Then ask, "Is the material in this essay well arranged?" Writing puts readers in possession of material in a temporal order: readers, that is, read from start to finish. Sometimes material that appears near the end of an essay might better appear near the beginning; sometimes material that appears near the beginning might better be postponed. Transitions between paragraphs may be unclear; when they are hard to specify, the difficulty may lie in the arrangement of the material.

Then ask, "Which sentences unfold smoothly and which sentences are likely to cause readers to stumble?" Readers who can point to what makes them stumble as they read your writing will teach you more about well-formed sentences than any set of rules for forming them.

Both reading and writing, then, can and should be shared. Collaborative exercises in writing classes create communities of readers to read the writing of professional and experienced writers in texts such as *The Norton Reader* as well as each other's writing. Learning to become a responsive and responsible reader of professional writing will teach you to respond helpfully to the writing of less experienced student writers in your classes.

PERSONAL REPORT

MAYA ANGELOU

Graduation

The Norton Reader, p. 1; Shorter Edition, p. 1

Maya Angelou's "Graduation," taken from the first volume of her auto-biography, *I Know Why the Caged Bird Sings* (1970), focuses on a single, significant event: her graduation from eighth grade in Stamps, Arkansas, in 1940. The essay is organized chronologically. Angelou begins with the town's, her family's, and her own preparation for graduation; describes the excitement and anticipation of the event; and ends with the ceremony itself, particularly the speech of the white politician that deflates the expectations of young blacks in the audience. Chronology is a natural ordering for autobiographical narrative and, in Angelou's hands, an effective one. You might ask students to look at the "real" time and the "fictional" time in "Graduation"; the "real" time of events leading up to the ceremony is compressed in relation to the "real" time of the ceremony itself, or, conversely, the "fictional" time of the ceremony is extended with description, dialogue, and the young Angelou's own responses.

Chronological narrative is a form that students can handle well, provided they see that "real" time is malleable and in their control. This form also offers students opportunities for significant reflection on their experience. The events of "Graduation" are told in the narrative voice that belongs to the mature Angelou looking back in 1969 at something that happened almost thirty years earlier. Like Alice Walker in "Beauty: When the Other Dancer Is the Self," Angelou uses adult language but maintains the perspective of a twelve-year-old. Students may need to be reminded of events between 1940 and 1969, notably the Supreme Court's school desegregation decision of 1954 that abolished "separate but equal" black and white schools in places like Stamps. One argument against segregated education was that it disadvantaged black children. Although the mature Angelou's sense of being disadvantaged undoubtedly differs from that of the young Angelou, in "Graduation" she re-creates the sense of her young self.

Analytical Considerations

1. Ask students to examine the structure of "Graduation" and diagram the relation of "real" to "fictional" time. How can we measure "real" time? How can we measure "fictional" time?
2. Alternatively, ask students to examine the structure of the essay in terms of "anticipation" and "fulfillment" or "reality." How does Angelou build the readers' sense of anticipation? How does she convey the disappointment she and her fellow students felt?

3. What information does "Graduation" offer about the elementary-school education of black students in Stamps? To what extent was it vocational? To what extent were they "tracked"?
4. In paragraphs 33 through 49 Angelou recounts the speech that Edward Donleavy, a white man running for political office in Stamps, gave at her graduation ceremony. How does Angelou convey both the racist assumptions of the speech and her own better-informed sense of black history?
5. How does Angelou use the valedictory address of Henry Reed to rebut Donleavy's speech and to convey her own determination to be "a proud member of the wonderful, beautiful Negro race" (paragraph 61)?

Suggested Writing Assignments

1. Write a retrospective account of an important event that occurred when you were young. Use adult language but maintain the perspective of a child; manipulate "real" and "fictional" time.
2. Using the content of Angelou's narrative to illustrate and support your points, write an argumentative essay against tracking students who are different by virtue of race, gender, ethnicity, or national origin.

ZORA NEALE HURSTON

How It Feels to Be Colored Me

The Norton Reader, p. 10

For many years Hurston was regarded by members of the African-American literary community as someone whose works could not be taken seriously or even discussed. (And of course during that time she, like the vast majority of African-American writers, was completely ignored by most white readers and critics.) In the past two decades Hurston's works have been revived, her biography written, and her status as a major American writer achieved. This essay provides an interesting insight into the ups and downs of Hurston's changing reputation. Perhaps she plays with the stereotypes too much; perhaps she makes "proper" or highly political people in the black community uncomfortable. At the same time, there's a spirit conveyed in the essay, a sense of life that shines as a beacon to writers so that they can feel comfortable in being different, and particularly to those proud of their African-American identity. (A major force behind Hurston's revival was the African-American writer Alice Walker, who became interested in Hurston's feminism and edited some of Hurston's out-of-print works.)

In paragraph 7 Hurston turns her back on the legacy of slavery—or at least claims to. In paragraph 14 she literally steps into the Harlem Renaissance, that outpouring of poetry, fiction, and music that influenced so much of both black and white America in the 1920s. Hurston is proud and defiant, exulting in the freedom she believes the times have granted her. As a black woman in 1920s America, she feels triumphant. One question for students might be, How much of this is genuine and how much is bravado, like whistling in a graveyard? It is useful to point out the extent to which Hurston's joy and anticipation are connected with place. She is happiest in Eatonville, the town of her African-American family home in Florida, and in Harlem, surrounded by black Americans in a time of prosperity and the building of a genuine community. She feels most uncomfortable at Barnard, where she is overwhelmed by "the thousand white persons" (paragraph 10). (Note that Barnard is just less than a mile from Seventh Avenue and 125th Street, the center of Harlem.) A careful reading reveals that Hurston is fully aware that she can be herself only where other black Americans are free. She is quite aware of discrimination (paragraph 16) even if she says it doesn't bother her.

Questions from the NR10

1. From the beginning Hurston startles us: "I remember the very day that I became colored." Why does Hurston insist that one *becomes* colored? What happened on that day to make her so?
2. Each section of Hurston's essay explores a different possible identity, some based on skin color, others emphasizing history, culture, or gender. What does Hurston accomplish by such an approach?
3. The final paragraph introduces a key metaphor: "like a brown bag of miscellany propped against a wall." How does Hurston develop this metaphor? What does she mean by it?
4. Like other writers in "Personal Report," including Bruno Bettelheim in "A Victim" and Nancy Mairs in "On Being a Cripple," Hurston chooses a label, "colored me," to explore questions of personal identity. Compare Hurston's use of "colored" with either Bettelheim's use of "victim" or Mairs's use of "cripple."

Analytical Considerations

1. In what sense is Hurston's manifesto a product of the optimism that characterized the boom years of the 1920s? (President Hoover promised, for instance, "A chicken in every pot, two cars in every garage.")
2. Try to pin down Hurston's tone. What kind of persona does she convey in this essay? Students will need to know that she was an accomplished novelist and writer who knew very well how to achieve an effect. In other words, she was consciously aiming to present herself in a particular way. The question is, exactly what way is that?
3. How do metaphors help Hurston articulate her sense of self? See, e.g., paragraphs 10, 14, 15, 17.

Suggested Writing Assignments

1. Write an essay that connects Hurston's outlook in the 1920s with Henry Louis Gates, Jr.'s in the 1990s (NR 334) and Alice Walker's in the 1980s (NR 44, SE 34). In what ways does Hurston's attitude toward race and participation in American society anticipate Gates and Walker?
2. Gates and Walker are great admirers of Hurston and have been instrumental in reviving her reputation. Write an essay that explains what in Hurston's work might have made Gates and Walker such admirers, using their own accounts of African-American life as evidence.

3. Write a Hurston-like essay, using a characteristic that some might view as a liability and treating it as an asset. Suggestions: short or tall, heavy or thin, from the "wrong" part of town (or the "wrong" state), Greek or independent, at a less than fashionable college.

BRUNO BETTELHEIM

A Victim

The Norton Reader, p. 13

"A Victim" is an excerpt from Bruno Bettelheim's account of his experience in a German concentration camp during World War II, *The Informed Heart: Autonomy in a Mass Age* (1960). It is, explicitly, a flashback: Bettelheim, a psychologist, recollects an event that occurred more than twenty years earlier. Students should notice that Bettelheim uses the event at the clinic to illustrate a point about relations between victims and their persecutors and that he adopts a structure of point, illustration, and elaborated point. His narrative thus functions as both illustration and demonstration.

The excerpt is brief. Nevertheless, Bettelheim narrates the event at the clinic with enough density and specificity to win our assent, to convince us that, yes, it could indeed happen this way. He does not re-create the event with the intricate detail of other authors in this section who shape events for thematic and emotional resonance, but neither does he reduce it to "mere" illustration. Students need to see what Bettelheim does as relevant to their writing, to ask (of themselves) what is enough and what is too much in the re-creation of personal experience. Bettelheim's narrative engages us in its own right, above and beyond the uses to which he puts it, and it is successful because it is well narrated.

Analytical Considerations

1. Ask students to consider Bettelheim's three-part structure of point, illustration, and elaborated point; also point out his simpler two-part structures of point-illustration and illustration-point. How does his announcing his point in advance of the illustration change our reading of it? How would we read the illustration if he withheld his point until later? How does the illustration permit and/or require him to elaborate (or qualify) his point?
2. Have students look at "A Victim" in connection with Maya Angelou's "Graduation" (NR 1, SE 1) or Alice Walker's "Beauty: When the Other Dancer Is the Self" (NR 44, SE 34). Two points of comparison might be made: first, between narrative as exploration and narrative as illustration; and second, between flashbacks from adulthood to childhood (Angelou) and from adulthood to adulthood (Bettelheim).
3. Bettelheim begins "A Victim" by making a large generalization about victims and persecutors. Can his illustration bear the weight of demonstrating it? Or does he, in his elaborated point, qualify his generalization? How can an individual case, or individual cases, demonstrate a generalization? Com-

pare Bettelheim's use of his personal experience with Bruce Shapiro's in "One Violent Crime" (NR 15, SE, 10).

Suggested Writing Assignments

1. Write an essay using Bettelheim's three-part structure of point, illustration, and elaborated point. Take an experience and present it as an illustration and, insofar as possible, as a demonstration of some larger point.
2. Write two variations on the same event, using Bettelheim's two-part structures: one of illustration followed by point, the other of point followed by illustration. Then write a paragraph of comment on the two structures and on whether you shaped your illustration differently in each variation. (First drafts of these essays might profit from being discussed in small groups.)

BRUCE SHAPIRO

One Violent Crime

The Norton Reader, p. 15 ; Shorter Edition, p. 10

As Bruce Shapiro explains in the opening paragraphs of his narrative, in 1994 he became the victim of a random attack in a neighborhood coffee bar. Seven people were stabbed, several so seriously that they barely escaped death. The attacker was not a hardened criminal, not a person high on drugs or a thief attempting to steal money, but a mentally unstable young man whose mother had been hospitalized and who thus felt he had been abandoned. Shapiro, a staff writer for the *Nation*, attempts to come to terms with the crime and its devastating effects on his own life by asking the question "Why didn't anyone stop him?"

Shapiro poses this question at several points in his essay, each time considering the mechanisms now in place to prevent crime and the crime bills currently proposed to be even more effective. His analysis focuses on the "rhetoric of restitution," a phrase that students will need to discuss carefully. Shapiro concludes that no current plan could have stopped this crime; American politicians, Shapiro argues, are pursuing by and large unworkable tactics and ignoring the social institutions that could serve as the most effective safeguards against violent crime.

Questions from the NR10

1. What do you think are the causes of violent crime in America? What do you think can be done to prevent violent crime? How did reading Bruce Shapiro's essay change your views on crime and its prevention?
2. Shapiro's essay interweaves personal experience and political debate. What advantages does he gain by beginning with personal experience? Where and why does he move to political issues? How does he make the transition?
3. How do Shapiro's references to television and movies contribute to his argument? What implicit argument does he make about the effect of popular culture on our political thinking?

4. Write an essay that interweaves a personal experience, your own or that of someone close to you, with a larger political issue.

Analytical Considerations

1. As Shapiro analyzes the crime that made him a victim, he introduces language from psychology and politics: "post-traumatic stress disorder" and the "rhetoric of restitution." What does he mean by these phrases? How do they help him understand his own experience and, more broadly, the problem of violent crime?
2. Published in 1994, Shapiro's essay engages with current debates about crime prevention. Have those debates changed? What issues have remained the same, and what has changed? If you wish to assign a research essay, you might ask students to find recent articles in newspapers and journals that put forth or criticize current plans for stopping crime.

Suggested Writing Assignments

1. In a longer version of his essay, Shapiro compares the press coverage of "his" crime with the coverage given to the shooting of Rashawnda Crenshaw in a poor black neighborhood in the same town. Using your local newspaper(s), compare the coverage of two similar crimes. Does Shapiro's suggestion that the press ignores crimes committed against the poor hold true? What other factors seem to influence press coverage?
2. In "A Victim" (NR 13), Bruno Bettelheim suggests that Jewish prisoners had some (though obviously not total) control over how they were treated. Does Shapiro's essay suggest that victims have any control? If so, what kind? If not, why might there be a difference between the "victim" in the two essays? Write an essay in which you compare and contrast Bettelheim's and Shapiro's presentation of the "victim."

WALLACE STEGNER

The Town Dump

The Norton Reader, p. 20

In this recollection of childhood, Stegner seems able to remember absolutely everything that occurred to him in connection with his town's dump. This essay was published in 1959, and the events it records took place between 1913 and 1919, as Stegner helpfully tells us in the opening paragraph. In other words, the remembrance spans at least forty years, yet events are portrayed with extraordinary vividness: the particular sound a leech made when it let go (paragraph 8), the reply to a letter from a St. Louis junk house (paragraph 11), the fate of the family Shakespeare (paragraph 17), among others. Students ought to ponder the source of that incredible power of recall. Some, the most naive, will think that Stegner just set himself to thinking hard and produced this account of his adventures in the dump. Others, more sophisticated, will realize that Stegner has shaped his memories and removed extraneous images and recollections. (He never claims that this is everything he remembers.) And the most sophisticated of all will speculate about how over time a novelist's imagination can build, shape, and produce an interesting memoir from just the fragments of memory. (In this sense Stegner's piece has much in common with Angelou's remembrance of graduation [NR 1, SE 1]).

It is useful to show that Stegner was aware of the culturally impoverished life on the Canadian plains. When he says, "The dump was our poetry and our history" (paragraph 20), he means both that the dump contained a literal Shakespeare and the detritus of decades of settlement, and that the dump itself, at least to a young boy, stood for both the romance of faraway places and the history of his community.

The remembered details are what make this piece so appealing. The technique is simple. It opens with the site, near a river, and the items in the first eight paragraphs have to do with water, an appealing attraction for a young boy. Paragraph 10, beginning ". . . it contained relics of every individual who had ever lived there, and of every phase of the town's history," serves to organize paragraphs 11 to 19, which all have textbook-perfect topic sentences. It is only with paragraph 20 that Stegner reveals the true import of his piece: "The dump was our poetry and our history." There, in the refuse of civilization, was all a young boy needed to form his picture of life.

Questions from the NR10

1. Through what details does Stegner portray the dump as a record of his childhood? How is it also a record of the town's history? Is it also a record of the North American West? In what sense?
2. How seriously do you take Stegner's claim (paragraph 21) that "I learned more from the town dump than I learned from school"? He has been making allusions to Coleridge and Virgil; what kind of learning is he thinking of?
3. Describe a "treasure" someone found and held on to.

Analytical Considerations

1. The phrase "kitchen midden" (paragraph 19) was deliberately not glossed. Students who look it up in the dictionary will find how this dump connects to the work of archaeologists searching through middens of different civilizations. The last two paragraphs make all the case that is necessary for the study of dump sites, whether dating from prehistoric times, the classical world, or the nineteenth-century Canadian prairie.
2. Students may not know that Stegner was a strong environmentalist, the conscience of the West to many people. Ask students to speculate on Stegner's attitude toward preservation of the environment, basing their thoughts on his ability to describe the natural and artificial world about him and his (implied) attitude toward humans' profligate use of resources.

Suggested Writing Assignments

1. Stegner says, "I think I learned more from the town dump than I learned from school: more about people, more about how life is lived, not elsewhere

but here, not in other times but now" (paragraph 21). Write an essay about how you or someone you know learned more about life from something other than school. Or, expanding on sentiments Stegner expresses in this sentence, write a critique of school by showing how it doesn't prepare students successfully for the real world.

2. Using "The Town Dump" and Lars Eighner's "On Dumpster Diving" (NR 25, SE 15) as models, write an essay about a "treasure trove," making a larger point about a family, a community, or consumer society. Suggested locales: a closet, basement, or attic; a storeroom; a dump.

LARS EIGHNER

On Dumpster Diving

The Norton Reader, p. 25; Shorter Edition, p. 15

Originally written as a separate essay, "On Dumpster Diving" later appeared in Eighner's first book, *Travels with Lizbeth* (1993). It gives an account of the time he spent homeless, getting much of what he needed from what people threw away in Dumpsters. Eighner's essay has five parts: (1) a brief introduction (paragraphs 1 to 6) about words: the derivation of *Dumpster,* the appropriateness of *scavenging* or *foraging*; (2) the inevitable question, as if posed by an imaginary interlocutor: "What is safe to eat?" (paragraphs 7 to 30); (3) a chronology of his own Dumpster diving, from beginning to scavenge to making the rounds of Dumpsters, with a concluding disquisition on what's wrong with can scroungers (paragraphs 31 to 48); (4) an examination of items found in Dumpsters (paragraphs 49 to 59); and (5) a philosophical conclusion that meditates on a throwaway society (paragraphs 60 to 68).

Questions from the NR10

1. How does Eighner organize his essay? What does such an organization imply?
2. Eighner's simple, understated tone suggests that anyone can adapt to Dumpster diving with a little practice. Why do you think he uses such a tone?
3. What shocked or surprised you most in this essay?
4. Write about someone who does what Eighner deplores in his closing paragraphs, "invests objects with sentimental value." Let your description reveal whether or not you agree with Eighner.

Analytical Considerations

1. "On Dumpster Diving" and "The Town Dump" (NR 20) are natural companion pieces. Their structures are remarkably similar: a brief autobiographical introduction that places the writer in the setting; an extended list of the "treasures" to be found in a dump or Dumpster, and a concluding reflection on what the experience has taught the writer. The key differ-

ence is that Stegner recalls his dump over a forty-year gap, whereas Eighner's experience is much more recent. Then, too, Eighner has a kind of consumer-guide flavor, a sense that he's instructing us on how to scavenge if and when we have to. Stegner sees the poetry in refuse; Eighner does not. Instead, his matter-of-fact consumer-guide approach suggests that a Dumpster might well be lying ahead in the lives of some of his readers.

2. Ask students to speculate on why Eighner doesn't tell what made him homeless or what precisely made him begin raiding Dumpsters. How would mention of the causes of his scavenging alter the essay?

Suggested Writing Assignments

1. Invent a name for something you do (as Eighner did for Dumpster diving) and describe its hazards and rewards.
2. Write three to five paragraphs (serious or humorous) defining and discussing the appropriate term for something you do, modeling them on Eighner's discussion of the proper term for his activities.
3. Eighner researched the term Dumpster. Do your own research on a trade name or the correct term for a well-known product. (Examples: boysenberry, Polaroid Land Camera, Oldsmobile, Bostitch stapler, Birds Eye frozen foods, shrapnel.) Explain how you went about your research as well as how you felt about what you found.

NANCY MAIRS

On Being a Cripple

The Norton Reader, p. 34; Shorter Edition, p. 24

Mairs has written extensively about disability, using her own experience as a starting point. This essay confronts her multiple sclerosis directly, beginning with a comic reflection on the relation of writing and disability: thinking about writing the essay makes her lose track of her disability, yet forgetting causes an accident that makes her think again about writing. There's a wry message here: writing may make one a more acute observer, but it can make one lose sight of the real situation as well. (There's a story about the Greek astronomer Thales who was so busy looking at the stars that he lost track of his way and fell into a ditch.) You may want to use this essay not only to discuss how people come to terms with disabilities (or fail to) but also to discuss how writing helps us understand the predicaments we find ourselves in, the experiences we must live through, the pasts we carry with us.

Questions from the NR10

1. How does Mairs organize her essay? What connects the different parts to each other?
2. What stereotypes of "disabled" people does Mairs expect us to believe in? How does she set out to counter them?

3. Mairs deliberately chooses to call herself a "cripple." Select a person or group that deliberately chooses its own name or description and explain the rationale behind the choice.

Analytical Considerations

1. Why is Mairs so concerned with terminology? Discuss the importance of naming or identifying with a specific term.
2. In the 1990s many people or groups have willingly accepted terms that not too long ago might have incensed them. Mairs calls herself "cripple"; Gates titles his book *Colored People*; Eighner invents "Dumpster diving." Back in the 1920s Hurston playfully dealt with "Colored Me." Gays speak of "Queer theory." What do these acts of appropriation suggest? What is gained in taking a term once used in derision and proudly accepting or claiming it?

Suggested Writing Assignments

1. Use a collegiate dictionary to examine the differences among words like *cripple, handicapped*, and *disabled*. Then have students ask three or four people what the terms mean to them. Ask students to use the results of their reading and the survey to write an essay about the nuances of such words.
2. Compare Mairs's attitude toward her impairment and Eighner's attitude toward Dumpster diving. Write an essay in which you discuss the ways their essays and attitudes are alike.

ALICE WALKER

Beauty: When the Other Dancer Is the Self

The Norton Reader, p. 44; Shorter Edition, p. 34

Walker writes about a wound she received in her eye when she was a child and its effect on her subsequent life. She chooses to write in the present, providing glimpses of separate moments from her life: before the accident, the years spent with a disfiguring white spot on her eye, after the spot was surgically removed. The perspective is extremely closeup. We never see Walker's affliction in any way but through her understanding of it. In a sense this approach mimics Walker's actual attitude: she cannot get out of her own feelings, her own "take" on her wound. When her mother tells her that there was no difference in her behavior before or after the accident, she is shocked. For years what Walker thought of as the central event in her life, the accident, has made little impression on those closest to her.

The essay exists in a world where readers are expected to know certain words of wisdom: "Beauty is in the eye of the beholder" and "How can we know the dancer from the dance," for example. Significantly, it ends with Walker's persona dancing to the music of a blind musician, Stevie Wonder, and embracing "another bright-faced dancer," herself.

Questions from the NR10

1. Throughout her essay, Walker refers to the "accident." Why does she put the word in quotation marks? Has Walker made her peace with the "accident" and its consequences?
2. Walker writes her essay by selecting particular moments in her life. What does each moment show? How do these moments relate to Walker's theme?
3. What is the effect of ending the essay by recounting a dream? How does the dream relate to the essay's title?
4. Write an essay comparing and contrasting Walker's essay and Mairs's "On Being a Cripple." Consider especially their responses to injury or illness and their attitudes toward those subjects.

Analytical Considerations

1. What is the effect of using the present tense throughout?
2. How do the white spaces help shape our reading of the essay?
3. This essay is about Walker "making peace" with the accident. To what extent is it also about making peace with other things? Is the accident some kind of metaphor, or by calling it one, do we diminish the impact it had on her life?

Suggested Writing Assignments

1. Take an event that helped shape your life, a "defining moment," and tell about it and its influence as a series of moments narrated in the present tense.
2. Read Annie Dillard's "Sight into Insight" (NR 1140) in connection with Walker's essay and then write an essay of your own that addresses the way these two writers use different meanings of the word *see*. You'll probably find yourself expanding on their notions, explaining what they're getting at, or agreeing or disagreeing with them.

JOAN DIDION

On Going Home

The Norton Reader, p. 50

In this short essay (of six paragraphs) Joan Didion describes returning to her family's home to celebrate her daughter's first birthday. Her husband remains in Los Angeles: she reenters the world of her father, mother, brother, and great-aunts. "On Going Home" proceeds by association: one experience reminds her of another, one question leads to another. What is "home"? Can you go home again? How does memory work to connect past and present, one home with another? Didion's essay links past and present by shifting incessantly back and forth between them.

Questions from the NR10

1. Didion speaks of herself at home as "paralyzed by the neurotic lassitude engendered by meeting one's past at every turn" (paragraph 3). What about the essay helps explain these feelings?
2. What does Didion mean by "the ambushes of family life"? (Besides "ambushes" note Didion's other highly charged language: e.g., "betrayal" in paragraph 1 and "guerrilla war" in paragraph 3.)
3. In paragraph 6, Didion says she would like to give her daughter "*home* for her birthday, but we live differently now and I can promise her nothing like that." In an essay, explain whether or not you think parents today can give their children "home." Include examples.

Analytical Considerations

1. How does the "vital although troublesome distinction" (paragraph 1) between home as the place where Didion lives with her husband and baby in Los Angeles and home as the place where her family lives in the Central Valley of California thread through "On Going Home"?
2. Ask students to look closely at "On Going Home" as an essay developed by association and, in particular, at how Didion maintains the illusion of free association while behaving responsibly toward her readers. She is careful to do two things: to let us know where she is, particularly with respect to present and past, and to provide thematic coherence. For the first, you might ask students to look at transitions between paragraphs and then within them; for the second, ask them to elucidate the several concerns that run through the essay.
3. Look at Didion's "On Keeping a Notebook" (NR 82, SE 40) in conjunction with "On Going Home" with respect to their development and rhetorical techniques. How do objects function in them? How do images function?
4. Consider the titles of both essays—"On Keeping a Notebook," "On Going Home." What does *on* followed by a participle serve to suggest about the kind of essay each will be?

Suggested Writing Assignments

1. Write a personal essay developed by associations radiating out from a return to a place. Give it a title beginning with "On" followed by a participle (a verbal ending in -*ing*).
2. One technique Didion uses is organizing her associations around objects. Write a personal essay in which you focus on objects. Attend to maintaining the illusion of free association while providing thematic coherence.

MARIANNA DE MARCO TORGOVNICK

On Being White, Female, and Born in Bensonhurst

The Norton Reader, p. 52

Marianna Torgovnick is an academic, a full professor and past chairman of the English department at Duke University. We learn these facts late in the essay, and in a sense, this essay traces the path by which its writer came to be where and what she is. Yet the essay also seeks to capture Italian American life in Bensonhurst (a section of Brooklyn) in the 1950s, before it became the site of racial tension in the 1980s. Just as Maya Angelou in "Graduation" (NR 1, SE 1) recalls growing up black in Stamps, Arkansas, or Henry Louis Gates, Jr., in "In the Kitchen" (NR 384) re-creates black life in rural West Virginia, so Torgovnick in the opening paragraphs paints a picture of her ethnic American childhood.

Discussion of Torgovnick's memoir might take one of several directions: it might focus on the changes that have occurred in American neighborhoods between the 1950s and 1980s and their causes; it might focus on an analysis of what features, positive and negative, contribute to ethnic "cohesiveness and provinciality" (paragraph 10)—not just of Italian Americans but of any ethnic group; or it might focus on the details of the memoir that anticipate Torgovnick's later career as a teacher and scholar and, indeed, on how well her past and present connect. If you pursue the final theme, you might ask students about the bracketed paragraph (14) and what it conveys about the link between academic and "ordinary" life.

Questions from the NR10

1. To what extent do the key terms of Torgovnick's title—"white" (race), "female" (gender), and "born in Bensonhurst" (region)—define her identity? What aspects of her identity escape these categories?
2. Torgovnick's essay is not divided, as one might initially guess, into three sections, each one emphasizing an aspect of her title. How, in fact, is the essay organized? Why might she have chosen this approach?
3. Write an essay using a title like Torgovnick's, "On Being _____." Emphasize whatever aspects of yourself you wish, and organize your account either categorically or narratively.

Analytical Considerations

1. Torgovnick's essay shuttles from past to present, from her ethnic childhood to her present life as a professor of English. How does she make transitions? Note that some transitions are made by leaving white space (blank lines) in the text, others by including dates or posing explicit questions (as in paragraph 16, "What has Bensonhurst to do with what I teach today and write?").
2. How many answers does Torgovnick give to her pivotal question: "What has Bensonhurst to do with what I teach today and write?" Are the three "scenes" (paragraphs 20–24, 25–30, and 31–36) the answers? What answers does Torgovnick exclude? (Consider paragraphs 17 to 19, plus other answers students might say she has failed to consider.)

Suggested Writing Assignments

1. Using the opening of Torgovnick's essay as a model, compose an "itinerary" through some neighborhood you know, stopping at people and places you want your readers to know more about.
2. In a longer essay, describe how a change came over a neighborhood or a place you know, and speculate about the causes of the change.

EDNA O'BRIEN

Waiting

The Norton Reader, p. 62

In traditional rhetorical terms, this essay illustrates the mode of "definition." Although O'Brien never provides a formal or dictionary definition (e.g., "remaining inactive or staying in one spot until something anticipated occurs"), she gives a sense of what waiting entails through numerous examples: how often it occurs in our lives, what it feels like, what our complicated responses to it might mean. If you use rhetorical modes in your teaching, O'Brien's example might provide an impetus for similar definitional essays (on such topics as watching, looking, seeing, talking, listening, hearing, thinking, meditating, debating, and so on). If you use generative techniques such as lists or cumulative catalogues, you might ask students to brainstorm on some of these topics by listing as many examples as they can think of.

O'Brien does not claim that waiting is exclusively a phenomenon of modern life, but she includes many examples that derive from modern, especially urban, existence. As a commentary on contemporary culture, her essay might have been included in the section "Cultural Critique." It might usefully be compared with Arthur Schopenhauer's "On Noise" (NR 343) or Maggie Helwig's "Hunger" (NR 318, SE 194) in terms of their tone, range of examples, and analytical strategies.

Questions from the NR10

1. This essay provides a definition of "waiting," not with a single sentence but rather with multiple examples. Choose one or two that in your opinion are the best, and explain why.
2. O'Brien's essay includes several literary allusions—to plays, poems, novels, and other books. Why do you think she includes them? What effect do they have? How do they relate to her final comment?
3. Are there any aspects of waiting that O'Brien has omitted? Write about your own example or experience of "waiting."

Analytical Considerations

1. O'Brien's essay, when first published, began with the sentence: "'Just you wait, Henry Higgins, just you wait,' Eliza Doolittle says, advancing the threat of equality, or maybe even superiority, over her cranky mentor, Professor Higgins." Ask students to discuss the advantages of this opening and to speculate on O'Brien's reasons for omitting the sentence in later versions.
2. What organizes O'Brien's essay? It is associative? Does it move from general to specific? From general to personal? From the category to the example?
3. Why does O'Brien conclude with the advice from Václav Havel's "Planting Watering and Waiting"? How does this organic metaphor "answer" some of the frustrating waiting we now endure in modern, mechanized societies?

Suggested Writing Assignments

1. Write a definitional essay on some other aspect of modern life—for example, watching, looking, seeing, talking, listening, hearing, thinking, meditating, or debating.
2. Write a response to O'Brien's question in paragraph 5: "Do women wait more than men?"

LOREN EISELEY

The Brown Wasps

The Norton Reader, p. 66; Shorter Edition, p. 45

Eiseley was an anthropologist, a historian of science, a nature writer, and a poet. "The Brown Wasps" gestures toward nature writing in its title, and wasps, field mice, and pigeons, along with human beings, appear in it. What humans share with such animals is a profound attachment to place. Eiseley develops "The Brown Wasps" by association of a particular sort, namely, analogy. By the time students have read the central vignettes—the field mouse, or mice, who burrowed in his flowerpot, the pigeons who hovered about the steelwork of the old El, and the man himself, who traveled two thousand miles to find the tree he and his father had planted—they should grasp how analogy links them.

The first section may seem somewhat puzzling: is Eiseley writing about the old men in the railroad station for whom the wasps are a metaphor or about the particular wasps for whom the old men are a metaphor? Neither, it turns out, but both. Humans and animals are related by their attachment to place and the support and consolation it affords them.

Eiseley's recourse to analogy leaves the meanings of "The Brown Wasps" to some extent open. Does analogy level humans and animals or open up differences between them? More specifically, does the analogy between the old men in the station and the brown wasps diminish the pathos of the humans or bestow pathos on the wasps? Is Eiseley's return to home as instinctive as that of the (faintly comic) mice digging in his flowerpot and the pigeons circling the deserted El? Or is it less instinctive than the return of the (somewhat pathetic) mice and pigeons because he understands what has happened in ways that they do not? Or is it both? Students, often impatient with ambiguity, may see some virtue, in this essay, of Eiseley's having it both ways.

Questions from the NR10

1. Eiseley writes of old men in train stations, brown wasps, a field mouse, pigeons near the El, and his own return to his boyhood home in Nebraska. What do these all have in common? State what you believe to be the essay's theme.
2. Some psychologists study animal behavior in order to learn about human behavior, but others write about animals in a very different fashion. Do

you think that Eiseley's way of relating the behavior of animals to human behavior makes sense?

3. From close observation of an animal's behavior, write two brief descriptions, one using animal-human comparisons and one simply sticking to what you see.

Analytical Considerations

1. Students should take some time to analyze Eiseley's keen observations and his power to render what he sees in words. You might divide up the essay according to what Eiseley observes and have groups of students work on its various sections and report on them.
2. Ask students to assess anthropomorphic elements in the language that Eiseley uses to describe wasps, field mice, and pigeons. And the reverse: have them assess the language of animal observation that he uses to describe humans.
3. How are we to understand the sentence in Eiseley's final paragraph: "I spoke for myself, one field mouse, and several pigeons"?

Suggested Writing Assignments

1. On the basis of your observation of a particular animal or group of animals, write an essay involving analogy with humans. Think carefully about how you want to use the analogy: to level humans with animals, to aggrandize animals, or to keep the two in an unstable relationship.
2. Write an essay about returning to a place that has disappeared or changed.
3. Write an essay in which you amplify Eiseley's remark: "It is the place that matters, the place at the heart of things" (paragraph 7). You may rely on personal experience alone or on experience, observation, and reading.
4. Write an essay in which you consider "The Brown Wasps" in conjunction with E. B. White's "Once More to the Lake" (NR 74, SE 53) as a meditation on last things. You may want to make this essay a formal comparison.

GARY SOTO

The Guardian Angel

The Norton Reader, p. 72; Shorter Edition, p. 51

This brief essay is a segment of Gary Soto's autobiographical book, *A Summer Life* (1990). Soto takes up the question, often difficult for autobiographers, of the "breaks" or special opportunities that he received versus the "tough luck" or lack of opportunities others around him (in this case, his brother) seem to have had. Other ethnic writers, most notably Brent Staples in *Parallel Time* (1994), have addressed this question of different fates using deep cultural analysis. Soto addresses it in a seemingly lighthearted way, invoking the old religious notion of a guardian angel. At the same time, it is worth considering with students how this notion allows Soto to take a more serious turn in the final three paragraphs of his essay and how it allows him to include the possibility of "providence" in an analysis of human lives.

1. What meanings of "guardian angel" did you bring to this essay? After reading Soto's personal account, how has your understanding of a "guardian angel" been revised or redefined?
2. Soto's essay turns on two contrasts: between his brother and himself and between his younger self and his older, present self. What does Soto accomplish with his double contrasts?
3. In the final paragraph Soto states, "Now I'm uncertain." About what? How do details convey and explain his uncertainty?
4. Do you believe in "guardian angels," or do you believe in other super-natural phenomena that others may doubt? If so, write a personal narrative that illustrates the basis for your belief. Think about the ways in which Soto's tone and evidence make his narrative appealing, even to those who don't believe in guardian angels.

Analytical Considerations

1. Soto's writing is spare: he often conveys a whole experience in a single sentence, an entire lifetime in a single paragraph. For contrast, ask students to compare a segment of Soto's essay, e.g., paragraphs 4–6, with a segment of Alice Walker's "Beauty: When the Other Dancer Is the Self" (NR 44, SE 34), e.g., paragraphs 8–14. What different effects do these writers achieve? How do their choices of details contribute to the effects?
2. How do writers' beliefs, whether political, philosophical, or religious, inform their writing? You might ask students to speculate about Soto's religious beliefs (we know he was raised in a Roman Catholic Chicano community in Fresno, California) and about how they inform his presentation and analysis. This topic is a complicated one, but important to students who hold firm beliefs but have difficulty expressing them in effective ways.

Suggested Writing Assignments

1. Write an essay in which you compare your experience—whether at home, in school, with friends, during a summer vacation, or in some other specific way—with that of a sibling or another family member, making it clear how you account for your different experiences.
2. Did Alice Walker have, in Soto's terms, a "guardian angel"? Explain why you think so, or why not.

E. B. WHITE

Once More to the Lake

The Norton Reader, p. 74; Shorter Edition, p. 53

"Once More to the Lake" is a classic essay on revisiting the past. With his son, E. B. White revisits the lake where he went as a child, and his account, shifting between present and past, measures the passage of time. Generations blur: as White sees his younger self in his son, so he sees his father in his present self. The final sentence—"As he [White's son] buckled the swollen belt, suddenly my groin felt the chill of death"—may startle readers at first, but on reflection, we realize that White prepares us for it. His narrative spans a natural cycle of life passing from one generation to the next; his rendering of natural landscape and pleasurable activity keeps the somber potential meanings of the cycle in the background until, at the very end, he foregrounds them.

In "Once More to the Lake," White combines particular and composite narrative. The particular narrative takes place in the present: White and his son return to the lake on a single occasion. The composite narrative takes place in the past: White recollects repeated episodes from the Augusts he vacationed at the lake. He moves easily but clearly back and forth in time. You might have students notice the shifts in the first paragraph: "One summer, along about 1904," "summer after summer," "A few weeks ago." These references mark transitions fluently, without emphatic breaks. You might ask students to continue to note how White marks them.

Questions from the NR10

1. What has guided White in his selection of the details he gives about the trip? Why, for example, does he talk about the road, the dragonfly, the boat's motor?
2. White speaks of the lake as a "holy spot." What about it was holy?
3. White's last sentence often surprises first-time readers. Go back through the essay and pick out sections or words or phrases that seem to prepare for the ending.
4. Write about revisiting a place that has a special meaning for you.

Analytical Considerations

1. How important is White's son to "Once More to the Lake"? How does his presence heighten the passage of time and the theme of mortality? Ask students to imagine the essay without him.
2. Comparison is an important device in this essay, as White again and again balances details from the past against details from the present. Sometimes things change, sometimes they don't. You might ask students which comparisons they remember and then ask them to reread the essay looking for additional ones.
3. Discuss what White reveals about himself (or his persona, his created self) in "Once More to the Lake." Ask what in the text enables us to construct an image of the author.
4. "Once More to the Lake" reveals familiar aspects of E. B. White—see also "Progress and Change" (NR 592) and "Democracy" (NR 882, SE 498). Yet it differs from these other essays as well. You might ask students how they differ and whether they differ in expected or unexpected ways? How are the differences evidence of White's range and flexibility?

Suggested Writing Assignments

1. Write an essay about revisiting a place you cherished as a child. Where does "change" lie? In the place? In yourself? Did the experience lead you to sober reflection on big issues? If so, structure your essay so that you can include reflection as well as narrative and description.
2. Write an essay in which you move retrospectively from the present to the past, drawing specific comparisons between them. Make your thematic emphasis that of loss through the passage of time.

JOAN DIDION

On Keeping a Notebook

The Norton Reader, p. 82

Joan Didion is best known for her nonfiction reportage of contemporary cultural and political trends and for her novels *Play It as It Lays* (1971), *A Book of Common Prayer* (1977), and *Democracy* (1984). "On Keeping a Notebook," one of the most personal of Didion's essays, reflects on the relation of fact and fiction in personal life.

This essay provides either a provocative beginning to a unit on journal writing or a useful interlude to students' own writing of journals. "Why did I write it down?" Didion asks in paragraph 4 of the essay—and that question might provoke a discussion about why people keep diaries, journals, and personal notebooks. Perhaps even before students read Didion's essay, you might ask if they have ever kept a journal and what they hoped to gain (or if not, why they did not). Their initial answers might be compared with Didion's, whether to confirm their practices as writers or to offer possibilities for kinds of journal writing they haven't considered before.

If you use this essay as an interlude, you might want to discuss some of Didion's detailed reflections on her "facts" to show students how to analyze their own experiences. (Paragraphs 4 to 5 and 16 to 17 are useful on this score.) If you read the essay as a conclusion to a unit on journal writing, you might ask whether Didion accounts for all the kinds of journals represented in this section. Didion concentrates, for example, on the personal and professional values of keeping a notebook: on persons afflicted with a sense of loss who for psychological reasons need to write things down, and on professionals who keep a writer's notebook for future use in constructing stories. She doesn't consider journals like Susanna Moodie's, written to record adventures in a new world for the reading of family and friends back home, or commonplace books like Henry David Thoreau's, kept to record his own and others' words of wisdom.

Questions from the NR10

1. What distinction does Didion make between a diary and a notebook? What uses does a notebook have for Didion?
2. Didion says she uses her notebook to "tell what some would call lies" (paragraph 7). Why does she do this? Would some people call these things truths? Why?

3. Didion says, *"How it felt to me:* that is getting closer to the truth about a notebook." What writing strategies does she use to convey "how it felt"?
4. Try keeping a notebook for a week, jotting down the sort of things that Didion does. At the end of the week, take one or two of your entries and expand on them, as Didion does with the entries on Mrs. Minnie S. Brooks and Mrs. Lou Fox.

Analytical Considerations

1. This essay is loosely structured: it begins with an incident once recorded in a notebook now recalled and reflected on, followed by two sections on the motives for keeping a notebook. Ask students about the purpose of each section and what they think is the "heart" of each.
2. At what point does the reader realize that the woman in the plaid dress is Didion herself? Why does Didion describe herself in the third person? How does this objective form of description, used in her notebook, help Didion understand herself and her situation?
3. Didion is a master of observing and analyzing details. Ask students what details they remember best from the essay, why they remember them, and what purpose these details serve. The discussion might usefully connect with the students' own writing and their use of details.
4. In an essay titled "Why I Write," Joan Didion has noted: "I write entirely to find out what I'm thinking, what I'm looking at, what I see and what it means." In the same essay she reveals that for her "certain images shimmer" and that these images determine the "arrangement of words." Apply these comments to "On Keeping a Notebook" as well as to "On Going Home" (NR 50).

Suggested Writing Assignments

1. Choose one of the journals in this section as a model for your own writing, and during the next week or two, keep a journal in a similar style and form.
2. Choose an incident or a detail from a journal you have kept, and expand it into a short story or nonfictional narrative. (Alternatively, let someone else read your journal and select the incident.) What extra details does such an expansion require?
3. Keep a notebook for a week or so; carry it with you and record what you like. At the end of the week review it, then write an analysis and commentary on your notebook. Do you share the same interests and motives in writing as Didion?
4. Write an essay in response to Didion's observation: "we are well advised to keep on nodding terms with the people we used to be whether we find them attractive company or not" (paragraph 16).

RALPH WALDO EMERSON

From Journal

The Norton Reader, p. 87

and

HENRY DAVID THOREAU

From Journal

The Norton Reader, p. 90

Emerson, one of America's most influential essayists, started a journal at age sixteen and kept it for over fifty years. Thoreau, his neighbor in Concord, Massachusetts, and an equally influential essayist, kept a journal for twenty-five years, from his late teens until his death at age forty-five. These entries represent what Didion calls, in "On Keeping a Notebook" (NR 82), "a series of graceful *pensées*." More generally, the journals of Emerson and Thoreau could be called "commonplace books" — that is, collections of quotations and maxims from other authors along with their own original, memorable sayings and observations. Before or after students read the selections, you might discuss the motivations for collecting maxims and memorable sayings, and you might also discuss what makes a maxim or saying memorable.

Questions from the NR10

1. Thoreau writes that "Nothing goes by luck in composition. . . . The best you can write will be the best you are." In what sense are his journal entries examples of this belief?
2. Both Thoreau and Emerson write journal entries on the subject of education, both using metaphorical language. Compare their beliefs on education, in part by comparing the metaphors they use.
3. Choose one journal entry from either Emerson or Thoreau and write an essay by expanding, amplifying, or showing exceptions to it.

Analytical Considerations

1. These selections are not narratives of the sort one finds in other journals in this section, but rather pithy maxims, observations, and reflections. Ask students to describe an entry they recall well and then, in small groups or together as a class, analyze its language. More often than not, the parallel construction or metaphorical language has contributed to its memorability.
2. Both Emerson and Thoreau comment on similar topics: religion, education, truth, ethics. Ask students to compare these writers' beliefs on one or more such topics. Does the highly metaphorical language create distinctions between the writers or suggest similarities in their views?

3. If you have taught "Apothegms," you might ask which of the entries are apothegms and what other kinds of entries Emerson and Thoreau include. Emerson, for example, reflects on personal experience (as in the 1835 entry) and on his reading (as in the 1841 entries). Thoreau often writes definitions (as in the 1850 and 1859 definitions of education).

Suggested Writing Assignments

1. Keep a commonplace book for a week or two in which you record witty or wise sayings, your reflections on your reading, and your own, original maxims.
2. Choose two entries, one from each writer, that seem to address the same topic: education, friendship, good writing, etc. By closely analyzing the language and content of each entry, write a brief essay that compares and contrasts the writers' views on the topic.

WALT WHITMAN

Abraham Lincoln

The Norton Reader, p. 92

Whitman, the American poet who wrote *Leaves of Grass*, was also a journalist for much of his life. *Specimen Days* (1882), from which these entries derive, consists partly of diary material and partly of newspaper articles that Whitman wrote during the 1860s and 1870s. We can see the traces of the journalist's reportage in some of the entries—as, for example, in the opening sentence for April 16, 1865, where Whitman lets us know that he is copying from his notes.

In these four entries, Whitman observes and reflects on President Abraham Lincoln, first on his actions (1863), then on his death and his character (1865). As a form, the entries represent an important kind of journal writing that observes historical persons, facts, and events as they happen. You might ask students what value such immediate, red-hot records of the moment have over other kinds of history that re-create events.

Questions from the NR10

1. The first entries in Whitman's journal record his personal observations of Abraham Lincoln. Which details best give a sense of the president? Why?
2. The last entries in Whitman's journal give an assessment of Lincoln's character. How are these entries different from the first ones?
3. If you have an opportunity to observe a public figure up close, write a journal entry like the first of Whitman's, perhaps followed by an entry that reflects on the person's character.

Analytical Considerations

1. Before students read this selection or, alternatively, before you analyze it in class, you might ask what facts they know and what impressions they have of Abraham Lincoln. Then ask students to consider how Whitman either confirms or corrects such impressions and how a public journal like his might be intended, almost by definition, to confirm impressions or set the record straight.

2. Questions 1 and 2 on p. 94 of the NR10 (reprinted above) are meant to help students distinguish between journal entries that record and those that reflect. Although this distinction may ultimately break down, you might help clarify the difference by comparing specific sentences in the entry for August 12 with the entry for April 16, 1865. For example, the sentence on p. 93 describing Lincoln's appearance as he rides might be contrasted with the sentence also on p. 93 beginning, "The tragic splendor of his death. . . ." What different versions of the president do these descriptions suggest? How does the language contribute to the differences?

3. Read Whitman's portrait of Lincoln in connection with Hawthorne's portrait of Lincoln (NR 110).

Suggested Writing Assignments

1. In the library find another biography of Lincoln or an account of his presidency. Compare Whitman's impressions of Lincoln with the second author's description.

2. Find a portrait or photograph of Abraham Lincoln and describe the character of the man the portrait suggests. Do you think Whitman is right to suggest that "the current portraits are all failures — most of them caricatures"?

SUSANNA MOODIE

A Visit to Grosse Isle

The Norton Reader, p. 94

Susanna Moodie, neé Strickland, was a younger sibling in a family of famous and financially successful writers. Her older sisters, Agnes and Elizabeth Strickland, published many works of fiction and history, including the popular *Lives of the Queens of England.* Susanna, like her sister and fellow writer Catherine Parr Traill, emigrated to Canada and wrote several books about Canada and settler life. Moodie also published a number of sentimental novels.

This excerpt from *Roughing It in the Bush* (1852) represents a journal entry intended for family, friends, and a wider public audience. Presumably Moodie knew, even as she wrote, that her account would later be published and read by others. Although it includes many personal details, its purpose is to convey to an English audience a sense of what it was like to emigrate to the New World: the hardships, the humorous experiences, the primitive life of the colonies. The chapter "A Visit to Grosse Isle" begins with an account of the cholera epidemic that was devastating Quebec just as Moodie's ship came into port. Grosse Isle is in the St. Lawrence River, just offshore from Quebec City; it served as a holding point for immigrants to Canada, much as Ellis Island did in the United States.

Analytical Considerations

1. This episode has the structure of a paradise found—and then lost on closer inspection. How does Moodie create a sense of the grandeur of the New World scene? How does she then deflate it?
2. Why does Moodie quote a fellow woman traveler, Mrs. Bowdich, rather than just explain her own desire for fresh bread? What sense of community does this anecdote (paragraph 3) create?
3. The passage ends with a contrast between the savage Irish immigrants and the noble Indian, "one of Nature's gentlemen" (paragraph 18). If you have time for extra research, ask students to find out about mid-Victorian attitudes toward the Irish and the Indian and to consider whether Moodie is reflecting or rejecting those attitudes in her account. For comparison, you might ask students to read Chief Seattle's speech in "Nature and the Environment" (NR 641, SE 351).

Suggested Writing Assignments

1. Do some research on nineteenth-century attitudes toward the Irish and the Indian. Is Moodie reflecting or rejecting such attitudes in her depictions of these people?
2. What does Grosse Isle look like today? Either by conducting a site visit or by finding illustrations and photographs, compare the landscape Moodie describes in paragraphs 6 to 9 with the current scene.
3. What were the experiences of other immigrants to the New World? Using a local library or a special collection within your university library, read about the experiences of immigrants to your state or province, and write a brief essay comparing and contrasting their responses with Moodie's.

MAY SARTON

From Journal of a Solitude

The Norton Reader, p. 98

As one learns from this selection, May Sarton was a poet, novelist, and journal writer. During her eighty years, she wrote over thirty volumes of poetry and fiction, plus a dozen volumes of nonfiction, most autobiographical. She began *Journal of a Solitude* just before she turned sixty, in part as an assessment of her life thus far, in part as an exercise in understanding and approaching the solitude of death. As she puts it in the entry for January 7, "I am proud of being fifty-eight, and still alive and kicking, in love, more creative, balanced, and potent than I have ever been" (paragraph 27).

This journal is a classic of modern spritiual introspection, a successor to the spiritual diaries of the Puritans and the journals of Transcendentalists like Emerson and Thoreau. Yet students may have difficulty "getting into" its ideas and concerns. To help them approach Sarton, one might begin by asking them what they hope to be like when they are old, what values they expect to have, and what issues they expect to confront. Such a discussion might provide an entrée not only into Sarton's journal but also into the uses of journal writing itself, especially the mode of the spiritual diary.

Analytical Considerations

1. Is there a pattern to Sarton's journal—or to these journal entries? Do we expect to find a pattern within a journal, as we do in a novel or autobiography? During the course of the year, Sarton moves from depression and despair to a reaffirmation of her life, yet it is worth discussing whether diaries and journals necessarily have such a pattern, whether positive or negative.
2. Throughout the journal, Sarton discusses her poetry and prose. Ask students to compare and contrast her views on these two genres: when she writes each, why she writes, what values she attaches to them.
3. What function do friends serve during Sarton's solitude and in her record of it in her journal? Perhaps in small groups, students might discuss the four friends mentioned in the entries: Perley Cole (paragraph 3), Arnold Miner (paragraph 9), Anne Woodson (paragraph 12), Laurie Armstrong and others (p. 101). Does the unnamed neighbor (paragraph 27) serve a different function?

Suggested Writing Assignments

1. Choose one entry in which Sarton makes statements with which you disagree, and write your own account of an experience that explains why you have a different point of view.
2. Is May Sarton the kind of journal writer Joan Didion describes in "On Keeping a Notebook" (NR 82)? Using paragraph 4 of Didion's essay, write a brief analysis of Sarton's motives as a journal writer as they do or do not fit with Didion's description.

WOODY ALLEN

Selections from the Allen Notebooks

The Norton Reader, p. 104

Woody Allen's "Notebooks" are a parody of the journal form, as we can tell from his prefatory note to the text: "Following are excerpts from the hitherto secret, private journal of Woody Allen, which will be published posthumously or after his death, whichever comes first." Because they *are* parodic, the entries provide a humorous means of understanding the journal as a form: what writers tend to include in their journals, why it might seem absurd or pretentious to an outside reader.

One way to conclude a unit on journals might be to ask each student to choose a favorite entry from Allen's "Notebooks," to analyze what makes it funny and what kind of journal writing it parodies, and then to compare it with a serious version of the same kind of entry. Particularly good for such a discussion are entries that begin with a serious philosophical question, such as "Do I believe in God?" or "Should I marry W.?" or "What is it about death that bothers me so much?" These allow students to see how parody works by disappointing the reader's expectations and deflating the classic form. You might then want to consider what makes the classic form of the journal successful.

Analytical Considerations

1. As suggested above, analyze several of the entries to show how parody works by means of raising expectations and then deflating them. Then consider what changes might make the entry into a serious reflection, whether on God, death, love, or marriage.
2. Discuss the entries in which Allen parodies the notebook of a writer. What attitudes or conceptions of the writer does Allen mean to poke fun at?

Suggested Writing Assignments

1. Reuse the beginning sentence of an entry from Woody Allen's "Notebooks," but write a serious reflection on the topic.
2. Take a serious entry from the journal of another writer included in this section, and try instead to write a humorous entry as Woody Allen does. What are the difficulties in writing parody?

PEOPLE, PLACES

THOMAS JEFFERSON

George Washington

The Norton Reader, p. 107

The opening selections in "People, Places" give students a chance to read about famous men and to think about how one writes a character sketch or biographical portrait from a position of knowledge but not intimacy (an intimacy Virginia Woolf has, for example, in writing "My Father: Leslie Stephen"). Jefferson knew Washington quite well; indeed, he sums up their acquaintance in the last paragraph when he explains how they worked together in the Virginia legislature before and during the Revolutionary War and later when he served as secretary of state during Washington's presidency. Yet his account of Washington does not include personal anecdotes or familiar details. Instead, it is a "character" sketch—that is, an account of the physical, mental, and moral qualities that distinguish George Washington as a man.

You might want to recall that Jefferson wrote this account for a historian who wanted to gather firsthand information and know more about Washington's role in the Federalist-Republican controversy. You might also want students to know that, when Jefferson uses the word *character* in the first sentence, the term carries the older sense of "integrity," the moral and ethical qualities that a person possesses.

Questions from the NR10

1. What, in Jefferson's view, are Washington's outstanding virtues? What are Washington's greatest defects? From what he writes about Washington, can you infer those qualities of character that Jefferson most admires?
2. Do we learn anything from Jefferson's portrait about what Washington looked like? About his family life? About his hobbies? About his religion? If not, are these important omissions in the characterization of a person in public life?
3. Write in the manner of Jefferson a characterization of an important figure in public life today. Consider whether this manner enables you to present what you think is essential truth, and whether the attempt brings to light any special problems concerning either the task itself or public life today.

Analytical Considerations

1. Before discussing Jefferson's portrait, you might ask students what they know about Washington and what qualities they associate with his character. What predictable details did they find in the portrait? What surprised them—either because it was a fact they hadn't encountered before or because they were surprised that Jefferson would mention it?

2. Look closely at the order in which Jefferson presents the details in paragraph 2: he moves from mental qualities and defects, to moral and ethical qualities, to physical features. Why might he have chosen this order?

3. Most modern writers would have broken paragraph 2 in the middle, after the description of Washington on horseback and before the account of Washington's behavior in private versus professional life. If we treat this second half as a unit, what contrast between Washington's public and private persona does Jefferson suggest? Does this make Washington seem more or less appealing as a person?

4. Why does Jefferson include the final paragraph, explaining how long and in what capacities he knew Washington? It might help to know that Jefferson wrote this account in response to an inquiry from a historian, fifteen years after Washington's death and five years after he completed his own term as president of the United States.

Suggested Writing Assignments

1. Find a modern character sketch or biographical portrait of a president, preferably one written by someone who knew the man. Compare and contrast the information included and the techniques used with Jefferson's portrait of Washington.

2. Read another biographical account of Washington from a modern source. What are the similarities and differences between its portrait and Jefferson's—and how do you account for them?

NATHANIEL HAWTHORNE

Abraham Lincoln

The Norton Reader, p. 110

Hawthorne wrote this sketch of Lincoln during the Civil War, when he visited the president as part of a delegation from Massachusetts. He published part of it in the *Atlantic Monthly*, although not paragraphs 3 through 7 included in *The Norton Reader* (and thus not the major portion of this selection). The editor of the *Atlantic* cut these paragraphs because, as he explained in the footnote to paragraph 3, "it lacks *reverence*." It might be useful and interesting to focus discussion on what is appropriate to include in a character sketch of an important person like the president of the United States, how attitudes have shifted during the past one hundred years, and what we now value in our reading of biography.

Questions from the NR10

1. In his final paragraph, Hawthorne seeks to prevent misunderstanding by stressing his respect for and confidence in Lincoln. Is there anything in the paragraph that runs counter to that expression? To what effect?

2. In the footnote to the third paragraph, the editor of the *Atlantic Monthly* explains his omission of the following four paragraphs. On the evidence of this statement, what sort of person does the editor seem to be? Is there anything in the omitted paragraphs that would tend to justify his decision as editor? Is the full description superior to the last paragraph printed alone? Explain.

3. What is the basic pattern of the opening sentence of the fifth paragraph? Find other examples of this pattern. What is their total impact on Hawthorne's description?

4. Write a paragraph of description of someone you know, using the same pattern for the entire paragraph that you discovered in the previous question.

Analytical Considerations

1. Jefferson's description of Washington unfolds as a sketch of his subject's character. Hawthorne's portrait of Lincoln unfolds as a narrative, as a story of what happened on the day he visited the White House. What different effects do these two approaches create?

2. Hawthorne calls Lincoln "the essential representative of all Yankees" (paragraph 4). What characteristics does he associate with Yankees? Why should he present the president as a stereotype or "pattern"?

3. Jefferson writes as a former president describing another president. Hawthorne writes as a New Englander observing and describing a "Western man" (paragraph 4). At what points does Hawthorne seem to distinguish himself from Lincoln? Does he seem to consider himself superior?

4. The editor of the *Atlantic Monthly* cut paragraphs 3 through 7 of this selection. Why? In the fifty years between 1814 when Jefferson wrote and 1862 when Hawthorne wrote, might there have been a shift in the way biography was written? The editor seems to think that Hawthorne's irreverence is partly a function of his age, that he is "falling into the characteristic and most ominous fault of Young America" (footnote to paragraph 3).

5. Look up the original article in the *Atlantic Monthly*. Might there have been other reasons for cutting five paragraphs out of Hawthorne's original submission?

Suggested Writing Assignments

1. Using some of the details from Hawthorne's sketch of Lincoln, write your own brief sketch but *without the irony and irreverence* of the original. In other words, write a positive, balanced sketch of the president.

2. Using Jefferson and Hawthorne as examples, and perhaps including Whitman's account of Lincoln (NR 92), write an essay in which you discuss your criteria for good biography. Try to answer the question, What should a good biography be and do?

3. If you have access to the original version of Hawthorne's article as published in the *Atlantic Monthly*, write an argument either for or against the editor's decision to cut five paragraphs from Hawthorne's original draft.

TOM WOLFE

Yeager

The Norton Reader, p. 113

Tom Wolfe's now-famous description of Chuck Yeager, the pilot who broke the sound barrier and became one of the first American astronauts, comes from chapter 3 of *The Right Stuff* (1979). In vivid, often breathtaking prose, Wolfe gives an account of a popular American hero and an analysis of what makes such a man popular, what charisma or mystique appeals to the public and makes a superman of an ordinary man. As a form of biography, "Yeager" allows students to see how a writer moves from specific details and facts to larger claims about character and historical significance. As a form of history, Wolfe's book depends on the interweaving of the personal, private lives of the astronauts with the larger public history of the American space program. It provides a good model for writing projects that ask students to connect their own or their families' experiences with some aspect of the public history of the United States or Canada.

Questions from the NR10

1. Before recounting Yeager's personal history or the story of breaking the sound barrier, Wolfe begins with the voice of an airline pilot. Why does he begin this way? What connection does the first paragraph have with the rest of the story?
2. Wolfe interweaves Yeager's personal history with a more public, official history of the space program. Make a flowchart or diagram to show how this interweaving works.
3. Write an essay that interweaves some part of your personal history with some larger, public story.

Analytical Considerations

1. The opening three paragraphs, what journalists call "the lead," establish interest and significance. Ask students what made them interested in Yeager and what significance Wolfe establishes by showing the influence of Yeager's voice and personal style.
2. Perhaps in small groups, ask students to chart the interweaving of Yeager's personal history and the history of the space program: paragraphs 4 to 8, Yeager; 9 to 14, space program; 15, Pancho's Fly Inn; 16 to 18, space program; 19 to 21, Yeager; 22 to 40, October 14, 1947, the day Yeager broke the sound barrier. What advantages does Wolfe gain by combining personal details with official history?
3. How does Wolfe describe places, planes, and other details unfamiliar to most readers? Ask small groups of students to choose one such detail—

whether the landscape at Muroc, Muroc air base, the X-1 plane, Pancho's Fly Inn, or some other detail—and figure out Wolfe's techniques.

4. Compare Wolfe's voice as an author with the voice he creates for Yeager. Ask students how they would describe Wolfe's voice (educated, ironic, intelligent, etc.) and why they think he chooses this voice for himself.

5. How does the ending echo—in style and content—the opening? After finishing the essay, what further significance do readers discover in the opening three paragraphs?

Suggested Writing Assignments

1. Write an account of some other person important to the U.S. space program, using some of Wolfe's techniques for presenting a character.

2. View the movie version of *The Right Stuff,* and write an account of how the movie adapts or uses Wolfe's account of Yeager's life and character.

3. Write an essay that connects some part of your personal history with some larger, public story.

DANIEL MARK EPSTEIN

The Case of Harry Houdini

The Norton Reader, p. 123

Epstein's account of Houdini provides an example of how a writer, intrigued by stories told to him as a child, goes on to learn more facts and discover the significance of a popular hero. Harry Houdini (1874–1926) was a legendary magician and escape artist, a rabbi's son born in Budapest, Hungary, and according to Epstein's grandfather, a man who "defeated the German Imperial Police." This larger-than-life significance is what intrigues Epstein; it makes him ask not only how Houdini's tricks actually worked but also why we are fascinated with heroes who seem able to defy and overcome reality. This essay was a commemorative piece, written sixty years after Houdini's death. It might provoke students to do research and write about some popular hero now dead but still remembered in family legend or local lore.

Questions from the NR10

1. What, according to Epstein, was the message of Houdini's career? What details in the essay exemplify that message?

2. How important to this account of Houdini is the fact that he was a Jew? What are some of the implications of that fact? What might Epstein mean to imply by his account of the confrontations between Houdini and the German police?

3. At several points in his account of Houdini, Epstein creates an effect of suspense. How does he manage that effect? What purposes does it serve?

4. Epstein's account of Houdini leaves some unanswered questions in, for example, paragraphs 3, 19, 30, and elsewhere. What are they? Why are

they unanswered? Choose one unanswered question and, through research or speculation, write an answer to it.

Analytical Considerations

1. Ask students if they find the figure of Houdini appealing—what appeals to them, what doesn't. Then consider whether Epstein's essay intends to re-create a popular hero, to deconstruct such a hero, or to present a balanced account of Houdini's life and significance.
2. Epstein connects the popularity of a figure like Houdini with the cultural context in which the man lived. Why does Epstein think Houdini might have had particular appeal to German working-class and Jewish audiences in the early twentieth century? Ask students to analyze esspecially paragraphs 7 to 15.
3. In the end Epstein wants to attribute Houdini's success to "good old American know-how" (paragraph 37). Ask students to consider what evidence fits this thesis, what does not, and why Epstein might wish to make such a claim.

Suggested Writing Assignments

1. Do research on a hero you have heard about from your family or friends. Write an account of his or her life, combining your research with family legend or lore.
2. Tom Wolfe and Daniel Epstein both write about popular heroes, yet they use somewhat different techniques. Write a comparison of the ways they present their heroes and make them appealing to the reader.

VIRGINIA WOOLF

My Father: Leslie Stephen

The Norton Reader, p. 134; Shorter Edition, p. 59

Virginia Woolf, one of the finest novelists and most sensitive literary critics of the twentieth century, was an acute reader and renderer of character. In this portrait of her father, a great philosopher and essayist in his own right, Woolf is able to bring the man to life. But we are certainly (and perhaps naturally) given a biased view of Leslie Stephen. Try as she might to leaven her praise with honest evaluation, the admiring daughter creates a glowing portrait of her father as a paragon of men. Perhaps Stephen was a paragon, a model scholar, father, and friend, but some students may feel that Woolf's portrait is a little too perfect. You might ask them to compare it with other portraits of family members in this section—say Annie Dillard's of her mother or Judith Ortiz Cofer's of her grandmother—to discuss the different purposes of these essays and to suggest how different purposes may lead writers to alternate approaches to biography.

Questions from the NR10

1. Would you like to have been Leslie Stephen's son or daughter? Why, or why not?
2. Giving praise can be a difficult rhetorical and social undertaking. How does Woolf avoid the pitfalls or try to?
3. In some of her other work, Woolf shows a deep and sensitive concern for women's experience and awareness. Do you find a feminist awareness here? In what way?
4. In her novel *To the Lighthouse*, Woolf creates the fictional character of Mr. Ramsey from recollections of her father. Compare the characterization in her essay with this passage from the novel: "What he said was true. It was always true. He was incapable of untruth; never tampered with a fact; never altered a disagreeable word to suit the pleasure or convenience of any mortal being, least of all his own children, who, sprung from his loins, should be aware from childhood that life is difficult; facts uncompromising; and the passage to that fabled land where our brightest hopes are extinguished, our frail barks founder in darkness (here Mr. Ramsey would straighten his back and narrow his little blue eyes upon the horizon), one that needs, above all, courage, truth, and the power to endure." (*To the Lighthouse*, Harcourt, Brace & World, 1927; © 1955 Leonard Woolf, pp. 10–11.)
5. Write a sketch about a father, real or fictional, adopting a tone similar to Woolf's in this sketch.

Analytical Considerations

1. As a class or in small groups, examine the essay for clues to Woolf's purpose in writing "My Father: Leslie Stephen." Direct attention to the original context of the essay—that of Woolf, the devoted daughter, writing her recollections for a general readership. In addition to Woolf's public purposes in writing, you might raise the idea that Woolf was writing for herself as a means of understanding her relationship with her father.
2. We know the audience for the original publication of this essay consisted of readers of the Times of London on November 28, 1932. (Leslie Stephen died in 1904, so this essay first appeared twenty-eight years after his death.) Ask students to look for textual clues that reveal Woolf's awareness of her audience, e.g., "Even today there may be parents . . ." (paragraph 10).
3. Analyze the design of the essay. Does it use chronology as an ordering mechanism? Does it organize details around abstract qualities that are taken up one by one? Or does it use some other principle of organization? Study and label what each paragraph contributes to the development of the essay. If you have read Dillard's essay "Terwilliger Bunts One" (NR 148, SE 74), you might compare and contrast her mode of organization with Woolf's.
4. Good description often coalesces around a dominant impression. Discuss the dominant impression Woolf creates about her father and how she creates it. Ask about specific assertions and kinds of support (anecdote, quotation, memory, etc.). Distinguish between the use and value of "objective" infor-

mation (the testimony of others; Stephen's remarks) and the use and value of "subjective" material (Woolf's own memories and opinions).

5. In paragraph 4, Woolf describes her father's habit of drawing beasts on the flyleaves of his books and scribbling pungent analyses in the margins; then she notes that these "brief comments" were the "germ of the more temperate statements of his essays." This aptly illustrates the process of composition for many of us. Encourage students to see that reading offers possibilities for establishing a dialogue between writer and reader, that careful reading involves annotation. You might devote some class discussion to fostering this sense of involvement with the text.

6. Woolf reveals, perhaps unconsciously, some rather unpleasant and dislikable aspects of her father here. Do such elements belong in a biographical sketch? You might recall, if you have read Nathaniel Hawthorne's account of Abraham Lincoln (NR 110), the editor's remarks on "irreverence," quoted in the footnote to paragraph 3.

7. When Woolf says of Leslie Stephen, "The things that he did not say were always there in the background" (paragraph 5) and "Too much, perhaps, has been said of his silence" (paragraph 7), she directs our attention to an oft-neglected dimension of the text: silences and absences. Ask students to reconstruct the image of Leslie Stephen based on the information Woolf leaves out of her essay.

Suggested Writing Assignments

1. Write a character sketch of a parent or grandparent. Strive for the concreteness and balance that Woolf has worked for in "My Father: Leslie Stephen."

2. Read two or three other biographical sketches in this section. Compare and contrast them with Woolf's on points of subject, purpose, content, and tone.

3. How does Woolf define *fatherhood* in her essay? Using examples from "My Father: Leslie Stephen," write an essay on Woolf's conception of fatherhood.

SCOTT RUSSELL SANDERS

Under the Influence

The Norton Reader, p. 138; Shorter Edition, p. 63

Scott Sanders's father was not, by most standards, an exemplary person: he drank too much, and his alcoholism did permanent harm to himself, his wife, and especially his children. Yet Sanders's essay is not a melodramatic account of the dangers of alcoholism or child abuse. It is an honest reminiscence and sensitive analysis of a father and his problem, and it contains thorough, relevant research on alcoholism as a disease and "public scourge" (paragraph 8).

Sanders provides an excellent model for treating a difficult biographical subject with fairness and candor. If you are also reading (or have read) Sanders's essay "Looking at Women" (NR 253, SE 132), you might want to compare and contrast his techniques in writing on a personal, but somewhat more distanced, topic with this vividly autobiographical essay in "People, Places."

Questions from the NR10

1. Sanders frequently punctuates his memories of his father with information from other sources—dictionaries, medical encyclopedias, poems and short stories, the Bible. What function do these sources perform? How do they enlarge and enrich Sanders's essay?
2. Why does Sanders include the final three paragraphs (53 to 55)? What effect do they create that would be lost without them?
3. Drawing on your memories of a friend or family member, write an essay about some problem that person had and its effect on your life.

Analytical Considerations

1. Using the responses to question 1 (above), chart the structure of Sanders's essay, especially his placement of external, objective sources and their relation to personal experience and memory.
2. One source that Sanders gives prominence is the New Testament story of the madman possessed by demons and the Gadarene swine. Ask students to read an original version of the story (Matthew 8, Mark 5, or Luke 8) and compare it with Sanders's retelling. What does Sanders emphasize? How does he apply the story? How does he later echo it (paragraph 51)?
3. Why does Greeley Ray Sanders drink? Consider those moments in the essay when Sanders seems ready to give an answer. Does he—or does he resist a final explanation?
4. Ask students what parallels Sanders sees between his own life as a "workaholic" and his father's as an "alcoholic." What are the differences between father and son? Why might Sanders want to draw parallels, even though the differences are significant?

Suggested Writing Assignments

1. Write a short sketch of a friend or family member who faced a serious problem, whether it was one he or she overcame or succumbed to.
2. Is alcoholism a "public scourge," as Sanders suggests in paragraph 8? Do research on this topic and write an "objective" report on your findings.
3. Is a "workaholic" really like an "alcoholic," as Sanders implies at the end of his essay? Write a brief essay comparing and contrasting the two types and pointing out differences as well as similarities.

ANNIE DILLARD

Terwilliger Bunts One

The Norton Reader, p. 148; Shorter Edition, p. 74

Taken from Dillard's autobiographical *An American Childhood* (1987), this selection might as readily have been titled "My Mother" as anything else, for in it Dillard attempts to characterize her mother—with all her amusing idiosyncrasies and annoying quirks, her remarkable strengths and forgivable weaknesses. Because Dillard depicts a person she knows well, her essay might be compared with Virginia Woolf's "My Father: Leslie Stephen" (NR 134, SE 59) or June Jordan's "For My American Family" (NR 154, SE 79) to raise questions about how a writer conveys a familiar subject to an audience unfamiliar with the subject (through anecdotes rather than adjectives, through the subject's favorite phrases as much as the writer's own words). In contrast, you might use Tom Wolfe's "Yeager" (NR 113) or Daniel Epstein's essay on Harry Houdini (NR 123) to ask about the techniques needed to characterize someone famous whom the writer has never met.

Analytical Considerations

1. You might ask students what anecdotes they remember best about Dillard's mother, why they remember them, and what the anecdotes reveal about the mother's personality.
2. Dillard's mother has many personal qualities her daughter admires. What are those qualities? Does she have qualities about which Dillard is ambivalent? How does Dillard convey her attitude?
3. Dillard's mother lived during a time when the possibilities for women were more limited than they are now, yet Dillard never belabors this point. She simply says, "Mother's energy and intelligence suited her for a greater role in a larger arena—mayor of New York, say—than the one she had" (paragraph 27). Why does Dillard work implicitly rather than explicitly? How does she make her point through examples and anecdotes?
4. This essay is constructed as a series of vignettes, each a page or two long. How does Dillard construct a single vignette? (You might compare the first with the last.) What organization does Dillard give to the series of vignettes— e.g., why does she begin as she does and end where she ends?

Suggested Writing Assignments

1. Write a character sketch about your mother or some other family member, using techniques from Dillard that you found particularly effective.
2. "Torpid conformity was a kind of sin; it was stupidity itself," according to Dillard's mother (paragraph 33). Write an essay in which you illustrate this thesis with examples from your own experience.
3. Take a phrase or common saying from your own family's history. Write a brief essay in which you convey what that phrase or saying means to you and your family.

For My American Family: A Belated Tribute to a Legacy of
Gifted Intelligence and Guts

The Norton Reader, p. 154; Shorter Edition, p. 79

June Jordan was born in Harlem, educated at Barnard College and the
University of Chicago, and now teaches at the University of California at
Berkeley. As the title suggests, this essay is a "tribute" to those family members
who helped her on her way and who were, on their own terms, gifted, intelligent, and courageous. It provides an excellent model for celebrating and
appreciating family members—without being negative, overly sentimental,
or saccharine. The essay also provides a critique of those social scientists who
refer to Harlem and its black communities as "breeding grounds of despair"
or "ghettos" or "culturally deprived" areas (paragraph 13). As a critique, it might
provide a model for students to respond personally to—and disagree with—
more formal, academic essays in other sections of *The Norton Reader*, such
as "Cultural Critique" or "Human Nature."

Questions from the NR10

1. Jordan's essay might be called an "appreciation"—of her parents, her aunt,
   and the community in which she grew up. What qualities in them does she
   appreciate? How does she make these qualities concrete for the reader?
2. Who is the "American family" referred to in Jordan's title? What do you
   think is Jordan's conception of a family?
3. Jordan quotes her aunt near the end of the essay. Why does Jordan present
   an important point through her aunt's words?
4. Write an essay of appreciation about some person or some group, taking
   into account Jordan's techniques for making personal qualities come alive
   through anecdote and action.

Analytical Considerations

1. In paragraph 6 Jordan uses the terms *immigrant* and *alien*. Ask students
   what each word connotes and which word Jordan associates with her family.
   How does the introduction—the imaginary scene in which Jordan's father
   photographs the Statue of Liberty—prepare for this later use of official terms?
2. The essay includes three portraits—of Jordan's father, mother, and aunt.
   What does Jordan accomplish with each? Why does she present them in
   this order?
3. Throughout the essay Jordan recalls and quotes the words of her father,
   mother, and aunt. How are their words and voices essential to this essay?
   What respect does Jordan implicitly show by not taking over their voices
   as narrator?
4. Many of Jordan's details offer specific evidence against the view that black
   persons growing up in Harlem are "culturally deprived" (paragraph 13).
   On their own or in groups, ask students to choose one black hero referred

to in paragraphs 11 to 12 or one aspect of life mentioned in paragraphs 14 to 15 and explain how it provides evidence of a "rich" cultural experience.

5. If you read any of the essays at the end of the "Cultural Critique" section— Brent Staples, "Black Men and Public Space" or Shelby Steele, "The Recoloring of Campus Life"—you might ask students to compare and contrast Jordan's experiences growing up in a black community with one or both of these writers' views.

Suggested Writing Assignments

1. Using Jordan as a model, write a "tribute" to a family member whose example or influence helped you.
2. Do research on one of the black heroes mentioned in paragraphs 11 to 12, and write an essay about his or her life that, at least in part, explains why Jordan's parents taught her about this figure.
3. How do parents and other relatives help to educate their children? Compare and contrast Jordan's essay with another in this section (such as Virginia Woolf's "My Father: Leslie Stephen" or Judith Cofer's "More Room") or in the "Education" section (such as Eudora Welty's "Clamorous to Learn").

JUDITH ORTIZ COFER

More Room

The Norton Reader, p. 158; Shorter Edition, p. 83

Born in Hormigueros, Puerto Rico, Cofer spent much of her childhood traveling between her Puerto Rican home and Paterson, New Jersey, where she also lived. This essay recalls her grandmother's bedroom: its sights, smells, symbols, and wonders. It also narrates the tale of a Puerto Rican woman who maintained control of her body and personal space. As such, it might be called a feminist parable, yet it is never so didactic that the message (made explicit in the final paragraph) intrudes upon the pleasure of the story. You might want students to use Cofer's essay as a model for their own exemplary tales: narratives and family stories that taught them a lesson about life.

Questions from the NR10

1. At the end of the essay, Cofer explains in fairly direct terms why her grandmother wanted "more room." Why do you think she uses narration as the primary mode in the rest of the essay? What does she gain by first narrating, then explaining?
2. Cofer uses many similes and metaphors—for example, in paragraph 1 she says that her grandmother's house was "like a chambered nautilus" or in paragraph 5 that grandmother's Bible was "her security system." Discuss the use of one or two such comparisons that you find particularly effective.
3. What are the possible meanings of the title?
4. Write about a favorite or mysterious place you remember from childhood.

1. This is a short essay, only eleven paragraphs, similar in length to many essays students are asked to write. You might ask students to map out the "flow" of the essay: what happens in each paragraph, where Cofer allows herself more space (paragraphs 5 to 6), where she creates suspense and picks up the pace (paragraphs 10 to 11).
2. In preparing Question 2, above, students will have identified some of the key metaphors in this essay: "like a chambered nautilus" (paragraph 1), "like a great blue bird" (paragraph 2), "like a wise empress" (paragraph 3), the Bible as "her security system" (paragraph 5), etc. List their findings on the board and discuss the way each metaphor either clarifies or enriches Cofer's description of *la casa de Mamá*.
3. Discuss the importance of the final paragraph, which explicitly states the reasons Cofer's grandmother needed her own room. If the students are writing essays similar to Cofer's, ask them to end with a similar explication of their story's meaning.

Suggested Writing Assignments

1. Retell a story often told within your family. Concentrate on a single person or place as Cofer does and suggest, either implicitly or explicitly, why this tale is so important to you or your family.
2. Write about a favorite place you remember from childhood, using details and metaphors as Cofer does to bring it alive.
3. Compare and contrast Cofer's depiction of her grandmother with N. Scott Momaday's of his grandmother in "The Way to Rainy Mountain" (NR 177, SE 87). Where they differ, suggest why their differences might reflect different backgrounds or intentions.

MARGARET ATWOOD

True North

The Norton Reader, p. 162; Shorter Edition, p. 91

Margaret Atwood is best known as a novelist, the author of such popular and award-winning works as *The Handmaid's Tale, Cat's Eye,* and *The Robber Bride.* Yet she also writes regularly as an essayist and contributes to a Canadian magazine called *Saturday Night,* in which this piece first appeared. Whether Canadian or from the northern parts of the United States, many students will remember the song with which Atwood opens the essay: "Land of the silver birch, Home of the beaver." (Like Atwood, I sang it as a child with my Brownie pack.)

If students recall the song, you might ask what emotions it evokes: do they think it corny? Or do they, like Atwood, find tears in their eyes? If they do not recall the song or if they think it corny, then you might need to find another way of explaining the nostalgia Atwood alludes to in the first paragraph.

(Perhaps simply asking about the "wilderness" will do it.) Like Noel Perrin in "Forever Virgin: The American View of America" (NR 643), Atwood means to explore our attitudes toward the wilderness, but unlike Perrin, she concerns herself with particularly *Canadian* attitudes. Indeed, comparing Perrin's essay, included in the "Nature and the Environment" section, with Atwood's provides a useful way to raise broad questions about North American attitudes toward nature and the environment—and whether or not there is a difference between Americans and Canadians on this score. Concluding this comparison with William Cronon's "The Trouble with Wilderness" (NR 651) adds a useful complication.

Questions from the NR10

1. What context does Atwood set for the opening section? How does her need to explain to American Southerners in a college classroom help her communicate with the readers of this essay?
2. Beginning in paragraph 16, Atwood reenacts a journey to the "north." What does this journey, re-created for the reader, help her achieve?
3. Why does Atwood include a section about "typical ways of dying" in a northern landscape? What qualities about northern Canada can she present through this unusual approach?
4. Write an essay about a geographical region that appeals to you but that may be unknown or unappealing to others. Using techniques learned from Atwood or other writers in this section, try to communicate the region's appeal as you write.

Analytical Considerations

1. Although this essay is a length common in sophisticated periodicals, it may seem slightly long to students accustomed to short pieces of 2,000 to 3,000 words. The questions (reprinted above) should help students begin to understand Atwood's approach and structure: the opening frame set in an Alabama classroom (paragraphs 1 to 7), the questions and definitions of "north" (paragraphs 9 to 13), the re-created journey (paragraphs 16 to 29), the discussion of acid rain (paragraphs 30 to 32), the comparison with Scotland (paragraphs 33 to 40), the imagined ways of dying in the Canadian wilderness (paragraphs 41 to 44), three scenes in the north "sitting around the table" or "on the dock" (paragraphs 45 to 56, 57 to 61, 62 to 64), the return to Toronto (paragraphs 65 to 67).
2. Atwood states that "everything in Canada, outside Toronto, begins with geography" (paragraph 3), and she shows a Canadian map to the American students she is teaching. It might help to show students a similar map, specifically to trace the route of the journey Atwood takes in paragraphs 16 to 27.
3. What happens in the essay after Atwood gets to "true north"? What do the three scenes "sitting around the table" (paragraphs 45 to 56, 57 to 61) or "sitting on the dock" (paragraphs 62 to 64) contribute?
4. When Atwood uses "us" and "we" in paragraph 10 and throughout the essay, to whom is she referring? Canadians only? Ask students whether Atwood's sense of the wilderness is similar to, say, Noel Perrin's in "Forever Virgin: An American View of America" (NR 643) or Edward Abbey's in

"The Serpents of Paradise" (NR 613, SE 331) or whether she describes a uniquely Canadian attitude toward the northern wilderness.

Suggested Writing Assignments

1. Do all North Americans share Atwood's attitudes toward the "north"? Write an essay in which you either show how your views differ or confirm your basic agreement with Atwood.
2. Write about your own region and the values you see embodied in it; write your essay to an audience of readers unfamiliar with that region.
3. In the final paragraphs, as Atwood traces the journey south back to Toronto and its pollution, she asks, "we're going into that?" Write an essay in which you analyze why you (or other people) choose to live in cities, even those hit hard by pollution.

KATHLEEN NORRIS

The Holy Use of Gossip

The Norton Reader, p. 172; Shorter Edition, p. 102

In the wrong hands Norris's essay could be a dangerous example, since it operates through assertions rather than extended demonstrations. Norris will tell a story or two, assert a claim, and move on. Nowhere does she stop to provide careful, step-by-step support for her statements and claims. She doesn't even seem to be aware that they are in need of further explanation. For example, the essay opens and closes with anecdotes. In between come rather large claims about her topic, gossip: "gossip done well can be a holy thing" (paragraph 10); "Gossip is theology translated into experience" (paragraph 22); "When we gossip we are also praying. . . ." (paragraph 22). Why doesn't Norris let on that these are huge, deliberately improbable claims?

Some composition teachers might be tempted to scorn Norris's approach as too superficial, too anecdotal. They will regard Norris as a bad example for college students, who need to learn how to handle a formal argument composed of claim and demonstration. To be sure, if all *Norton Reader* essays employed this type of example there would indeed be a problem. Fortunately, *The Norton Reader* is large and rich enough to encompass all kinds of essays, and this particularly nice example of anecdotal arguing can be opposed by many more orthodox examples of traditional arguments.

Ask students what they think of this type of approach, the anecdotal. Where wouldn't it work? What subject matter lends itself to this kind of anecdotal style? What kind of person would be convinced by this type of essay? Who would resist it? (A thought experiment: imagine what kind of formal argument could ever support one of those three claims Norris makes about the religious nature of gossip. Can we see any of those claims being the subject of formal proof?) Interestingly, a professional theologian, one whose job it is to think about the divine, might find Norris's essay seriously wanting as theology but perfectly fine as an interesting kind of writing about ethics, spirituality, or small-town living.

Questions from the NR10

1. Exactly how is Norris using the word *gossip*? How do you use the word yourself? What range of meanings of gossip do you usually encounter? Check a collegiate dictionary to pin down the most common meanings.
2. Norris situates her essay in a small town in a rural part of the country where population is decreasing. Can you imagine her doing something similar in a suburb? In the heart of a large city? Would some of the strengths Norris discerns be lost in the translation to a different setting?
3. Norris sees the religious value of what is often regarded as human failing. In an essay of your own, take a similar "failing" and, like Norris, show its good side, though it doesn't have to be religious. (Some possible examples include: silence, nosiness, jealousy, pride.)

Analytical Considerations

1. Does Norris fall back on overused language at times? How else would you interpret sentences like "the town breathed a collective sigh of relief" (paragraph 20) and "the whole town rejoiced" (paragraph 23)? They both sound like clichés. Are they? Do they work in their settings?
2. What is theology? Look it up in an encyclopedia. (A dictionary entry would be too short.)
3. Students can consider why Norris chooses to end with a series of anecdotes. (Rachel Carson does something similar in her otherwise very different essay, "Tides" [NR 598].)
4. By connecting this essay to its epigraph by noted short story writer Grace Paley, students can test the claim that gossip is "the way all storytellers learn about life." Is Norris, a storyteller herself, doing something like that in her essay?

Suggested Writing Assignments

1. Write about a situation in which many people were hoping a friend or neighbor or admired figure would "pull through."
2. Describe an incident of gossip, making it as vivid as you can through quotes and detailed descriptions of faces, tones of voice, and physical reactions.
3. Tell how the values of these small-town and ranch people seem to be similar to or different from those of the people where you live.

N. SCOTT MOMADAY

The Way to Rainy Mountain

The Norton Reader, p. 177; Shorter Edition, p. 87

Momaday's description of his grandmother and his return to Rainy Mountain, a place sacred to the Kiowa Indians, employs a structure common to many cultures: the journey as an actual and metaphorical quest. You might ask students about their own journeys and journeys they have read about in literature—whether in Homer's *Odyssey* or Jack Kerouac's *On the Road* or some even more recent book of travel writing. Why do we travel? What do we expect to gain from travel? What did Momaday hope to discover by returning to his grandmother's house and retracing the traditional movements of the Kiowas? Such questions might help students to think about the journey structure as a possible one for their own personal reports or for their descriptions of a place of special interest to them. The journey Momaday describes in "Rainy Mountain" beautifully links realistic descriptions of the West, sacred myths of the Kiowas, and memories of his grandmother and her stories to evoke a sense of the importance of place in his own life.

Analytical Considerations

1. What is the structure of this essay? You might ask students to compare Momaday's actual journey (introduced in paragraph 2 and again in paragraph 5) with the historical journeys of his ancestors, the Kiowas. How are the two journeys linked?
2. Why does Momaday begin and end with descriptions of Rainy Mountain? How and why are the two descriptions different?
3. Where does Momaday include cultural myths, historical events, or his grandmother's stories in this essay? How do these enrich our understanding of the places Momaday revisits?
4. To what extent are "people" essential to our understanding of "place"? Discuss the ways in which Momaday describes his grandmother both as grandmother (i.e., a real person, a family member) and as Kiowa Indian (i.e., a representative of an older culture that no longer exists). Why do we need both views of his grandmother to understand the significance of Momaday's return to his ancestral home?
5. Look closely at sentences in which Momaday chooses words with metaphorical or symbolic significance—e.g., in paragraph 1, where he links Rainy Mountain to the place "where Creation was begun," or in paragraph 5, where he refers to his journey as a "pilgrimage," or in paragraph 9, where he refers to the soldiers stopping of Indian rituals as "deicide." Discuss the connotations of such words and how they enrich the literal journey that Momaday takes.

Suggested Writing Assignments

1. Write about a journey you took to a place important in your family's history—whether an ancestral home, the home of a relative, or a home you lived in as a child.
2. Write about a place with historical and cultural significance, combining your own observations with history, legend, and/or myth.
3. Write a descriptive essay about a person and place that seem intertwined. In doing so, think about why the person seems so essential to understanding the place.

JON KRAKAUER

Club Denali

The Norton Reader, p. 181

Jon Krakauer's "Club Denali" recounts his failure to achieve a quest he admits is foolish and dangerous. He makes the drudgery and danger of mountain climbing seem obvious—interestingly, he doesn't spend any time at all analyzing why he or any of his fellow climbers actually pursue this strange quest. It may be useful to ask the class for opinions of the quest itself: Is it crazy? Rational? Worthwhile? Foolish? A complex mixture? A question closer to home: Would you do this yourself? What would you think of a loved one who wanted to climb Denali?

"Club Denali" is part of a growing trend in non-fiction writing: the tale of danger and death in the elements, either at sea, in the forests, or on mountains. Krakauer is something of a specialist in this genre; readers interested in this text can be directed to his other books exploring the desire to tempt nature in extreme circumstances: *Into the Wild,* about a young man's deadly Alaska adventure, and *Into Thin Air,* an account of the disastrous 1996 Everest expedition on which Krakauer himself came close to perishing.

Students should note the ironic understatement of the title, a play on Club Med, no doubt. And they should note the juxtapositions of highly syllabic, "elevated" language—"inhalations" (paragraph 53) "premises" (paragraph 33), "the maelstrom" (paragraph 33), "creatures of the subterranean gloom" (paragraph 37)—with very down-to-earth language—"there were seven or eight very strange guys in there" (paragraph 35). This is a calculated effect that appears throughout. Students can find other examples in the rest of this essay.

In connection with Question 3 from the NR10, about women's perspectives, students can start by looking at Ruth Anne Kocour with Michael Hodgson, *Facing the Extreme* (1998), an account of her 1992 Denali climb. Other relevant accounts are by Arlene Blum, Stacey Allison, and in *Leading Out* (1992), a collection of women's mountaineering essays.

Questions from the NR10

1. How does the fact that Krakauer himself was a participant affect his observations about mountain climbing?
2. What details in Krakauer's writing help readers understand why anyone would do something such as climb Denali?
3. Plenty of women climb mountains, but this piece is almost all about men. What elements seem the most stereotypically male? Speculate about whether women might write differently about mountain climbing.
4. The names climbers call themselves don't sound particularly humorous as we read closer to sea level. What other sports or activities give rise to similarly silly and/or inventive names? Why are such names popular?

Analytical Considerations

1. Exactly what does Krakauer admire in people as disparate as Dr. Hackett on the one hand and the Throbbing Members on the other? Does Krakauer have any of that admiration and respect for Adrian the Romanian?
2. Krakauer drops the names of some famous climbers—Bradford Washburn, Reinhold Messner, etc. What role do these names play here? What's the purpose of such name-dropping?
3. "Club Denali" starts by associating the impact of warnings to mountaineers with similar warnings about VD as a menace to new army recruits. Does it surprise you to have mountaineering associated with VD? Does this opening linkage connect to the tone or the details in the rest of the essay? Point out other "low" elements in the essay.
4. It's worth focusing on Krakauer's rueful tone here and trying to pin down his consistent technique of a flat presentation of terribly daunting facts: "everyone above 15,000 feet is going to die"; "a vertical mile above."
5. Krakauer writes for climbing enthusiasts as well as armchair mountaineers. Why would climbers enjoy this, since he's so unrelievedly grim about the actual climbing itself? What's the attraction?

Suggested Writing Assignments

1. Write about how someone "failed" at some demanding, hopeless, yet important task. Take a rueful attitude toward the attempt, much as Krakauer does in "Club Denali."
2. Write an essay describing how people who have been through difficult or life-threatening situations later talk about them. Do they use understatement, as Krakauer does? Do they dramatize, making the event into a good story? What is the range of responses to danger, and why do some people choose to recount it in one way instead of another?
3. Write to Krakauer and try to persuade him that his desire to climb is foolish.

CHARLOTTE GRAY

The Temple of Hygiene

The Norton Reader, p. 193

Who has not wanted to visit a Japanese or Turkish bathhouse—or some other exotic place that, through photographs or drawings, has filled our imagination with mystery and excitement? In this essay, Gray takes us on a trip to a Japanese *sento* (bathhouse), and it turns out to be more utilitarian and less exotic that she expected.

The structure of this essay is straightforward: after a brief explanation of how and why she went to Japan, Gray takes us chronologically through the ritual of bathing in a sento, along the way recording her responses and the responses of Japanese patrons to her. Because it is relatively simple, the essay provides an excellent model for students' writing about place. One interesting assignment would be to ask students to visit a local place they have never seen before and to record their experiences and impressions. (If nothing else, churches provide interesting sites of cultural difference, but if your class is ethnically or nationally diverse, your students may be able to suggest many such places.) Peer groups can easily respond to such essays by noting what details they liked and what they would want to know more about.

Questions from the NR10

1. Much of Gray's essay reflects on the differences between Canadian and Japanese cultures. List some of those differences and Gray's techniques for portraying them.
2. After reading the title of this essay, "The Temple of Hygiene," did the opening paragraph startle you? What different perspectives on the Japanese bathhouse are presented by the title versus Gray's description of the picture? Which one dominates the essay?
3. If you have visited another country, or a region in your own country different from the one in which you live, write about the experience of encountering cultural difference by, as Gray does, focusing on a *place*.

Analytical Considerations

1. Why does Gray begin by describing a Japanese print? You might show such a print to students and ask how it arouses our expectations.
2. Where does the actual trip to the *sento* (bathhouse) begin? What is the function of the first six paragraphs?
3. Ask students to list the cultural differences that Gray's essay reveals—both within the bathhouse and before the visit. Then consider how she portrays those differences and with what tone.

4. Why does Gray end with the detail about Ben Johnson, the Canadian sprinter who, after winning a gold medal in the Olympics, was disqualified for anabolic steroid use? Is it just a current reference—or does it relate closely to the theme of cultural difference?

Suggested Writing Assignments

1. Visit a place you have heard about but never before seen, and write about your experience and impressions.
2. With a group of peers, decide on an "exotic" place you would like to know more about. Collect photos and drawings of that site, and then write about what in those pictures captures your imagination and makes you want to visit.
3. Is there a place you have visited where others in your class have never been? If so, write an informative account of your memories and impressions.

FRED STREBEIGH

The Wheels of Freedom: Bicycles in China

The Norton Reader, p. 198

An experienced journalist goes to China to report for a cycling magazine on how bicycles are omnipresent. While there, Strebeigh witnesses the start of the 1989 Tiananmen Square uprising, the outpouring of democratic spirit that would end with brutal government repression. So Strebeigh has a problem. How to fulfill the original intent of his trip, to produce a report on bicycles in China for his audience of cycling enthusiasts, while remaining true to his own instincts as a reporter witnessing history being made in a student revolt? He solves it brilliantly by regarding the bicycle as a cultural symbol of China. It represents the one way to gain anonymity and, paradoxically, freedom to meet people in a time of troubles.

The opening is a model for students to examine and steal ideas from. Strebeigh places us in the midst of the flow of cyclists in Beijing, meeting a stranger who feels empowered to talk to him, knowing she will be free from suspicious eyes. The simple quote at the opening and the ominous "as we rode together we broke the law" frame a paragraph that introduces readers to Strebeigh's two themes: the ubiquity of bicycles and their key presence in the lives of participants in the uprising.

It would be helpful to a class to have some understanding of bicycle technology; perhaps a class member knows enough to serve as a guide. Strebeigh was writing for a highly knowledgeable audience who all ride sleek chromoly road bikes with lightweight Shimano components that make the clunky, heavy Chinese bicycles seem from another century, hopelessly outclassed by the modern machines found in American bike shops. How is Strebeigh to make those bikes interesting to his readers? He finds a simple way: connect them to the lives of the people who ride them, and focus on their cultural significance, not their outdated technology. For the Chinese have something hard-core American cyclists can only dream of: a society where the bicycle is the central mode of transportation. The actual kind of bike doesn't matter; their role is what counts.

Analytical Considerations

1. Ask students to imagine what the illustrations to Strebeigh's essay looked like. What about the ads in such a magazine?
2. Have students bring in similar "lifestyle" magazines with their complement of ads for the appropriate, expensive implements: skis, snowboards, stereos, sports cars, boats. The question is, What's the context in which Strebeigh's essay would have been seen?
3. Fang Hui's story is of triumph over discrimination, inexperience, and great physical obstacles. Ask students if they think Strebeigh might be making a subtle point about American reliance on fancy machinery and expertise.

Suggested Writing Assignments

1. Describe the significance to your own life of a form of transportation. Ask, as Strebeigh does, what the bike, bus, car, plane, or train does to human interaction.
2. Write about someone who excelled at a physical activity against great odds. (It doesn't have to be as dramatic as Fang Hui's story.)
3. Take a seemingly utilitarian implement, appliance, or tool and describe it to show the meaning it has for the people who proudly use it.

DAVID GUTERSON

Enclosed. Encyclopedic. Endured: The Mall of America

The Norton Reader, p. 206

Guterson's essay, published in *Harper's Magazine*, is a thorough report on—and devastating critique of—the American shopping mall. It begins in classic journalistic form by establishing the interest and significance of its subject: the 4.2 million miles of floor space, the 12,750 parking spaces, the 10,000 employees, the 44 escalators and 17 elevators, and so on. Then (in paragraph 4) it poses the question: "What might it [the mall] tell us about ourselves?" The answer is a chilling one about loss of community, a feature of ancient marketplaces like the Greek agora or the Persian bazaar but absent in modern America.

This essay might be read in conjunction with Anthony Burgess's "Is America Falling Apart?" (NR 304, SE 171).

Analytical Considerations

1. Ask students what details they remember from Guterson's essay and why those details are significant to them and/or to the essay. If there is a difference in terms of significance, you might ask how Guterson wants his

readers to interpret his facts and what obstacles their own impressions might create for him as writer.

2. It's helpful to create a diagram or outline of this essay and its parts: introduction (paragraphs 1 to 3), sense impressions (paragraphs 4 to 5), interviews with shoppers (paragraphs 6 to 14), a history of marketplaces in various cultures (paragraphs 15 to 19), an extended description of the stores and their contents (paragraphs 20 to 26), a history of the American shopping mall (paragraphs 27 to 33), a descent into the basement of the mall (paragraphs 34 to 40), upstairs in the "woods" (paragraphs 41 to 45), religious services (paragraph 46), concluding analysis (paragraphs 47 to 50). For any one of these sections, ask what Guterson hopes to achieve with it.

3. Why does Guterson descend to the basement, what he calls the "underbelly"? What negative features and false facts does he expose? Why is his survey of Camp Snoopy linked to this section?

4. *Community* is a word that recurs in Guterson's analysis and takes prominence in his conclusion. Ask students what he means by "community" and why he thinks the mall doesn't have it.

Suggested Writing Assignments

1. Visit another place of commerce and, using some of Guterson's techniques, write your own analysis of it.

2. If you have access to recent periodicals or on-line data sources, report on the success of the Mall of America. Look especially at the projections in paragraphs 31 to 32.

3. Guterson argues that modern shopping malls do not create a sense of community. Do you agree or disagree? Why?

4. Compare Guterson's characterization of the mall with Joseph Addison's of the royal exchange. Are their attitudes toward these symbols of commerce similar or different?

HUMAN NATURE

WILLIAM GOLDING

Thinking as a Hobby

The Norton Reader, p. 218; Shorter Edition, p. 118

In this essay, William Golding uses a three-part classificatory scheme, rather casually introduced, to shape an autobiographical account of his development, from school to university in learning what it means to think. Although the essay proceeds in chronological order, his classificatory scheme—three kinds of thinking classified by value and presented in ascending order—overrides its narrative development. Yet because Golding illustrates "grade-three" and "grade-two" thinking with a couple of comic figures each and turns even his illustration of "grade-one" thinking, an encounter with Einstein, into comedy, his discussion of thinking is light and amusing. A serious discussion would require more analysis and different illustrations; it might also require a less easy and tidy classificatory scheme.

In addition to his three-part "made" scheme, Golding introduces a "found" scheme (at least according to what he tells us in the essay): the three statuettes on the cupboard behind his headmaster's desk. The "found" scheme is more arbitrary than the "made" scheme and contributes to the essay's comedy. "Found" schemes, in their arbitrariness, often make good writing exercises: students are likely to perform well—and be pleased with themselves—when challenged with difficult or impossible writing tasks that come with built-in excuses for failure. As a whole, however, "Thinking as a Hobby" may not be an easy model for students, inasmuch as many will be unable to reproduce Golding's wry perception and tonal subtlety.

Analytical Considerations

1. How does Golding's title, "Thinking as a Hobby," signal his comic intent? You may want to ask the same question about his categories: "grade-three thinking," "grade-two thinking," and "grade-one thinking."
2. How does Golding use his "made" classificatory scheme of three kinds of thinking and his "found" scheme of three statuettes on the cupboard? Consider other kinds of "made" and "found" categories. What are their differences?
3. Golding's "made" and "found" schemes both contain three categories. How frequent are classifications by three? How do they differ, say, from classifications by two or four? How many ways can three categories be arranged? ("Goldilocks and the Three Bears" will remind students of means and extremes.)

Suggested Writing Assignments

1. Write a satirical account of at least two individuals you know who exemplify Golding's "grade-three" and "grade-two" thinking.
2. Write a serious account of an individual you know or have read about who exemplifies Golding's "grade-one" thinking; you may want to give it another name. You may want to read the description of Einstein in Jacob Bronowski's "The Nature of Scientific Reasoning" (NR 901, SE 517) and use him.
3. Write an essay in which you use a "found" and arbitrary classificatory scheme. Find or invent one that challenges your ingenuity.

ISAAC ASIMOV

The Eureka Phenomenon

The Norton Reader, p. 223; Shorter Edition, p. 123

Discussion of "The Eureka Phenomenon" can begin with form or content. A formal approach may involve a transition from William Golding's "Thinking as a Hobby" (NB 218, SE 118). Like Golding, Asimov uses a classificatory scheme, though he uses his less emphatically than Golding does. Asimov's scheme contains two categories: voluntary and involuntary thinking, reason and intuition, call them what you will. You may want students to mark the places in the essay where Asimov describes each and notice how often his descriptions involve contrast, explicit and implicit. You may also ask the class to list as many of the pairs as they can and distinguish between these two kinds of thinking. You will want to point out their interdependence. First, the names are usually linked, often conventionally: we do not, for example, ordinarily pair voluntary thinking with intuition, or reason with involuntary thinking. Second, each term of the pair is ordinarily defined by what it is not as well as by what it is. Third, in most pairs, one term will be more or less approving, one term more or less pejorative. This exercise dramatizes binary thinking and, usefully, makes students aware of how conventional it is, how ingrained it is in our language and habits of thought. It also makes them aware of how it invariably involves value judgments. A formal approach shows Asimov, in "The Eureka Phenomenon," reclaiming and transvaluing involuntary thinking or intuition.

An approach focusing on content might begin with the hardest section of the essay, Kekule's discovery. I usually read it with students and point out that Asimov includes it in order to show that Kekule, after seven years of trying to conceptualize the structure of a benzene molecule, came upon the model of a ring—rather than a chain—while sleeping. But I also want students to see how Asimov's prose explanation of the structure of a benzene molecule is virtually unintelligible without diagrams—and thus to appreciate the power of images. (Instructors for whom his explanation is virtually unintelligible even with diagrams will usually find some students in the class who understand Kekule's theory and be able to turn to them for help; demonstrating a transition from incomprehension to comprehension can be a valuable lesson in reading.) Then I go back to an easier section of the essay, Archimedes' discovery, and ask students to generate and even to draw their own images. Experienced readers use imagery habitually but may not be aware that they do; inexperienced readers often need to learn consciously to make and deploy images as an aid to comprehension.

"The Eureka Phenomenon" might well have appeared in the section called "Science." It raises issues explored in that section about the increasing unintelligibility of science to nonscientists and the difficulties of writing about modern science for a popular audience. These issues are also raised in Jacob Bronowski's "The Reach of Imagination" (NR 233) and in another essay by Bronowski, "The Nature of Scientific Reasoning" (NR 901, SE 517) in "Science."

Questions from the NR10

1. Consider Asimov's narrative of Archimedes' and Kekule's discoveries. What elements does he heighten and how? How does he include the scientific information necessary to understand them? How does he make (or attempt to make) this information accessible to nonscientists?
2. Scientists, Asimov concludes, "are so devoted to their belief in conscious thought that they . . . consistently obscure the actual methods by which they obtain their results" (paragraph 81). Consider your own experiments in science courses and the way you have been taught to report them. Do you agree or disagree with Asimov? Why?
3. Have you ever had a "Eureka" experience? Does Asimov's account of the "Eureka phenomenon" help you to understand it? Write about your experience with reference to Asimov's essay.

Analytical Considerations

1. Consider the role of mathematics in both Archimedes' and Kekule's discoveries.
2. William Wordsworth, in the 1800 Preface to the second edition of the *Lyrical Ballads*, wrote: "The remotest discoveries of the Chemist, the Botanist, or Mineralogist will be as proper objects of the Poet's art as any upon which it can be employed, if the time should ever come when these things shall be familiar to us, and the relations under which they are contemplated by the followers of these respective sciences shall be manifestly and palpably material to us as enjoying and suffering human beings." Was Wordsworth's confidence misplaced? How was he wrong about the future of science? Thomas S. Kuhn's "The Route to Normal Science" (NR 905), in "Science" (paragraphs 16 to 18), provides a useful discussion. How was Wordsworth wrong about the future of poetry?
3. Read (at least the section on methodology) John Henry Sloan et al., "Handgun Regulations, Crime, Assaults, and Homicide: A Tale of Two Cities" (NR 913, SE 521) in "Science" and/or Carl Cohen, "The Case for the Use of Animals in Biomedical Research" (NR 707) in "Ethics"; both come from the *New England Journal of Medicine*. Consider their form and how it must, as Asimov puts it, "consistently obscure the actual methods by which they [i.e., scientists] obtain their results" (paragraph 81).

1. Choose a set of paired terms in Asimov's essay and identify the approving and pejorative term. Write an essay in which you reclaim and transvalue what the pejorative term refers to. Some suggestions: reason and emotion, mind and body, order and disorder, masculine and feminine, sacred and secular.
2. Do library research on one or more of the scientists Asimov mentions in paragraphs 75 to 80. Construct an explanation of Asimov's decision not to feature their discoveries in this essay.

JACOB BRONOWSKI

The Reach of Imagination

The Norton Reader, p. 233

The late Jacob Bronowski wrote about both science and literature and was responsible for a television series that you (and perhaps some of your students) may have seen, "The Ascent of Man" (1973–74). He held that scientific and poetic thinking are essentially the same, both originating in the imagination and both tested by experience. "The Reach of Imagination" may be read in conjunction with his essay "The Nature of Scientific Reasoning" (NR 901, SE 517) in "Science"; although written for independent publication, the second extends the concept of imagination that appears in the first. In the first, Bronowski defines the imagination by its nature and scope. His illustrations from science and from literature exemplify his general argument, affirm similarities between scientific and poetic thinking, and buttress his authority.

Students may (legitimately) recognize Bronowski's magisterial range of illustrations as beyond their resources. What kinds of authority, then, are available to them? Many kinds, it's important to emphasize, so long as they learn to moderate their claims to pronounce on large issues, stake out smaller ones, and deploy the authority of others in developing their own, without at the same time losing a personal voice. You may wish to require Suggested Writing Assignment 2 and then use both successful and less successful student papers to illustrate problems of authority.

Questions from the NR10

1. "To imagine," according to Bronowski, means "to make images and to move them about inside one's head in new arrangements" (paragraph 9). How do his illustrations support and expand this definition?
2. Bronowski argues that the imagination works similarly in artists and in scientists. List his illustrations and references in two columns, one for science and one for literature. Why do you think he demonstrates the working of the imagination in science more fully than in art?

3. Read Bronowski's "The Nature of Scientific Reasoning" (NR 901, SE 000). Write an essay in which you describe his illustrations from the work of Newton in both "The Reach of the Imagination" and "The Nature of Scientific Reasoning." Could he have interchanged them? Why or why not?

Analytical Considerations

1. Ask students to list Bronowski's illustrations and references in two columns, one labeled science, the other literature. What does the range of each list indicate about him?
2. Which illustrations does Bronowski explain, and which does he simply refer to? What does his handling of illustrations and references indicate about his intended audience?
3. "Indeed, the most important images for human beings," Bronowski claims, "are simply words, which are abstract symbols" (paragraph 11). Read Erich Fromm, "The Nature of Symbolic Language" (NR 568) in "Language and Communication," and compare his and Bronowski's conceptions of language as symbolic representation.
4. "Animals do not have words," Bronowski observes (paragraph 11). Read Carl Sagan, "The Abstractions of Beasts" (NR 673, SE 344). How would Bronowski respond to Sagan's claims that animals are capable of abstract thought?

Suggested Writing Assignments

1. Write an essay in which you imitate, on a smaller scale, Bronowski's procedures. Take the simplest definition available (in a dictionary) of some abstract term of your own choosing: you may wish to try terms such as *harmony, knowledge, paradox,* or *similarity.* Extend this definition with at least three illustrations, one of which is drawn from experience, another from reading.
2. "Imagination," Bronowski claims, "is a specifically *human* gift" (paragraph 1). Argue against or qualify this claim. Draw your evidence from and buttress your own authority with other authorities by using one or both of the following: Alexander Petrunkevitch, "The Spider and the Wasp" (NR 630, SE 340), Carl Sagan, "The Abstractions of Beasts" (NR 634, SE 344), and/or Edward Abbey, "The Serpents of Paradise" (NR 613, SE 331). While you use the voices and authority of Petrunkevitch, Sagan, or Abbey through quotation and paraphrase, don't let their voices drown out yours or their authority inhibit you from claiming your own.
3. Bronowski, writing in 1967, predicted that "on the day when we land on the moon . . . it will be not a technical but an imaginative triumph, that reaches back to the beginning of modern science and literature both" (paragraph 25). Read one of the works of fiction Bronowski mentions in paragraph 23 and a newspaper or magazine account of the first actual landing on the moon, and then argue for or against his assertion.

SVEN BIRKERTS

Homo Virtualis

The Norton Reader, p. 240

Has the nature of man—of humankind—changed since the advent of computer technology? Almost everyone would say yes, but not everyone would say for the good. In *The Gutenberg Elegies* (1995), of which this essay is a part, Birkerts fears that the current deluge of Internet information may leave us drowned, lost, or abandoned on the "information highway." He presents himself as a modern-day Luddite, "the last man" not to understand computers, "the one to whom everything needs to be explained" (paragraph 1).

Yet in the opening section of the essay (paragraphs 1 to 9) Birkerts give us a description of what the Net can and does currently do, what the "visionaries" claim and what the more moderate "engineers" say. (He obviously did some research and interviewing to gain the information he lacked.) Then he poses the question: "How can anyone argue that computer and Net are just tools, just ways to manage information and facilitate its transmission? . . . It must, in time, alter the humans themselves" (paragraph 9). You might ask students, both those comfortable with computers and those not, whether the changes Birkerts imagines in the remainder of the essay are likely to occur, whether some have already occurred, and whether Birkerts make the case for a shift in the basic human conception of self: "from a belief in a sovereign, bounded self (the Renaissance ideal) to a belief in transpersonal process" (paragraph 16).

Questions from the NR10

1. For years the human species has been called *Homo sapiens*. What is the effect of reclassifying us *Homo virtualis*?
2. The essay begins by noting an "us/them mentality" about the "Net." When you began this essay, were you an "us," knowledgeable and optimistic about the Internet, or a "them," uninformed and distrustful? Did reading the essay change your view? If so, why and how?
3. To what extent does Birkerts's argument depend on personal experience? generalizations about modern culture? facts about technology? Why does he need all three kinds of evidence?
4. Birkerts ends with the argument that "the system is not only inhospitable to the spiritual impulse, it works against it" (paragraph 30). What evidence has he provided to support this position? Has he omitted any important considerations?
5. Write an essay about how the computer has changed the way you think or behave, whether for good or ill.

Analytical Considerations

1. Ask students to consider the language (especially the metaphors) associated with the "visionaries" versus the language associated with the "engineers" (paragraphs 4–9). Does the language fall into predictable binaries? Does anything about the language surprise you and your students?

2. For all or perhaps just two different segments of the essay, ask students to identify the sources of Birkerts's evidence: personal experience, facts about technology, information (whether fact or opinion) gained from interviews, and generalizations about modern culture. What kind of evidence dominates? Does the kind of evidence used change from the beginning to the end of the essay?

3. Consider the final five paragraphs in which Birkerts summarizes what the Net can and cannot do. What positive things does he mention? What negative things? Why does he raise the symbol of "home" in the penultimate paragraph?

Suggested Writing Assignments

1. Interview several people, ideally a combination of students, faculty, and technical personnel, who are closely involved with computers. Write a report on the changes they see in the way(s) human beings will think and live as a result of computer technology.

2. Write a biographical portrait of someone who is either a computer "visionary" or, like Birkerts, a modern Luddite, afraid of and skeptical about technology. Incorporate the person's views but also how you think he or she came to hold them.

HENRY DAVID THOREAU

Observation

The Norton Reader, p. 250

This selection from Thoreau is part of a journal entry he made on May 6, 1854. The section "Journals" contains a series of short excerpts from his journal: pithy maxims, observations, and reflections (NR 90). In this selection Thoreau writes disjunctive segments rather than a sustained argument. More often than not, Thoreau uses parallel construction and metaphorical language. You may want students to mark some memorable sentences that exhibit one or both of these stylistic features.

Many of Thoreau's statements in this journal entry are extravagant: he makes one sweeping generalization after another, each calling for qualification. An exercise in qualifying them may be done collectively or in groups and will stand students in good stead when they are asked to scrutinize their own sweeping generalizations. In a journal, however, extravagance is often appropriate. It facilitates rapid thinking and, with luck, fresh and original ideas.

Rather like Isaac Asimov in "The Eureka Phenomenon" (NR 223, SE 123), Thoreau's journal entry reclaims and transvalues the more or less pejorative term *subjectivity*. This journal entry usefully opens up discussion about the shifting and interdependent relations between objectivity and its opposite, subjectivity. It will be useful to elicit from students some of the anecdotes that lead them to consider *objectivity* preferable to *subjectivity*; they invariably have some, if only the delivery of injunctions to avoid the pronoun *I*. Whether they really believe that objectivity is preferable to subjectivity or merely recite the conventional wisdom may or may not emerge from this exercise. Students' belief that objectivity is the appropriate stance for a writer is apt to impoverish and conventionalize their writing. Thoreau provides a useful antidote.

Analytical Considerations

1. "Every important worker will report what life there is in him," Thoreau observes. In what ways might Asimov in "The Eureka Phenomenon" (NR 223, SE 123) or Bronowski in "The Reach of Imagination" (NR 232) be said to agree with him?
2. "Anything living," Thoreau observes, "is easily and naturally expressed in popular language." What does Thoreau mean by this statement? How many ways can it be interpreted? Do any of these interpretations contradict one another?

Suggested Writing Assignments

1. Write a brief essay in which you qualify one of Thoreau's extravagant generalizations.
2. Write some journal entries of your own in which you make sweeping generalizations, preferably extravagant generalizations about a controversial topic.
3. Write a brief essay in which you qualify one of your own extravagant generalizations.

PAUL THEROUX

Being a Man

The Norton Reader, p. 250

Paul Theroux is a novelist and essayist known for his writing on travel, particularly by train. "Being a Man" was published in a collection called *Sunrise with Seamonsters* (1985). Theroux takes a calculatedly strong and unqualified line that is both personal—"I have always disliked being a man" (paragraph 2)—and general—"Any objective study would find the quest for manliness essentially right-wing, puritanical, cowardly, neurotic and fueled largely by a fear of women" (paragraph 7). Midway through the essay he discloses an ax to grind, his desire to be a writer when in the United States to write, especially fiction, is considered unmanly. His personal involvement, however, does not lead him to qualify his assertion that the quest for manliness is bad for everybody. It is possible to argue that Theroux's strong line is subverted by his involvement. But is that necessarily the case? Academic writing, which minimizes personal involvement, is usually qualified writing, but it is only one kind of writing, and its rules are the rules of a specialized discourse.

Analytical Considerations

1. Ask students to mark Theroux's generalizations and consider how he makes them. You may also ask them to rewrite one or two as qualified generalizations.
2. Call attention to Theroux's illustrations. Ordinarily he uses one for each point he makes. The exception comes in paragraphs 10 and 11, where he surveys a number of writers. What are the uses of single and multiple illustrations?
3. Theroux asserts that men, at least in America, aren't expected to be writers; Evelyn Fox Keller, in "Women in Science: A Social Analysis" in the section called "Science" (NR 989, SE 565), asserts that women aren't expected to be scientists. To what kind of thinking do they attribute these expectations?

Suggested Writing Assignments

1. Both Theroux and Herb Goldberg, in "In Harness: The Male Condition" in the section called "Cultural Critique" (NR 349, SE 198), look at the condition of being a man, one with personal engagement, the other with a degree of clinical detachment. Write an essay in which you consider the advantages and disadvantages of each strategy.
2. Do library research on one or more of the writers Theroux mentions in paragraphs 10 and 11. Write an essay in which you test his assertion that the quest for manliness is particularly destructive for writers. In qualifying his generalization, be sure to qualify your own.
3. Write an essay called "Being a Student" in which you argue forcefully that being a student constitutes a hardship.

SCOTT RUSSELL SANDERS

Looking at Women

The Norton Reader, p. 253; Shorter Edition, p. 132

Scott Russell Sanders tells us in the course of "Looking at Women" that he was eleven when he saw the girl in the pink shorts and that, thirty years later, he is married and the father of two. We even learn his wife's name: Ruth. If we are interested in him as an author as well as a looker at women, we can further learn that he is also a professor of English at Indiana University (which may explain his quoting the improbable Miss Indiana Persimmon Festival) and that he has published scholarly works, science fiction, and nonfiction. In an essay called "The Singular First Person," he talks about the rules for writing he was taught as a schoolboy and his impatience with them: among them, using linear development (that is, thesis sentences and transitions) and avoiding *I*, the "singular first person" of his title. He prefers what he calls "dodging and leaping," "the shimmer and play of mind on the surface and in the depths a strong current." He is also fond of metaphor, as when he likens his preferred essay form to a stream.

Much of "Looking at Women" is personal report and, if Sanders does not succeed in making his experiences and his perceptions interesting, readers will find it hard going. Students may find it repetitive; instructors will appreciate the way Sanders circles, thickens, and complicates his perceptions. Sanders's essay, however, is more than personal report. In it he treats a timely and loaded question: how the gaze, directed at women by men, by construction workers as well as by artists, can reduce them to objects of desire. Through his reminiscences and musings, Sanders looks at men's looking at women and women's being looked at. He wants to exempt himself (and other men like him?) from reducing women to objects, to demonstrate that he views them not as "sexual playthings but as loved persons" (paragraph 31). Because the essay is wide-ranging, Sanders suggests the complexity of male gazes other than his and the complexity of female self-presentation. The responses of students, both male and female, to Sanders's essay should raise questions about making the personal representative, about using the *I* for analysis, both particular analysis—about Sanders himself—and general analysis—about men and women. This essay, with its focus on the personal and particular, gestures toward inclusiveness and generality. Sanders's success in combining the particular and the general is an open question, as is, indeed, what we mean when we say that a piece of writing is a success.

Questions from the NR10

1. Several sections of this essay are grounded in specific episodes from Sanders's life. Identify the episodes and explain how he uses them.
2. The five sections of this essay are separated by typographical space rather than connected by prose transitions. Determine the content of each section and explain its relation to the content of the section that precedes it. Describe Sanders's strategies of organization and development.
3. In paragraph 12 Sanders asks: "How should a man look at a woman?" What is his answer? Where does he provide it?
4. Write an essay in which you answer, in your own terms, Sanders's question, "How should a man look at a woman?"

Analytical Considerations

1. What kind of development does Sanders provide in place of linear development? You may direct students to his statement, "What I present here are a few images and reflections that cling, for me, to this one item" (paragraph 13).
2. Have students read Dorothy Allison's "Gun Crazy" (NR 275, SE 149). Allison, like Sanders, presents a series of scenes, but without reflecting on them, without "the shimmer and play of mind on the surface and in the depths a strong current." Her essay and Sanders's stand in instructive contrast.
3. What does the pronoun *I* entail for Sanders? How is self-presentation as he uses it both risk-taking and self-protective?
4. What kinds of metaphors does Sanders use? To what extent are they subsumed into the essay? To what extent are they showy, calling attention to themselves?

Suggested Writing Assignments

1. Write an essay with at least four sections developed by association in which you use, as Sanders puts it, "images and reflections that cling" (paragraph 13). Begin the first section with an incident and return to it in the fourth.
2. Locate and read the *Playboy* interview with Jimmy Carter that Sanders mentions (paragraph 20) and some of the responses to it. Write an essay in which you analyze the interview and the responses. Use *I* in a way that seems appropriate to you. Think about how much of your experience will go into your essay, and how you will include it.
3. Look at Sanders's definition of pornography: "making flesh into a commodity, flaunting it like any other merchandise, divorcing bodies from selves" (paragraph 37). Do library research on the Supreme Court's definition of pornography. Write an essay in which you contrast Sanders's definition with the Supreme Court's definition.

ANNA QUINDLEN

Between the Sexes, A Great Divide

The Norton Reader, p. 263; Shorter Edition, p. 142

Anna Quindlen begins this brief essay with a *perhaps* — "Perhaps we all have the same memory of the first boy-girl party we attended" (paragraph 1) — and expands it into an exploration of gender differences. If students haven't paused over the *perhaps*, ask them about it. Is the memory shared, or is it gendered female? Is it gendered uniformly female? What would be a male memory — or male memories — of such a party? How might the entire essay be rewritten from a different memory of a similar event? Instructors may profitably move from this discussion to a discussion of the "great divide" of the waxed floor: how it originates as a real object of somewhat indeterminate meaning and then takes on complex meanings through Quindlen's embedding it within a context. Students like to say "this symbolizes that," as if to symbolize means to equal. This essay illustrates the making of a symbol, the loading of that "great divide" with more meanings than can simply be predicated of it. Quindlen makes much out of little; her essay, which contains approximately one thousand words, appeared as a "Hers" column in the *New York Times*, as did Gloria Naylor's "'Mommy, What Does "Nigger" Mean?'" in "Language and Communication" (NR 525, SE 271).

Anna Quindlen joined the *New York Times* in 1977 as a reporter. She became metropolitan editor, columnist, and writer for the Op-Ed page; in line to become an editor, in the early 1990s, she resigned to have time to write fiction. As she explains in "Altogether Female," the introduction to a collection of her essays, *Thinking Out Loud* (1993), she benefited from affirmative action in both her hiring and promotion: six women brought a class-action suit against the *Times* in 1974 that was settled in 1978, and as a result the *Times* began to hire and promote women.

Questions from the NR10

1. Mark the places in this essay where Quindlen, after describing "the first boy-girl party we attended" (paragraph 1), returns to it. How does she turn an event into a symbol of male-female differences?
2. "I've spent a lot of time telling myself that men and women are fundamentally alike, mainly in the service of arguing that women should not only be permitted but be welcomed into a variety of positions and roles that only men occupied" (paragraph 4). Does her admission that they are not fundamentally alike mean that women should not be welcomed into male positions and roles? Why?
3. As Quindlen, in this essay, casts men as the Other, so Scott Russell Sanders, in "Looking at Women" (NR 253, SE 132), casts women as the Other. How do they present and try to decipher what they do not fully know or understand?
4. Write an essay in which you turn an event into a symbol.

Analytical Considerations

1. Ask students to look at the amaryllis in the bathroom (paragraph 8) as another example of Quindlen's symbol-making.
2. "I've always been a feminist," Quindlen writes (paragraph 4). How, in the course of this essay, does she define feminism? Are there other definitions of feminism? Where do they come from? Who uses them? Why is *feminism* a term whose meaning needs to be stipulated when it is used?
3. Does Quindlen lock herself into binary thinking about gender differences? See, for example, the discussion of binary thinking with respect to Isaac Asimov's "The Eureka Phenomenon" (*Guide*, p. 52).

Suggested Writing Assignments

1. Everybody engages in binary thinking about gender differences: as Quindlen points out, they help children "classify the world" (paragraph 10). Catch yourself doing it or hearing someone else doing it until you locate an instance you interpret as damaging, another you interpret as innocuous. Write an essay in which you reflect on what each instance entails and the differences between them.
2. What does Quindlen mean by "linear thinking" (paragraph 9)? What would be its opposite? Write an essay in which you offer one or more examples of each and discuss their advantages and disadvantages. You may also wish to consider whether these two kinds of thinking are necessarily gendered.
3. Read four or five additional essays on gender issues by Quindlen—a number of them can be found in her collection *Thinking Out Loud: On the Personal, the Political, the Public, and the Private* (1993)—and write an essay in which you trace several concerns of Quindlen's that run through them.

ANDREW SULLIVAN

What Is a Homosexual?

The Norton Reader, p. 266; Shorter Edition, p. 145

This essay comes from Andrew Sullivan's autobiographical book about gay identity, *Virtually Normal* (1995); it represents his attempt to define for himself and others what it means to be homosexual in late twentieth-century society. Sullivan does not attempt a scientific or social-scientific definition (although he refers to such research in paragraph 10 with the phrases "in a string of DNA" and "in a conclusive psychological survey"). Instead, he analyzes his personal experience and its effects, beginning with the need for "self-concealment" (paragraph 1) and the sense of rejection, of being "forlorn" (paragraph 4). You might ask students why they think Sullivan does not turn to scholarly research, why his notion of "evidence" (paragraph 9) is insistently personal. If you wish to extend discussion beyond the bounds Sullivan sets, you might ask them to gather "evidence" from scientific or social-scientific studies and consider why Sullivan might have chosen to exclude it from his essay.

Questions from the NR10

1. Throughout this essay Sullivan distinguishes between the "human experience" of all adolescents and experiences particular to or common among "homosexuals." Make a list of each. Were there features that you would have listed in the opposite column? Were there features you expected Sullivan to mention that he did not?
2. Sullivan notes that it is currently unfashionable to think in terms of "stereotypes" of any group, whether based on race, gender, sexuality, or some other classification (paragraph 11). Even so, he has set himself the task of answering the question "What is a homosexual?" How does he define this key term without resorting to stereotypes?
3. Although Sullivan does not advance a political agenda or a set of social reforms, his essay implies actions that would be beneficial to homosexuals and, more generally, to American society. What are these?
4. Write an essay that attempts to define the characteristics of a particular group, using a variation of Sullivan's title, "What Is a _____?"

Analytical Expectations

1. Why does Sullivan begin with the example of the locker room? How does it serve both to rivet our attention and introduce a key concept?
2. How does Sullivan handle opposing views? For example, he raises the issue of choice in sexual orientation in paragraphs 9 to 10. What is his attitude toward others, including gays and lesbians, whose views differ from his own? What does Sullivan gain by his stance? What does he lose?

3. Why does Sullivan move to the issue of "diversity" and "stereotyping" in the final third of the essay (beginning with paragraph 11)? What argument about homosexuality does it allow him to make? You might ask students who are members of minority groups that Sullivan names whether they agree with his argument.

Suggested Writing Assignments

1. Do all homosexuals share the traits Sullivan treats as fundamental? Do some nonhomosexuals share them (for instance, self-concealment)? Write an essay in which you either take exception to one of Sullivan's fundamental traits or show that it applies to nonhomosexuals.
2. Do research in the sciences or social sciences on theories of homosexuality. What explanations do researchers give that are compatible with Sullivan's essay? What explanations do they offer that are different from, or even contradictory of, his views?
3. Discuss Sullivan's essay with a gay or lesbian friend or acquaintance and write about his or her views of it. You may wish, in particular, to discuss Sullivan's relative silence about lesbian relationships and consider whether homosexual women offer a different view.

CHARLES LAMB

A Bachelor's Complaint of the Behaviour of Married People

The Norton Reader, p. 270

Depending upon their experience of literary genres, students may or may not have encountered the familiar essay, which is both intimate in its address to readers and also self-regarding. Those who have—and those who have not—may or may not be put off by Lamb's to-modern-ears quaint diction and his somewhat fusty and calculated charming manner. With luck, some students will have strong responses to Lamb's essay, and instructors will be able to follow up on the issues students themselves raise. Confronted with silence, instructors may wish to try an extravagant response of their own—perhaps that Lamb is a misogynist whose charm disguises his gloating over never having married; perhaps that he's a closeted gay in love with his friends and jealous of their wives—that will provoke discussion about how we make meaning when we read.

Instructors may wish to talk about Lamb's construction of a persona, Elia, mentioning other essays by Lamb and how they contribute to our sense of Elia. Lamb's biography also raises questions about and allows for teasing speculation on the relations of personae to selves and, of course, the problems biographers have attempting to reconstruct their subjects' selves. Certainly it's possible to see Lamb's resolutely cheerful Elia both as a psychic defense against the melancholy of his life and as a literary projection.

Questions from the NR10

1. Mark the divisions of this essay. How many aspects of the behavior of married people does Lamb consider? What kinds of transitions does he provide?
2. Lamb published his essays under a pen name, Elia. On the basis of this essay, describe the character (or persona) of his creation, Elia.
3. In this essay Lamb criticizes marriage, children, and family life, which are ordinarily respected, even venerated. What makes his criticism gentle rather than harsh, comic rather than severe?
4. Lamb concludes this essay: "But I am weary of stringing up all my married acquaintances by Roman denominations." *Testacea*, who saves the oysters for her husband, has a name derived from the Latin for shell; *Cerasia*, who sends the morellas to her husband, has a name derived from the goddess Ceres, the patron of agriculture. Write an essay in which you invent English "denominations" appropriate to several of your acquaintances and provide sketches of their character and behavior.

Analytical Considerations

1. See the questions about style in the "Introduction" to "An Album of Styles" (*Guide*, pp. 149–50), and use them for this essay.
2. Ask students to mark the words that are strange to them in Lamb's essay: *palliative* and *usufruct* (paragraph 6) are likely candidates. Use their words as the basis of a dictionary exercise: have students, singly or in groups, look up selected words in the *Oxford English Dictionary* and report on their history. How does the history of words contribute to their meaning? What words would we use in place of the words Lamb uses? What differences would these substitutions make in the meaning and tone of this essay?

Suggested Writing Assignments

1. Create a female persona of some sort and rewrite Lamb's essay, focusing on husbands rather than wives and criticizing the behavior of married people.
2. Read Betty Rollin, "Motherhood: Who Needs It?," in the section called "Cultural Critique" (NR 354, SE 203), and notice how she creates an overtly aggressive persona. Try out two personae, one with Lamb's calculated charm, another with Rollin's aggression, and use them to write two brief critiques of something you dislike. Append a note in which you consider how you expressed each persona and the advantages and disadvantages of using each in your critiques.

DOROTHY ALLISON

Gun Crazy

The Norton Reader, p. 275; Shorter Edition, p. 149

Dorothy Allison, in "Gun Crazy," transgresses gender roles by wanting to own and shoot guns. The force of her transgression will be assessed differently by students, depending upon regional as well as personal and familial attitudes toward guns. Allison (author of a novel called *Bastard Out of Carolina*) grew up in South Carolina; the setting of "Gun Crazy," though not named, is specifically southern and rural. Nevertheless, as Allison makes plain, shooting, acceptable for men, is forbidden to women.

Another transgressive figure is Anne's mama, the narrator's role model, who not only gives her sixteen-year-old daughter a rifle but also drinks, smokes, and refuses to cook. Students will probably approve of her sentiment that "a woman should be able to take care of herself" (paragraph 24) while disapproving of her behavior. Instructors may wish to assign this essay in conjunction with Anna Quindlen's "Between the Sexes, A Great Divide" (NR 263, SE 142). Quindlen plays out her gendered roles of wife and mother, yet declares herself a feminist; Anne's mama, who violates these roles and has no label for herself, is presented in many respects as eccentric.

In "Gun Crazy," shooting is literal and symbolic. Allison develops this essay in five dramatic vignettes. Dialogue predominates, and instructors may profit from focusing on the interpretive strategies necessary to read it. Stage directions in the third vignette, from uncle Bo's smile when he says "Girls don't shoot" (paragraph 14) to its disappearance at the end, will provide an exercise. So too will Allison's most explicit interpretation of shooting in the fifth vignette: among other things, guns signify power. Students, who will find Allison's condensed presentation attractive, need to discover how carefully it elicits close reading and attentive response.

"Gun Crazy" appeared in a collection of Allison's essays called *Skin: Talking About Sex, Class, and Literature* (1994); other essays in the collection announce her lesbianism. Will students who do not know Allison's sexual preference read "Gun Crazy" as coded for lesbian desire? When they do know, will they feel compelled to read it this way? Is it necessary to take the narrator's characterization of both Anne shooting and the rifle itself—"sexy" (paragraph 27)—as sexually explicit? What other meanings of "sexy" does the essay make possible? Instructors may also wish to ask why, if Allison appears as a self-identified lesbian in other essays in the collection, she omits the identification here.

Analytic Considerations

1. Have students choose one vignette in this essay and look carefully at Allison's dialogue and stage directions in order to interpret it. The five vignettes may be divided up among groups of students.
2. Have students read Andrew Sullivan's "What Is a Homosexual?" (NR 266, SE 145) and consider, in conjunction with Allison's "Gun Crazy," some of the differences that emerge from reading an essay in which the author stays closeted and one in which the author comes out. How do public controversies over and personal beliefs with respect to homosexuality affect reading and interpretation?

Suggested Writing Assignments

1. Write a personal essay about policing gender roles that includes someone's telling you "Girls don't _____" (or "Boys don't _____").

2. Write an essay in which you bestow the epithet "sexy" on something not conventionally regarded as erotic.
3. Read four or five additional essays in Allison's *Skin: Talking About Sex, Class, and Literature* (1994), and write an essay in which you trace several concerns that run through them.

MALCOLM GLADWELL

The Sports Taboo

The Norton Reader, p. 278; Shorter Edition, p. 152

If you have an opportunity to introduce this essay in class before your students read it, you might ask them if they believe that some racial or ethnic groups do better in some sports than others—and why. For example, do they think it's true that "white men can't jump"? Or how do they explain the relative dominance of white men and women in golf (Tiger Woods being the obvious recent exception)? Asking students to articulate their views, some based on biology, others on sociology, will prepare them for Gladwell's essay.

Gladwell takes on the biological question, arguing that "elite athletes are elite athletes because, in some sense, they are on the fringes of genetic variability. As it happens, African populations seem to create more of these genetic outliers than white populations do" (paragraph 13). But he also addresses the sociological or "nurture" question, often referring to his own experience as a runner but more seriously considering this issue in terms of country of origin (beginning in paragraph 14). Students interested in this question of national influence might want to do further research, including reading biographies of athletes or histories of an individual sport.

Questions from the NR10

1. To discuss the "racial dimensions of sports" can be, Gladwell notes, "unseemly." What strategies does he use to introduce controversial issues? How does he minimize the tensions readers might feel? Does he always choose to minimize tensions?
2. What theories about the dominance of blacks in sports does Gladwell consider and reject? Why?
3. After Gladwell rejects inadequate explanations (paragraphs 1–7), he offers alternatives. What are they, and how are they developed?
4. Gladwell begins and ends with personal experience. What is the effect of his final story?
5. Write an essay on a topic that is "taboo," using some of the writerly strategies you have learned from Gladwell.

Analytical Considerations

1. The essay begins with personal experience. How does this introduction help Gladwell establish his credentials?

2. The essay is divided (by means of white space) into four sections, the first and last using personal experience. Ask students to identify the argument and evidence in the second and third sections, one focusing on racial stereotypes and using genetic and anthropological research, the other focusing on national or regional influences. How does Gladwell's interpretation of this evidence further establish his credentials?
3. Why does Gladwell return in the last section to personal experience? Does it merely complete the essay as a literary piece? Does it introduce another factor not covered by the research in sections two and three?

Suggested Writing Assignments

1. Do your own research on an issue of race or ethnicity and sports by reading a biography of an athlete or a history of an individual sport (for instance, Roberto Gonzalez Echevarria's history of Cuban baseball, *The Pride of Havana*). What explanations, explicit or implicit, does the author give for the success of the individual or racial group in the particular sport?
2. In the penultimate paragraph of his essay, Gladwell states, "To be a great athlete, you have to *care*." Write an essay in which you agree or disagree with Gladwell about this criterion as the basic one for success in sports.
3. Use Gladwell's concept of "learned helplessness" (paragraphs 17–18) to explain the relative failure of some person or group in a sport or some other area of endeavor such as academics, business, or politics.

ELISABETH KÜBLER-ROSS

On the Fear of Death

The Norton Reader, p. 286; Shorter Edition, p. 160

Three essays in this section of *The Norton Reader* discuss dying and death: Elisabeth Kübler-Ross's "On the Fear of Death" (NR 286, SE 160), Stephen Jay Gould's "Our Allotted Lifetimes" (NR 292, SE 166), and Sherwin B. Nuland's "The Strangled Heart" (NR 297). All are critical of the way we have made dying and death into medical problems instead of accepting them as natural occurrences, and they adopt various strategies to allay our fears. You may wish to assign all three essays and ask students to assess the extent to which they think each succeeds and why.

Dr. Elisabeth Kübler-Ross, a Swiss psychologist, was a pioneer in examining attitudes toward dying and death; her book *On Death and Dying*, from which this essay comes, was published in 1969. In it Kübler-Ross announces as her intended audience professionals who work with the dying, like chaplains and social workers (paragraph 2), and her excursus on the communications of the dying may be of particular interest to them. The book, however, was a best-seller that clearly transcended the particular audience she had in mind. In the selection reprinted here, Kübler-Ross presents and analyzes various kinds of material—experience, observation, and reading—to make a series of related points about patients and their needs and the often competing needs of those who take care of them and the families who arrange for their care. Her psychiatric orientation—what she claims as the unconscious motives that impel the behavior of the dying and the living—may need careful scrutiny. Do students understand the claims she makes and the Freudian psychology that warrants them, which she takes for granted?

Since the publication of *On Death and Dying*, medical technology has made it possible to prolong life almost indefinitely, and court cases have complicated what Kübler-Ross regards as patients' rights. Students will probably have some familiarity with these issues; they may need prompting to discuss them with reference to the rights that Kübler-Ross articulates.

Questions from the NR10

1. In this essay Kübler-Ross incorporates various kinds of evidence: experience, observation, and reading. Mark the various kinds and describe how she incorporates them.
2. In this essay Kübler-Ross attends to the needs of the living and the rights of the dying. Describe where and how she attends to each and how she presents the conflicts, actual and potential, between them.
3. In paragraphs 24 to 27 Kübler-Ross describes the experience of the trip by ambulance, the emergency room, and the hospital from a patient's point of view. What does this shift in point of view contribute to the essay?
4. Imagine a situation in which a child or children are not isolated from death. What might be the consequences? Using this situation and its possible consequences, write an essay in which you agree or disagree with Kübler-Ross's views.

Analytical Considerations

1. You may ask students to reread paragraphs 15 to 17 and consider what Kübler-Ross's vignette—her personal report, so to speak—enables her to say and to imply about dying and death. Implication may be of two sorts: the texture and emotional resonance of the episode she recollects and its modern obverse. How would this farmer die today?
2. Consider what Kübler-Ross has to say about the mechanical prolongation of life. Ask students to gather other material—newspaper or magazine articles, scientific studies, etc.—about this issue and try to articulate the various different views that exist today.
3. Look at Kübler-Ross's discussion of avoidance techniques (paragraph 22). You may wish to ask students to discuss these and other techniques for avoiding unpleasant truths. What would be the consequences of speaking plainly and acting openly?

Suggested Writing Assignments

1. Write an essay in which you focus on your own experience of the death of someone you love. Frame it by considering Kübler-Ross's point that our treatment of the dying ordinarily reflects the needs of the living.
2. Do library research on one court case involving the mechanical prolongation of life. Look in particular at who is on each side and what arguments their lawyers make. Write an essay in which you describe and analyze the

arguments of each side with respect to the rights of the dying and the needs of the living as Kübler-Ross conceives of them and as you conceive of them.

3. Read sections of Philippe Ariès's *The Hour of Our Death* (1981). Giving proper credit to both Ariès and Kübler-Ross, describe and analyze a set of customs that once surrounded death with reference to Kübler-Ross's scheme, that is, the rights of the dying and the needs of the living.

4. Kübler-Ross's attention to death and dying is repeated now in college courses on death and dying. If your institution offers one, get a copy of its syllabus, interview a couple of students who are taking or have taken it, and write an essay in which you describe the course and analyze what you understand to be Kübler-Ross's influence on it.

STEPHEN JAY GOULD

Our Allotted Lifetimes

The Norton Reader, p. 292; Shorter Edition, p. 166

Three essays in this section of *The Norton Reader* discuss dying and death: Elisabeth Kübler-Ross's "On the Fear of Death" (NR 286, SE 160), Stephen Jay Gould's "Our Allotted Lifetimes" (NR 292, SE 166), and Sherwin B. Nuland's "The Strangled Heart" (NR 297). To different degrees, all are critical of the way we have made dying and death into medical problems instead of accepting them as natural occurrences, and they adopt various strategies to allay our fears. You may wish to assign all three essays and ask students to assess the extent to which they think each succeeds and why.

Stephen Jay Gould is a biologist, an historian of science, and a superb popularizer; this essay, like others by him in *The Norton Reader*, was first published in the column he writes for *Natural History* magazine. You will want to make sure that students understand his explanations of scaling theory and relative (and absolute) time. (Instructors for whom they are virtually unintelligible will usually find some students in the class who understand them and be able to turn to them for help; demonstrating a transition from incomprehension to comprehension can be a valuable lesson in reading.) You may also want to consider Gould's presentation of mathematical information through both equations and words. But it's Gould's larger strategy that deserves most attention. Considering humans under the category "mammal," he reframes and provokes us to rethink death: "We live," he observes in an arresting parenthesis, "far longer than a mammal of our body size should" (paragraph 7).

Gould may be said to draw reductive parallels between humans and mammals, emphasizing similarities and neglecting differences. He neglects our feelings with respect to our own deaths; when he alludes to our feelings, it is with respect to the death of a pet mouse or gerbil, and he writes them off in a parenthesis: "our personal grief, of course, is quite another matter; with this, science does not deal" (paragraph 8). Nevertheless, his conclusion that we distort the way we interpret events measured on a large-scale geologic clock, trying "to bend an ancient world to our purposes," indicates that he is aware of tension between accepting the natural order of things and experiencing it as alien to us.

Questions from the NR10

1. In paragraph 7 Gould observes: "We live far longer than a mammal of our body size should." Describe, first, how he leads up to this statement, and second, what consequences he draws from it.
2. Explain, first in Gould's words and then in your own, Galileo's example (paragraph 3), the scaling of brain weight versus body weight (paragraph 4), the scaling of heart rate versus body weight (paragraph 5), the scaling of metabolic rate versus body weight (paragraph 6), the scaling of mammalian lifetime versus body weight (paragraph 7), the equations for mammalian breath time and heartbeat time versus body weight (paragraphs 13 to 14), and the deviance of human lifetimes (paragraph 15).
3. In this essay Gould describes three kinds of time: Newtonian time, metabolic time, and geologic time. Consider how you experience each one. Then write an essay in which you describe your experience of all three and their relative importance to you.

Analytical Considerations

1. Have students, probably in groups, take one another's pulse and measure one another's rate of breathing. Are they in accord with Gould's ratios of four to one? Have them explain the ratios; also have them explain how many heartbeats and breaths they can anticipate in their allotted lifetimes.
2. Have students mark Gould's arresting formulations and look at his use of words, sentence structure, and analogies. You may also have students experiment with rewriting them to diminish their force.
3. Direct students to locate Gould's parenthetical remarks. What characterizes all of them? Does he use parentheses conventionally both to interrupt and to subordinate?

Suggested Writing Assignments

1. Locate and read the essay on "neoteny" that Gould refers to in paragraph 7. Write an essay in which you explain it with reference to "Our Allotted Lifetimes." You should also add a paragraph of conjecture about why he skirts the subject in "Our Allotted Lifetimes."
2. Describe what you take to be Gould's views on the mechanical prolongation of life. Write an essay in which you use (and credit) evidence of his views in "Our Allotted Lifetimes."
3. Read Gould's other essays in *The Norton Reader*: "The Terrifying Normalcy of AIDS" (NR 727, SE 398) and "Darwin's Middle Road" (NR 982, SE 558). Describe some of his strategies in writing about science.
4. Read Gould's other essays in *The Norton Reader*: "The Terrifying Normalcy of AIDS" (NR 727, SE 398) and "Darwin's Middle Road" (NR 982, SE 558). Write an essay in which you consider what he thinks science includes, what he thinks it excludes, and the consequences of his views.

SHERWIN B. NULAND

The Strangled Heart

The Norton Reader, p. 297

Three essays in this section of *The Norton Reader* discuss dying and death: Elisabeth Kübler-Ross's "On the Fear of Death" (NR 286, SE 160), Stephen Jay Gould's "Our Allotted Lifetimes" (NR 292, SE 166), and Sherwin B. Nuland's "The Strangled Heart" (NR 297). To different degrees, all are critical of the way we have made dying and death into medical problems instead of accepting them as natural occurrences, and they adopt various strategies to allay our fears. You may wish to assign all three essays and ask students to assess the extent to which they think each succeeds and why.

Nuland's essay focuses not so much on the patient's fear as on the young doctor's. Using his own first experience with death, he describes the first patient he "lost," a fifty-two-year-old man named James McCarty. Nuland describes in detail the medical procedures used for cardiac arrest and his initial self-confidence (or at least calm) in the emergency room. But the essay focuses on his failure, on his loss of a patient, on our inability to stop death, and on the false certainty that "modern biomedicine" gives by seeming to deny "the certain advent of our own individual mortality" (paragraph 25).

Questions from the NR10

1. Nuland's essay is half narrative, half reflection. What is the relation between the narrative of his first encounter with a dying patient and his reflection, years later, on death itself?
2. What details in the narrative did you find most gripping? Why?
3. What general observations or reflections did you find most enlightening? Why?
4. If you have experience of death or another dramatic human experience— a birth, an accident, or a violent crime—write about it. Use a similar combination of personal narrative and reflection.

Analytical Considerations

1. Ask students to mark instances in the opening narrative where Nuland anticipates his failure in the emergency room. How do these add suspense? How do they contribute to Nuland's later argument?
2. As a follow-up to Question 3 in the NR10 (reprinted above), bring in (or assign students to bring in) one of the paintings Nuland mentions in the second half of his essay: Luke Fildes's *The Doctor* or Francisco Goya's *Diphtheria* or *The Croup*. Ask students to dicuss the influence of art, or more broadly visual images, on our understanding of disease and death.

Suggested Writing Assignments

1. Using one of the paintings Nuland alludes to or another visual image of death and dying, write a brief essay about how visual imagery contributes to the "mythology [that] has grown up around the process of dying" (paragraph 19). (Attach a photocopy of the image to your essay.)
2. Nuland mentions that, at the time of this episode, "closed-chest cardiopulmonary resuscitation, or CPR, had not yet been invented" (paragraph 11). Do research on CPR, and explain how it is different from the technique Nuland used on James McCarty.

CULTURAL CRITIQUE

ANTHONY BURGESS

Is America Falling Apart?

The Norton Reader, p. 304; Shorter Edition, p. 171

Anthony Burgess, an Englishman (as he makes clear in the course of his essay), offers an outsider's response to the title question, "Is America Falling Apart?" You might ask students how they think Burgess acquired the authority (in 1971, when he spent his year in America) to estimate that nearly 50 percent "of the entire American population" think that their country is "coming apart at the seams" (paragraph 21): whom did he talk to, and what did they tell him? Research and documentation are not among the personal experiences that serve as evidence for his strictures on America. He situates himself, vaguely, in New Jersey. Where in New Jersey? Newark? Princeton? Ho-Ho-Kus? It would make a difference. Students can try to reconstruct Burgess's year in America from the evidence he provides in the essay.

Burgess's essay is loosely connected. Although individual paragraphs are coherent and bear some relation to his title question, the connections between them are as often associative as consecutive. He divides the essay into five sections through the use of blank space: paragraphs 1 through 5, 6 through 8, 9 through 13, 14 through 18, and 19 through 21. These spatial divisions don't really mark units within the essay except in the most impressionistic of ways. What then is their function? Ask students to speculate. Also call their attention to Burgess's reversal at the end of the essay (paragraph 21), in which he owns that he finds America "more stimulating than depressing" and expects to return. Does he prepare us for this reversal in the course of the essay, or is it something of a surprise?

Students will probably need to be encouraged to pull apart an essay by a professional writer and see how many of the principles of "good" writing they dutifully learn can be, and at times should be, violated. They will probably have been engaged by Burgess's essay; if they haven't been, or won't admit to having been, then you'll have to dramatize your own engagement. You might turn the discussion to the differences between having an opinion and being opinionated. Opinionated writers can be boring and tedious; for most people, Burgess isn't, and that's why they think him worth reading.

Questions from the NR10

1. This essay appeared in 1971. What might Burgess leave out, add, or modify if he were to write it today?
2. Burgess says that in his son's school, there was "no readiness to engage the individual child's mind as anything other than raw material for statistical reductions" (paragraph 10). Precisely what is he referring to? Does your own experience support or counter Burgess's claim?

3. Visitors like Burgess can sometimes see things natives miss; they can also overlook the obvious. Write a response to Burgess, pointing out where he is on target and what he has missed.

Analytical Considerations

1. Burgess's exaggerations, such as his assured estimate of the percentage of Americans who agree with him, fall under a technique called hyperbole. You might ask students to identify other hyperbole in the essay and consider their effect. How does the frequent hyperbole characterize Burgess's style as a writer? What kind (or kinds) of responses do they elicit from readers? In what kinds of writing is it legitimate to use hyperbole, in what kinds illegitimate?
2. Ask students to identify some of Burgess's criticisms of America that they find valid. Do they find them valid in Burgess's own terms or by toning down his hyperbole? You might ask them, perhaps in small groups, to rewrite some of Burgess's claims in more moderate language.

Suggested Writing Assignments

1. Write an opinionated essay of your own in answer to some provocative question.
2. Burgess describes Americans as guilty and masochistic, eager to confess their national faults and accept blame for them (paragraph 13). Write an essay in which you play this kind of American. (You might, in a coda, discuss whether this kind of role-playing is easy or difficult for you.)
3. Burgess calls America "a revolutionary republic based on a romantic view of human nature" (paragraph 20) and refers to the "dangerous naiveté of the Declaration of Independence" (paragraph 12). Read the final version of "The Declaration of Independence" (NR 874, SE 490) in conjunction with these statements; try to reconstruct his reading of the document and respond with your own.

PICO IYER

The Contagion of Innocence

The Norton Reader, p. 310

In contrast to Anthony Burgess, Pico Iyer concerns himself not with the decline of American culture but with how American pop culture has spread throughout the world, dominating the consciousness even of people who consider themselves superior to its influences. Iyer, a staff writer for *Time* magazine, argues by means of examples he has drawn from all over the world, concentrating most of his attention on Vietnam (paragraphs 1–4), Japan (paragraphs 18–19), and the phenomenon of Madonna worldwide (paragraphs 12–14). Indeed, one rhetorical technique students can learn from Iyer is how to accumulate example upon example to argue a point. Yet since most students will lack the range of knowledge and references that Iyer brings to this essay, it may be easiest to concentrate discussion on his treatment of Madonna to understand the argument he makes. Why does Iyer believe that Madonna has been so successful as an icon? To what extent does her success depend on her being American? How do students answer his seemingly rhetorical question: "Can one picture a Madonna from Stockholm, or Tokyo, or even London?" (paragraph 14). It might turn out that they can indeed picture a popular, non-American icon.

Questions from the NR10

1. What does Iyer's title mean? Where does he provide a thumbnail explanation? What effects does he initiate by thinking about popular culture as both "innocent" and a "contagious" disease?
2. Iyer gives multiple explanations for American dominance in the realm of popular culture. List them, ideally in the order they occur, and then consider why he ends with "the hunger for innocence" that American movies and songs satisfy in "the common viewer" (paragraph 19).
3. This essay was written in 1991. Have any of the American "icons" that Iyer discusses lost their appeal? If so, why? Can this loss be explained within Iyer's framework, or does it undermine his argument?
4. Choose a current media star or icon of popular culture and, in a brief essay, analyze his, her, or its appeal.

Analytical Considerations

1. Have students discuss the significance of the title and its apparent origin in Graham Greene's novel *The Quiet American*. It might help students to sort out who is innocent (the American Pyle), who is apparently more sophisticated (the Englishman Fowler), and how innocence becomes "contagious." How does the Vietnamese character Phuong figure into the equation—if not in the novel, then in Iyer's introduction of the phenomenon of cultural contagion?
2. To understand two different ways that Iyer advances his argument, compare a paragraph with multiple examples (perhaps paragraph 3 on Vietnam) with a paragraph that focuses on a single example (perhaps paragraph 14 on Madonna). What does Iyer achieve with multiple examples? What does he achieve by concentrating on a single example? What are the limitations of each kind of paragraph?

Suggested Writing Assignments

1. Write an affirmative answer to Iyer's question: "Can one picture a Madonna from Stockholm, or Tokyo, or even London?" (paragraph 14). Explain why.
2. Can you think of examples of resistance to American pop culture? If so, write about how and why such resistance occurs.

MAGGIE HELWIG

Hunger

The Norton Reader, p. 318; Shorter Edition, p. 194

Helwig writes of a problem afflicting not just individuals but a whole category of people, in this case well-off women in their teens and twenties: anorexia and bulimia. She herself has been a victim, as paragraph 26 makes clear ("I nearly died"). But Helwig writes less as a survivor than as a committed observer. That is, she does not make use of her own experience in anything like the way that, say, Nancy Mairs does in "On Being a Cripple" (NR 34, SE 24). A comparison of opening paragraphs—Mairs's versus Helwig's—displays two very different ways of treating material one has experienced personally. Helwig has just as much right to do an "engaged" or "you are there" opening, but she chooses instead to be a more distant narrator. Students might speculate on the gains and losses from each approach.

Helwig regards anorexia as a form of communication: the desire to be thin, though it has some connections to the world of fashion, is more spiritually based, a criticism of the existing order. It is, for Helwig, "the nightmare of consumerism acted out in women's bodies" (paragraph 4), and thus her long, admiring portrait of Simone Weil's self-abnegation. For Helwig, anorexia is both a life-threatening condition and an anguished cry about the nature of life in the present.

Questions from the NR10

1. Psychologists, social workers, or medical doctors would describe eating disorders according to their own professional criteria and in their own style. What particular language, style, and tone does Helwig use?
2. Helwig says that anorexia and bulimia are particularly feminine statements about consumption and consumerism. What evidence does she offer for this claim?
3. Helwig says that "women's magazines" claimed that anorexia was "understandable, almost safe really, it was just fashion gone out of control," while it was really something deeply symbolic of what is wrong in the culture. Write about something else that people are often told is simply a matter of lack of proportion.

Analytical Considerations

1. Paragraph 23 contains a critique of feminist understandings of anorexia. Have students refer to ads and illustrations of the type the feminists were relying on, and then explain why Helwig is not satisfied with such explanations.
2. Students should ask what more they'd need to know in order to agree totally with Helwig's main point. What ultimately would convince them that anorexia is communication?

1. People often treat eating and drinking disorders as trivial. Describe examples of serious disorders that are, or were, laughed at or scorned rather than addressed as the problems they in fact represent.
2. Based on a comparative examination of reference sources (general purpose dictionaries and encyclopedias are best) from the 1960s and the present, write an account of the growing awareness or changing notions of eating disorders.

JOHN MCMURTRY

Kill 'Em! Crush 'Em! Eat 'Em Raw!

The Norton Reader, p. 322; Shorter Edition, p. 187

John McMurtry, a Canadian professor of philosophy, writes in this essay about his experiences as a professional football player. He moves smoothly from personal report to impersonal generalization. He starts in the present, with the flaring up of an old injury, and moves back to his love of athletics, the increasing professionalization of his participation in sports, and the injuries that finally led him to quit the game. He then broadens his scope to consider the social role of professional sports, particularly violent and damaging ones like football.

Although his arguments for and against professional sports may seem familiar, indeed overrehearsed, McMurtry derives his authority from his unusual career as both player and philosopher. He condemns professional football, but judiciously. Perhaps what is most engaging about his essay is his depiction of himself as a player caught up in the ethos of the sport, accepting its rules and hazards with some sense of disquiet but without much questioning.

Questions from the NR10

1. What similarities does McMurtry see between football and war? How persuasive do you find the linkage?
2. Is McMurtry's essay mainly about his personal experiences in football or is it about some larger point, with his experiences as examples?
3. Draw connections between "real life" and some kind of game or play familiar to you. Does this illuminate any social arrangements and help you to see them in a new light? How far can one generalize?

Analytical Considerations

1. Ask students to consider the various dimensions of McMurtry's overarching analogy between football and war. What claims about football does the analogy make? And, conversely, what claims about war? Are both these sets of claims acceptable to them?

2. Herb Goldberg, in "In Harness: The Male Condition" (NR 349, SE 198), argues that men are imprisoned by "traditional definitions of masculine-appropriate behavior" (paragraph 13). To what extent do these definitions figure in McMurtry's account?

Suggested Writing Assignments

1. Perhaps you have found yourself in a situation similar to McMurtry's, participating in an activity that you later decided you should not have participated in or did not want to participate in. Write an essay in which you reconstruct your state of mind during your participation and the process that led you to change your mind about participation and/or to give it up.
2. Critics from a number of spheres are calling into question the professionalization of sports on college campuses. What is the status of sports on your campus? Write an essay in which you argue for their lesser or greater professionalization.
3. Write an essay in which you consider why becoming a professional athlete is so attractive to some men or women. You can develop your essay through experience or research. If your own experience or the experience of a friend is relevant, use it. Or do library research, either on a particular athlete or on the general topic, to expand your range of examples.

JESSICA MITFORD

Behind the Formaldehyde Curtain

The Norton Reader, p. 328; Shorter Edition, p. 180

Mitford's essay is drawn from her brilliant book, *The American Way of Death* (1963), a biting analysis of American funeral practices. Now in her eighties, Mitford has revised and updated her book for a new edition (1998).

The masterful opening warrants attention. The metaphor of stage presentation governs the entire essay (as the title suggests), so the *Hamlet* quote is apposite. The object of the behind-the-scenes drama is to prepare the body for "public display," the ultimate objective a "Beautiful Memory Picture" (paragraph 1). Contrasted with this use of metaphor is her litany of verbs: "sprayed, sliced, pierced, pickled, trussed, trimmed, creamed, waxed, painted, rouged. . . ." (paragraph 1). (Bismarck's remark that anyone without a strong stomach should not watch sausages or laws being made might usefully be extended to "Memory Pictures.")

Mitford's British background gives her the distance that is needed to survey American funeral practices with a traveler's eye; what seems normal to us seems quite odd to her. Interestingly, this was not the only British send-up of America's funeral industry. Evelyn Waugh's *The Loved One* (1948) focused on pet cemeteries and extravagances such as Los Angeles's famous Forest Lawn Memorial Park. (It was made into a movie starring Robert Morse and Jonathan Winters.)

Analytical Considerations

1. Paragraph 4 is typical of Mitford's attitude, which some might find disagreeably superior. Students can look closely at how her word choice denigrates the people who pay so much money for embalming. One might usefully ask why she omits any mention of the survivors' state of mind at the time they decide such matters.
2. As the essay proceeds, it takes its order from the chronology of embalming, the steps the funeral home takes to prepare the remains. Ask students to explain the source of Mitford's comedy here.
3. A close look at names reveals Mitford's scornful delight in incongruities. The "Vari-Pose Head Rest" (paragraph 8), the Eckels College of Mortuary Science (paragraph 9), Flextone (paragraph 11), and "Lyf-Lyk tint" (paragraph 11) are only a few of the odd names Mitford mentions in her deadpan style. Ask students to list more from the essay. The next step would be to come up with some odd-sounding names for commonly used Amercian products and ask about the source of amusement in them. (Examples: Dr Pepper; Oil of Olay; Oldsmobile; Pepsodent; fancy British-sounding cigarettes, such as Sir Walter Raleigh, Parliament, Marlboro [its crest reads "*veni, vidi, vici*"], Philip Morris, Herbert Tareyton, Pall Mall [its crest reads "*in hoc signo vinces*"], Chesterfield, etc.) With Mitford's sardonic eye for incongruity, such slightly odd names turn up everywhere.

Suggested Writing Assignments

1. Take a common American practice and describe it from the perspective of someone from a distant country who doesn't automatically get it. Suggestions: engagement rings, football pep rallies, cheerleading, hanging out in malls, school newspapers.
2. Write an account of a procedure in the Mitford style, going step by step and providing both the main actions as well as suggesting alternatives.

HENRY LOUIS GATES, JR.

In the Kitchen

The Norton Reader, p. 334

Gates, a literary critic and professor of African American studies at Harvard University, published his memories of growing up in *Colored People*; this section of that memoir appeared in the *New Yorker*, not usually an outlet for university professors.

Gates's subject is hair in the African American community during the 1950s and 1960s. Students should note that he does not discuss the well-known reactions to these hairstyles, the Afros of the late 1960s and 1970s, as worn by such cultural icons as Jimi Hendrix and the young Michael Jackson. Gates's essay can be seen as an act of recovery. Those cultural practices he celebrates have mostly fallen into disuse; during the 1970s they were vigorously opposed by activists who denounced the "process" as too imitative of white styles. Gates's essay is not a refutation of such denunciations but an attempt to pin down exactly what styles existed, set in the context of his family life in West Virginia of the 1950s. Interestingly, though he starts out with an extensive portrait of his mother's hair preparation, his real subject is men's hair, especially his own in relation to the figures he admired.

Analytical Considerations

1. Note the colloquial air to paragraph 2, the back-and-forth movement of "I liked that smell. Not the smell so much, I guess, as what the smell meant for the shape of my day." What reactions do students have to that movement? What kind of mental operation is suggested by it? What kind of relationship to the reader does Gates assume by writing this way?
2. Students might consider if Gates's obvious admiration for hair like Nat King Cole's "magnificent sleek black tiara" (last paragraph) indicates that he favors such hair for himself today or, on the contrary, that he regards it as an impressive achievement for the 1950s but not to be imitated.
3. Analyze the elements that make the concluding paragraph so effective. Include Nat King Cole, the African setting (Zanzibar is off the east coast of Tanzania), the hair itself. (Some students will not know what Cole looked like; they might need to see a photo.)

Suggested Writing Assignments

1. How were hair and hairstyles regarded in your family? Write about hair-care incidents, pleasant or unpleasant, you remember from growing up. Connect them to the kind of family you had or the type of person you were then.
2. Report on hairstyles and practices among identifiable communities and/or subgroups. Suggestions: nursing homes, military bases, punk rockers, farmers, teenage Latina girls, sports figures. (Just make sure the group you pick is well defined.)

DANIEL HARRIS

Light-Bulb Jokes: Charting an Era

The Norton Reader, p. 340; Shorter Edition, p. 177

Harris's essay, which appeared as a brief article in the *New York Times Magazine*, represents a common but important genre of contemporary American writing: the analysis of a seemingly trivial cultural phenomenon that, under scrutiny, becomes deeply revealing. Other examples in this section show variations on this form: Jessica Mitford's more extended analysis of American funeral practices in "Behind the Formaldehyde Curtain" (NR 328, SE 180) and Calvin Trillin's humorous critique of American tax laws in "The Alice Tax" (NR 347).

Virtually all students have heard light-bulb jokes; indeed, they can probably add several more to the list printed at the head of the essay. (In the original article, these jokes encircled a photo of an illumined bulb.) You might ask students to consider how some of Harris's analysis works by extracting a single feature of the joke (the words "how many" in paragraph 2, the use of contrasting groups in paragraph 6), and how some of it proceeds under a general rubric (the age of consumerism in paragraph 3, "our aging democracy" in paragraph 5, "social unrest" in paragraph 9). You might then ask them if Harris's opening statement—that light-bulb jokes are "uniquely political" in contrast to knock-knock, dead-baby, and dumb-blonde jokes—holds true. Could one analyze these other types of jokes in similar terms?

Analytical Considerations

1. Ask students to note the various categories in which Harris "reads" the light-bulb joke: for example, within the age of consumerism in paragraph 3, within "our aging democracy" in paragraph 5, within the computer age in paragraph 8, and as "social unrest" in paragraph 9. Can students suggest other categories? What might these additional categories add to Harris's analysis?
2. Ask students to engage with Harris's argument (paragraphs 6–7) that the light-bulb joke is "an equal-opportunity leveler" that belittles minorities and the intelligensia alike. Are there other ways to interpret such belittlement?
3. If students know other light-bulb jokes, ask them to analyze the jokes either in Harris's terms or in their own.

Suggested Writing Assignments

1. What does another type of joke reveal about American culture? Choose a category that Harris doesn't consider (knock-knock, dead-baby, dumb-blonde jokes, etc.) and show its meaning(s).
2. Choose something ordinary in American culture and write a Harris-like essay showing what it really expresses. Suggestions: bread, sneakers, backpacks, CDs, MTV, gourmet takeout.

ARTHUR SCHOPENHAUER

On Noise

The Norton Reader, p. 343

A delightful quirky piece of major-league complaining, Schopenhauer's "On Noise" displays all the characteristics that have come to typify his outlook on the world: annoyance with careless people; a sense that his work is subject to great difficulties; loneliness; an insensitivity to others' feelings; an ability to say what he thinks, regardless of what other people might conclude. In this essay the writer comes across as a whiner, a complainer who raises ordinary city noise to heights of anger and anguish few would have thought possible. Yet there is a sense in which he is right, that he is saying things many people have felt but were afraid to say. We all know that life in a crowded city would be intolerable if everyone were free to make as much noise as possible. Neighbors and travelers need to have some restraint, some sensitivity to the other person's inconvenience. And this shows up not in the large issues—robbery, mayhem—but in the everyday intrusions that degrade the quality of life: the cracking of whips has as its modern equivalent the honking of taxi horns or the blare of car alarms in cities and the barking of dogs in suburbs.

Questions from the NR10

1. Does Schopenhauer think noise affects everyone or just a certain type of person?
2. Imagine what Schopenhauer expected to accomplish with this essay. Why, do you think, does he conclude with some references to comic treatments of noise? Just how serious is he?
3. The cracking of whips annoys Schopenhauer most, especially since the noise made is totally useless. Write about what noises annoy you the most; or describe a sensitive person in a noisy environment: attending a hockey game, being forced to listen to car alarms, working a cattle roundup.

Analytical Considerations

1. Schopenhauer's essay is about finding a quiet place to work. Ask students what they have found works well for them.
2. What risks has the writer taken? Has he successfully avoided looking foolish or seeming far too sensitive?
3. In paragraph 6 Schopenhauer suggests that those who crack whips ought to get whippings, a sort of "let the punishment fit the crime" attitude. Ask students to think of some everyday analogues they'd like to see. (They might enjoy the Gilbert and Sullivan song of that name, "Let the Punishment Fit the Crime," from the Mikado, particularly for the gusto the Mikado expresses for fiendish punishments.)
4. In paragraph 6 Schopenhauer distinguishes between laborers and thinkers, the former being "beasts of burden." He knows this is an outrageous thing to say; the question is, Do many other people act as if this were true? For instance, do people in rich countries treat people in poor countries this way, though of course from afar?

Suggested Writing Assignments

1. Schopenhauer says certain types of people are affected the most by noise, e.g., thinkers like himself. Do a survey of people you know who are affected by noise and write up the results in a report to the class.
2. Tell about an incident involving intrusive noise. Describe what was happening before the first occurence of the noise, what kind of person was bothered, what was thought, what was said, and the outcome. (In an age when people have been murdered over parking spaces, getting up the gumption to complain about noise might be harder; address this issue in your essay.)

The Alice Tax

The Norton Reader, p. 347

Everyone complains about taxes, but not everyone complains the way Trillin does: with a satire on a money-grubbing society and a humorous yet serious critique of a culture that doesn't understand what it means to have "enough." Trillin's short column, collected in the volume *Too Soon to Tell* (1995), might have been included in the "Op-Eds" section or in "Politics and Government." We have placed it here, with other short examples of cultural critique such as Harris's "Light-Bulb Jokes" and Schopenhauer's "On Noise," to emphasize the way it focuses on a single phenomenon to illumine a larger cultural pattern. Trillin's argument—presented as if it were his wife Alice's idea—is that tax laws might put large surcharges on "income over a million dollars a year" (paragraph 1). As he presents this argument in Alice's name, he introduces (and exposes the absurdity of) many counterarguments made against high taxes on the rich.

Questions from the NR10

1. Trillin presents his tax proposal as if it were his wife's idea and he were merely repeating her arguments. What advantages does he gain by this strategy?
2. What does Trillin mean by "the concept of enoughness"? Try to define "enoughness" for yourself and speculate about whether your definition would be compatible with Alice's.
3. Several essays in this cluster—including Schopenhauer's "On Noise," Harris's "Light-Bulb Jokes," and Mitford's "Behind the Formaldehyde Curtain"—focus on a single phenomenon of American culture to analyze our values (or lack of them). Choose some aspect of contemporary culture that intrigues you and write an essay in which you reveal the values and beliefs that it embodies.

Analytical Considerations

1. Ask students to formulate as many counterarguments as they can recall that oppose a large tax surcharge on the rich. Then ask them to note how many of these counterarguments Trillin embeds in his satire and how he dismisses them (e.g., that a large tax surcharge is "confiscatory" in paragraph 2, that it is "foreign to the current American notions of capitalism" in paragraph 3, that it would rob "people vital to the economy" of their "incentive" in paragraph 5). Consider how humor implicitly becomes a form of argument.
2. In paragraph 4, Trillin introduces the notion of "direct democracy"? What does this phrase ordinarily mean? How does Trillin use it?

1. Choose a law or government regulation that you think privileges one group of Americans. Write an analysis, either humorous or not, that explains why you think it is inappropriate or unfair.
2. Rewrite "The Alice Tax" as a straight (that is, nonhumorous) Op-Ed piece.

HERB GOLDBERG

In Harness: The Male Condition

The Norton Reader, p. 349; Shorter Edition, p. 198

Herb Goldberg is a psychologist, professor, and writer. "In Harness: The Male Condition" bears the marks of his therapeutic practice. It begins with a long example, a case study of a man who was probably his patient. Then, after generalizing about the male condition, Goldberg includes three vignettes, obtained by a request that these men (who may or may not have been his patients) write to him: a forty-six-year-old businessman, a thirty-nine-year-old carpenter, and a fifty-seven-year-old college professor (paragraphs 26–29). The fourth vignette is his own: at thirty-five he devoted himself to his family, and at fifty-seven he feels unrewarded. What is the effect of this delay in Goldberg's announcing his own involvement with his subject?

While Goldberg includes individual cases to illustrate his generalizations, when he generalizes he speaks of men collectively, as if gender unites them more than other circumstances—such as social or economic class, race and ethnicity, or small circumstances of infinite variety—divide them. He creates a universal that may well be false. A similar error is often charged about some statements propounded by feminists. On the one hand, Goldberg argues that the women's movement offers men little for achieving their own liberation; on the other hand, he is clearly aware of the movement as a model both to emulate and to react against.

Questions from the NR10

1. Exactly what does Goldberg mean by "in harness"? Is it a condition you have felt yourself? Are there women as well as men who can be said to be "in harness"?
2. What evidence does Goldberg have to support his conclusions? What problems might arise from basing conclusions on men who seek help from a psychotherapist?
3. Write about the extent to which males you know are or are not in situations Goldberg would describe as "in harness."

Analytical Considerations

1. Given Goldberg's clinical, detached presentation, his delayed announcement of his own involvement with his subject (and perhaps with his patients' predicaments) can be misleading. Be sure to make the point that personal involvement itself is not the problem: students are too often caught up in the notion that clinical detachment is better, truer. The problem is Goldberg's detached presentation and tone.

2. Sigmund Freud asked a much-quoted question with respect to women: what do women want? Get your students to ask Goldberg (at least as he is presented in this essay): what do men want? He's more articulate about their discontents than their contents. Apparently what he wants for himself is to do research, publish, teach, administer, play tennis, and travel.

Suggested Writing Assignments

1. Write an essay in which you analyze Goldberg's construction of a false universal. What characteristics do the individual men included in his essay share? What characteristics individualize them? Suggest some additional characteristics that need to be included for him to speak to and for a more representative, if still not universal, group of men.

2. Androgyny is a condition in which both male and female qualities are incorporated and valued. Does Goldberg see men becoming androgynous as a way of liberating them? Are there characteristics of women he would like to appropriate for men? Are there characteristics of women he would not like to appropriate for men? Write an essay on the role of androgyny in Goldberg's thinking.

BETTY ROLLIN

Motherhood: Who Needs It?

The Norton Reader, p. 354; Shorter Edition, p. 203

Although Betty Rollin never says so, the answer to her question "Who needs motherhood?" is "Nobody." This essay, written in 1970 for *Look*, a mass-circulation magazine now defunct, still generates strong responses. Virtually all students disagree with her argument and object to the tough way she argues; very few admit even to enjoying the essay. It's hard for students to imagine anyone taking her uncompromising position and calculatedly choosing to antagonize readers.

What students need to see is that Rollin makes her case against motherhood like a debater: she illustrates her argument with clear-cut evidence—no one she quotes has anything good to say about motherhood—and apparently she is out to win. If she brings up counterarguments, she dismisses them as propaganda and brainwashing. But does she really expect us to agree with her position? Think of a debate. The case for motherhood has been made often enough, as strongly and with as little qualification as Rollin makes the case against it. In place of all the goo that has been spread on the subject, Rollin throws acid. Somewhere between goo and acid must lie a reasonable viewpoint.

Questions from the NR10

1. Why does Rollin use the term "myth" to describe what she believes is the common attitude toward motherhood?
2. Arguing against motherhood is likely to cause problems in persuading an audience. How does Rollin go about dealing with those problems?
3. Rollin allows that "nothing could be worse or more unlikely" than "a world without children" (paragraph 30). Does this contradict her previous argument?
4. Choose a common "myth" in contemporary society and argue against it.

Analytical Considerations

1. Ask students, individually or in groups, to look at Rollin's language, particularly at her exaggerated, frequently outrageous statements (or hyperboles). Can they hear her as quotable and appreciate the wit of her formulations?
2. You might ask students to consider their antagonistic response to Rollin as gender based. Do they identify argument and debate as a masculine form, persuasion as feminine? Is a tough style legitimate for men, illegitimate for women?
3. Direct students to paragraphs 30 through 32, the last three paragraphs of Rollin's essay. How are they different from the rest of the essay? Why did she include them?

Suggested Writing Assignments

1. Write a debater's argument against some generally revered custom or institution. You might try "Fatherhood: Who Needs It?"
2. Try thinking of "Motherhood: Who Needs It?" as an example of sustained irony. Write an essay in which you compare it to Swift's "A Modest Proposal" (NR 848, SE 477). Consider how both Swift and Rollin may be seen as creating a putative author who offers proposals that violate feeling.

GLORIA STEINEM

The Good News Is: These Are Not the Best Years of Your Life

The Norton Reader, p. 363; Shorter Edition, p. 212

This essay first appeared in *Ms.* magazine, of which Steinem was a founder, in 1979. Steinem asks a question she is now ready to answer: why are younger women, college-age women in particular, not actively feminist? The genre of her essay is persuasion, and of a particular sort: she wants readers not only to understand her position but also to understand why she once believed something else and then changed her mind. By taking a second look, she not only questions her mistaken beliefs but also looks at the false expectations and assumptions that underlay them.

The structure of the essay is well marked. After describing her former beliefs, she turns to what she believes now. "Consider a few of the reasons," she concludes in paragraph 3; in paragraphs 4 through 15 she considers the contemporary scene; in paragraphs 16 through 18, the first and second women's movements, throughout regularly devoting one paragraph to developing and explaining each reason. Then she concludes with the inverse of what her present position implies: if college-age women are not actively feminist, older women are.

Women students, both younger and older, may or may not accept Steinem's view of their lives. They may need to be reminded that Steinem, rather than criticizing them, explains and excuses them. Moreover, the developmental scheme she traces in their lives she sees as also present in her own (paragraph 3).

Women students may or may not be willing to talk about this developmental scheme, although older women are usually more willing to talk about such things than are younger women. Men students may be only too willing to talk about the pressures on them. At some point, you will probably want to turn the discussion back to the false assumptions that Steinem sees underlying her former views: single-sex models of cultural pattern, including, in this essay, human development and revolution.

Analytical Considerations

1. Steinem creates four categories to describe college-age women's responses to feminism (paragraph 15). Discuss the adequacy of her classificatory scheme. You might also ask students to imagine this scheme, which appears in only a minor way in Steinem's essay, as the organizing scheme of another essay. What kind of essay would it be?
2. Particularly if you've had students analyze Herb Goldman's construction of a false universal—see "In Harness: The Male Condition" (NR 349, SE 198; Suggested Writing Assignment 1, *Guide*, p. 86)—you will want to have them look at Steinem's qualification with respect to women: "every generalization based on female culture has many exceptions" (paragraph 3). Is this qualification sufficient to exempt her from constructing a false universal about women?
3. Ask students to read Casey Miller and Kate Swift, "Who's in Charge of the English Language?" (NR 550, SE 289) for a discussion of how language creates many of our concepts. Does their essay shed light on differing responses to the word *feminist*?

Suggested Writing Assignments

1. Taking a second look: write an essay in which you look at something you've changed your mind about, accounting for what you used to believe, what you believe now, and how you changed your mind.
2. Steinem claims a "depth of feminist change" on campus that observers often miss (paragraph 26). Assemble what evidence of change you can, through your own experience and by interviewing at least one woman of another

generation. Depending on whom you interview, you can compare the present with the past of ten, twenty, thirty, or even more years ago.

3. Carol Gilligan's *In a Different Voice* (1982) is an extended study of a single-sex model of moral development. Read it and write a brief essay in which you explain Gilligan's theory of how single-sex cultural patterns affect women.

VANESSA OCHS

Not in My Backyard

The Norton Reader, p. 368

We usually associate the phrase "Not in my backyard" with the opposition of one racial or ethnic group to a different racial or ethnic group that wishes to live in the same neighborhood. Ochs begins with an instance of conflict between two Jewish groups in Hewlett Harbor, Long Island, New York, where she grew up. When Orthodox Jews bought property in the neighborhood to establish a girls' yeshiva, more liberal and (in Ochs's terms) assimilated Jews opposed their invasion. Ochs narrates the event and analyzes the underlying beliefs and fears that motivate the opposition, including different responses to the Holocaust and its aftermath. This essay, like James Baldwin's "Stranger in the Village" (NR 375), provides an opportunity for discussing ways that writers handle potentially (or actually) explosive topics. An important consideration is how Ochs, the writer, situates herself as both a member and an outside observer of the Long Island community.

Questions from the NR10

1. The phrase "Not in my backyard" has been used by many different groups to express resistance to change in their neighborhoods. Which reactions that Ochs describes are specific to the differences between Jewish groups in her hometown? Which reactions have you observed in other communities?

2. The first half of Ochs's essay narrates a controversy over the "Yeshiva High School for Girls at Hewlett Bay Park." In paragraph 16, Ochs then asks herself about the "deep, true meaning of this controversy." What answers does she consider? What answers does she finally develop?

3. If there is (or has been) a controversy among neighborhood groups in your region, write about it using a similar combination of narrative and reflection.

Analytical Considerations

1. The first half of the essay (paragraphs 1–16) describes Hewlett Harbor, Long Island, and narrates the controversy over the Orthodox girls' yeshiva. Ask students to look at those places in which Ochs describes herself or her memories of Hewlett Park. What kind of persona does she convey? How does this persona help her in the remainder of the essay, where she must analyze (sometimes critically) the responses of neighbors and family?

2. After Ochs asks about the "deep, true meaning of this controversy" (paragraph 16), she responds, "Many possibilities present themselves." What possibilities does she consider only to dismiss? What possibilities does she consider more seriously? Ask students if they can see a logic to the order of the remaining paragraphs.

3. Why does Ochs end with the example of her mother's "Steinway grand piano"? What does it symbolize?

Suggested Writing Assignments

1. Write about an incident in your ethnic or religious community that caused controversy. Describe the controversy and analyze its causes.

2. Write an Op-Ed piece—for a newspaper like the *New York Times* or the *Nassau Herald*—in which you either present Ochs's argument (or some of it) in condensed form or argue the position of one of the groups involved: the longtime residents of Hewlett Harbor or the Orthodox Jews who wish to establish a yeshiva. What can you accomplish in a short Op-Ed? What can Ochs accomplish in a longer essay?

JAMES BALDWIN

Stranger in the Village

The Norton Reader, p. 375

This classic essay is a product of James Baldwin's stay in a Swiss village, where he went to live in a friend's family chalet to get some writing done. Baldwin's experiences with the Swiss villagers' reaction to a black man in their midst causes him to see a paradox. In the normal course of things, the relationship of Europeans to Americans is straightforward: Europeans came first; Americans are of the New World; therefore, Europeans are more worldly, more sophisticated, more complex. But in matters of race, Baldwin argues, it is the Europeans who are naive, simple, and somewhat foolish. They have a few unsophisticated attitudes toward a black visitor in their village: fear and wonder, or at most a grudging acceptance. In fact, it turns out that these Swiss are much like the stereotypical Africans who first encountered white-skinned Europeans (though Baldwin knows there is a difference between an American black in Europe and whites in nineteenth-century Africa).

For Baldwin, America, more than anyplace else, is where black and white citizens have had the most interaction, the most to do with one another. Difficult as that relationship has been, Baldwin sees America as the only place where racial interactions are likely to continue to make progress.

Questions from the NR10

1. Baldwin begins with the narration of his experience in a Swiss village. At what point do you become aware that he has a larger point? What purpose does he make his experience serve?

2. Baldwin relates white people's language and legends about black people to the "laws" of the white man's personality. What conviction about the source and the nature of language does this reveal?
3. Describe some particular experience that raises a large social question or shows the working of large social forces. Does Baldwin offer any help in the problem of connecting the particular and the general?

Analytical Considerations

1. For Baldwin, America is unique: "no other people has ever been so deeply involved in the lives of black men, and vice versa" (paragraph 26). Ask black studies students if contemporary scholars of black history might dispute Baldwin's claim, perhaps citing the long history of multiracial relations in Brazil or the Sudan or in Spain under the Moors.
2. Baldwin's picture of Africa is drawn from what he knew in the 1950s, just about half a century ago. Recent developments in recapturing the past might have given him a somewhat different attitude toward African history, though without altering his main point. What knowledge about the African past is missing from Baldwin's picture?

Suggested Writing Assignments

1. Describe the experience of being an outsider in a community.
2. In an essay, show whether or to what extent American attitudes have changed since 1955, when Baldwin published his essay. Is his basic point still valid, or have conditions altered so much that this essay has more value as history and literature than as contemporary commentary?

BRENT STAPLES

Black Men and Public Space

The Norton Reader, p. 384; Shorter Edition, p. 217

In this short essay Brent Staples writes about himself as an individual and as a universal, that is, as a well-educated and nonviolent black man who, by virtue of his gender and race, is perceived as belonging to a class: violent black men. He is not unsympathetic to women who avoid him on the streets at night: "the danger they perceive is not a hallucination" (paragraph 5). The essay provides an account of his initiation into awareness and his attempts to distinguish himself from other members of his putative class.

"Black Men and Public Space" is an episodic narrative with commentary. You might call students' attention to the four times and places of the essay—childhood in Pennsylvania, graduate school in Chicago, Chicago of the late 1970s and early 1980s, and New York City now—and how Staples manipulates chronology. You can also have them note how the particularized narrative of the opening (his first encounter with a "victim" as a graduate student in Chicago) reverberates against his more generalized narrative of other times and places.

Questions from the NR10

1. Staples writes of situations rightly perceived as threatening and of situations misperceived as threatening. Give specific instances of each and tell how they are related.
2. Staples's essay contains a mixture of rage and humor. Does this mix detract from or contribute to the seriousness of the matter?
3. Write of a situation in which someone was wrongly perceived as threatening.

Analytical Considerations

1. Ask students to distinguish between narrative and commentary in this essay—and to notice how Staples combines them. Whereas many essays frame personal experience with generalizing commentary, Staples's does not. Yet it is more than a personal report; it calls attention to larger problems.
2. The pressure of the unspoken in this essay generates irony. Students might consider verbal irony, such as Staples's describing the woman he encountered in Chicago as his "victim," and dramatic irony, such as whistling Vivaldi and Beethoven when he walks the streets late at night. Another irony would be Staples's "solution": his precautions against being taken for a mugger and a rapist. Are they a solution? How does the unspoken exert pressure? What are the advantages and disadvantages of irony in this essay?

Suggested Writing Assignments

1. Rewrite Staples's essay as an unironic indictment of America as a racist society.
2. Write a personal essay about your experience of reading (and discussing) "Black Men and Public Space."
3. A longer version of this essay appeared in the September 1986 issue of *Ms.* magazine as "Just Walk on By." Find it in the library, read it, and write an analysis in which you focus on two things: the relation of "Black Men and Public Space" (excerpted for *Harper's Magazine*) to the longer "Just Walk on By" (published in *Ms.*) and the question of audience in both essays. How does Staples engage with his presumably different readers in each essay?

SHELBY STEELE

The Recoloring of Campus Life

The Norton Reader, p. 387

In "The Recoloring of Campus Life," Shelby Steele, a professor of English at San Jose State College in California, addresses a volatile and controversial subject: race relations and affirmative action on college campuses. Whether or not you decide to have students read and discuss it will depend on the situation on your campus and the dynamics of your class. The essay was published in *Harper's Magazine* in 1989; in other words, it wasn't written with student readers in mind. Nevertheless, it is exemplary in Steele's judicious evenhandedness and careful assumption of authority. If you do assign this essay, you will probably notice its tight structure: Steele presents his credentials, explains how he gathered his evidence, and then divides his presentation of it—black students speak, then white students speak—before presenting his own proposal for a politics of commonality rather than a politics of difference. Although he has a proposal, the essay is not primarily an argument for it. Steele devotes more attention to analyzing the social and psychological dynamics of campus unrest than to advancing his solution.

Students will probably begin discussion in their own terms: after all, when someone generalizes about a group of which you are a member, your first response is, Is this true of me? The question of constructing universals has surfaced in other essays in this section: Herb Goldberg's "In Harness: The Male Condition" (NR 349, SE 198) and Gloria Steinem's "The Good News Is: These Are Not the Best Years of Your Life" (NR 363, SE 212). You might consider this concept again as you discuss Steele's essay. Has Steele constructed false universals—black students, white students? How might he construct true universals? How much qualification would be necessary? Is the entire enterprise of constructing universals doomed to fail? You will probably need to remind students that talk about groups rather than individuals is characteristic of academic disciplines other than literature: it is something they can expect to hear a lot of and do a lot of in college. Perhaps, then, universals are most problematic when we write about contemporary issues, when we read as individuals, when we look for signs of the times.

Questions from the NR10

1. What are the differences Steele cites between black-white campus relations in the 1960s and the 1980s?
2. What leads Steele to say that today's campus is given over to "politics of difference"? What are the "politics of difference"?
3. Using the same kind of interviewing approach that Steele does, write about the extent to which his conclusions apply to your own campus today.

Analytic Considerations

1. Steele tends to highlight what he sees as paradoxes: for example, "I think racial tension on campus is the result more of racial equality than inequality" (paragraph 6). You might ask students to consider his evidence and his formulation of this paradox by the use of antitheses: equality versus inequality. They should be able to locate other instances of paradoxical formulations in the essay.
2. How does Steele incorporate personal experience in his analysis and to what ends? Would he argue for its importance as strongly as Paul Fussell does in "Thank God for the Atom Bomb" (NR 735, SE 401)?

Suggested Writing Assignments

1. Ask yourself: Is this true of me—i.e., is Steele's construction of a group to which I belong by virtue of my race accurate? Write a private journal entry (for yourself), a semi-private journal entry (to be shared with the class), and a public essay (to be read to an audience that does not know you) in response to this question.

2. In a footnote Steele refers to an earlier essay of his also published in *Harper's Magazine*: "I'm Black, You're White, Who's Innocent? Race and Power in an Era of Blame" (footnote 2). The title suggests that he treats at greater length the theme of innocence that appears in "The Recoloring of Campus Life." Read this earlier essay and write an analysis of its relationship to the later essay. Does Steele demonstrate similar evenhandedness and careful assumption of authority in both, and how?

DEBRA DICKERSON

Who Shot Johnny?

The Norton Reader, p. 398; Shorter Edition, p. 220

Debra Dickerson defines herself in the opening paragraph: she is black, single, middle-class, feminist, Harvard-educated, and well-read in contemporary American politics. What happens to her nephew is not what she (or we) would expect: he is shot and paralyzed in a random and still unexplained attack by another black man.

Given her background, students might expect Dickerson to write a certain kind of essay, especially to write in a certain kind of style. In a sense, she gives us what we expect in the first two-thirds of her essay: a careful narrative of the episode and her frustrated attempt to make sense of it. Yet the final four paragraphs startle the reader. Dickerson shifts to the language of the streets, a language of rage and a style of derisory parody. Students will inevitably want to discuss the shift; it will be important for them to see the relation of both styles, the effectiveness of the shift, the use of the "colloquial" in the face of the limitations of the "academic."

Questions from the NR10

1. Why did *The New Republic* include the first paragraph? Do you think the essay would be more or less effective if it began simply with the sentence "On July 27, 1995, my sixteen-year-old nephew was shot and paralyzed"?
2. Dickerson feels—and expresses—anger throughout this essay. How? Against what or whom?
3. Why does Dickerson use the term "brother" in the final paragraphs? How does this composite characterization work? How does it answer the question "Who shot Johnny?"

Analytical Considerations

1. Why is it important for Dickerson to describe her immediate reaction to the shooting as well as the routine in its aftermath? That is, how does she gain *pathos* and establish *ethos*?

2. Is Dickerson's use of the category "brother" in the final four paragraphs a "false universal"? (See the entry in the *Guide* for Herb Goldberg's "In Harness: The Male Condition" [p. 86] for a discussion of this term.) Ask students why Dickerson might choose to universalize at this point.
3. Dickerson does not conclude with a sociological analysis, with a discussion of the economic, social, or historical sources of violent crime. Yet her enraged commentary shows that she is aware of such sources. Ask students to discuss sentences that show her awareness.

Suggested Writing Assignments

1. "Who Shot Johnny?" Ask students to write a sociological analysis of the causes of the crime that Dickerson describes.
2. Ask students to read Bruce Shapiro's "One Violent Crime" in "Personal Report" (NR 15, SE 10). Write a comparison of the two writers' responses to crime and of their means of "coping" with the crime through writing.
3. Read Molly Ivins's "Get a Knife, Get a Dog, but Get Rid of Guns" (NR 404, SE 192) and/or Sloan et al., "Handgun Regulations, Crime, Assaults, and Homicide: A Tale of Two Cities" (NR 913, SE 521). Write a brief essay in which you explain how the proposals of either or both writers might have prevented the crime Dickerson describes.

MOLLY IVINS

Get a Knife, Get a Dog, but Get Rid of Guns

The Norton Reader, p. 404; Shorter Edition, p. 192

If Op-Ed ranges from dull and earnest to witty and smart-alecky, Ivins is firmly in the latter camp. Agree or disagree with her, everyone is pretty clear about exactly where she stands. Here her title says it all. You don't need to read on to find out what she thinks of guns. But when you do read on, you find out why.

For many readers, Ivins provides a short, sharply argued "take" on a subject. Here she sets out to skewer Second Amendment traditionalists by quoting them the entire amendment and telling exactly what she thinks it means by glossing it with statements such as "Fourteen-year-old boys are not part of a well-regulated milita" (paragraph 5).

This is not subtle writing. It's not meant to be. In fact, some can argue that Ivins is simplifying a difficult and complex subject, one that was until recently considered closed but now seems to have some life in it. That is, the Second Amendment was considered to govern group rights, not the rights of single individuals. (Courts almost always rule that the government can regulate firearm possession and use.) Now, however, legal scholars are having another look at the amendment, and even liberals are agreeing that there seems to be some room in it for the rights of individuals to possess guns.

By taking a complex issue and simplifying and condensing it to the length of a short newspaper column, Ivins (and her newspaper opponents as well) seems intent on arguing the case in sound bites, which is what tends to happen in television ads at election time. Her column and Anna Quindlen's "Evan's Two Moms" (NR 410) stand in contrast to the longer, less clever, and and much less lively think pieces by Michael Sandel (NR 415) and Michael Walzer (NR 417).

Questions from the NR10

1. What do you think of Ivins's examination of the Constitution? What kind of evidence would make you be convinced even more? Why doesn't Ivins provide more evidence?
2. Characterize Ivins's language. What words, phrases, or structures seem typical of her style?
3. Examine the analogy between guns and cars. How does it hold up? Where does it break down?

Analytical Considerations

1. Ask students to examine the Second Amendment, which Ivins quotes (paragraph 5). Does the second clause depend on the first? What is the linkage

between "militia" and "the people"? How do we decide precisely what the amendment means? Whose interpretation gets to "count"?

2. Ivins says the Second Amendment is clear. Many disagree with her. What arguments do her opponents give? Many students in the class, no matter what their beliefs, should be able to lay out the two sides of the argument.
3. Examine Ivins's diction to pick out the words that make her writing seem sharp and down-to-earth.
4. Ivins lives in Texas, where guns have historically been highly popular and readily available. Are there any signs of her Texas roots in this essay?

Suggested Writing Assignments

1. Answer Ivins in a debate-style piece of your own, trying for a similarly brisk, no-nonsense style.
2. In an essay, compare Ivins's essay with Dorothy Allison's "Gun Crazy" (NR 275, SE 149), which assumes the right of women to use guns. Who seems to have the more sensible approach?
3. Research some of the material supplied by pro-gun and gun-control advocacy groups and explain how their approachs are different from or similar to the way Ivins argues.

BRENT STAPLES

Why Colleges Shower Their Students with A's

The Norton Reader, p. 405

With its strong opinions about the deterioration of American colleges, Staples's editorial can provoke some sharp reaction among students, who will not always see things the way he does. A teacher can turn that student reaction into valuable writing assignments.

The first issue is getting to Staples's real point: that the rules of economics force colleges to keep the customers satisfied by raising grades. The experience of a class of first-year students might not reach to grade inflation, but they can do some research on their own. It is not hard to find out which departments and programs on campus are hard and which are easy. It's the kind of research students will be doing on their own anyway, so it's relatively easy to channel it into composition assignments.

Staples's essay also lets students examine some of the rhetorical strategies good writers employ. One is the generalization. Staples employs the terms "colleges," "departments," "students," and "teachers" but is rather short on specific examples, on individual cases. Is that permissible? Don't generalizations need support? What constitutes sufficient support? (Short opinion essays often don't supply much support, as Staples and the *New York Times* demonstrate here, and as Molly Ivins does in her Op-Ed column on gun control [NR 404, SE 192].)

Another useful term is analogy. For Staples, the college is a "product" and the students are the "customers." Class members can trace this commodity *analogy* throughout the essay and then decide how accurate it is. Do they think of themselves as customers? Just what happens when we think of college as a product? Is the market analogy a sign of the rising prominence of business in American life?

Questions from the NR10

1. What is the grade situation on your campus? Have you been showered with A's recently? Have you noticed professors inflating grades?
2. Staples writes, "An Ivy League professor said recently that if tenure disappeared, universities would be 'free to sell diplomas outright.'" Analyze this statement. What are its implications? Why does the professor think tenured faculty serve as protection against the "selling" of diplomas? What level of confidence does this professor have in the administration?
3. A Duke University statistics professor proposed "recalculating the grade point average to give rigorously graded courses greater weight." He was opposed by humanities professors. What might have been the source of their opposition? What do you think is meant by "rigorously graded"? What is the situation on your campus: do math profs grade more "rigorously" than English profs? Who are the hardest graders?
4. How broad is Staples's range of examples? Would he need to adjust his position if he considered other colleges? Write an analysis of the situation at your college either to confirm or to contest Staples's argument.

Analytical Considerations

1. Staples's market analogy does not include the notion of college as a brand name. Do some students regard colleges like designer labels? Are these students making an informed judgment about the value of different colleges? What can go wrong in such thinking? This train of thought can lead to excellent discussion, since students are likely to have their own college searches fresh in their minds.
2. Are there any traces of elitism in Staples's essay? The University of Phoenix, a for-profit school with a job-focused, "superficial" curriculum, is his first example of a "less rigorous" college. On what evidence does he brand Phoenix as watered-down? Does Staples supply any evidence that Phoenix gives higher grades? His other examples are strictly Ivy League, which often but inaccurately serves as a convenient stand-in for "college." (For instance, Staples's essay doesn't reflect the fact that most first-year students begin at a community college, and that the large majority of students attend public universities.)

Suggested Writing Assignments

1. Write about the college searches conducted by people you know, including yourself if you wish. What kind of information did prospective students get? How did they make up their minds?
2. Describe a campus tour you took while considering a particular college. Was that tour helpful in making up your mind? In light of Staples's essay, what information could you have used in making your decision?

3. Conduct a survey of the grading practices among some departments in your college. Which have the highest percentages of A and B grades? Which mark on curves? Which have the highest dropout rates? (If departments discourage marginal students early on, they don't have to give so many low grades.)
4. Write a response to Staples's depiction of college as product and student as customer, basing it on your own experience.

MICHIKO KAKUTANI

Portrait of the Artist as a Focus Group

The Norton Reader, p. 408; Shorter Edition, p. 609

Kakutani's 1998 column is a defense of a critic's high standards in the face of a growing tendency for artists and producers to pander to the audience. She imagines a future of nothing but focus groups, with the audience totally in charge, when "Pop Art gives way to Poll Art" (paragraph 10). In a way, she's restating a classic argument that goes back to Plato's *Gorgias*: truth (Kakutani's "artist") needs to be defended against rhetorical manipulation (Kakutani's "focus group").

In thinking about the ostensible subject of Kakutani's column, the poll of Americans' favorite subjects for paintings, it helps to introduce students to the concept of "the straw man." Kakutani's opening depiction of poll-driven art seems merely a pretext, a proxy target that is very easy to dispatch. Pollsters Komar and Melamid could well be celebrated as sly jokers who poke fun at Americans' low tastes in art. Instead, Kakutani uses them to condemn the whole concept of poll-driven art, which is hardly a clear and present danger today outside of Hollywood and Broadway. But note that Kakutani quickly drops the Komar and Melamid poll and moves her aim to a larger target, what she terms "the sales imperative" (paragraph 5). And one needs to remember that she is a critic of literature, not painting. Her concern is not pictoral art at all, but the relationship between critics and the public.

To Kakutani, the *New York Times*'s regular book reviewer, the concept of poll-driven art seems ludicrous, and at bottom the prospect must be threatening. Most newspaper and magazine critics are used to being arbiters, judges whose superior taste helps educate their readers as well as inform them of particularly important events and trends. They also see themselves as protectors of the public interest, bridges between artist and consumer. The notion of a poll directly attacks such an exalted stance, since it raises the audience to the level of the ultimate arbiter, while at the same time rendering the critic superfluous. If the public decides, who needs a critic?

Classes can go well when asked to define the appropriate role for the critic. Some students will ask why a poll is bad: This is a democracy, right? Others will resent the assumption of superiority that goes with the critic's territory.

Students as a rule resist being told what to like or dislike. Good discussion can result when students are asked exactly when and where a critic can be helpful. Surely they rely on the critical intelligence of others. When and to what extent?

(For the record, Broadway impresario Garth Drabinsky (paragraphs 7–8), the poll-driven producer of *Ragtime*, was charged with criminal fraud for misstating his company's financial picture, that is, for cooking the books [*New York Times*, January 14, 1999].)

Questions from the NR10

1. The "hook" in this Op-Ed is the "Painting by Numbers" poll, what Kakutani calls "a sly comment on the democratization of creativity and America's mania for polls." How seriously is this poll taken in the rest of the essay?
2. What are the specific examples of artists or organizations that Kakutani cites as examples of poll-driven art? How would you characterize them? What kinds of art is Kakutani leaving out?
3. Since Kakutani is herself a professional critic, what might be her own stake in this issue? Why might she be opposed to the "democratization" of artistic judgment?
4. How successful a case has Kakutani made against polls? Would you commission a poll if you were producing a $5-million musical or aiming to write a best-selling thriller? Why or why not?

Analytical Considerations

1. Examine how Hollywood gets treated as a source of infection throughout this essay.
2. Based on this single essay, what inferences can one make about Kakutani's opinion of most popular culture?
3. Ask students what is wrong with market testing. Surely some things need it. Is market testing only wrong when "major" genres like painting and literature are involved? Is it permissible for certain less-exalted arts?

Suggested Writing Assignments

1. Write a 350- to 500-word critical essay on a recent film, concert, or episode of a TV show. Include a one-paragraph cover memo explaining what kind of readers you are trying to reach and how you want them to think about the critic's role.
2. Choose a critical piece from a newspaper or magazine about a performance or artist you know and respond to it, either disagreeing with it or, if you agree with it, choosing a different point to emphasize.
3. Teachers can assign groups of students to write individual critiques of the same event or work and then have the critiques brought to class and discussed in pairs or groups.

ANNA QUINDLEN

Evan's Two Moms

The Norton Reader, p. 410

Famous for her witty, engaging newspaper columns and her popular novels, Anna Quindlen has championed liberal issues by making them seem like commonsense notions, much the way the more flippant Molly Ivins does in her piece on gun control (NR 404, SE 192). Reasoned argument is not part of Quindlen's technique here. Clever positioning and a strong emphasis on the down-to-earth verities of love, fairness, and plain dealing characterize this essay.

Quindlen's essay consistently places love and devotion ahead of a narrow, rigid interpretation of the law, making it seem that there is no contest: a couple's love and devotion are far more important than narrow rules, she claims, and she quite cleverly assumes that no one thinks differently. In other words, Quindlen proceeds on the assumption that her "answer" to the issue of gay marriage is sensible, down-to-earth, and shared by all right-thinking people. The only disquieting moment comes with her sharply written sentence: "Gay marriage is a radical notion for straight people and a conservative notion for gay ones" (paragraph 4). This well-crafted sentence admits what everyone has known all along: that Quindlen's position is the minority one, that the fifty states have consistently ruled against gay marriage, that gay Americans do not share the right to marry the person they choose. As the sentence acknowledges, Quindlen is arguing for a right that most Americans oppose as too radical.

Thus the brief column is a nice example of making the "radical" seem sensible, commonplace, rooted in traditional values. And Quindlen does a fine job in foregrounding the positive aspects of her case: having two moms, rooting marriage in love and commitment, fostering the conservative desire to formalize a bond that already exists. When you want to argue for something radical, it is often a good strategy to make it seem safe and traditional.

Questions from the NR10

1. What is the precise subject matter of Quindlen's column? How far afield does she stray from that subject matter?
2. What do you think of the personality that lies behind this piece? What seem to be Quindlen's values? Compare them to the values espoused by Brent Staples, her fellow *New York Times* writer, in his Op-Ed in this section.
3. Compare Quindlen to Molly Ivins in "Get a Knife, Get a Dog, but Get Rid of Guns," both journalists writing columns. How does Quindlen begin? What is her hook? Why doesn't Ivins provide a similar hook to an event in the news?

Analytical Considerations

1. Why doesn't Quindlen put the argument in terms of partisan politics?
2. What's the effect of the closing comparison with interracial marriage? Spell out each aspect of the comparison Quindlen is making.
3. Is there anything underhanded in trying to make a "radical" notion seem safe and ordinary? Or is Quindlen confident her readers will understand that she is simply positioning her subject in a new, more favorable light?

Suggested Writing Assignments

1. Write an comparison of the two pieces by liberal women columnists, Anna Quindlen and Molly Ivins. Both make commonsense arguments in favor of very large shifts in public policy. How do they both treat the central issue?
2. Research and write an essay explaining why almost all governments have traditionally banned same-sex marriages.
3. Taking Quindlen's approach for a model, write an essay making something "radical" seem safe and ordinary.

RUSSELL BAKER

American Fat

The Norton Reader, p. 412

This is a light, witty update on the same general subject as Orwell's "Politics and the English Language" (NR 575, SE 304), though here the evil is depicted in terms of obesity and poor style rather than political manipulation. Could it be that Baker, a World War II veteran writing in the 1980s, is forty years away from Orwell's close-up familiarity with the Stalin and Hitler period? For historically minded students, it's worth reflecting on the change in language of criticism from Orwell to Baker. Both of them have devoted a good deal of thought to how in the twentieth century those in power used the media in an attempt to manipulate popular opinion. Orwell imagined it in sinister ways, Baker comically.

If the political angle is played down, except for the presence of one of Baker's heroes, Truman, the style angle is played up. Orwell and Baker both locate the source of fat, evasive language in the bureaucracy—and heap particular scorn on professionals who aim to make everything seem grander or more diffuse than it is. Baker's key example is the doctor. Students can no doubt find similar examples all around them, in the world of education, where searching for examples of overblown language is always fun and revealing. A college catalogue or Web site are usually good places to start: names of departments and programs are a fertile ground; so too are the pompous mission statements that often precede course descriptions or describe the university's overall philosophy. Other good hunting grounds are law enforcement, the funeral industry, and psychology.

Questions from the NR10

1. Examine Baker's first paragraph closely. Do you find any examples of "lard" in his own writing, if only added for humorous effect?
2. Examine the way Baker alternates short and long sentences. What is the ratio? Can you discern a method in Baker's style?
3. Baker cites the Truman campaign of 1948 as the last example of plain talk. What do you think has happened since then to account for our supposed love of fancy, overdone language?
4. Read Baker's essay in connection with Orwell's "Politics and the English Language" (NR 575). On what points do they agree? Do they cover the same ground?

Analytical Considerations

1. Use *facilitate* in a sentence, seeing if you can get it to sound appropriate. What are the problems involved in making it work?
2. To what extent is Baker's a serious attack? Do you think this essay works to make people change, or only to make them a bit more worried?
3. Besides doctors, what kinds of professionals use words like *facilitate*?
4. Many students will have their own lists of words that they find repellent. A good class discussion can ensue from students asking each other what is wrong with some words on their own lists. Some will be quite surprised to see what their classmates dislike.

Suggested Writing Assignments

1. Write a column-length essay (500–800 words) telling what would happen if everyone followed Baker's advice and removed the lard. What would prose be like? Would life be better?
2. How worried are people you know about their use of English? Outside of English classes, are people terrorized by the language police? Write about this subject, basing your essay on interviews.
3. Using a collegiate dictionary, check the current status of the word *presently* (paragraph 14). Then ask people you know what the word means. Make sure you keep track of their responses when you explain what the dictionary says. Write up the result of this little experiment.
4. Interview five similar people (all students, all from comparable occupations, or all from the same neighborhood) about the overused, empty words they come across. Write up your results.

MICHAEL J. SANDEL

Last Rights

The Norton Reader, p. 415

Sandel's article fuses policy and morality, bringing disciplined intelligence to a burning moral issue. The tone is cool, detached, restrained, yet Sandel never lets us forget that lives are at stake.

Students might have trouble seeing that Sandel deliberately limits himself to a small, very specific part of this complex debate. The wrenching moral decision embodied in Barbara Huttmann's first-person approach in "A Crime of Compassion" (NR 420) is replaced by a cool argument about the premises underlying the moral philosophers' argument. Essentially the question is, Do we have the right to dispose of our own lives? Sandel takes issue with the moral philosophers whose argument, he claims, says we do. To counter the "Dream Team" of moral philosophers, Sandel assembles a smaller team of two, John Locke and Immanuel Kant, two of the most eminent moral philosophers of all time. Through selective quotation from the Dream Team and his own "experts," Sandel presents a very strong case against the notion that our lives are ours to dispose of as we wish.

One question for students is, What guarantees that Sandel is accurately presenting the views of the Dream Team and of Locke and Kant? The answer is something that many students will not have thought of: the only "guarantee" lies in the notion of public discourse, here embodied in the ongoing discussion of the issue in the pages of the *New Republic* and other journals. If Sandel mischaracterizes the case of his experts or of the Dream Team, the *New Republic* will most likely receive and print letters from attentive and angry readers. If the mischaracterization is particularly underhanded, Sandel is likely to weaken his reputation. He is likely to be cited for many years to come, so he cannot afford to be seen as arguing in bad faith or wildly stretching the truth. In other words, the rules of the game are created by the journal and the reading public. There really is a court of public opinion, though in many cases the public is fairly small, much less than a million. And if a prominent thinker like Sandel or an influential magazine like the *New Republic* is caught in an inaccuracy or a bold-faced lie, the rest of the media will pick up that fact and spread it to the wider American public. Thus when the *New Republic* was discovered to have a writer who was fabricating stories, it immediately apologized amid a stream of very bad publicity. The only thing a magazine has is its reputation, and the *New Republic* would have lost its very quickly had it not owned up to the misdeeds of its writer.

Questions from the NR10

1. Sandel calls assisted suicide a "wrenching" moral issue. Is there anything in his essay's content or tone that reveals the "wrenching" qualities of the debate? How would you characterize the way Sandel makes his case?
2. The first sentence of the last paragraph suggests that Sandel is not against assisted suicide "in all cases." What is he arguing against? State his argument in a sentence or two.
3. Count the times Sandel uses the word "autonomy" or some variation of it. What does this tell you about his point of view?

Analytical Considerations

1. Some students could be assigned the task of looking up information about Locke and Kant. There may be a few students taking a moral philosophy class who can explain Kant and Locke's position. At the very least, the term "moral philosopher" might be investigated and explained for the class.

2. What would be gained if Sandel were to engage in scorning or rebuking his Dream Team opponents? What would be lost?
3. Why does Sandel make it clear at the end that in some cases he might not be against assisted suicide?

Suggested Writing Assignments

1. Are our lives our own to dispose of? Find out what others think and write an essay explaining what the range of beliefs seems to be.
2. What do you think the result will be of this extended argument over assisted suicide? Can you make an educated guess on what the law will be in five years?

MICHAEL WALZER

Feed the Face

The Norton Reader, p. 417

Walzer is deferential to Michael Sandel ("Last Rights") in his first paragraph, but in his second suggests that the particular disagreement between Sandel and "the philosophers" represents only one, and a less important, argument about assisted suicide. To Walzer, the issue is not some abstract philosophical or moral question, but a case of who gets what kind of care and when. And he imagines that in a world that permitted assisted suicide, the poorest and most helpless would be encouraged to take advantage of it rather than wait around for their inevitable, expensive end. Thus Walzer's argument is rooted in the down-to-earth, practical necessities of who will pay for care. As he argues, ". . . the chief problem with assisted suicide may not be moral or legal so much as financial: it is just too cheap relative to the available medical alternatives" (paragraph 9).

Walzer later calls Sandel's article and the philosophers' argument "briefs," that is, statements submitted to a court to help judges make up their minds. Students will benefit from learning that briefs are a special type of argument that focus particular attention on precedence, the record of prior decisions in cases of a similar nature. Briefs also spend a great deal of time specifying the issue at hand with clairty, which is Walzer's task in this article. (Walzer's court is the readers of the magazine, many of whom are policymakers in Washington and at law schools.) Walzer and Sandel both know that if your explanation of what the issue is gets accepted by the court, you've already come close to winning your case.

Questions from the NR10

1. Do you think Walzer's first paragraph provides a fair and accurate characterization of Sandel's argument?
2. Why might Walzer have been dissatisfied with Sandel's attack on physician-assisted suicide? What perspective does Walzer provide that is missing from Sandel's treatment?

3. Compare the levels of Sandel's and Walzer's discourse. Who is arguing on a higher, more abstract level? Whose tone is more elevated? What evidence leads to your conclusion? (Note that both Sandel and Walzer wrote for the same magazine, and that their articles are the same length.)

Analytical Considerations

1. The title of Walzer's essay, drawn from the Brecht quote, is much more slangy, much less neutral, than Sandel's. Does this difference in titles get reflected in differences in the style of argument in these two pieces? Is Sandel's "higher," Walzer's "lower"?
2. Students can determine why Walzer, like Sandel, avoids personal anecdotes. (Huttmann's essay is all anecdote, a telling difference in approach.)

Suggested Writing Assignments

1. Bring Walzer's warnings to life by writing a scenario that portrays an ill elderly person being urged to take advantage of assisted suicide. Include dialogue. (You can do this as a brief play as well.)
2. Do you know of a case in which finances made terminating an ill person's life a real possibility? Write about it in a way that addresses Walzer's essay.

BARBARA HUTTMANN

A Crime of Compassion

The Norton Reader, p. 420

Nurse Barbara Huttmann puts a human face on the abstract arguments propounded by policymakers like Michael Sandel and Michael Walzer. She's on the front lines of this issue, dealing with life and death decisions every day. Her perspective mixes practical issues of negligence and liability with the moral, humanitarian questions of the patient's and family's wishes.

Since this piece was written in 1983, most states have permitted the patients themselves (or those who have their medical power of attorney) to determine whether care may be withdrawn. There are still legal disputes about some thorny issues, but most of the time a patient's clearly stated wishes have a good chance of being followed. The case Huttmann describes, in which a patient and his family want no extraordinary measures taken to prolong life, was often the norm; it has now become considerably rarer.

In such a deeply felt piece as Huttmann's, it seems insensitive to bring up the subject of money. Yet Huttmann herself reveals that the doctor who refused to write a "no code" order mentioned the idea of negligence (paragraph 9). In other words, he was at least in part worried about being sued if he didn't keep his patient alive. Add to this the fact, unmentioned by Huttmann, that doctors get paid a substantial amount of money for running a code. The truth is, codes are both profitable and a means of avoiding lawsuits. (Walzer's paragraph 9 confronts the financial issues directly.)

Analytical Considerations

1. In paragraphs 10 and 11 Huttmann asks four questions that she does not attempt to answer. What kinds of answers do they call for? You may want to assign Tom Regan's "The Case for Animal Rights" (NR 696, SE 376) in this section in conjunction with Huttmann's essay: in it Regan subordinates experience and emotion to ethical principles that can be defended generally and rationally. What principles would enable Huttmann to justify what her experience led her to do? What principles would justify the man who called her a murderer on "Donahue" and the man who accused her of playing God?

2. Elisabeth Kübler-Ross, in "On the Fear of Death" (NR 286, SE 160) in the section called "Human Nature," distinguishes between the needs of the living and the rights of the dying. How might these concepts have provided Huttmann with a framework for a different kind of essay, an analysis or an argument, instead of the narrative she wrote?

3. What difference does it make to Huttmann's narrative that Mac was young and strong? Would the point be different if the ill person were old, fat, and ugly? How different would the effect be? (Would the legal point be any different? How about the moral point? How about the readers' sympathies?)

4. Huttmann says, "Every morning I asked his doctor for a 'no code' order" (paragraph 9). Why doesn't she give us the dialogue that ensued, or even indicate her tone of voice? What do you make of this absence of drama at what a novelist or playwright would consider a key moment?

5. Codes are tied into the very definition of good hospital medicine: they actually save lives. Everyone can see that without the doctors' intervention, someone would die. That has to be an impressive achievement; it goes to the heart of the positive motivation for becoming a doctor in the first place — saving lives. So it seems particularly hard for medical professionals to relinquish the power they have, even though all would admit that their power has very obvious and definite limits.

6. Male-female issues abound in Huttmann's piece: have students list the players and their characteristics to see what they discover.

Suggested Writing Assignment

1. Do library research on living wills. If Mac had made one, would he or his wife have had a legal right to refuse artificial resuscitation? Explain.

2. Write a narrative about your experience of the death, in a hospital, of someone you knew, or use the experience of a friend as your own; that is, write in the first person. Focus on the emotional impact of the experience on all the people involved.

3. Convert the material in your narrative, above, into an analytic essay, a persuasive essay, or an argumentative essay. Append a paragraph in which you explain your decision to write one kind of essay rather than another.

4. Describe how the practices Huttmann describes in her 1983 essay have changed in the medical world of the twenty-first century. Exactly what are the rules now? Explain the situation to someone who only knows Huttmann's piece.

The Physician-Assisted Suicide Debate: Sandel, Walzer, and Huttmann

The stakes in these three pieces are quite different. Sandel and Walzer are arguing against assisted suicide, that is, the right of terminally ill people to receive help in ending their lives. This help can take the form of a physician giving an injection or a lethal dose of pills, or it can involve more active euthanasia, such as that performed by Dr. Jack Kervorkian in many cases in Michigan. With Huttmann the issue is starkly different: a terminally ill patient wants people to stop keeping him alive through heroic measures. He does not want or need pills or active assistance; he will die as soon as doctors stop running "codes" on him in the hospital.

Some will argue that at bottom both cases are the same: in both, a terminally ill person wants to end the suffering. In the past, both cases were often treated in exactly the same way: doctors and hospitals insisted on keeping the patient alive and refused to cooperate in ending a life. In the one case, the refusal consisted of withholding the means to end it; in the other, the refusal consisted of not withholding the normal procedures, that is, hospitals would insist on acting normally, which for them meant prolonging, not ending, life. The moral distinction between the two approaches has become enormous, but just in the last few decades. Hospital withholding of heroic measures has now become perfectly ordinary, as long as the patient approves. Moralists and religious leaders all approve of this approach, and all states have laws recognizing medical powers of attorney or health-care advance directives spelling out what care patients wish to receive.

But *active* assistance in ending life is still illegal in most states, and moralists and religious leaders still oppose it strenuously. In the year 2000, Oregon is the only state that allows physicians to prescribe life-ending doses of pills. Sandel and Walzer argue against the practice of assisted suicide that has now become legal in Oregon. Huttmann does not deal at all with assisted suicide; when she wrote her essay in the 1980s she was arguing for the withholding of heroic measures. And she was excoriated for this by the audience of "The Phil Donohue Show," a popular television program at the time. Times have certainly changed.

General Questions on Op-Eds from the NR10

1. What characteristics do the Op-Ed pieces in this section have in common? Consider technique, argument, and attitude.
2. Examine the five column-length Op-Ed pieces: those by Ivins, Quindlen, Huttman, Staples, and Baker. What features do they have in common? What kind of arguments do they tend to make? How would you characterize their language? From your reading of these five, discuss the range available to the writer of a newspaper Op-Ed column.
3. Read Wechsler's article on binge drinking (NR 942). What does it share with the Op-Eds in this section? Might it usefully be considered an Op-Ed?
4. Look for three other essays in other parts of *The Norton Reader* that also fit into the category "Op-Ed."

EDUCATION

EUDORA WELTY

Clamorous to Learn

The Norton Reader, p. 423

"Clamorous to Learn" and "One Writer's Beginnings" (NR 998, SE 573) both come from Eudora Welty's best-selling memoir *One Writer's Beginnings* (1985). Taken together, they comprise an account of her curricular and extra-curricular education and may well be read together. Welty was fortunate to grow up in a family of readers, in a house rich with books and music. While her formal schooling was rich in books as well, she was not dependent on it for her acquisition of literacy. Rather, she was permitted to enroll in school at age five (when, today, a child would be enrolled in kindergarten) because she already knew how to read.

"Clamorous to Learn" is memorable for its portrait of Welty's elementary-school principal, Miss Duling. The other adults Welty talks about are minor characters: Mrs. McWillie, the stern fourth-grade teacher; other teachers; and her parents. Miss Louella Varnado, her own fourth-grade teacher, gets short shrift. Welty depicts Miss Duling from a significant distance. She remembers her as a figure of power and authority, much larger than life. Miss Duling tells the governor how his daughter will be named, and she calls on old grads when she wants to right some obvious wrong. It's clear that Welty admires Miss Duling's exercise of authority in a good cause, educating the children of Jackson. In retrospect, she sees Miss Duling's life as one of denial; as a child, "this possibility was the last that could have occurred to us" (paragraph 4). From the perspective of a child, authority figures are all-powerful and complete in themselves.

Analytical Considerations

1. Welty doesn't mention that the schools in Jackson were segregated, that the Jefferson Davis School was for whites only. The black school was, no doubt, considerably less impressive; see Maya Angelou's "Graduation" (NR 1, SE 1) in the section called "Personal Report" for a description of a black school in a small southern town. Ask students what effect this omission has on Welty's account.
2. Why does Welty describe Miss Duling's physical characteristics and clothing so thoroughly?
3. According to Welty, "I did nothing but fear her [Miss Duling's] bearing-down authority, and did not connect this (as of course we were meant to) with our own need or desire to learn, perhaps because I already had this wish, and did not need to be driven" (paragraph 7). This complex state-ment needs unpacking: Welty makes some connections between fear and learning and implies others. Ask students what they believe about the

relation between fear and learning, what they think most people believe, and what beliefs were embedded in their own educations.

4. Welty's left-handedness was "broken" when she entered the Jefferson Davis School, though her parents were not in agreement (paragraphs 14–15). Why are children no longer forced to write right-handed? What does it signify about schooling that they once were?

5. Both Edward Rivera, in "First Communion" (NR 1096, SE 618) in the section called "Philosophy and Religion," and Eudora Welty, in this essay, mention "deportment." Ask students if the word has any resonance for them. Some will never have heard it, while others are likely to have had it engraved on their consciousness. Ask them if they know the word *conduct*. Then ask them the significance of different schools naming concepts differently.

Suggested Writing Assignments

1. Write a Welty-like piece on memorable teachers or coaches or authority figures you have known, keeping an eye out for the telling detail or quotation.

2. Write an essay in which you compare Welty's description of her teachers with Adrienne Rich's description of hers, in "Taking Women Students Seriously" (NR 482, SE 258). Pay particular attention to questions of gender stereotyping.

3. According to Welty, the people of Jackson, Mississippi, believed in "the value of doing well in school"; see paragraph 16 for details. Write an essay in which you consider how much emphasis your own community puts on doing well or, alternatively, compare your own community and Jackson, Mississippi, in this respect.

4. Write an essay in which you analyze the role of fear in one or more particular episodes in your own education; see Analytical Consideration 3 (above).

FREDERICK DOUGLASS

Learning to Read

The Norton Reader, p. 428; Shorter Edition, p. 224

This essay is chapter 7 of the *Narrative of the Life of Frederick Douglass, An American Slave, Written by Himself*, published in 1845. "Written by Himself" is important: as Douglass tells us, it was "almost an unpardonable offence to teach slaves to read in this Christian country" (paragraph 4). He was taught, as we discover elsewhere in the *Narrative*, by Sophia Auld, until her husband put a stop to lessons. There were obvious practical reasons for keeping slaves illiterate: reading and writing made information accessible to them and multiplied their opportunities to escape. But there were also symbolic reasons: the ability to read and write was evidence of their rationality and humanity. Douglass escaped to the North when he was eighteen. His powerful *Narrative of the Life of Frederick Douglass* gave powerful support to the Abolitionists in their campaign to end slavery. He wrote two additional autobiographies, one, *My Bondage and My Freedom*, before the Civil War, and another, *The Life and Times of Frederick Douglass*, after.

In this selection Douglass tells how he learned to write as well as read. Like Eudora Welty (in "Clamorous to Learn" [NR 423]) and William Scheick (in "Books Oft Have Such a Charm" [NR 432]), Douglass, after his introduction to literacy, virtually taught himself to read. But, unlike Welty and Scheick, he was actively discouraged from reading, indeed forbidden to read. His account, dignified in presentation, has moments of high drama, sharply rendered. It also contains passages of impressively subtle analysis that students should be asked to look at with some care.

Analytical Considerations

1. Slavery, according to Douglass, gave Sophia Auld "irresponsible power" (paragraph 1). Ask students to look carefully at Douglass's analysis of the corruption that accompanies such power.
2. Look at the selections from "The Columbian Orator" Douglass names (paragraphs 5–6). Why were they important to him?
3. Ask students to look carefully at Douglass's analysis of why learning to read "had been a curse rather than a blessing" (paragraph 6).

Suggested Writing Assignments

1. A number of people helped Douglass in his attempts to read and write. Who were they? Why do you think they helped him? Locate all the evidence that appears in Douglass's narrative and write an essay in which you answer this question.
2. Look in either *My Bondage and My Freedom* or *The Life and Times of Frederick Douglass* to see what Douglass says about learning to read. Write an essay in which you consider how and why these accounts differ from the account in the *Narrative of the Life of Frederick Douglass, An American Slave, Written by Himself*.
3. Write your own literacy narrative, an account of how you learned to read. If suitable, include details about the specific book or books you remember as important.

WILLIAM J. SCHEICK

Books Oft Have Such a Charm

The Norton Reader, p. 432

The young William Scheick's inability to read and inattentiveness to what was said to him, which earned him the epithets *Dummkopf* and *Dummerjan* from his father and favorite uncle, were taken as signs of obstinacy (paragraph 2). Today he would be diagnosed as having dyslexia (and perhaps attention-deficit disorder); these learning disabilities were unknown when he was growing up.

In the summer of 1953, when he was almost twelve, his mother took charge and ordered him to read a book. He chose *Amos, The Beagle with a Plan* because of the picture of a beagle on the cover. It spoke to his condition, one might say, and the rest is history. He read *Amos* again and again and again; he taught himself to read without being aware of doing so, and, as his dyslexia abated, read his way through high school and went on to earn a Ph.D. in literature from the University of Illinois.

Questions from the NR10

1. The first three essayists in this section describe their entry into literacy, their "learning to read." What do their learning processes have in common? How are they different?
2. In paragraph 7 Scheick refers to two methods of teaching reading: phonics and look-and-say. Which method does he think preferable? How do you know? What does he imply that both methods leave out?
3. One book is fundamental to Scheick's narrative, just as the titles of specific books appear in the accounts by Eudora Welty and Frederick Douglass. Of what importance to their development are the specific books they mention?
4. Write your own literacy narrative, an account of how you learned to read. If suitable, include details about the specific book or books you remember as important.

Analytical Considerations

1. According to Scheick, his mother believed that "some magical combination of tactics would exorcise her son of the demon of perversity" (paragraph 2). How did she diagnose his problem?
2. Scheick uses a series of military metaphors to describe his education with the Sisters of Notre Dame (paragraph 3). Ask students to look at them and analyze how they work.
3. One might argue that the young Scheick was the victim of emotional abuse: he was called names; he lost a dog he loved without being told that the family was getting rid of it; he was left to believe that his inability to read was his own fault. What strategies does Scheick use in narrating this episode in his life that cut off possibilities for pathos?
4. When the young Scheick began to read on his own there was no one around "to measure my progress, to critique my failures, to patronize me" (paragraph 9). In what ways does Scheick's narrative support John Holt's analysis in "How Teachers Make Children Hate Reading" (NR 436, SE 228)?
5. Reading exerted its power over the young Scheick through "the fantasy of my own involvement in the narrative" (paragraph 9). To what extent do you think involvement is necessary in order to learn to read? How do we read nonfiction texts that do not involve our fantasies?

Suggested Writing Assignments

1. "Never before in my life had I wanted to read a book," Scheick writes (paragraph 7). Revise the sentence to read "I have never wanted to read a book."

Write an essay in which you describe someone you know who might say it, or imagine someone saying it. What would be your response?

2. Does dyslexia abate, as Scheick says his did? Do research and write an essay in answer to this question.

3. Use Scheick's epigraph from Thomas Carlyle—"All that mankind has done, thought, gained or been: it is lying as in magic preservation in the pages of books"—as the epigraph to an essay of your own. Scheick of course agrees with Carlyle; you need not agree with either of them.

JOHN HOLT

How Teachers Make Children Hate Reading

The Norton Reader, p. 436; Shorter Edition, p. 228

John Holt, after ten years as a teacher, wrote *How Children Fail* (1964), a critical analysis of American education, followed by *How Children Learn* (1967). "How Teachers Make Children Hate Reading," which appeared in *Redbook* magazine in 1967, is a compendium of both: how children fail to learn and yet how they succeed in learning that complex of subjects referred to in elementary school as language arts (Holt's editorial comment on that term, in paragraph 33, is "ugh!"). Holt writes for a general rather than a professional audience: in paragraphs 44–45, for example, he addresses parents. He includes a lot of information about what works and what doesn't through vignettes, a few of them about particular students, most of them about particular classes. His essay disperses itself into a set of precepts, how-not-to and how-to. You may want to ask students to trace Holt's assumptions about learning, about children as learners, and about the value of reading and writing through these precepts.

Running through Holt's essay is another theme: the education of John Holt, the teacher. Most revealing, probably, is the opening vignette, in which Holt's professional wisdom is challenged by his sister's experiential wisdom. As the essay proceeds, Holt again and again invents new and more successful modes of teaching that run counter to professionally sanctioned modes; only after he invents the writing derby, for example, does he find that S. I. Hayakawa has invented Non-Stop writing (paragraphs 28–29). Holt's inventions always succeed. Ask students to consider his antiprofessional bent. Is it possible to codify his wisdom as professional wisdom? Some twenty-five years after Holt published "How Teachers Make Children Hate Reading," has any of his wisdom become professional wisdom?

Questions from the NR10

1. Mark the anecdotes that Holt uses and describe how he orders them in time and by theme. Consider the advantages and disadvantages of his organizing this essay to reflect his own learning.

2. "[F]or most children," Holt observes, "school was a place of danger, and their main business in school was staying out of danger as much as possible" (paragraph 12). Locate instances in which he makes this point explicit and instances in which he implies it.

3. What Holt calls a composition derby is now usually called free writing. Have your teachers used free writing? In what grades? In your experience, how much has the teaching of writing changed since 1967, when Holt wrote this essay?

4. Holt begins this essay by describing the "game of wits" played by teachers and students alike: teachers ask students what teachers want students to know and students ask teachers for clues about what teachers want (paragraph 1). Do you recognize this game? Do you remember learning to play it? Do you think you play it well? Do you like playing it? Write an essay that answers these questions. Be sure to include anecdotes from your own experience.

Analytical Considerations

1. Ask students to look at Holt's advice to parents (paragraphs 44–45). What assumptions does he make about parents' circumstances and their involvement with their children's education? Are these assumptions legitimate? What kind of families does he take for granted?

2. Ask students about their own education in reading and writing, particularly with respect to how much of Holt's experiential wisdom has become professional wisdom since 1967, when "How Teachers Make Children Hate Reading" was published. The results are hard to predict. In general, since Holt's essay appeared, the teaching of writing has changed more than the teaching of reading, but not uniformly.

3. Follow up Analytical Consideration 2 (above) with students' responses to Holt's methods of teaching reading and writing. What force does their experience have, individually and collectively?

4. What do students think about Holt's advice on reading: "Find something, dive into it, take the good parts, skip the bad parts, get what you can out of it, go on to something else" (paragraph 21)?

5. If a high school English course ran on Holt's principles, what would it be like? Describe a typical week in such a course: assignments, classroom arrangements, teaching style, discussion of reading, work on writing, homework.

Suggested Writing Assignments

1. Two antitheses are often used with respect to pedagogy: teaching versus learning, teacher-centered versus student-centered. Write an essay in which you define these antitheses using Holt's essay and amplifying them with your own experience. Is Holt firmly on one side or the other? Are you?

2. According to Holt, "we make books and reading a constant source of possible failure and public humiliation" (paragraph 13). Write an essay based on your experience, observation, and reading in which you discuss education as failure and humiliation. Are failure and humiliation chiefly associated with reading?

3. Imagine yourself sending Holt's "How Teachers Make Children Hate Reading" to one of your English teachers. Write a letter to accompany the essay.
4. Locate two or three instances from your own education where your experiential wisdom ran counter to the apparently professional wisdom of your teachers. Use them in an essay in which you evaluate the nature and importance of personal experience, at least of the instances you choose, versus professional wisdom.
5. Do research on Whole Language teaching, which involves many of Holt's precepts (such as invented spelling). Has education in your state or locality moved toward Whole Language? Write an essay in which you discuss Whole Language and some of the controversies associated with it.

CATHY DAVIDSON

From the Best of Japanese Families

The Norton Reader, p. 444

Cathy Davidson teaches American literature at Duke University and has published extensively on literature by American women. "From the Best of Japanese Families" is a chapter in *36 Views of Mount Fuji: On Finding Myself in Japan* (1994), an autobiographical account of a year of teaching in Japan. The "finding myself" in the title has two senses: the literal ("I found myself stuck in traffic") and the metaphoric. The latter is the important sense in this selection, for cross-cultural experience invariably leads to seeing oneself in new and different ways, to finding oneself. Davidson's experience teaching at Kansai Women's University, a liberal arts college for women founded by alumnae of the Seven Sisters, undoubtedly led her to see American women students in new and different ways as well. Certainly her essay makes readers consider what American women students have in common with the women Davidson taught in Japan. Older women are likely to recognize in these young Japanese women versions of their preliberation selves. Younger women may or may not recognize themselves, but responding to these unassertive, well-mannered young Japanese women may lead them to find themselves more liberated than they thought.

Davidson's essay also raises questions about the role of teachers. Should education prepare students to fill their roles in society or to rebel against them and work for social change? Or are these alternatives too schematic? Adrienne Rich, in "Taking Women Students Seriously" (NR 482, SE 258) suggests the latter—education should prepare students, if not to rebel against their roles, at least to understand the history that accounts for the strictures placed upon them. Davidson, at the end of this essay, raises explicit questions about her role (paragraphs 65–70). She temporizes in her answers: on the one hand, she writes, "I like to think I give my Japanese students the same thing I try to give my American students back home: a space in which to speak and be heard," and on the other hand, "I don't think you can be a teacher unless you believe in the possibility of change" (paragraph 68).

Analytical Considerations

1. Ask students if they think Davidson transmitted her belief in the possibility of change to her students. Do students expect to change in college? Do they think teachers change them? Do they think teachers should try to change them?
2. Davidson found that Japanese culture encourages individual reticence and Japanese education encourages passivity, but working together made her Japanese students more outgoing and active. What perspective on American culture and education did these perceptions give her?
3. Davidson observes: "all language learning is childish, inherently infantalizing," and "Learning a language means returning to a state of near idiocy" (paragraph 34). Do you agree? Why?
4. What careers are open to Davidson's Japanese students?
5. Ask students to consider what Davidson's students say about arranged marriages. If you have students who come from cultures where marriages are arranged, ask them what they have to say about them. What assumptions about marriage undergird arranged marriages? What assumptions about marriage undergird marrying for love?

Suggested Writing Assignments

1. Davidson provides American students and students from cultures other than Japanese with vicarious cross-cultural experience. Write an essay in which you consider what her essay showed you about yourself and your culture.
2. In "To Be a Woman and a Scholar" (NR 488, SE 264), Dorothy Gies McGuigan also provides American students and students from other cultures with what might be called vicarious cross-cultural experience. Write an essay in which you consider what McGuigan's essay showed you about yourself and your times.
3. When Davidson considers her role as a teacher in Japan, she offers several possibilities: to represent America, to provide a model, to divert and entertain. Write an essay in which you consider these as possibilities for teachers in America. What do you expect of your teachers, and why?

BENJAMIN R. BARBER

America Skips School

The Norton Reader, p. 453

There are two strands in Barber's argument: the first, that Americans don't value education; the second, that education is the foundation of what he calls "civic literacy: "It encompasses the competence to participate in democratic communities, the ability to think critically and act with deliberation in a pluralistic world, and the empathy to identify sufficiently with others to live with them despite conflicts of interest and differences in character" (paragraph 21). You can start class discussion with either strand. Students will undoubtedly be more taken with the first, with its fierce indictment of adult hypocrisy, its defense of children as excellent learners ("Our children's illiteracy is merely our own, which they assume with commendable prowess" [paragraph 13]), and its multiple-choice Real-World Cultural Literacy Test. Barber does a good job of filling students in on ten years of complaints about what they don't know and why they don't know it. They can be asked to list the complaints and explanations and test them against their own experience of education, perhaps in groups.

The second strand of Barber's argument, civic literacy, is less developed, less lively, and probably less accessible to students. Indeed, when students are vocationally oriented, educational goals like "global competition and minimal competence," which Barber criticizes, make sense (paragraph 16). They will have encountered concepts of democracy and citizenship; most of them will have studied American history. Do they value democracy the way Barber does? Can they understand Barber's valuing it? Would "America Skips School" have been a more successful essay had Barber attended only to the first strand of his argument? Why did he feel compelled to add the second?

Questions from the NR10

1. What is the function of Barber's Real-World Cultural Literacy Test in the larger argument of his essay?
2. Write three additional questions for the Real-World Cultural Literacy Test.
3. Mark some of the passages in whcih Barber expresses strong feelings about American education. What are some characteristic ways he expresses these feelings?
4. What is "civic literacy"? How does Barber define it? Why is it so important to him? Do you share his sense of its importance? Why or why not?
5. Barber concludes this essay with the observation "We have given up on the kids . . ." (paragraph 33). Write an essay in which you use your experience, observation, and reading to agree or disagree with him.

Analytical Considerations

1. Ask students if they value education and why? Or have they learned the lesson that school doesn't matter? If they are part of the problem, can they also be part of the solution?
2. According to Barber, "the pundits, instead of looking for solutions, search busily for scapegoats" (paragraph 7). Does the evidence he present support this sweeping generalization? Ask students what solutions they have to suggest.
3. According to Barber, children spend 900 hours a year in school and 1,200 to 1,800 hours watching television (paragraph 9). Ask students to estimate their own division of time between school and television, in elementary school, in high school, and in college. Does education "compete" with television? Can it ever win out over television? What has this competition meant for students' lives? What does it mean for their children's lives?
4. Barber's remedy is simple—money. What does he argue more money will do? How might he answer the argument that throwing more money at schools won't help?

5. Focus the above question on Barber's proposal to pay starting kindergarten teachers $70,000 to $80,000 a year. What arguments for and against such salaries can students provide?

6. Try reading paragraph 22 (beginning "Civility is a work of the imagination. . .") closely with students as an illustration of the role of education in civic literacy.

7. Barber is a master of irony achieved through sentence construction. Look, for example, of the sentence beginning "We honor ambition . . . " (paragraph 10); how does it work? Ask students to locate similar examples.

Suggested Writing Assignments

1. Barber considers class size important, claiming that fewer students in the classroom make for better learning. Write about this issue, using your experience and observation as evidence. Have small classes benefited you? How? Have you had good learning experiences in large classes? What made them work?

2. Investigate the research that has been done on the relation of class size to learning. Write an essay in which you consider what the research is, what it shows, and whether or not it is conclusive.

3. Read one of the pundits Barber alludes to. Write an essay in which you consider the fairness of Barber's account. Plainly all of them present more complex arguments than can be encompassed in a brief summary. But would you describe Barber's summary as essentially fair or distorted for polemical reasons?

4. Barber claims that "The classroom, however, should not be merely a trade school. The fundamental task of education in a democracy is what Tocqueville once called the apprenticeship of liberty: learning to be free" (paragraph 17). Write an essay in which you describe what you think Barber's ideal of a school would look like in operation at, say, the high-school level. What subjects would be offered? What would classes be like? What kind of teachers would work there? What would exams be like? What kind of student behavior would be encouraged?

5. Read Jonathan Kozol's *Savage Inequalities*, which Barber refers to as part of his argument for spending more money on education (paragraph 26). Write an essay in which you consider what money would do to remedy the situation Kozol describes.

CAROLINE BIRD

College Is a Waste of Time and Money

The Norton Reader, p. 463

In *The Case Against College* (1975), Caroline Bird argues that the college experience, good though it may be for many young people, is not good for all of them. In this chapter, also published as an essay, Bird argues that while providing a college education to all high-school graduates is "a noble American ideal" (paragraph 3), many students don't want to be there, and college itself is a bad investment for them and their parents. Her evidence? Plenty of anecdotes from faculty and students.

Your students may share her bleak outlook; asking them what they think of Bird's essay may lead to lively discussion. Although it was written over twenty years ago, Bird's arguments are still relevant. Indeed, today there seems to be a kind of disenchantment with college—and certainly resistance on the part of parents and taxpayers to assume its costs.

Analytical Considerations

1. Ask students to list Caroline Bird's bad reasons for attending college. How many of them do they take seriously? This exercise may well be done in groups.
2. Bird is frank to admit that she addresses the issue as a journalist, not as a scholar or policy analyst. Ask students to point to examples of what Bird calls "the journalistic tools of my trade" (paragraph 11).
3. Bird relies heavily on anecdotes to support her generalizations. Ask students if they have anecdotes of their own that confirm or contradict Bird's? How do we weigh the evidence of anecdotes when agreeing or disagreeing with arguments?
4. Paul Tillich, in "The Riddle of Inequality" (NR 1132, SE 647) in the section called "Philosophy and Religion," speaks of students who came to college eager to learn but somehow lost the spark (paragraph 6). Compare his analysis of students' discontent with Bird's. Is hers as subtle as his?

Suggested Writing Assignments

1. Interview students, teachers, and college officials you know and write an essay that updates Bird's. Are conditions still the same as they were twenty years ago? Is the outlook for someone without a college degree still the same?
2. Some regard a college degree as a necessary kind of license, a union card, a piece of paper they have to have. Write about people who believe this, showing how such a belief colors their attitude toward learning, classes, and interaction with other students.
3. According to Bird, in 1970 colleges were spending more than 30 billion dollars annually to educate half of America's high-school graduates. Do research to ascertain the comparable figures today, or figures for as recent a time as they are available. Write an essay in which you consider how economists justify such an expenditure. Are there other economists who regard it as a bad investment?

JAMES THURBER

University Days

The Norton Reader, p. 4671; Shorter Edition, p. 236

James Thurber is known for his stories, fables, and cartoons. "University Days," published in 1933, is an example of deadpan humor. Thurber creates himself literally and metaphorically as a near-blind innocent who stumbles through the strange world of the university, trying to understand its odd customs without much success. The essay is a series of vignettes: botany lab, economics, gym, journalism, and ROTC. The other undergraduates who figure in it are even dimmer than Thurber. You might, for example, look at Bolenciecwcz's adventures in economics class as a stripped-down sequence of cartoons (paragraphs 5–12).

"University Days" is a comic essay, not a critique of higher education, and few students will take it as seriously critical. Considering how we know how to take it can be a useful exercise. You might take it as a critique yourself and let students argue against your view. They should be able to point to Thurber's exaggerations, his use of idiosyncratic and extreme examples as representative; they will be less likely to point to his verbal wit, to the comic precision of his language.

Questions from the NR10

1. Analyze Thurber's creation of a comic persona with reference to his literal and metaphoric blindness. What, in the various anecdotes that constitute the essay, does Thurber not see?
2. In an essay called "Some Remarks on Humor," E. B. White says: "Humorists fatten on trouble. . . . You find them wrestling with foreign languages, fighting folding ironing boards and swollen drainpipes, suffering the terrible discomfort of tight boots. They pour out their sorrows profitably, in a form that is not quite fiction nor quite fact either. Beneath the sparkling surface of these dilemmas flows the strong tide of human woe." Discuss this quotation with reference to Thurber's essay.
3. Ethnic stereotypes are often a staple of humor: in this essay, Bolenciecwcz, the dumb football player, has a Polish name. Is the anecdote offensive? Would it be more or less offensive if he were African American? Why?
4. Find some incident that will yield to a Thurberesque treatment, that is, that can be told from the point of view of a "blind" narrator, and write about it.

Analytical Considerations

1. What do the incidents Thurber writes about have in common?
2. Is it possible to determine, on the basis of this essay, what Thurber might have thought an ideal liberal arts education to be?
3. Look also at the comedy in Thurber's fable "The Owl Who Was God" (NR 1111). Can students generalize about Thurber's comic techniques?
4. Students need help apprehending Thurber's verbal wit. Probably they read with such attention to content that sentences like "He would wander around the laboratory pleased with the progress all the students were making in drawing the involved and, so I am told, interesting structure of flower cells, until he came to me" (paragraph 1) slip by them. Try the sentence without "so I am told"; try putting "so I am told" in other places in the sentence. Ask students to find additional carefully modulated sentences in "University Days"; ask them to "spoil" Thurber's verbal wit by rewriting them. This exercise can be done successfully in groups.

5. Compare Professor Bassum with John Holt's portrait of himself in "How Teachers Make Children Hate Reading" (NR 456, SE 228). Is Bassum an example of "How Teachers Make Students Hate Economics"?

Suggested Writing Assignments

1. Rewrite Thurber's essay as a serious critique of some elements of higher education. Use his material and add to it, using idiosyncratic and extreme examples as representative makes for comedy, not critique. You may find Caroline Bird's "College Is a Waste of Time and Money" (NR 463) helpful.
2. Find one incident from your university days that will yield to a Thurber-like treatment and write about it.
3. Do research on Thurber's university days at Ohio State University; a recent biography—*James Thurber: His Life and Times* (1995) by Harrison Kinney— has information about them. Write an essay in which you consider this question: were they a waste of time and money?

WILLIAM ZINSSER

College Pressures

The Norton Reader, p. 475; Shorter Edition, p. 241

William Zinsser, a writer and journalist, taught at Yale University from 1971 to 1979 and served, he explains, as master of Branford College. "College Pressures" was published in 1979; students will probably notice that room, board, and tuition in most private colleges then cost as much as $7,000 and that students might leave college with a debt of as much as $5,000. What are room, board, and tuition now?

Zinsser introduces "College Pressures" with notes from students and then, in an odd maneuver, first generalizes and then limits their relevance: "students like the ones who wrote those notes can also be found on campuses from coast to coast—especially in New England and at many other private colleges across the country that have high academic standards and highly motivated students" (paragraph 2). Does Zinsser restrict the relevance of this essay to elite colleges? Are most/many/some students still harried, driven by the same external and internal pressures he describes? Which students, and where are they to be found? Among the pressures Zinsser does not mention are work and family. How do these exert pressure on students, and on which students?

"College Pressures" appeared in a little-known magazine, *Blair and Ketchum's Country Journal*. Who does Zinsser think his audience is? What evidence is there in the essay? Is it written to students, to professors, to parents, to outsiders? Which elements of it seem directed to each of these groups?

Zinsser uses a four-part classificatory scheme in characterizing the pressures on students as economic, parental, peer, and self-induced. His scheme does not provide structure for his entire essay. It is, however, elaborately framed, and the divisions according to kinds of pressure are not only weighted with illustrations but also cross-referenced (see, for example, paragraphs 15–19 and 24). Zinsser apparently sees his classificatory scheme as rhetorically useful in ordering his material but distorting in compartmentalizing it. You may want to discuss the value of using classification within an essay rather than as the framework for an entire essay.

Questions from the NR10

1. What are the four kinds of pressure Zinsser describes for the 1970s? Are they the same kinds of pressure that trouble students today? Or have new ones taken their place?
2. Some people believe that students perform best when subjected to pressure, others that they perform best when relatively free of pressure. How do you respond to pressure? How much pressure is enough?
3. Write an essay in which you compare your expectations of college pressures with the reality as you have experienced it to date.

Analytical Considerations

1. Zinsser combines personal experience with description, analysis, and both explicit and implied prescription. Ask students to locate personal passages and discuss their contribution to the essay. What is Zinsser's authority to describe, analyze, and advise, and how does he claim it in this essay?
2. Ask students to imagine Zinsser's four-part classificatory scheme as organizing this entire essay. What parts of "College Pressures" would remain, what parts would go? What would be the effect of these omissions?
3. "Where's the payoff on the humanities?" Zinsser inquires (paragraph 20). Ask students to define the payoff Zinsser illustrates.
4. Pressures, according to Zinsser, lead students to do more than asked (paragraphs 27–29). Do you think this is still true at Yale? Is it true at other institutions?

Suggested Writing Assignments

1. What are the pressures on college students today? Write an essay in which you describe and analyze them, perhaps using evidence from Zinsser's essay to suggest that some pressures remain the same.
2. "Where's the payoff on the humanities?" Zinsser asks (paragraph 20). Write your own answer to this question, drawing on experience, observation, and reading.

ADRIENNE RICH

Taking Women Students Seriously

The Norton Reader, p. 482; Shorter Edition, p. 258

Adrienne Rich is a poet as well as an essayist. Born in 1929, she graduated from Radcliffe College in 1951, the year her first book of poems was published; her early poetry antedates the women's movement. In "Taking Women Students Seriously," an address given to teachers of women, Rich professes her intention not to lecture but to "create a context, delineate a background" for discussion (paragraph 1). She begins with her own education and her experience teaching minority students as well as her own women students. "The personal is political"—this is a maxim of the women's movement and an enabling principle of consciousness-raising. It is also a strategy of feminist writing.

Rich sets in parallel form the questions discussed by instructors of minority students and the questions she came to ask about teaching women. Both minorities and women are disadvantaged, she believes, and the pedagogy appropriate to one has parallels with the pedagogy appropriate to the other. Note Rich's emphasis on activity versus passivity, questioning rather than accepting. Her discussion of women as students leads to a discussion of women in society: the academy mirrors society at large in putting women down or not taking them seriously.

Analytical Considerations

1. Ask students to review the personal elements in Rich's essay and their political meanings. "The personal is political"—political in what sense or senses?
2. For Rich, as for Patricia Williams (see "The Death of the Profane: A Commentary on the Genre of Legal Writing" [NR 556]) "the personal is political": in the events of a single person's daily life can be seen larger political forces operating in society. Ask students to compare the positions of the two narrators in their respective pieces, looking at how they use their individual lives to make larger social points.
3. Deborah Tannen (in "Conversational Styles" [NR 545]) quotes those who think they're being fair and then argues that they're wrong: "'I treat everyone the same.' But treating people the same is not equal treatment if they are not the same" (paragraph 20). Would Adrienne Rich agree? Do you?
4. Rich discusses what she calls "the precariously budgeted, much-condescended-to area of women's studies" (paragraphs 8–9). What does women's studies teach, and why, according to Rich, do women need to learn these things?
5. Rich speaks of women (and men) as if gender unites them more than other circumstances—large circumstances of social and economic class,

of race and ethnicity, or small circumstances of infinite variety—divide them. She creates universals that may well be false. Consider the following: "Men in general think badly; in disjuncture from their personal lives, claiming objectivity where the most irrational passions seethe" (paragraph 16). Does Rich's generalization suggest a counter-generalization about how women think? Are there familiar generalizations about how women think?

6. "Feminists are depicted in the media," Rich says, "as 'shrill,' 'strident,' 'puritanical,' or 'humorless,' and the lesbian choice—the choice of the woman-identified woman—as pathological or sinister" (paragraph 12). The last became Rich's choice. Does she run the risk of such labels in this essay? Does she care? Who is her audience, and what assumptions does she make about them?

Suggested Writing Assignments

1. From your experience and observation (of high school or college or both), are women students taken seriously? Do teachers and faculty members treat them the same way as male students? Do male students regard them as equals? Write an essay addressing these questions. You might also consider differences between male and female teachers and between fields of study, for example, between education and engineering, or English and physics.

2. He: "Women take everything personally." She: "The personal is political." Write an essay in which you make a case for or against the personal. Use this essay of Rich's, her essay "When We Dead Awaken: Writing as Revision" (NR 1036) in the section called "Literature and the Arts," and any other essays you find useful.

3. Read Rich's "When We Dead Awaken: Writing as Re-Vision," (NR 1036) published in *On Lies, Secrets, and Silence: Selected Prose, 1966–1978* (1979), in which she reviews her education while tracing her development as a woman poet and a feminist poet. Write an essay in which you discuss how she presents and links the personal and the political. What, in Rich's view, are the politics of poetry?

4. Write an essay on a larger issue in which you focus on your own experience as evidence and illustration.

5. Read Gloria Steinem's "The Good News Is: These Are Not the Best Years of Your Life" (NR 363, SE 212). On the face of things, Steinem and Rich take opposing views of women's college experience. Write an essay in which you discuss how you think their views are opposed, why you think they are opposed, and the extent to which you can reconcile them.

6. If you have a women's studies program at your institution, find out more about it. What are its aims, what courses does it teach, and who teaches them? Interview some students, some faculty, and/or both who are active in women's studies. Write an essay in which you discuss women's studies at your institution. Enunciate your own position with respect to women's studies as part of your discussion.

DOROTHY GIES MCGUIGAN

To Be a Woman and a Scholar

The Norton Reader, p. 488; Shorter Edition, p. 264

In the biography of the Renaissance Italian scholar Elena Cornaro, McGuigan sees a way of making centuries of barring women from intellectual pursuits by denying them education particularly vivid. This learned woman was not able to attend school or college without special permission and was denied the right to earn her doctorate until higher authorities intervened. She was of course not permitted to teach at the university that granted her the doctorate (or any other university)—she would have had to teach men!

Students need to know that outright gender discrimination in education existed until recently. Women were barred from colleges and universities in the United States until the nineteenth century, from law and medical schools until the twentieth century, and from elite undergraduate colleges such as Harvard, Princeton, and Yale, which were single-sex institutions until the 1970s. Although they were permitted to earn doctorates, women never taught at all-male colleges and seldom taught at research universities.

Questions from the NR10

1. McGuigan frames her essay on women scholars with accounts of the doctoral examination and the death of Elena Cornaro. What is the usefulness of this framing? Can you locate other "framed" essays in this reader and explain the purpose of the frames?
2. Choose five women scholars mentioned by McGuigan and find out if people you know have heard of any of them. Which ones do people know and what do they know about them?
3. McGuigan herself was a scholar; yet she omits her own experience from this essay. Look at the details of her biography in "Authors." What experiences do you think she shared with the women scholars she describes?
4. Compare McGuigan's exclusion of personal detail with Adrienne Rich's inclusion of it in "Taking Women Students Seriously" (NR 482, SE 258). Consider the advantages and disadvantages of each strategy. What does each writer gain, what does each lose?
5. Research the admission of women either to American colleges and universities or to Oxford and Cambridge. In a brief essay consider whether McGuigan's four basics (paragraphs 5–9) hold true for them.

Analytical Considerations

1. To what extent does McGuigan explain what a scholar is? Why do you think she is so sketchy about the meaning of the term?

2. Do the salons of seventeenth-century France sound much like a university? Why has McGuigan included them?
3. Examine McGuigan's essay in light of Adrienne Rich's "Taking Women Students Seriously" (NR 482, SE 258). What does Rich gain by using herself as an example? Would the two writers agree about the causes of the discrimination they chronicle? What about the solutions?

Suggested Writing Assignments

1. Interview three or four women scholars to find out what barriers, if any, they had to overcome. Write up your results as an essay on whether or not the problems faced by the earliest women scholars still persist today.
2. Look up the word *scholar* and describe how its meaning has changed over time. Try to pin down when changes occurred and, in particular, if contradictory meanings coexisted.
3. In "From the Best of Japanese Families" (NR 444), Cathy Davidson provides American students and students from cultures other than Japanese with vicarious cross-cultural experience. Think about McGuigan's essay as also providing contemporary students with what might be called cross-cultural experience. Write an essay in which you consider what this essay showed you about yourself and your times.

WAYNE C. BOOTH

Boring from Within: The Art of the Freshman Essay

The Norton Reader, p. 495; Shorter Edition, p. 247

Although Booth focuses on how to teach students to write well, his ultimate objective is to guide students to think for themselves. Booth views his two aims—good writing and cogent thinking—as complementary; only "thinking boys and girls" (paragraph 16) will write papers that aren't boring or in other ways frustrating to teachers. As he elucidates the problem of boring essays and potential remedies for them, Booth himself attempts to be not only organized and clear but also interesting and controversial.

Questions from the NR10

1. What is the occasion for Booth's address? How does it shape his language, structure, and evidence?
2. Divide the essay into sections and explain what Booth does in each and how each functions as part of the whole.
3. Select three essays from other sections of this reader that you think would engage Booth. Explain his criteria and how the essays meet them.
4. When you write, do you consciously attempt not to bore your reader? If so, list your strategies. Or, if the obligation not to bore your reader is a new idea to you, think of some strategies you might employ and list them. Use

the list to develop an essay on strategies for generating interest and the circumstances in which they are appropriate.

Analytical Considerations

1. The occasion for Booth's address is a conference of college teachers of English; students in your class are overhearing him talk about their writing to other teachers. How much blame for boredom does Booth assign to teachers? How much to students?
2. How do paragraphs 5 and 6 set up the rest of his essay?
3. Are Booth's attacks on the *Reader's Digest, Time,* and *Newsweek* still justified? Bring in recent issues (or ask your students to) in order to test the legitimacy of Booth's remarks (paragraph 8).
4. Extract three principles for good writing from "Boring from Within." Then compare Booth's philosophy of composition with George Orwell's in "Politics and the English Language" (NR 575, SE 304). Would Orwell agree with Booth's principles?
5. Point out examples of exaggeration and satiric humor in Booth's essay. Is the tone that these elements create geared to Booth's audience and thesis? Explain.
6. In light of some of his comments, would you call Booth an elitist? If so, what statements make him seem so?

Suggested Writing Assignments

1. Read the Op-Ed page in the *New York Times* or another major newspaper for a week and select a column that isn't boring. (You may want to look at the "Op-Eds" section in *The Norton Reader* to see Op-Ed pieces the editors thought weren't boring, but you are responsible for finding your own.) Analyze it and write an essay that explains why and how the writer avoids the pitfalls of "boring from within."
2. Test the validity and accuracy of Booth's criticism of popular magazine journalism by reading several issues of the *Reader's Digest, Time,* or *Newsweek,* choosing representative articles and writing an analytic essay.
3. Select and write about a model of "genuine narration, with the sharp observation and penetrating critical judgment that underlies all good story telling. . . ." (paragraph 28).
4. Booth does not soft-pedal his criticism of typical freshman writing. Does this essay offend you? Does it contain a fair assessment of students' abilities and productivity? Does it offer ideas that may help you to write better, more interesting essays? Write a closely argued response to Booth's assessment of student writing in "Boring from Within."
5. Booth seems to believe that topics concerning "social problems and forces, political controversy, and the processes of everyday living around them" can personally engage most college students (paragraph 19). Make up a list of topics that engage you and topics that don't; this can best be done in groups. Then write, individually, essays that aren't boring on one of the topics the group agrees on as engaging and share them with the group.

WILLIAM G. PERRY, JR.

Examsmanship and the Liberal Arts:
A Study in Educational Epistemology

The Norton Reader, p. 505

William G. Perry, Jr.'s urbane and erudite discussion of examsmanship, while it contains much of interest to students, is not addressed to or written for them; it was published in *Examining in Harvard College: A Collection of Essays* (1964), a volume written by members of the Harvard faculty and addressed to faculty. Perry approaches "educational epistemology"—ask students, after they have read his essay, to define it—through a story that, were it told simply, is comic: "the picture of a bright student attempting to outwit his professor while his professor takes pride in not being outwitted," Perry observes, "is certainly ridiculous" (paragraph 4). Perry's elaborate irony and extended explanations defuse its comedy. What students will understand are the surprising uses to which Perry puts the story of Metzger's prank: he not only defends it as harmless but also, and more importantly, defends the section man's grade of A on Metzger's examination. A less complicated telling might have turned the story into a trickster tale.

Perry's educational epistemology involves framing, in which a fact becomes "'an observation or operation performed in a frame of reference'" (paragraph 40). With this statement in mind, direct students back to Perry's account of Metzger's examination: he wrote exclusively about framing because he had no facts to frame. Be sure students can discriminate between Perry's educational epistemology and their own cruder one, which Perry describes as finding "the right mean" between particulars and generalizations. They are not the same: "The problem is not quantitative," Perry writes, "nor does its solution lie on a continuum between the particular and the general" (paragraph 25).

Perry calls framing "bull" and facts "cow." The first comes from "bull session": shooting the breeze, talking loudly and authoritatively. "Cow" is Perry's invented opposite, and the genders of the pair are unfortunate, inasmuch as thought becomes male, facts female. Perry, again surprisingly, defends "bull," redeeming it in an academic context from its pejorative sense. While framed facts are best, if it comes to choosing between them, framing is better—even though students who present unframed facts are seldom given grades as low as they deserve. Perry also analyzes the mistaken educational epistemology of elementary and high schools: students are given high grades for remembering facts and graded down for misremembering them.

Questions from the NR10

1. Perry divides this essay into four sections, an introduction and sections numbered I, II, and III. Identify the focus of each and its relation to what precedes and what follows.

2. Perry makes the point that "bull" and "cow" are not the equivalent of generalizations and particulars, not "poles of a single dimension" (paragraph 25). Explain how, according to Perry, they differ from generalizations and particulars.

3. Perry's essay appeared in a volume on examinations written by members of the Harvard University faculty and presumably addressed to them and to others like them. How does Perry address his audience? What kind of persona does he construct? Point to evidence for it.

4. Have you found the grading practices of your teachers mysterious or confusing? Write an essay in which you describe the practices of two or three of your teachers and try to discern the theories of knowledge that account for them.

5. Perry proposes that his colleagues "award no more C's for cow" (paragraph 52). Write an essay in which you argue for or against his proposal.

Analytical Considerations

1. What does Perry mean by *bull* and *cow*? How does he oppose them to each other? Ask students first to locate Perry's definitions and then to write their own. Is it necessary to provide examples to define terms? This exercise can profitably be done in groups.

2. How necessary are Perry's terms *bull* and *cow*? Can students find gender-neutral terms to fit Perry's and their definitions? See Analytical Consideration 1, above.

3. Ask students to look at paragraph 44, the "productive wedding" of "bull" and "cow." How do Perry's gendered terms lend themselves to metaphoric expansion? What are the consequences?

4. How might the audience of Perry's essay have determined its shape and tone? What changes might Perry make if he were writing for a group of high-school teachers? A group of educators from developing nations? First-year college students?

5. Perry, confronting the moral issues that "bull" raises, asserts: "Too early a moral judgment is precisely what stands between many able students and a liberal education" (paragraph 5); education of the right sort leads "not away from, but *through* the arts of gamesmanship to a new trust" (paragraph 40). Ask students to discuss these assertions with reference to the essay as a whole.

6. See Perry's account of the history examination that entering students at Harvard and Radcliffe are asked to grade (paragraphs 48–49). How do the results warrant his generalization that "better students in the better high schools and preparatory schools *are* being allowed to inquire"? Is this a demonstrated generalization or an elitist one?

Suggested Writing Assignments

1. Write an essay addressed to college freshmen in which you pass on what is important in Perry's essay. You may of course include what Perry says as advice

about getting good grades. But grades, Perry observes, reflect an educational epistemology (paragraph 2). Do not slight epistemological issues.

2. Write an essay in which you describe and analyze the educational epistemology underlying your high-school education. Introduce the essay with a fully developed incident.

3. Perry suggests that educational epistemologies differ according to field of study, with English teachers privileging "bull" and science teachers, "cow" (paragraph 38). Is this true of your experience? Write an essay in which you contrast your experience of "bullish" and "cowish" fields of study.

ALFRED NORTH WHITEHEAD

The Rhythmic Claims of Freedom and Discipline

The Norton Reader, p. 515

This essay, drawn from Whitehead's *The Aims of Education* (1929), calls for revitalized educational practices: scrapping the modern notion of studying subjects and returning to the ancients' quest for wisdom. It bears some of the marks of its original appearance in a lecture series, as well as its British origins. (The spelling and some of the punctuation remain in British form, as in the original.)

Whitehead's prose is seldom lively. He writes like an elderly sage—which, in 1929, he was: sixty-eight years old, with a record of major contributions to the study of both mathematics and philosophy. Nor are the terms of his argument immediately engaging. But the issues he discusses are vital to any consideration of education, and the practices he suggests are in fact attractive to many students. The stage of romance, where Whitehead says education must begin, particularly interests them; you may find yourself hard-pressed to get equal time for precision and generalization.

Questions from the NR10

1. Whitehead addresses his audience as "you." Mark the instances where he does so and make what inferences you can concerning his imagined audience. Who, collectively, do you think they are?

2. Whitehead often uses the language of biology to describe education, as in "the natural mode by which living organisms are excited towards suitable self-development is enjoyment" (paragraph 5). Locate other examples of this language. How does it define his conception of education? Do you find such language usual or unusual?

3. Although Whitehead constructs a sequence—the stage of romance, the stage of precision, the stage of generalization—he describes education as cyclical. His essay is also organized circularly rather than linearly. Identify repetitive passages.

4. Look carefully at Whitehead's concluding paragraphs (18–21). What does he see as the values of education in art? Do you accept his arguments?

5. Both Whitehead and Perry, in "Examsmanship and the Liberal Arts: A Study in Educational Epistemology" (NR 505), regard the goal of education as more than the acquisition of facts, though they describe the process in different terms. Write an essay in which you consider the extent to which they agree about the goal of education. You will have to consider the terms each uses, especially the different meaning each gives to "generalization."

Analytical Considerations

1. Compare Whitehead's definition of "wisdom" with William J. Perry, Jr.'s definition of "framing" ("Examsmanship and the Liberal Arts" [NR 505]). How close to each other are they?
2. Define in your own words what Whitehead calls the "stage of Romance," the "stage of Precision," and the "stage of Generalisation."
3. Ask students if and when they have had ideas and subjects presented "romantically"? At what stage of their education? What do they remember about these presentations?
4. Whitehead says that schoolmasters "are apt to forget that we are only subordinate elements in the education of a grown man; and that, in their own good time, in later life our pupils will learn for themselves" (paragraph 9). Do you agree? If so, what is the role of a teacher?
5. At a rough estimate, according to Whitehead, the years till age thirteen or fourteen are for romance, fourteen to eighteen for precision, and eighteen to twenty-two for generalization (paragraph 16). Why do you think he came up with these years? Do you agree with his calculations?
6. Whitehead confidently pronounces that "you can never greatly increase average incomes" (paragraph 20). He was wrong. What are the consequences for his argument that art, drama, and music should be included in the curriculum? Are there other reasons for studying them?

Suggested Writing Assignments

1. Whitehead writes of the "evil" of "barren knowledge" (paragraph 6). Write an essay in which you describe what you consider "barren knowledge" in your own education, using Whitehead's discussion to help you think through what the term means to you. Is Whitehead's term *evil* too strong?
2. Wisdom is the end of education for Whitehead, as it was for the ancient philosophers. Write about someone you know who you think has wisdom. Describe this wisdom in action and explain how this person developed it.
3. Choose a subject and describe what it would be like if it were presented according to Whitehead's concept of romance. Or tell how you or someone you know became excited about a subject through something like Whitehead's concept of romance.
4. "To speak the truth" Whitehead writes, "except in the rare case of genius in the teacher, I do not think that it is possible to take a whole class very far along the road of precision without some dulling of the interest" (paragraph 11). Write an essay in which you agree or disagree, using evidence from your experience and observation.

LANGUAGE AND COMMUNICATION

GLORIA NAYLOR

"Mommy, What Does 'Nigger' Mean?"

The Norton Reader, p. 525; Shorter Edition, p. 271

A graduate of Brooklyn College and Yale University, now a novelist, Gloria Naylor takes up the question of racially loaded language in this essay reprinted from the "Hers" column of the *New York Times*. For Naylor the term *nigger* can, when used by whites, be an insulting, destructive epithet; yet, when used within black communities, it can become a term of endearment, even pride. Analyzing the examples Naylor gives from her childhood will help students draw out the principles by which she makes this distinction and the position against which she argues.

If it seems relevant, you can discuss the problem of racially biased language on campuses today. Many colleges and universities have adopted—or are considering adopting—a "code" that would prohibit insulting language based on race, class, gender, sexual orientation, or ethnicity; others have given them up or are considering giving them up. If your campus has (or had) such a code, analyze it to determine whether it is consonant with the principles underlying Naylor's argument or whether it takes the oppositional position to which she alludes at the end of her essay (paragraph 14). If your campus has faced any alleged violations of the code, or if students can cite incidents that might violate such a code, ask them to imagine what Naylor's analysis of the incident(s) might be.

Analytical Considerations

1. Like other pieces written for the "Hers" column, Naylor's essay uses a combination of "personal" experience and "impersonal" generalization. Why does Naylor choose to begin with two paragraphs of generalization rather than with her third-grade experience?
2. What makes Naylor's narrative of her third-grade experience so powerful? Help students analyze the concise, objective style, the effect of words such as *nymphomaniac* and *necrophiliac*, as well as the unstated assumptions about black students that Naylor writes against.
3. The bulk of Naylor's essay recounts memories in which *nigger* occurs in nonderogatory contexts. What are the possible connotations of the term as used by blacks? Why does Naylor wish to show the richness of this term within the black community? How does this richness contrast with the starkness of the white third-grader's language?
4. In paragraph 14, Naylor summarizes a position against which she is arguing: "the use of the word nigger at this social stratum of the black community [is] . . . an internalization of racism." Ask students what evidence they

might bring to support the opposing argument—and why Naylor treats it only briefly when and where she does.

5. Naylor never tells us how her mother answered the question, "What does 'nigger' mean?" Instead, she simply concludes: "And since she [her mother] knew that I had to grow up in America, she took me in her lap and explained." Why does Naylor end this way?

6. What persona does Naylor create in this essay—and how? What kind of person do we imagine her to be? Why is this persona important to her argument?

Suggested Writing Assignments

1. Write an essay about the use of the term *nigger* in which you disagree with Naylor and take the opposing position that she alludes to: "the use of the word nigger at this social stratum of the black community [is] . . . an internalization of racism" paragraph 14).

2. If you come from a racial or ethnic minority, write an analysis of a term that can have negative or positive meaning, depending on the context in which it is used.

3. Write an essay about your own experiences with a word that someone used to insult or denigrate you. As you analyze your experience, try to draw out the various connotations of the word used, as Naylor does.

MAXINE HONG KINGSTON

Tongue-Tied

The Norton Reader, p. 527; Shorter Edition, p. 273

Maxine Hong Kingston's *The Woman Warrior* (1976) combines autobiography with family history, cultural myth, and fictional tale to capture the meaning of growing up female and Chinese American. As in other sections of her autobiography, Kingston here retells a story originally told by her mother to probe the problem of silence and speech. Though painful, even cruel as Kingston retells it, the story prepares for the complexity of Kingston's linguistic responses, a paradoxical combination of refusing speech and speaking out, depending on the context.

If students have read Gloria Anzaldúa's "How to Tame a Wild Tongue" (NR 537, SE 283), you may ask them whether her position that language is a form of political dominance and social control applies to Kingston's situation: why can't Kingston speak in English school, for example, when she can speak, shout, even scream in Chinese school? If students have read Richard Rodriguez's "Aria" (NR 531, SE, 277), you may compare the essays to explore the complex patterns of gender, ethnicity, and class that affect students' ability to speak. Such discussion will prevent students from assuming that only one factor creates a condition of silence. Both Kingston and Rodriguez, female and male, suffer from an inability to speak in school; yet Kingston can speak at home and in Chinese school, whereas Rodriguez notes the growing silences at the family dinner table. In addition, learning a new language affects family members in different ways: the mothers in these two families learn to speak out in English, whereas Rodriguez's father (Kingston does not mentions hers) becomes quiet, almost shy as his family learns its second language. Anzaldúa talks different "home tongues" with different members of her dispersed family.

Analytical Considerations

1. Encourage students to interpret the story that Kingston's mother tells. What meanings do they see? What meanings does Kingston emphasize?
2. As Kingston tells it, her mother cut her frenum to loosen her tongue. Nevertheless, her essay includes a Chinese proverb to the effect that "a ready tongue is an evil" (paragraph 2). Gloria Anzaldúa's "How to Tame a Wild Tongue" (NR 537, SE 283) contains additional proverbs about tongues. Do other cultures have similar proverbs? Why is the tongue a universal metaphor for speech? Why are loose tongues attributed to women, and why are women chastised for them?
3. How does Kingston convey the differences between being a person, an "I," in English versus being one in Chinese? What other strategies does she use to explain the differences between Chinese and Americans?
4. Compare Kingston's experiences in grade school with Rodriguez's ("Aria" [NR 531, SE 277])? How and why are they similar or different?

Suggested Writing Assignments

1. If you had difficulty speaking in school, write an essay in which you describe and analyze your experience. Did you face obstacles similar to or different from those Kingston describes?
2. Retell a story that your mother, father, or grandparent told to communicate appropriate (or inappropriate) behavior within your ethnic community. Try to capture the richness of the story, as well as your responses to it.
3. Is silence always a mark of social control? Can it also be a form of resistance? Analyze Kingston's or Rodriguez's account to suggest ways in which they are both being controlled and resisting control.

RICHARD RODRIGUEZ

Aria

The Norton Reader, p. 531; Shorter Edition, p. 277

"Aria" is the first chapter of an autobiography, *Hunger of Memory: The Education of Richard Rodriguez* (1982). This selection comes from the end of that chapter, in which Rodriguez draws on the memories he has narrated and makes a case, explicitly and forcefully, against bilingual education. When *Hunger of Memory* was first published, it provoked heated controversy among

Spanish-speaking Americans. Rodriguez opposes bilingual education not only because he believes that it delays the acquisition of English crucial to American citizenship but also, more importantly, because he believes that all education requires the assumption of a "public" voice and the loss of "private" language. To avoid the process of loss and gain is, for Rodriguez, to undermine or sentimentalize education.

If you have students whose first, "public" language is not English, this essay provides an occasion for allowing them to speak for—or against—bilingual education. If they agree with Rodriguez, you might ask them to narrate incidents that support his views and the analysis he provides. If they disagree, you might help them find alternate modes of analysis or counterarguments to define their own positions. Even with classes of students whose only language is English, the issue of the "private" language of home versus the "public" language required at school can provoke an excellent discussion of education.

Questions from the NR10

1. What, according to Rodriguez, did he lose because he attended an English-speaking (Catholic) school without a bilingual program? What did he gain?
2. Rodriguez frames this section of his autobiography with an argument against bilingual education. How convincing is his evidence? Does he claim that all nonnative speakers of English educated in English would have the same losses and gains as he did?
3. According to Rodriguez, what are the differences between private and public languages, private and public individuality? Can both exist when the family language and the school language are English? How might a native speaker of English describe the differences?
4. Make a case, in writing, for or against bilingual education using material from Gloria Naylor's "Mommy, What Does 'Nigger' Mean?", Maxine Hong Kingston's "Tongue-Tied," and Gloria Anzaldúa's "How to Tame a Wild Tongue"—as well as your own experience, observation, and reading.

Analytical Considerations

1. What is Rodriguez's thesis? How does he use the arguments of opponents to define and support his own view? After the opening paragraphs, at what other points does he introduce the arguments of his opponents in order to refute them?
2. How does this essay incorporate personal narrative within an argumentative structure? To get at this question, try analyzing the opening sentences of paragraphs 1 through 4, in which Rodriguez articulates his position on bilingual education, and the opening sentences of paragraphs 5 through 10, in which he condenses his educational experiences.
3. Rodriguez's account shows both Spanish and English to be "rich" languages. How—and why—does he accomplish this?
4. Have students read Gloria Anzaldúa's "How to Tame a Wild Tongue" (NR 537, SE 283). Compare the ways in which Rodriguez and Anzaldúa show Spanish and Chicano Spanish, respectively, to be "rich" languages.

5. Rodriguez's autobiographical account of his education might be subtitled "Loss and Gain." What are the gains Rodriguez discusses? What are the losses? Are there some losses or gains that Rodriguez might have avoided mentioning? Why? What are they?

6. What persona does Rodriguez create in this essay—that is, what kind of person do we as readers imagine him to be? In classical rhetoric persona involves the issue of *ethos*, argument the issue of *logos*. How do the two interact in this essay?

Suggested Writing Assignments

1. Is the transition from the private language of the home to the public language of the school a necessary part of education? Write an essay, based on your experience, observation, and reading, in which you address this question.

2. If your first language is something other than English, recount your own experience(s) of learning English in school, either implicitly or explicitly agreeing or disagreeing with Rodriguez's position on bilingual education.

3. Should bilingual education in America be continued—or abandoned? Do research on the subject and write an essay arguing your own view.

GLORIA ANZALDÚA

How to Tame a Wild Tongue

The Norton Reader, p. 537; Shorter Edition, p. 283

Gloria Anzaldúa is a Chicana, that is, an American of Mexican descent born in south Texas; she is also a Latina, the more general term for Spanish-speaking Americans. She is a writer, a poet, a lesbian feminist, and a social activist. This essay, "How to Tame a Wild Tongue," comes from a collection whose title, *Borderlands/La Frontera* (1987), is bilingual, like the essay itself. Anzaldúa mixes English and various forms of Spanish, often without translating the Spanish. Call students' attention to her statement near the end of the essay: "Until I am free to write bilingually and to switch codes without having always to translate, while I still have to speak English or Spanish when I would rather speak Spanglish, and as long as I have to accommodate the English speakers rather than having them accommodate me, my tongue will be illegitimate" (paragraph 24). In this essay she claims that freedom for herself.

Readers without Spanish are likely to be put off and see Anzaldúa's use of untranslated Spanish as an act of linguistic terrorism—which it probably is: she compels them to accommodate her. Much of the essay, however, can be understood without translating the Spanish. Although it is translated in the editor's notes, you may want to ask students to read the essay, at least the first time, without looking at them. Anzaldúa defies the convention that, in writing, one translates from a subaltern language to the dominant language, and by doing so, she registers her protest against Anglo dominance.

In this essay Anzaldúa explains—and celebrates—varieties of Chicano Spanish, the five "home" tongues on the list of eight that Chicanos speak (paragraph 11). However, she begins this essay by complaining about the Chicano culture that silences women and even, grammatically, excludes their bonding. The word she didn't know existed, *nostras*, is the female form of *we*; in Chicano Spanish the masculine form, *nosotros*, is used by women and men alike (paragraph 15). Yet the gendered inflections of Chicano Spanish allow her to make distinctions that English does not: have students note when she uses the masculine singular *Chicano* and *Tejano*, the feminine singular *Chicano* and *Tejana*, and the gendered plurals *Chicanos* and *Chicanas*.

Questions from the NR10

1. Anzaldúa includes many Spanish words and phrases, some of which she explains, others which she leaves untranslated. Why does she do so? What different responses might bilingual versus English-only readers have to her writing?
2. The essay begins with an example of Anzaldúa's "untamed tongue." What meanings, many metaphorical, does Anzaldúa give for "tongue" or "wild tongue"? How does the essay develop these meanings?
3. Anzaldúa speaks of Chicano Spanish as a "living language" (paragraph 8). What does she mean? What is her evidence for this point? What other languages do you know that are living, and how do you know?
4. If you speak or write more than one language, or if you come from a linguistic community that has expressions specific to itself, write an essay in which you incorporate that language and/or alternate it with English. Think about the ways that Anzaldúa uses both English and Spanish.

Analytical Considerations

1. A patois is a regional dialect. Ask students what other patois they have encountered or know of.
2. Ask students how many of them think they speak with an accent. What does it mean, in the United States, to speak with an accent? Do some accents have a higher status than others? Have any students been told to get rid of their accents? Have any tried to get rid of their accents? Why?
3. According to Anzaldúa, Chicano Spanish is necessary "for a people who live in a country in which English is the reigning tongue but who are not Anglo" (paragraph 9). Why?
4. Richard Rodriguez, in "Aria" (NR 531, SE 277), apparently agrees with many of Anzaldúa's points about "home" languages. Nevertheless, he argues that children must give them up as soon as possible to learn the "reigning tongue." Why? Do you think Anzaldúa would agree?
5. "By the end of this century," according to Anzaldúa, "English, and not Spanish, will be the mother tongue of most Chicanos and Latinos" (paragraph 23). What do you think this development will mean for Chicano Spanish and other "home" languages?
6. Those who grew up speaking Chicano Spanish "have internalized the belief that we speak poor Spanish" (paragraph 19), Anzaldúa writes. How

widespread is mistrust of one's ability to speak "good English"? How many people feel uncomfortable about their English? What are some of the reasons?

Suggested Writing Assignments

1. "Language is a male discourse" (paragraph 5). Use Anzaldúa's piece in conjunction with Casey Miller and Kate Swift's ("Who's in Charge of the English Language?" [NR 550, SE 289]) to write an essay in which you explore features of speech and the gendered power relations they reflect. Or, alternatively, take issue with Anzaldúa and Miller and Swift.
2. Do research on the French language spoken in Canada, particularly its incorporation of anglicisms, and write an essay in which you discuss parallels between the Spanish in the United States as Anzaldúa describes it and French in Canada.
3. Write a personal essay in which you describe one or more occasions when your "incorrect" speech made you uncomfortable, or one or more occasions when you heard someone else's "incorrect" speech. You may use Anzaldúa's "How to Tame a Wild Tongue," but you need not.

JOHN TIERNEY

Playing the Dozens

The Norton Reader, p. 543, Shorter Edition, p. 295

John Tierney is a reporter for the *New York Times* who frequently writes the column called "The Big City," from which this essay comes. Students may notice the journalistic "hook" of the opening: Tierney plunges right in with a person (Alfred Wright, 19), a place (Longwood Avenue in the South Bronx), an incident, and a "snap," an exchange of insults also called "playing the dozens." In the course of his essay Tierney includes a number of snaps. He also names his informants: Monteria Ivey, 35, and Stephen Dweck, 33; Ivey first developed a nightclub act based on playing the dozens, and then the two turned to collecting the dozens and produced a book.

Tierney describes playing the dozens as "an African-American oral tradition that developed among slaves and evolved in urban ghettos" (paragraph 6). The insults exchanged are not formulaic profanities but imaginative inventions, competitive hyperboles, each one, if the game is played skillfully, more outrageous than its predecessor. They are also, among the younger generation "astonishingly crude" (paragraph 12); Tierney manages to convey an idea of their crudity while still conforming to the rules of what the *New York Times* will print. In his brief essay Tierney manages to suggest regional as well as generational differences in playing the dozens.

Analytical Considerations

1. Ask students if they have heard snaps among African-Americans. Does their culture or their family have a tradition of insults? Or some other oral tradition? What is it? Who participates?
2. Snapping, Tierney writes, is "more egalitarian than status competitions based on money or clothes or sports ability" (paragraph 12). Do you think verbal ability is more equally distributed than athletic ability? Or is it just easier to acquire through practice?
3. Tierney half-jokingly attributes the fact that playing the dozens is a male pastime to testosterone (paragraph 12). Deborah Tannen, in "Conversational Styles" [NR 545]), talks about differences between male and female conversational styles (paragraphs 3–5). How does testosterone figure in them?
4. Do women have their own verbal games? See, for example, Gloria Naylor's "Mommy, What Does 'Nigger' Mean?" (NR 525, SE 271).

Suggested Writing Assignments

1. Write some snaps. This assignment may profitably be done in class in groups. (Afterward, ask the women in the class if they participated and if they enjoyed their participation.)
2. Look at Ivey and Dweck's book *Snaps*. Choose a couple of snaps you find particularly successful and analyze what makes them work.
3. In Chicago, according to Tierney, playing the dozens is still called "signifying" (paragraph 11). Do research and write a paper on signifying in black culture.

DEBORAH TANNEN

Conversational Styles

The Norton Reader, p. 545

Deborah Tannen represents the unusual case of a well-regarded academic who also writes books for popular audiences. (Can students name others? Carl Sagan and Stephen Jay Gould come to mind.) Her field is a "hot" one: human interaction, especially between men and women. It has implications for people's personal lives, for schools, for businesses, and for legal cases. Tannen won a measure of fame for the best-selling book *You Just Don't Understand: Women and Men in Conversation* (1990).

This article was commissioned by the *Chronicle of Higher Education*, a weekly newspaper for college administrators and faculty. Tannen's task was to draw out the implications of her research for college classrooms. She does so not only by referring to some of the research that underlies her studies of interactions but also by drawing on her own experience as a teacher. This makes the piece more vivid, less a review of research—though it is undergirded by a lot of research, Tannen's and others'—and more the conclusions of an experienced teacher with years of classroom experience.

Questions from the NR10

1. As a student, you probably have thought of some of the issues Tannen considers. Does she strike you as basically right about her subject? Is what she says true to your experience?
2. Tannen's essay is a journalistic piece written for an audience of college teachers, not linguistic researchers. Identify some places where a scientific report or scholarly argument would be more precise: for example, "more" in sentence 4 of paragraph 2 or "many" in paragraph 7. What kind of evidence does Tannen employ? Would it be acceptable in a scientific report or scholarly argument?
3. John Tierney's "Playing the Dozens" (NR 543, SE 295) is a journalistic piece written for a general audience. He and Tannen make some similar points. Identify them. What kind of evidence does Tierney employ? How do their different audiences seem to require different kinds of assertions and different kinds of evidence?
4. Test Tannen's observations against your own in three different college classes. Write an essay in which you present your evidence and interpret it in conjunction with hers. Do you have any points to add to her argument? to contradict her argument? to refine or complicate it? For example, does the type of course or student make a difference?

Analytical Considerations

1. John Tierney, in "Playing the Dozens" (NR 543, SE 295), half-jokingly attributes an aggressive male conversational style to testosterone (paragraph 12). How does testosterone figure in Deborah Tannen's account of male and female conversational styles?
2. Tannen quotes those who think they're being fair and then argues that they're wrong: "'I treat everyone the same.' But treating people the same is not equal treatment if they are not the same" (paragraph 20). Ask students what they think of the opening statement and Tannen's rejoinder. Students will have an interesting (and difficult) time deciding who is and who is not the same, or at what point real differences justify different treatment. This neat little two-sentence statement-and-riposte has powerful implications for valuable classroom discussion about what makes a convincing statement.
3. Tannen describes what she calls "different ethics of participation" for men and for women (paragraph 14). Ask male and female students if they share these ethics, not only with respect to how often they speak but also with respect to their assumptions about those who speak often and those who speak seldom.
4. As a teacher, Tannen says she's learned that "small-group interaction should be part of any class that is not a small seminar" (paragraph 23). Ask students if they share this view. Why or why not? Do they have examples or counterexamples to offer from their experience?

Suggested Writing Assignments

1. In paragraph 17 Tannen writes: "No one's conversational style is absolute; everyone's style changes in response to the context and others' styles." Support or dispute Tannen's observation in an essay, using as evidence some situations you have witnessed.

2. Write a letter to a teacher—an elementary-school, secondary-school, or college teacher—who seems not to notice that the girls or women in her class are largely silent and the boys or men do all the talking. What do you want to point out to him or her?

3. According to Tannen, "one's sense of timing, of one's rights and obligations in a classroom, are automatic, learned over years of interaction" (paragraph 22). A recent study by the American Association of University Women, *How School Shortchanges Girls: A Study of Major Findings on Girls and Education* (1995), suggests that the gendered styles Tannen observed in college classrooms are laid down early. Read the AAUW study and write an essay in which you argue for changing the dynamics of elementary- and high-school classrooms. Should women's styles prevail? Or should girls learn to adopt men's styles?

4. Compile a bibliography of Tannen's books (she writes a lot) and choose one scholarly and one popular book to compare. Write a brief analysis of some telling differences between them.

CASEY MILLER AND KATE SWIFT

Who's in Charge of the English Language?

The Norton Reader, p. 550; Shorter Edition, p. 289

This essay, excerpted from an address given at the annual meeting of the Association of American University Presses (June 1990), argues for gender-neutral language. The argument has been made before, but Miller and Swift provide a tightly organized, well illustrated version of the doctrine of gender significance in (the English) language and the need for conscious change. Because their audience is academic, Miller and Swift choose their examples from academic sources (the dictionary, literary criticism, philosophy, history); you may want to point out this relation between audience and example to your students and see if they can contribute examples from nonacademic sources.

Most students will have encountered the issue of gender bias in language—and perhaps even rules for avoiding it in their writing. Ask them, if they write about "a student," whether they use the pronoun *he* or *she*. Or do they write about "students" and use the pronoun *they*? What are the consequences of these choices? You may want to bring to class a guide to nonsexist usage, such as Francine Wattman Frank and Paula A. Treichler's *Language, Gender, and Professional Writing: Theoretical Approaches and Guidelines for Nonsexist Usage* (1989), Marilyn Schwartz and the Task Force of the Association of American University Presses' *Guidelines for Bias-Free Writing* (1995), or Miller and Swift's own *Handbook of Nonsexist Writing* (1988); look, in particular, at "generic he."

Questions from NR10

1. What is the structure of this essay? How does each of its three sections — "Female-Negative-Trivial," "The Slippery Slope," and "Resistance to Change and the Problem of Precision" — advance Miller and Swift's argument?
2. From what sources do Miller and Swift draw their evidence? Make a list. How are these sources appropriate to their audience, members of the Association of American University Presses?
3. Miller and Swift emphasize resistance to language change. Is this resistance restricted to academics? Take some of their examples, try them out on people you know who are not academics, and report on what you find.
4. In the section "Female-Negative-Trivial" Miller and Swift look at definitions of *manly* and *womanly* as examples of gender bias. Locate another pair of gendered terms, look up their definitions in a modern dictionary (preferably an unabridged rather than a collegiate dictionary), and write an analysis of how gender bias does or does not figure in them.

Analytical Considerations

1. In preparation for discussion, ask students about the connotations they bring to the following sets of terms: *male-female, masculine-feminine,* or *manly-womanly* (the pair used by Miller and Swift).
2. Miller and Swift's analysis of *manly* and *womanly* provides a good model for close reading. You might point out its structure — thesis statement, followed by evidence, followed by detailed analysis — and ask students to do a similar close reading of another set of gendered terms (those listed above in Analytical Consideration 1 or others from the essay such as *hero-heroine, actor-actress*).
3. Why do Miller and Swift begin with an illustration from the Book of Genesis about Adam's naming of the animals? Why do they follow up, in the next section, with an analysis of the definitions of *manly* and *womanly* in *Webster's Third New International Dictionary*?
4. From what sources do Miller and Casey draw their evidence? You might ask students to make a list — and then perhaps compare it with the sources of evidence that Nancy Mairs (in "On Being a Cripple" [NR 34, SE 24]) and Gloria Naylor (in "Mommy, What Does 'Nigger' Mean?" [NR 525, SE 271]) use in their essays. How do writers' audiences shape (or even demand) certain kinds of evidence?
5. Try posing this question: "If we eradicate sexism, then language will take care of itself. Meanwhile, why not fight sexism rather than try to reform usage?" George Orwell's argument that corruption in language and corruption in politics are interrelated (in "Politics and the English Language" [NR 575, SE 304]) may be useful here.

6. Miller and Swift quote from George Orwell's "Politics and the English Language" (NR 575, SE 304) in their conclusion (paragraphs 23–24). Ask students to analyze Orwell's essay in terms of Miller and Casey's criteria for gender-neutral language.

Suggested Writing Assignments

1. Analyze an essay from *The Norton Reader* that you think may be guilty of gender-biased language, such as Alfred North Whitehead's "The Rhythmic Claims of Freedom and Discipline" (NR 515) or Paul Tillich's "The Riddle of Inequality" (NR 1132, SE 647). What effect does the writer's choice of words have upon the meaning the reader takes from the essay?
2. In the section "Female-Negative-Trivial," Miller and Swift use *manly* and *womanly* as their example of terms revealing gender bias. Choose another set of gendered terms, look them up in a modern dictionary, and do a close reading of their connotations.
3. For the next week or two, listen to the language of teachers and students in your classes. Do you hear examples of gender-biased speech? Use your observations in an essay in which you consider gender-biased speech at your institution.

PATRICIA J. WILLIAMS

The Death of the Profane: A Commentary on the Genre of Legal Writing

The Norton Reader, p. 556

As an African American lawyer (and law professor), Patricia Williams is in a privileged position to see legal issues in the context of race and gender. This essay describes one. It seems at first to be a simple narration about discrimination, a store clerk refusing permission to enter to a woman with the wrong color skin. But Williams is after larger issues, the ways such a common discriminatory act can be discussed within the legal community. She argues that the law, because of the particular kind of writing expected by the legal community, drains the life and force out of issues. The story Williams tells with such narrative skill becomes convoluted and washed out when the details are omitted. Why can't she name the store that refused her entrance, Benetton's? How can she omit mention of her race without appearing paranoid? Her emotional state when she is refused permission to enter has to go also. The law wants a skeleton account: as Sergeant Friday used to say, "Just the facts, ma'am."

Questions from the NR10

1. Williams tells of the original experience three times. What changes occur in the telling of the incident itself?
2. List the gains and the losses in the change between Williams's lively telling and the law review account she decries. How real are the gains? The losses? What standards were the law review people trying to uphold? What is Williams trying to uphold?
3. What might those law review sentences or paragraphs have looked like before they were edited? Find a law review article or two or rewrite paragraph 2 of her essay in the neutral, "law review" style that Williams despises.

Analytical Considerations

1. For Williams, as for Adrienne Rich (see "Taking Women Students Seriously" [NR 482, SE 258]), "the personal is the political": in the events of a single person's daily life can be seen larger political forces operating in society. Ask students to compare the positions of the two narrators in their respective pieces, looking at how they use their individual lives to make larger social points.
2. Also ask students to compare Williams's and Rich's respective rhetorical stances toward using their own lives this way. How do their apologies and justifications and protests indicate that certain kinds of writing—in these essays, legal writing and writing about education—are, by convention, impersonal? What other kinds of writing do students expect to be impersonal?
3. Students can be asked to argue against Williams. What is the problem with injecting personal details into legal cases? Why should the law actively try to remain impersonal? What is there about details of individual cases that may sow confusion?
4. William concludes this essay with a series of questions she has been asked after delivering it as a talk on various occasions (paragraphs 16–23). How many of these questions would students want to ask her? Why? How do they think she would answer them?
5. What does Williams gain or lose, first, by including these questions, and second, by leaving them unanswered?

Suggested Writing Assignments

1. Write about a time someone you know was accused or suspected of shoplifting or a similar crime. Or describe a situation in which someone was denied admission to a store, bar, sporting event, dance, or concert. Try writing two different accounts, one personal, the other impersonal.
2. Ask people who work in shops how they decide which customers to watch most closely. Write about the responses you get, making a larger point about access and discrimination.
3. Williams belongs to a school of legal interpretation known as Critical Legal Studies. Do research and write an analysis of this essay: which of its features are representative of Critical Legal Studies?

GARRISON KEILLOR

How to Write a Letter

The Norton Reader, p. 561; Shorter Edition, p. 297

and

Postcards

The Norton Reader, p. 563; Shorter Edition, p. 299

Garrison Keillor offers sound advice about writing in these two easy, seemingly off-the-cuff essays. He is an accomplished monologuist, as listeners to *A Prairie Home Companion*, his long-running show on National Public Radio, will know. You may want students to listen to a broadcast; you may want to tape part of one to play in class. Students should be able to hear Keillor's diffident, breathy voice behind these essays, as in "We shy persons need to write a letter now and then, or else we'll dry up and blow away" (paragraph 1).

Keillor's instructions for writing letters are applicable to writing in general, freewriting and first drafts in particular, and they may make more of an impression coming from the sage of Lake Woebegone than from a writing instructor. You may assign this essay early in the semester so students can get instructions from Keillor first. If you assign it later in the semester, ask them which instructions have been working for them and which haven't; you (or Keillor) may even persuade them to try again instructions that haven't been working.

Analytic Considerations

1. Mark Garrison Keillor's self-deprecating statements. What is their effect? What does he gain and what does he lose by making them? Is making such statements in a piece of writing ordinarily risky?
2. What are Keillor's reasons for writing letters rather then telephoning? How many of these reasons also apply to using E-mail rather than telephoning?
3. "The telephone is to shyness what Hawaii is to February," Keillor observes (paragraph 1). His riddling comparison provokes suspense—until he resolves it, wittily and somewhat enigmatically: "it's a way out of the woods." Ask students to mark Keillor's metaphors in both essays and to look at the ways he handles them. (This exercise can be done in small groups.)
4. Are women more likely to write letters than men? Why?

Suggested Writing Assignments

1. Try handing out small, postcard-size pieces of paper at the beginning of the semester and assigning students five or so other students each to write a postcard to in the first week or two of class. According to Keillor, letters

are saved, reread, and "improve with age" (paragraph 15). You can follow up this exercise by asking if the same holds true for postcards.

2. "Writing is a means of discovery, always," Keillor writes (paragraph 14). Write an essay in which you discuss Keillor's observation in relation to something you have written this semester.

3. Read around in the collected letters of some nineteenth- or twentieth-century figure who interests you. Choose a couple of letters you would have enjoyed receiving and analyze what makes them good letters. Use Keillor's instructions for writing letters if they help your analysis.

LEWIS THOMAS

Notes on Punctuation

The Norton Reader, p. 566; Shorter Edition, p. 301

"Notes on Punctuation" provides a lighthearted and witty supplement to classwork on punctuation. Thomas's conversational tone and obvious delight in learning give life to the arguably dry topic of punctuation. His "rules" are likely to be remembered longer than those in any grammar handbook, for they are simple, nontechnical, personal, and wittily illustrated. Students may be interested to know that Thomas was a medical doctor and researcher as well as a science writer, not an English teacher.

Questions from the NR10

1. The title of this piece begins with the word "Notes." Is that the right word? Is this a series of notes or something else?

2. How long did it take you to realize that Thomas is playing a kind of game with his readers? (For instance, paragraph 1 is a single sentence.) Is punctuation the kind of thing people usually play games about?

3. Choose one or two writers in "An Album of Styles" and describe how they employ commas, colons, and semicolons. Do any of the semicolons serve as "a wooden bench just at a bend in the road ahead" (paragraph 9)?

4. Compare Thomas's technique of illustrating his points as he explains them with Garrison Keillor's similar technique in "Postcards" (NR 564). What other forms of writing might be treated this way? Consider writing a piece that, like Thomas's "Notes" or Keillor's "Postcards," merges form and content.

Analytical Considerations

1. What is the difference between the comma, semicolon, and period, on the one hand, and the question mark and exclamation point, on the other? How does Thomas communicate this difference?

2. In one sentence, summarize Thomas's sense of the purpose and value of punctuation. Why is his essay more effective in making this point than a single sentence can be?

3. Thomas's first and last paragraphs are one sentence each. Ask students to sort out the twelve parentheses that close the first paragraph and the structure of the last paragraph. What goes on in each sentence?
4. Thomas writes paragraphs that conform to traditional principles of unity, coherence, and emphasis. Ask students to analyze, for example, paragraphs 2 or 5.
5. Thomas's tone is particularly important because his topic is potentially dry. Locate some passages in which his wit and personality come through (e.g., paragraphs 2, 5, and 9) and use these to work toward a description of his persona. In the end what makes "Notes on Punctuation" an interesting and engaging essay on a rather dull subject?
6. Does Thomas really believe there are "no precise rules about punctuation" (paragraph 1)?

Suggested Writing Assignments

1. Select an essay you like in *The Norton Reader* and analyze its author's use of commas, semicolons, and exclamation points according to Thomas's guidelines. Turn your analysis into an essay on punctuation.
2. Test Thomas's principles of punctuation on several poems. Write an essay on your discoveries.
3. Do you agree with Lewis Thomas that "the essential flavor of language . . . is its wonderful ambiguity" (paragraph 1)? Write an essay in which you elaborate on or disagree with this point.

ERICH FROMM

The Nature of Symbolic Language

The Norton Reader, p. 568

Erich Fromm's many books and articles made him a popular interpreter of twentieth-century psychology. His career began in Germany and then continued in America after Hitler's accession to power.

What characterizes Fromm's writing is a touch for the clear explanation, as this essay makes plain. He takes on a notoriously difficult subject, symbolic language, and explains it simply and effectively, breaking the subject into three distinct parts, then applying the newly explained distinctions to an interpretation of a story everyone has heard, Jonah and the Whale. It's an impressive performance that students should understand as a fine case of exposition.

Questions from the NR 10

1. Fromm begins his essay by classifying symbols. Identify each class, the name he gives to it, and his definition of it. List his examples and add one of your own to each.
2. In paragraph 16 Fromm speaks of "the universal character of symbols"; in paragraph 17 he acknowledges that the "foregoing statement needs qualifi-

cation." Identify other instances of statement followed by qualification in his essay. How do you as a reader respond to this strategy? Is it one that you as a writer would use?

3. The "accidental symbol cannot be shared by anyone else except as we relate the events connected with the smbol," Fromm observes (paragraph 11). Write an essay in which you share the events that made some object, person, or scene powerfully symbolic to you.

Analytical Considerations

1. Examine Fromm's notion of "dialects" in paragraph 18. Some might claim that calling the sun the life giver in one culture and the destroyer in another means that the sun is not at all a universal symbol. Ask the students how Fromm attempts to get around this difficulty.

2. Does Fromm seem consistent in his notion of universal symbols and the particular meaning they may take on, "in terms of the predominant experiences of the person using the symbol" (paragraph 19)? What problems is he trying to overcome?

Suggested Writing Assignments

1. Fromm's essay interprets a well-known story, Jonah and the Whale. Interview people of different backgrounds about what they think of this story's accuracy. Is it literally true, as many people believe? Is it true to human nature? Is it true to "the way things are"? Is Fromm's interpretation the one people believe? Write up the results of your survey in a report to the class.

2. For group work: Take a well-known story and examine it the way Fromm does for its symbolic content. Then ask how plausible the interpretation is to other class members who have read Fromm's essay and are interpreting their own stories.

GEORGE ORWELL

Politics and the English Language

The Norton Reader, p. 575; Shorter Edition, p. 304

This essay on language and meaning from one of the twentieth century's best English prose stylists is justifiably famous. Most of us share a belief that "language is a natural growth and not an instrument which we shape for our own purposes" (paragraph 1). Orwell, on the other hand, refuses to take a passive stance; rather, he actively seeks to purge the English language of errors, obfuscation, cant, and corruption. He does more than diagnose its illnesses; he offers prescriptions that are practical—though not painless. Implicit in his proposals for the reform of the English language is the need to reform political systems as well, for, as Orwell sees the matter, corruption in the use of language and corruption in politics are interrelated.

Questions from the NR10

1. State Orwell's main point as precisely as possible.
2. What kinds of prose does Orwell analyze in this essay? Look, in particular, at the passages he quotes in paragraph 3. Where would you find their contemporary equivalents?
3. Apply Orwell's rule iv, "Never use the passive where you can use the active" (paragraph 19), to paragraph 14 of this essay. What happens when you change his passive constructions to active? Has Orwell forgotten rule iv or is he covered by rule vi, "Break any of these rules sooner than say anything outright barbarous"?
4. Orwell wrote this essay in 1946. Choose at least two examples of political discourse from current media and discuss, in an essay, whether Orwell's analysis of the language of politics is still valid. If it is, which features that he singles out for criticism appear most frequently in your examples?

Analytical Considerations

1. Describe Orwell's goals and methods in "Politics and the English Language." Which methods do you find most effective?
2. Orwell turns a passage from *Ecclesiastes* into "modern English of the worst sort" (paragraphs 9–11)? Why do you think Orwell uses the Bible to illustrate his point?
3. Does Orwell seem to lose his way in the first half of this essay, particularly after paragraphs 1 and 2, in which he discusses politics and language? Is his deliberate postponement of his analysis of the five writing samples an effective device?
4. Orwell writes, "In our time, political speech and writing are largely the defence of the indefensible" (paragraph 14): he names as indefensible British rule in India, Russian purges and deportations, and dropping atom bombs on Japan. Did his readers agree? What contemporary equivalents can students name? Do they agree?
5. Ask students to find and evaluate some of Orwell's metaphors. Are they fresh and lively? Are they dated or drawn from a cultural context too far removed from those of the students? Ask students which metaphors they find most powerful—and why.
6. Ask each student to summarize Orwell's essay by extracting six statements that best represent the spirit and intention of the writer. Then ask students to compare their choices of the six statements. What does it mean that we, as readers, make so many of the same choices?
7. Ask students to bring in examples of the problems discussed by Orwell and to rewrite at least one passage for consideration in class.

Suggested Writing Assignments

1. Revise an essay written for this course by following Orwell's six rules.
2. Locate a speech made by a politician on an issue you consider indefensible; the *New York Times* is a good place to look, since it is a newspaper of record. Write an analysis of the speech based on Orwell's ideas in "Politics and the English Language."

3. Give the speech and your analysis of it (see Analytical Consideration 4, above) to a classmate who finds the issue defensible. Have the classmate write his/her own analysis, either taking issue with or not taking issue with yours.
4. Select another essay by Orwell and analyze it according to his principles and standards.

What is style? The question eludes easy answers. *"Le style est l'homme même,"* the Count de Buffon observed in 1753, in an address on his admission to the French Academy, and his words, translated into English, have become proverbial: "The style is the man." Or, perhaps, to avoid the false generic man, we ought to translate: "The style is the woman." (Is there a woman's style? some recent critics have asked, without reaching a conclusive answer.) Or, perhaps, to use gender-neutral language, it should be: "The style is the person." (Proverbial sayings tend to lose their punch when altered.)

Regardless of how we translate Buffon, his gnomic statement suggests that we can gain insight into a person's character by considering his or her self-presentation, whether in action or in words. In class we can work toward an understanding of a writer's style by examining the elements—diction, syntax, rhetorical techniques and maneuvers—that create it. For now, let's say that a writer's style is a recognizable sense of self that permeates a text, the clear, distinct, and individual voice that readers "hear."

There are different types of prose style: Renaissance or Augustan, for example, Baroque or plain. Reading the selections from older writers in "An Album of Styles," students may mistake the conventions of the period for the writer's individual voice, and it can be difficult to sort out convention from invention (and perhaps it's not necessary to do so). The selections from recent writers tend to be strongly, even idiosyncratically, voiced. So be it. The purpose of this section, in spite of its chronological organization, is not to provide students with a brief history of English prose but rather to provide them with examples that focus attention on, even force attention to, their stylistic features. Readers reading for content extract meanings and discard texts (like Kleenex, I sometimes observe when I ask students to notice and hold on to texts and take them as more than transparent embodiments of meanings). Readers reading as writers also need to notice and hold on to texts, for self-conscious attention to others' texts will help them be self-conscious readers of their own.

When we ask students to notice writers' styles, we need to provide them with ways of identifying and talking about stylistic features. You may want to add questions to those below. You may also want to encourage students, individually, in groups, or as a class, to develop their own checklists for style.

1. What kinds of words does the writer use? From what sources (Anglo-Saxon, Latin, French, Greek, etc.)? How does a dictionary, even a collegiate dictionary, enable us to trace the derivation of words? What more can be learned from an unabridged dictionary and from the *OED*?

2. What types of sentences does the writer prefer? Long or short? Loose or periodic? Exercises that ask students to turn their own loose sentences into periodic ones are a useful introduction to types of sentences.

3. What kinds of sentence patterns does the writer employ? Do the sentences have rhythm and balance or not? What kinds of parallel constructions provide rhythm and balance? How do repetition, variation, and contrast contribute to rhythm and balance?

4. What features of sound are evident in the writer's prose? Are alliteration and assonance important? Are there noticeable differences between prose designed for oral delivery and prose designed for silent reading?
5. What conventions of punctuation does the writer follow? What commas appear in the prose of older writers that recent writers would eliminate?
6. What conventions of paragraphing does the writer follow? To what extent are paragraphs determined by meaning, to what extent by sight? Can paragraphs that seem long be split? To what effect?
7. What is the writer's characteristic voice or tone? How does the writer use voice or tone to create a persona? What kinds of personae are there? How do we as readers respond to them? How do we talk about them?
8. How do writers create readers? What strategies do they use to address them? Are some strategies preferable to others?
9. What adjectives are available for describing styles? Are any self-explanatory? Which need to be defined, stipulatively, with examples?

The classical tradition of imitating stylistic models may be helpful for some students. (An alternative exercise is to ask students to obliterate the stylistic features of others' prose, to mess it up, so to speak.) Imitation is an exercise that has fallen out of fashion, yet you may want to read to students Ben Jonson's advice on imitation (from *Timber*) or Benjamin Franklin's account of reading and imitating the essays of Addison and Steele (in the *Autobiography*). Both advocate imitation not as an end in itself but as a means to discovering a style of one's own. My students, I hope, will learn to write a cleaner, crisper, clearer style than they bring from high school in the course of a semester of college writing; that in itself will give them an individual voice. Learning to revise sentences is a slow and difficult process. As usual, Samuel Johnson's reflection on revision speaks volumes: "What is written without effort is in general read without pleasure."

The following exercises are appropriate to all the selections in "An Album of Styles." They may be done in class or given as written assignments to be done at home.

1. Write a paragraph or two in deliberate imitation of this selection.
2. Take a paragraph or two from this selection and alter it so that it sounds different. What stylistic features have you obliterated?
3. Enter this selection into a computer program designed to revise and improve texts. Compare the original and the new text. What has been gained, what lost? What can be learned from this experiment in style?

FRANCIS BACON

Of Youth and Age

The Norton Reader, p. 585; Shorter Edition, p. 314

Francis Bacon's essays appeared in 1597, 1612, and 1625. The 1597 edition contained ten essays, the 1612 edition thirty-eight (twenty-nine new essays and nine of the original ten, altered and enlarged), and the 1625 edition fifty-eight (twenty new essays and the earlier thirty-eight, altered and enlarged). This essay, "Of Youth and Age," appeared in the 1612 edition and again, altered and enlarged, in the 1625 edition; we reprint the 1625 version in its entirety. You may want to reproduce the 1612 version from Edward Arber's parallel texts in *A Harmony of the Essays* (1871 and 1895) in order to consider what Bacon added to enlarge what is still a remarkably brief essay.

Bacon's essays are thought to derive from his commonplace book, a book in which, as his schoolmasters would have recommended, he took notes on his reading, copying down, in particular, wise sayings (or *sententiae*). The 1597 essays are the briefest: pithy, discontinuous, sparing in illustrative material. In all versions he uses parallel constructions and figurative language. In this version of "Of Youth and Age," he also develops contrasts through antitheses.

JOHN DONNE

No Man Is an Island

The Norton Reader, p. 586; Shorter Edition, p. 315

John Donne, a preacher as well as a poet, was notably attentive to oral delivery in his prose. While this selection comes from a series of meditations in which he traced the course of an illness rather than from a sermon, its cadences are evidence of Donne's attention to sound. You will certainly want to read it aloud or have students read it aloud. It is sonorous, melodic, and demands slow, emphatic reading; it concludes, memorably, with "and therefore never send to know for whom the bell tolls; it tolls for thee." Donne develops the idea of human interconnectedness through a single metaphor: man as a continent rather than an island. You will probably want to ask students how many of Donne's phrases and sentences they have heard before. Their familiarity reminds us that some styles are more memorable and quotable than others.

SAMUEL JOHNSON

The Pyramids

The Norton Reader, p. 587; Shorter Edition, p. 316

Samuel Johnson's *The History of Rasselas, Prince of Abyssinia* (1759) is a philosophical fiction in which Rasselas, his sister Nekayah, and her maid, Pekuah, travel in the company of a guide, Imlac, to see the world and make what Rasselas calls "a choice of life." In Egypt they wonder at the pyramids; this selection is Imlac's answer to their questions about them. Imlac, like Johnson himself, makes general statements: he speaks of "that hunger of the imagination" that belongs to everyone; of the pyramids as "a monument of the insufficiency of human enjoyments"; and concludes by applying his remarks generally to "Whoever thou art." You will want to draw students attention to Johnson's frequent use of parallel structure (as in the clauses that modify "Barbarians" in paragraph 1 or those that qualify "king" in paragraph 3); to his use of "King James" English ("imaginest" and dreamest" in the final sentence); and to his use of dual nouns ("the satiety of dominion and tastelessness of pleasures") and verbs ("survey the pyramids, and confess thy folly").

ADAM SMITH

The Watch and the Watch-maker

The Norton Reader, p. 588

Most students know Adam Smith, if they know him at all, as a political economist and the author of *The Wealth of Nations* (1776). Smith, a Scotsman educated at Glasgow University, in fact began his career with an appointment to lecture in rhetoric and belles-lettres in Edinburgh. Before the age of thrity, he had moved back to Glasgow, where he was appointed professor of logic in 1751 and of moral philosophy in 1752. His revolutionary work in economic theory came much later in his career in the 1770s.

This selection from *The Theory of Moral Sentiments* (1759) gives a nice example of workman-like eighteenth-century prose. Its subject—the watch and the watchmaker, or how to read the creator in the creation—was a familiar one, though Smith's treatment is original. Students may need to know the difference between "efficient" and "final" causes: the "efficient" being the force, instrument, or agency by which a thing is produced; the "final" being the purpose or end for which it is produced. The other two "causes," as defined by Aristotle, are the "formal" (the form or essence of the thing caused) and the "material" (the elements or matter from which it is produced). See the *OED*, s.v. *cause*, n. 5. This example raises the question of specialized vocabulary and its advantages (or disadvantages) in writing for a knowledgeable audience.

JOHN HENRY NEWMAN

Knowledge and Virtue

The Norton Reader, p. 588

This selection comes from a series of lectures delivered in Dublin in 1852 and published the same year. Newman converted to Roman Catholicism in 1845; he was not elevated to cardinal until 1879. The lectures were delivered after he had been named rector-elect of what was to become a Catholic university in Dublin. Newman's *Idea of a University* is a classic statement of the nature and value of a liberal arts education. In this paragraph, however, he deprecates "human knowledge and human reason" by paraphrasing what he sees as overblown claims made for them and by discriminating between knowledge and virtue.

Selections like this from *Idea of a University* are difficult for students who see education primarily as a way to a better job and a better life defined in economic terms. It takes careful explication to persuade them that Newman, contrasting knowledge and virtue, nevertheless thinks highly of knowledge; they apprehend his antithetic structures better than his conceptual oppositions. You might begin by disentangling overblown claims from the real claims that Newman himself makes and the values he attributes to gentlemanliness. You might also explain, briefly, the kind of university education young men (not young women) received in the nineteenth century and how it was thought to embody the classical tradition that knowledge makes good men. Ask students what courses in the present curriculum resemble those Newman took for granted and whether we still think of them as embodying his values—albeit values that we subsume under terms other than *gentlemanliness*.

In addition to his use of antithesis, Newman was a master of parallelism, of metaphor, and of catalogues that define or elaborate a term (as in his sentence on the "gentleman," which includes a list of gentlemanly features from "a cultivated intellect" to "a noble and courteous bearing in the conduct of life").

ABRAHAM LINCOLN

The Gettysburg Address

The Norton Reader, p. 589; Shorter Edition, p. 317

As legend has it, Abraham Lincoln's brief, moving address was scribbled on the back of an envelope. In fact, it was the result of considerable revision, not just sudden inspiration. Moreover, Lincoln was widely read in the classics of English prose and steeped in principles of oral delivery. He knew the power of repetition, variation, and parallel structure and brought all these devices to bear in crafting a brief and memorable address. You will certainly want to read it aloud and, perhaps, set it beside John Donne's "No Man Is an Island" (NR 586, SE 315) in this section. Donne, like Lincoln, was a master of oral composition, and both created memorable prose, literally memorable because they are quoted so often.

ERNEST HEMINGWAY

From A Farewell to Arms

The Norton Reader, p. 590; Shorter Edition, p. 317

Ernest Hemingway's style may be the most easily recognized in English prose, and this passage is typical of it: crisp, conversational, dominated by nouns standing free of adjectives, and developed by accumulation. Hemingway's preferred conjunction is *and*. This selection also provides a rationale for Hemingway's style, that things are themselves and the resonances we project on them through language are fraudulent. Name—that's all; don't try to invoke phony feelings.

VIRGINIA WOOLF

What the Novelist Gives Us

The Norton Reader, p. 590; Shorter Edition, p. 318

In this excerpt from an essay in *The Second Common Reader* (1932), Virginia Woolf provides advice on how to read a book. "Do not dictate to your author; try to become him. Be his fellow-worker and accomplice." The style is informal, conversational, as evidenced by the pronouns. Parallelism that in works by other authors seems formal, even ponderous—as, for instance, in Johnson's or Newman's—here seems natural, even simple.

Initially, Woolf makes common cause with her readers, speaking of "we" before modulating to an advisory "you," after which she returns to "we" and concludes with "you." You may want to have students mark her pronouns and discuss their effect, particularly the "we-you" variations. At the same time, she refers, easily and knowingly, to a range of literary works that assume considerable knowledge on the part of the reader. Is her rhetorical stance at odds with the content of her essay? Or is she trying to introduce her own readers to books they might enjoy?

E. B. WHITE

Progress and Change

The Norton Reader, p. 592

This selection, one of E. B. White's columns for *Harper's Magazine*, was written over fifty years ago. White makes sharp and witty observations about reactionaries and sentimentalists who resist change, among whom he includes himself. After his opening generalizations, he moves from one homely, matter-of-fact particular to another. Is he for or against progress and change? The answer probably is "against . . . but . . . " or perhaps "for . . . but . . . ." This selection invites comparison with White's "Democracy" (NR 882, SE 498) in its use of massed particulars and with his "Once More to the Lake" (NR 74, SE 53) in its reflection on past and present.

WILLIAM FAULKNER

Nobel Prize Award Speech

The Norton Reader, p. 592; Shorter Edition, p. 319

In this speech William Faulkner describes himself as on "a pinnacle" (paragraph 1). On the one hand, he deprecates himself: the award is not for him but for his novels. On the other hand, he aggrandizes himself: as a writer he works "in the agony and sweat of the human spirit" (paragraph 1, partially repeated in paragraph 2). The speech, written in what most of us would consider a ponderous and self-important tone, was written for an important international occasion, the awarding of the Nobel Prize for literature. Speaking in 1949, just after World War II, Faulkner characterized "our" tragedy as the fear of annihilation, ostensibly through atomic warfare. Nevertheless, the greater subject he recommends to young writers—and offers as his own—is "the problems of the human heart in conflict with itself" (paragraph 2). This speech invites comparison with Virginia Woolf's "What the Novelist Gives Us" (NR 590, SE 318) and her easy characterization of novelists as world-makers. Which writer's apologia do students find more appealing? Do they do so because of what the writer says or how he or she says it?

JAMES THURBER

A Dog's Eye View of Man

The Norton Reader, p. 593

James Thurber works by juxtaposition: see, for example, the series of woes inflicted by Man (uppercase) on the dog (lowercase). How, in the first paragraph, does Thurber put, one beside another, woes of differing intensity and awfulness? How does his language dignify and enlarge even the most trivial of the dog's woes? The first paragraph should make readers attend to the relative size and seriousness of things. In the second paragraph Thurber reverses serious, reasonable Man and frivolous, unreasonable dog to look at laughable Man from the dog's point of view. Thurber's strategies for creating humor are palpable. How funny is this selection? Or is it not funny at all? Or, perhaps, how does Thurber make what may be Man's deadly foolishness at least tolerable, if not amusing? You may want to set this selection beside Swift's "A Modest Proposal" (NR 848, SE 477) in the section called "Politics and Government" as an exercise in discriminating between kinds of satire.

JOHN UPDIKE

Beer Can

The Norton Reader, p. 594

Apparently John Updike was not the first person unhappy with the new, "improved" beer can; we are now on the second "improved" can. How much of what he says of the plastic tab can be said of the metal tab? How much of this selection needs to be rewritten? Can students update Updike's essay while matching his disdain for progress, or rather for Progress (uppercase)? Are there other objects that make them yearn, as Updike does, for "Progress with an escape hatch"?

Updike's reflection on a beer can is not the lighthearted selection it first seems; rather it is a serious reflection on social and cultural change, cleverly focused on a mundane object. It invites comparison with E. B. White's "Progress and Change" (NR 592) in the simplicity of its focus and the complexity of its development.

JOSEPH MITCHELL

The Rivermen

The Norton Reader, p. 595

Joseph Mitchell is the "dean" of American literary journalists, a longtime feature writer for the *New York Herald Tribune* and then a staff writer for the *New Yorker* until his death. His quiet, seemingly simple, almost flat style influenced a whole generation of nonfiction writers and still dominates the essay style of the *New Yorker*. You will want to call students' attention to his use of *I* as a way of establishing his presence and point of view; to his use of repetition ("I like to look at it") as a way of cataloguing the various seasons and moods of the Hudson River; to the careful choice of adjectives when he finds his object of interest (the sturgeon); and to his preference for simple, often single-syllable words that nonetheless convey a range, depth, and precision of meaning.

JAMAICA KINCAID

The Ugly Tourist

The Norton Reader, p. 595; Shorter Edition, p. 320

Jamaica Kincaid was born in the West Indies and lives in the United States. Her ugly tourist is an American (an ugly American, as Graham Greene called him) who vacations in a tropical "paradise." Kincaid reports from both sides: how the American (you) sees the natives and how the natives see the American. She is not kind to either; she is unkinder to the American. Moreover, her direct address to the reader turns the selection into a challenge and a taunt: I am going to tell you some unpleasant truths about yourself.

Kincaid begins with a generalization: "The thing you have always suspected about yourself the minute you became a tourist is true: A tourist is an ugly human being." She follows it with a torrent of particulars, a heap of inclusive details. Her sentences are less emphatically parallel than those of other writers in this section, her particulars more disjunctive. Kincaid uses repetitions in blocks and frequently interrupts the patterns she sets up with parentheses. Her prose is easy to get lost in, and her heaping up of details concerning *your* ugliness becomes vindictive rather than, for example, Charles Lambs's comic details about married people in "A Bachelor's Complaint of the Behaviour of Married People" (NR 270).

NATURE AND THE ENVIRONMENT

RACHEL CARSON

Tides

The Norton Reader, p. 598

Carson's essay was written and published in the middle of the twentieth century, but it will very likely seem old fashioned indeed to many students of the early twenty-first. Some of the questions below aim to get at the sources of Carson's powerful, classical-sounding style, a style very different from that of her contemporaries George Orwell, Wallace Stegner, and Arthur C. Clarke.

One source of Carson's style is her use of sweeping assertions, the large claims she makes with practically every sentence. She's explaining complex events in nature to an unspecialized audience. As the title of her book, *The Sea Around Us* (1951), suggests, she is looking at something that is familiar, yet upon close examination is really quite amazing. [This has been a tried-and-true approach to science writing for centuries; see Richard Conniff's "Spineless Wonders: Leapers" (NR 622) and Alexander Petrunkevitch's "The Spider and the Wasp" (NR 630, SE 340), for other examples.]

Carson ends her essay with a series of illustrations of "the influence of the tide over the affairs of sea creatures" (paragraph 17). She provides a little story about many of these sea creatures, including oysters, palolo worms, grunion, all leading toward her striking conclusion on the Convoluta. Richard Conniff, a fellow science writer, concludes his essay with a single extended anecdote. A very different writer, Kathleen Norris, concludes her essay the same way Carson does, with a series of striking illustrations. No wrap-up, no finales: all three state their points at the beginning, expand upon them, and conclude with illustrations that make their points. It's a narrative technique worth exploring in other essays as well.

Questions from the NR10

1. No one would call Carson's prose style lively. (Look closely, for example, at her verbs.) How, then, does this piece work? What accounts for its overall impact?
2. *The Sea Around Us* was translated into over thirty languages. Do you think it was easy or difficult to translate? On what characteristics of Carson's writing do you base your opinion?
3. Compare Carson's use of sources with Richard Conniff's and E. O. Wilson's, later in this section. A good place to start is paragraph 5, in which Carson discusses "mathematicians," and paragraph 6, in which she refers to H. G. Wells. How are these "authorities" different from the ones referred to by Conniff and Wilson?

Analytical Considerations

To get a good sense of Carson's style, it might help to take apart the first few sentences. Her opening reads: "There is no drop of water in the ocean, not even in the deepest parts of the abyss, that does not know and respond to the mysterious forces that create the tide." This is a periodic sentence, with the main action ("know and respond") deliberately placed later, in the second half. With this sentence structure, Carson links herself to classical stylists, especially the masters of the English sentence such as Johnson in the eighteenth century and Macaulay and Stevenson in the nineteenth.

Carson's third sentence is equally interesting: "Compared with the tide the wind-created waves are surface movements felt, at most, no more than a hundred fathoms below the surface." The movement here is notable: no comma after "tide," where most classical and modern writers would place one. And the interpolated phrase "at most" is inserted to slow down the motion so carefully built up in the first half of the sentence, whose pace was hastened by the absent comma after "tide," which forced us to read the first half in one breath.

These two sentences alone demonstrate the presence of a carefully crafted style operating in conjunction with a subject matter, the ebb and flow of the tides in the ocean, that has always given inspiration to poets and stylists. It is somehow fitting that the naturalist Carson deliberately crafts her sentences to depict the complex, ever-changing world of the sea.

Suggested Writing Assignments

1. Try rewriting the first sentence in a way that conveys the most information in the fewest words. Retain all of Carson's ideas, but shorten the sentence. What is gained? What is lost?
2. Follow the instructions in Suggested Writing Assignment 1, above, for another two sentences in Carson's essay. Then use all three rewrites to make some tentative conclusions about the resources of Carson's prose style compared with a purely information-based style.
3. Write about the role that mystery, the unknown, plays in Carson's essay. Think of this question in light of the fact that Carson is dealing with super-human forces—the influence of the sun and the moon on the behavior of what she calls "sea creatures."

GRETEL EHRLICH

Spring

The Norton Reader, p. 605; Shorter Edition, p. 323

The next three selections in "Nature and the Environment" represent the work of contemporary nature writers from different regions of North America: Gretel Ehrlich from the Northwest, Edward Abbey from the Southwest, and

Robert Finch from New England. Ehrlich is a much-admired writer from Wyoming, the author of essays (*The Solace of Open Spaces* [1985]), poetry (*To Touch the Water* [1981]), and fiction (*Heart Mountain* [1988], and *Drinking Dry Clouds* [1991]). "Spring," perhaps the most lyrical but also the most difficult essay in this section, is an attempt to come to terms with what spring means—to Ehrlich personally and more universally to the human race.

Students may find it easiest to discuss the personal narratives Ehrlich embeds within the essay: her bout with pneumonia and her use of spring as a metaphor for recovery; her discovery of an injured eagle and the personal significance she attaches to its survival; the proposal of marriage from Joel, his death in a pickup accident, and her spring-inspired dream of his riding across the range on "a black studhorse." In each of these episodes Ehrlich sees the restorative power of the natural cycle, of spring following winter. It is also important to ask, however, why Ehrlich includes allusions to time in Julius Caesar's reign and discussions with physicists about the illusoriness of human concepts: what is the significance of an Einsteinian concept of time in which past, present, and future become meaningless notions? You might ask whether Ehrlich successfully blends these different concepts of time, whether they stand in opposition to each other, or whether she finally privileges one over another.

Analytical Considerations

1. In paragraph 3, Gretel Ehrlich writes, "It's spring again and I wasn't finished with winter." How does the opening of her essay reflect this reluctance to come to terms with spring?
2. What does spring mean to Ehrlich? You might ask students to find places where Ehrlich uses metaphorical language to get at its significance. Why does Ehrlich rely on metaphors? Does any single metaphor capture spring's essence?
3. Why does Ehrlich include discussions of time—time in Julius Caesar's reign, Einsteinian time, cyclical time?
4. This essay works by association as much as by logical progression. Ask students to plot out the movement of the essay, trying to explain what each section achieves.
5. How does Ehrlich create a sense of unity? You might ask students to look for details—such as the conversation with the physicist or the injured eagle—that keep recurring and that give a sense of unity to the essay.
6. What is the significance of Ehrlich's ending—the dream of Joel riding a black horse north across the range? Does it successfully bring together the various strands of "Spring"?

Suggested Writing Assignments

1. Write your own essay about spring and its significance to you.
2. Write about another season—summer, fall, or winter—by blending your own experiences with meanings that human beings have traditionally attached to the season.

EDWARD ABBEY

The Serpents of Paradise

The Norton Reader, p. 613; Shorter Edition, p. 331

Edward Abbey served for fifteen years as a fire lookout and park ranger in the American Southwest, much of the time at Arches National Monument, where he wrote this section of *Desert Solitaire* (1968). His later novel, *The Monkey Wrench Gang* (1975), which portrays a group of environmental guerrillas, became so famous that it inspired the formation of the radical environmental group *Earth First!* Abbey's love of the desert and his respect for the natural world emerge in this essay—as does, to some extent, his anger with human institutions that despoil nature. In conjunction with Robert Finch's "Very Like a Whale" (NR 618, SE 336), this essay provides a good springboard for discussing our fascination with nature and the current popularity of the environmental movement.

Questions from the NR10

1. Why is the word "paradise" included in the title? What does it reveal about Abbey's attitude toward the desert in which he lives?
2. "I'd rather kill a *man* than a snake," writes Abbey in paragraph 12; yet three paragraphs later he threatens, "If I catch you around the trailer again I'll chop your head off" (paragraph 16). What are the rhetorical purposes of these statements? How do they articulate the thematic concerns of the essay?
3. Write an essay in which you use your own experience in nature to defend an ecological or environmental cause.
4. Write about your own encounter with an animal, whether domesticated or wild.

Analytical Considerations

1. How do nature writers portray nature? Discuss the first four paragraphs of Abbey's essay, perhaps in comparison with the opening section (paragraphs 1–8) of Ehrlich's "Spring" (NR 605, SE 323) to discover the combination of specific detail, generalization, and metaphorical language. Why include specific detail? Why turn to metaphor?
2. Does Abbey anthropomorphize—that is, does he interpret and value animals in human terms? Consider different parts of the essay, including his introduction of the morning doves (paragraphs 5–8), his domestication of the gopher snake (paragraphs 20–22), and the final discussion of anthropomorphism (paragraphs 29–30).
3. Both Abbey and Finch quote poetry, each in evidence of his very different propositions about human attraction to animals. Compare their quotations and the function of each: paragraph 29 in Abbey and paragraph 15 in Finch.

4. Ask students to check the various definitions of "sentimental" in a good dictionary. Can any sentimentality be applied to Abbey's essay? This question might lead to a discussion of why writers wish (or do not wish) to arouse emotions via their writing.

Suggested Writing Assignments

1. Write about your own encounter with an animal, whether domesticated or wild.
2. Compare and contrast the views of Edward Abbey and Robert Finch toward anthropomorphism, taking into account their stated views and their actual practice in writing about nature.

ROBERT FINCH

Very Like a Whale

The Norton Reader, p. 618; Shorter Edition, p. 336

Robert Finch is, by vocation and avocation, a nature writer, coeditor of *The Norton Book of Nature Writing*, and author of such works as *Common Ground: A Naturalist's Cape Cod* (1981) and *Outlands: Journeys to the Outer Edges of Cape Cod* (1986). In this essay Finch tries to explain why human beings are attracted to large mammals like whales. For him, the answer lies not in the conventional wisdom that points out "their similarities to human beings" (paragraph 11) or their usefulness to us. Rather, Finch argues that our attraction results from their difference from us, their "Otherness." And he quotes Robert Frost that what the human spirit wants "Is not its own love back in copy-speech, / But counter-love, original response" (paragraph 15).

This essay can be helpful, on its own or in conjunction with the two essays that precede it, for raising questions about "anthropomorphism"—that is, our tendency to interpret and value nature in terms of human beings and their needs. Finch presents a compelling case against this common perspective.

Analytical Considerations

1. At the beginning of paragraph 4, Finch poses the key question: "What was it? What had we seen?" He poses it again in paragraph 10. Ask students where they think he finally answers it.
2. In the introduction and throughout the essay, Finch frequently uses the rhetorical question (not just in paragraphs 4 and 10, as mentioned above, but also in paragraphs 5, 6, 7, and 8). Look closely at two or three of these examples, and suggest how Finch answers each question (often within the paragraph, in a series of sentence fragments) and why he relies on the question as a fundamental rhetorical technique.
3. Finch's essay argues against a common view about man's attraction to whales and other large mammals—i.e., the view that we see ourselves in such

mammals and hence invest them with meaning and value (paragraphs 11–12). How and why does Finch propose a different argument?

4. This essay uses a simple frame: a visit to a Cape Cod beach where a dead whale has washed up (paragraphs 1–3 and 20–22). Ask students why they think this simple frame is effective, and show them how Finch moves out of it to raise larger questions about our relation to nature.

Suggested Writing Assignments

1. Write about an animal with which you have had some personal contact; in addition to your own experience, incorporate the views or written accounts of others.

2. Why do human beings anthropomorphize animals? Think about Finch's discussion of why we identify with whales (paragraphs 11–12) or another account of animal behavior that similarly attributes human characteristics to animals, and speculate on this human tendency.

3. Write about another, smaller animal that you have found dead, whether an insect, a fish, or a small mammal. Did it provoke the same responses that the whale did for Finch? Why or why not?

RICHARD CONNIFF

Spineless Wonders: Leapers

The Norton Reader, p. 622

The artist's exclamation in paragraph 7 of Richard Conniff's essay — "Dear God, what wonders there are in so small a creature" — foreshadows Conniff's basic approach: to show us "wonders" about the infinitesimal flea. Like many other nature writers, he's mainly interested in what used to be called "curiosities." That has been an extremely popular way of proceeding, and Conniff shows us why. Wonders exist in small packages, prodigies abound in an insect we thought beneath our notice. The flea is a sexual prodigy, an amazing athlete, and a dangerous predator.

Conniff's essay is a nice blending of art and science, somewhat akin to Rachel Carson's account of the tides (NR 598) in that it envelops its "scientific" information with highly stylized literary language. Having students focus on that language is a good way to show them the constituents of style, from the information-based, factual approach to the highly literary. Conniff's piece certainly lies toward the more elevated end of the scale.

Another issue for a class to consider is authority. Conniff is clearly not a working scientist himself, so he has to base his essay on information readily available (in articles, in textbooks, in encyclopedias, on the Internet) and then go on to interview "experts." This is a standard journalistic technique: the reporter is not an expert about the subject but is an expert in amassing and passing on information. But here Conniff is a bit more. He draws on the knowledge of experts to convey information, but he presents it in a literary way that makes his essay a work of art as well.

Questions from the NR10

1. Who seems to be the intended audience for this essay? What about the essay makes you think so?
2. What is "scientific" about "Leapers"? What is not scientific? If some parts are not "science," how would you categorize them?
3. Try to pin down Conniff's peculiar kind of humor in the first five paragraphs. Look, for example, at the endings of paragraphs 1 and 2, and the way "dull" and "merry" are used in paragraphs 4 and 5.
4. Write a brief comparison of Conniff's approach to the flea and Alexander Petrunkevitch's to the spider or wasp.

Analytical Considerations

1. What is the effect of the description of Professor Neville (paragraph 8)? Would it matter if Neville looked like a rock musician or a diplomat?
2. Compare the depictions of Neville (paragraph 8) and Traub (paragraph 36). Are both these scientists examples of recognizable types?
3. How should readers interpret the concluding statement from Theresa Howard: "The most important thing . . . is to be understanding"? Does it connect to Conniff's overall point?

Suggested Writing Assignments

1. Take something small and describe it in great detail, showing readers what they perhaps never saw before.
2. Write about the perspective of some other authors in *The Norton Reader* writing about bugs. Besides Conniff these include Alexander Petrunkevitch, in "The Spider and the Wasp" (NR 630, SE 340); Edward O. Wilson, in "Krakatau" (NR 975, SE 551); Virginia Woolf, in "The Death of the Moth" (NR 1138, SE 656); Jonathan Swift, in "The Spider and the Bee" (NR 1089); and Henry David Thoreau, in "The Battle of the Ants." (NR 762, SE 414). (Obviously there is an enormous range of topics and intentions among this group of essays.)
3. Describe Conniff's essay in connection with the section in James Thurber's "University Days" (NR 471, SE 236) that describes looking through a microscope to see some more "wonders" of nature.

ALEXANDER PETRUNKEVITCH

The Spider and the Wasp

The Norton Reader, p. 630; Shorter Edition, p. 340

Two fascinating, if repellent, creatures allow Petrunkevitch to discuss animal instinct versus intelligence, the same issue that excites Carl Sagan in the essay that follows. The structure of Petrunkevitch's essay differs, however, from that of Sagan's. Whereas Sagan mounts a formal argument using chimpanzees and other primates to illustrate his points, "The Spider and the Wasp" begins with a detailed description of the physiological makeup of the tarantula, continues with an account of what happens when it encounters the digger wasp Pepsis, and concludes with deductions about animal reasoning versus instinctive behavior. You might discuss these different organizations that writers choose—and suggest that students, too, should consider a range of options in their own work.

Questions from the NR10

1. Why is Petrunkevitch's initial description of the tarantula longer than his initial description of the wasp?
2. What are the major points of contrast between the spider and the wasp? Why does Petrunkevitch emphasize these particular points rather than others?
3. Petrunkevitch suggests more than one hypothesis for the behavior of the tarantula; indeed, he says that "no clear, simple answer is available." How does he test the possible explanations? Which one do you think he prefers?
4. What evidence is there that Petrunkevitch sees the tarantula and the wasp at least partly in human terms? In a brief essay explain why you think this is or is not legitimate for a scientist.

Analytical Considerations

1. Ask students to describe Petrunkevitch's opening paragraph, perhaps comparing it to other opening paragraphs in this section. What advantages do they see in his straightforward, workmanlike statement of purpose?
2. Plot the organization of this essay. Where do descriptive paragraphs tend to occur? Argumentative paragraphs? Why?
3. What details about the tarantula or the digger wasp were the most fascinating? How does Petrunkevitch's style contribute to the effect?
4. Is there any evidence that tarantulas behave intelligently? How does Petrunkevitch treat possible evidence against his case?

Suggested Writing Assignments

1. Write an essay about the spider or the wasp, using facts from Petrunkevitch's article but also including more information on human responses to the animal (whether personal, historical, or mythological). In other words, write an essay that is closer in style to Edward Abbey's "The Serpents of Paradise" (NR 613, SE 331) or Robert Finch's "Very Like a Whale" (NR 618, SE 336).
2. Rewrite some of the material from Carl Sagan's "The Abstractions of Beasts" (NR 634, SE 344) or Edward Abbey's "The Serpents of Paradise" (NR 613, SE 331) so that it follows the form of Petrunkevitch's essay: description of animal, narration of its behavior in a specific situation, conclusions about its "instinctive" or "reasoning" ability.

CARL SAGAN

The Abstractions of Beasts

The Norton Reader, p. 634; Shorter Edition, p. 344

A professor of astronomy and space science, Carl Sagan (1934–1996) earned a reputation as a controversial and imaginative thinker whose ideas challenged the anthropocentrism underlying traditional scientific and philosophical thought. Sagan was perhaps best known as a scientist with solid academic credentials who publicly aired his belief in extraterrestrial life.

In this essay, taken from *The Dragons of Eden* (1977), Sagan argues that the distinction humans rely on to set themselves apart from and above other animals—the ability to reason and imagine—is false. He bases his assertion on evidence that at least some beasts, notably primates, seem to have abstracting powers. Though less extensive than in humans, primates' ability to "reason" demands that we reevaluate ourselves and our ethical views. Perhaps threatening, certainly controversial, Sagan's essay is lively and forceful in its skillful interweaving of theory, anecdote, and illustration.

Questions from the NR10

1. Instead of a traditional thesis statement, Sagan uses two rhetorical questions in his opening paragraph. What advantages—and disadvantages—does this technique have? Try writing a thesis statement to replace Sagan's questions.
2. Sagan's essay divides into two parts: paragraphs 1 to 14 and paragraphs 15 to 26. Why does he choose this arrangement? What is the function of each part?
3. At the end of his essay Sagan raises some questions about the legal rights of apes. Respond to those questions in a journal, a brief essay, or class discussion.
4. Sagan begins with quotations from three philosophers: John Locke, Bishop George Berkeley, and Michel de Montaigne. Choose one of the three quotations and write an essay in which you agree, disagree, or correct the philosopher. Use evidence from Sagan's essay as well as from your own experience or research.

Analytical Considerations

1. Who said of animals, "The defect that hinders communication betwixt them and us, why may it not be on our part as well as theirs?" Why does Sagan quote this philosopher early in his essay?
2. Consider spending some class time on a careful analysis of the introduction. Is there a thesis statement? Does it predict the scope of the essay?
3. Analyze the ways in which Sagan develops his argument, leading students to recognize the function of the two parts (paragraphs 1–14 and 15–26).
4. Ask students about Sagan's tone. Is he belligerent or provocative? For reasons of conviction or rhetoric?
5. What paragraphs constitute the conclusion? Is it expected? Do students find it effective?

6. Like Robert Finch's "Very Like a Whale" (NR 618, SE 336), Sagan's essay provides an opportunity to teach the technique of the rhetorical question. Ask students to note where they occur (paragraphs 1, 2, 5, 14, 23, 25, 26) and how they function.
7. Although this essay is included in the "Nature and the Environment" section, some readers might feel that it represents "scientific reporting" rather than "nature writing." Ask students if they think this essay is different in approach, style, or tone from others in the section—and whether they think it is closer to "science" than to "nature" writing.

Suggested Writing Assignments

1. Two abilities—abstract thinking and language use—seem to be the most important factors in intelligence. Define "abstraction" and "language," and explain their relationship to each other. Why do these elements seem crucial in a consideration of the value of species?
2. Write an essay in response to either of Sagan's questions (paragraph 23):
   a. "How smart does a chimpanzee have to be before killing him constitutes murder?"
   b. "If chimpanzees have consciousness, if they are capable of abstractions, do they not have what until now has been described as 'human rights'?"

CHIEF SEATTLE

Letter to President Pierce, 1855

The Norton Reader, p. 641; Shorter Edition, p. 351

Chief Seattle's "Letter," like the essays by William Cronon (NR 651, SE 352) and Joseph Wood Krutch (NR 655) that follow, argues for the interdependence of man and the natural world—in Seattle's words, that "All things are connected" (paragraph 3). Yet these three writers argue their case in quite different ways, using different styles and rhetorical strategies. Seattle's "Letter," for example, abounds in maxims: "Continue to contaminate your bed, and you will one night suffocate in your own waste" (paragraph 5) or "Whatever befalls the earth befalls the sons of earth" (paragraph 3). Krutch's article, in contrast, draws heavily on scientific and historical data; indeed, his term for interdependence, *cybernetics*, comes from modern science: a "self-regulating mechanism."

You might also use Seattle's "Letter," and the essays that follow, to discuss how a writer gains authority to speak out on an issue of public importance. Today, we might assume that Seattle, chief of the Dwamish, Suquamish, and allied Indian tribes, would be respected for the wisdom about the natural world he and his people had accumulated; but, speaking in 1855, Seattle knew that many Americans considered the Indian to be only "a savage." Seattle takes this common view and recasts it ironically—repeating the phrase "the red man is a savage and does not understand" in somewhat different variations at moments when the white man's behavior seems most foolish and destructive. His speech, transcribed and edited by a white man, shows the way that a minority point of view can become an effective and necessary counterpoint to majority opinion.

Questions from the NR10

1. Chief Seattle repeatedly refers to the red man as "a savage" who "does not understand," yet in the course of this letter he gives evidence of a great deal of understanding. What is the purpose of such ironic comments and apparently self-disparaging remarks?
2. Scholars have recently suggested that Chief Seattle's "Letter" is in fact the creation of a white man, based on Seattle's public oratory. If so, what rhetorical techniques does the white editor associate with Indian speech? Why might he have done so?
3. A surprisingly modern note of ecological awareness resounds in the statement "[W]hatever happens to the beasts also happens to man. All things are connected." Locate two or three similar observations, and explain their effectiveness.
4. Chief Seattle says that the red man might understand the white man better "if we knew what it was that the white man dreams, what he describes to his children on the long winter nights, what visions he burns into their minds, so they will wish for tomorrow." Write a short essay explaining, either straightforwardly or ironically, how "the white man" might reply. If you prefer, write the reply itself.

Analytical Considerations

1. Listeners who heard Chief Seattle speak said that he was an impressive public orator. What elements of his style would contribute to this effect?
2. Ask students to compare/contrast Chief Seattle's ironic style with Terry Tempest Williams's attempt to blend traditions of feminine, western American, and Indian rhetoric (NR 663, SE 356).

Suggested Writing Assignments:

1. Choose a maxim from Chief Seattle's "Letter" as the thesis for an argument you wish to make about a topic of environmental importance. Examples: "Continue to contaminate your bed, and you will one night suffocate in your own waste" (paragraph 5) or "[A]ll things share the same breath—the beasts, the trees, the man" (paragraph 2). Add your own evidence and experience to support the argument.
2. Write a letter to the President on an environmental issue of relevance today, or recast the material from another essay in this section into the form of a letter to the President.
3. In many essays on environmental topics, a member of a minority group (or a person holding a minority opinion) must persuade the majority to alter its course. Write an argument on an environmental topic that concerns you deeply, using your position as a minority writer as part of your strategy for persuading the majority to change its view.

NOEL PERRIN

Forever Virgin: The American View of America

The Norton Reader, p. 643

Noel Perrin lives in New Hampshire and teaches at Dartmouth College. For years he has recorded and meditated on his experiences as a New England farmer, contributing regularly to *Blair and Ketchum's Country Journal* and collecting his essays in such books as *First Person Rural* (1978), *Second Person Rural* (1980), and *Third Person Rural* (1983). This essay takes on a larger, more sweeping topic than many of Perrin's local pieces: how Americans view the landscape and why they see it as they do. It makes a useful conclusion or counterpoint to the essays by other regional writers included in this section (Ehrlich, Abbey, Finch). It also works well in conjunction with Margaret Atwood's "True North" (NR 162, SE 91), which considers how Canadians view their large expanses of northern wilderness.

Analytical Considerations

1. Perrin begins with a reference to Fitzgerald's *The Great Gatsby*. Ask students why he begins with this reference, what kind of audience he assumes, and whether they have read the novel (and, if not, whether Perrin provides enough information so all readers can understand his point). This opening can provide an occasion for discussing how, when, and why to make use of allusions—and when and why not to.
2. After the opening discussion of Fitzgerald's novel, Perrin gives a clear statement of purpose and plan (paragraphs 3 and 4). Ask students to locate the statement of purpose, the outline of his plan, and the major sections of the essay (the "short" and the "long" things he says he will do).
3. Definition is often a difficult task—especially when the thing to define is large, ambiguous, or multivalent. Consider how Perrin neatly handles the business of defining "nature" in paragraphs 5 to 9.
4. The body of Perrin's essay analyzes the attitudes toward nature in key texts of American nature writing. Ask students to list the key writers (Crèvecoeur, Lewis and Clark, Thoreau, Muir) and the attitudes Perrin finds in their works. When does he think the American attitude changed significantly? Why?
5. At the end of the essay, Perrin divides American attitudes to nature into two basic categories. Ask students what view they hold, whether they think there are other views, and why Perrin might have oversimplified to make his argument.
6. On the uses of digression: in his account of Crèvecoeur's *Letters of an American Farmer*, Perrin includes a paragraph on Nantucket women and their addiction to opium (paragraph 15). Why does he include it? If it is just a digression without a larger purpose, what value does it have?

1. In small groups or on your own, read more from one of the writers Perrin analyzes: Crèvecoeur, Lewis and Clark, Thoreau, or Muir. Write a brief account of how your reading does or does not conform to the general impression Perrin gives of this writer.

2. Near the end of the essay Perrin asserts that "the present United States government" operates under an illusion—that is, "to deny that anything has changed significantly since the days of Hector St. John de Crèvecoeur and Lewis and Clark" (paragraph 34). Has the attitude of the government changed since 1986 when Perrin first published this essay? Write an essay in which you explain whether it has or has not.

WILLIAM CRONON

The Trouble with Wilderness

The Norton Reader, p. 651; Shorter Edition, p. 352

This essay, particularly the first part, will seem oddly contrarian to many students; Cronon himself says his argument seems at first glance to be "perverse." He argues that we should understand the concept of "wilderness" as a human creation, and as soon as he makes this claim, some readers will get it, and many will scratch their heads in puzzlement. This is not to say that Cronon in any way disparages or denounces wilderness, only the quick assumptions that allow humans to easily demarcate such a concept from their everyday lives. As he reminds us, those who helped create the concept were often city folks with little or no understanding of what it is like to work the land.

If your class contains a good mix of rural and urban students, have them compare their own notions of wilderness with both the strict definition and the looser one Cronon seems to be employing throughout, a definition that encompasses Great Plains ranches as well as trackless forests in the Sierras. Rural students will usually have a much more familiar, more comfortable, and less mystical view of wilderness. (That doesn't mean they won't love it more, of course. Just that their love might be less misty-eyed.)

The last three paragraphs witness a turn toward a lesson. This is where Cronon tells us what we ought to do about wilderness, how we ought to react. Some will find the tone a bit preachy, but a careful reading will demonstrate that this tone has been carefully prepared for earlier on. In fact, the entire essay has the form of a classic sermon, one that examines a single word, in this case *wilderness*, and derives a moral lesson from its conclusions.

Questions from the NR10

1. In paragraph 12 Cronon writes: "We live in an urban-industrial civilization, but too often pretend to ourselves that our real home is in the wilderness."

Cronon gives no examples. What examples might back up Cronon's statement? Can you think of counter examples as well?

2. Who is Cronon's "we" throughout this essay? Why does he use "we" so frequently?

3. Paragraph 2 raises the issue of whether wilderness provides us with a "mirror." Look through the essay for similar visual imagery; then explain what role such imagery plays.

4. If you found significant counter examples in response to question 1, write a letter to the editor in which you question or object to one aspect of Cronon's argument.

Analytical Considerations

1. This essay is taken from a book entitled *Uncommon Ground: Toward Reinventing Nature*. Show how this essay's subject matter and approach are appropriate for a book with such a title.

2. Cronon talks of "a natural landscape that is also cultural" (paragraph 14). Explain what he means.

3. Does Cronon show much awareness that his readers might have a very different view of the word *wilderness*? How does he meet his readers' expectations?

4. If wilderness is a construct, mainly mental, what are the rules for deciding what is wilderness and what is not? Who gets to decide?

Suggested Writing Assignments

1. Write about a place that would fit Cronon's notion of wilderness so your readers can decide if his main point is accurate.

2. There are many specifically designated "wilderness areas" in national parks and national forests. Is it contrary to the spirit of the term *wilderness* to have foot trails through these areas? Bicycle trails? Horse trails? Snowmobile trails?

3. Interview people about what the term *wilderness* means to them. Write up your findings.

JOSEPH WOOD KRUTCH

The Most Dangerous Predator

The Norton Reader, p. 655

What is "the most dangerous predator"? The title leads us to expect a large ferocious animal, perhaps a lion, tiger, or jaguar, or even a small deadly insect we have heard little about. But the answer, we soon discover, is *Homo sapiens*, the human being. This essay, based in facts about the Baja Peninsula of Mexico, which stretches 760 miles south of California, is an early example of environmentally conscious nature writing and writing for environmental advocacy.

Joseph Wood Krutch began as a drama critic and professor of literature in New York; during a midlife crisis of conscience, he reread his Thoreau, moved to the southwestern desert, and began to write about nature and natural history. It might be interesting to ask students whether things have changed since Krutch wrote thirty years ago—and, if so, whether for better or for worse.

Questions from the NR10

1. What is the distinction Krutch makes between predation within the non-human world of nature and predation on the creatures of that world by man?
2. Krutch obviously feels disdain for men who shoot and kill wild animals. Locate sentences in which he expresses that disdain, and analyze how they work.
3. Krutch wrote this essay over thirty years ago. Have any of the facts changed? If he were writing today, would he need to modify any of his conclusions in paragraph 27?
4. Taking the gulls and terns as a kind of model, explore the similarities and differences in some other relationship of predation—for instance, birds and mosquitoes, mosquitoes and people, hunters and deer—and write a brief account of how the relationship works.

Analytical Considerations

1. Like many other writers on science and natural history, Krutch must simplify. Using students' responses to Question 1, above, you might ask them to suggest why Krutch creates simple dichotomies (this versus that) and to compare his dichotomy with, say, Noel Perrin's at the end of "Forever Virgin: An American View of America" (NR 643, paragraphs 32–35).
2. Krutch calls the story of the gulls and terns of Rasa Island "absurd" and adds, "How decisively it gives the lie to what the earliest idealizers of nature called her 'social union'" (paragraph 17). Ask students to explain the concept of "nature's social union" and the point Krutch makes here.
3. Analyze the rhetorical effectiveness of the opening sentence of paragraph 3: "Someday—probably a little too late—the promoters of Baja as a resort area will wake up to the fact that wildlife is a tourist attraction and that though any bird or beast can be observed or photographed an unlimited number of times it can be shot only once." Find and analyze two or three similar examples of Krutch's style.
4. Near the end of the essay, Krutch explicitly states "three truths" he derives from the example of Guadalupe (paragraph 27). Discuss with students why he makes his points so directly and obviously, perhaps in comparison with other writers in this section who are more implicit or suggestive (e.g., Ehrlich or Carson).

Suggested Writing Assignments

1. Write an essay in which you consider whether things have changed since Krutch wrote his essay—for example, whether the tourist industry now recognizes the importance of preserving wildlife or whether the "three truths" mentioned in paragraph 27 still hold.

2. If you have access to information about some ecological problem or issue in your region, write an essay in which you, like Krutch, advocate a position on that issue.

TERRY TEMPEST WILLIAMS

The Clan of One-Breasted Women

The Norton Reader, p. 663; Shorter Edition, p. 356

Williams explains the literal meaning of her title in the first paragraph: the women in her family suffer from breast cancer, and mastectomies are a frequent, devastating result. Students may also want to know about the mythological tribe of women warriors, the Amazons, who according to some legends cut off their right breasts in order to wield their bows and arrows more freely. This allusion prepares for Williams's discussion, later in the essay, of her dilemma about whether or not she, as a Mormon woman, should fight governmental authorities and risk imprisonment. Should she, like other Mormons, accept passively the risks that threaten her, or should she, like the Amazons, fight actively against them?

Williams served as naturalist-in-residence at the Utah Museum of Natural History and published several books of nature writing: *Pieces of White Shell: A Journey to Navajoland* (1984), *Coyote's Canyon* (1989), and *Refuge* (1992). This essay combines powerful personal experiences with research into historical and environmental issues to argue against nuclear testing in the desert. Students may find the combination of personal experience and research data rhetorically useful if they choose to write essays that take a stand on environmental issues. You might suggest that they use Williams's essay as a model for structure and for argument.

Questions from the NR10

1. Williams uses a variety of evidence in this essay, including personal memory, family history, government documents, and other sources. List the evidence and the order in which she uses it. Why does Williams present her material in this order?
2. The essay begins with what Williams calls a "family nightmare" and ends with a dream vision. What is the rhetorical effect of this interactive opening and closing?
3. What does Williams mean by the statement "I must question everything" (paragraph 36)?
4. Do some research on an environmental issue that affects you or your family and, using Williams as a model, write an essay that combines your personal experience and your research.

Analytical Considerations

1. The first section of Williams's essay narrates family history and personal memory. How does Williams shape her narration to build to a startling revelation?

2. How—and why—does a writer incorporate factual evidence into what is essentially a personal essay? In the second section (paragraphs 20–29), Williams condenses facts from several historical and governmental studies (see footnotes 1–10). You might ask students to look up these sources and explain how Williams uses evidence from her research, especially the quoted phrases. You might also discuss with them why Williams does not quote her research materials in some places, whether because she can assume knowledge on the part of her readers or because her personal rendition of the material is more compelling.

3. What influence does Mormon culture and religion have on Williams's personal behavior? How does she convey her attitude toward her religious background, especially in the third section?

4. Williams's rhetorical strategies include many that might be called "feminist": naming her mother and grandmothers (paragraph 34), recounting her "dream" and the song of the Shoshoni women (paragraphs 38–39), metaphorically comparing the pangs of women giving birth with the death pangs of the desert (paragraph 42), referring to her memory of the Joshua trees (paragraph 57), and, more generally, as in her title, alluding to women's history and myth. Instructors interested in the possibilities of feminist rhetoric might want to consider the use of women's history and myth as an alternative to more traditionally "masculine" modes of argument in pieces of environmental writing, such as Abbey's.

Suggested Writing Assignments

1. Choose an environmental issue for which you have personal experience and factual data to draw on. (If you don't have factual data when you start, do research to collect the relevant evidence.) Write an essay about that issue in which you, like Williams, combine personal experience and objective facts.

2. Use an incident or story in your family's history as the starting point for an essay that makes an argument (explicit or implicit) about some important public issue.

3. Consult one of the sources Williams cites in her footnotes to learn more about nuclear testing in Utah and other western states. Instead of a personal essay, write a historical summary of the events that lie behind Williams's family experience. What purpose might your version of the events have that Williams's does not?

LORD CHESTERFIELD

Letter to His Son

The Norton Reader, p. 670

Lord Chesterfield, in a "Letter to His Son," attempts to do what most parents wish they could do: pass on to their children the wisdom they have accumulated by experience. Students should be able to identify what Chesterfield takes for granted, that his son needs to acquire the "art of pleasing" (paragraph 1) in order to flourish in the station that is his by birth, the "great society of the world" (paragraph 10). They are likely to lack information about Chesterfield's social class and historical era and to need help in understanding how his wisdom reflects both. Chesterfield's advice is hardly stuffy and moralistic. It might be described as *urbane*, provided the word is stipulatively defined in relation to Chesterfield's *urbs*, eighteenth-century London.

Chesterfield's "Letter to His Son" has what the New Critics called tonal complexity. You might want to work on paragraph 9 to illustrate it. How did Chesterfield expect his son to hear his remark about "that degree of pride and self-love, which is inseparable from human nature"? When he writes of "those whom we would gain," whom and what does he have in mind? Chesterfield passes over questions of morality and immorality, except to enjoin his son to distinguish between vices and crimes, weaknesses and vanities (paragraph 8). This selection may, of course, be paired with Mark Twain's more humorous "Advice to Youth" (NR 673, SE 363), though it is worth noting how both Chesterfield and Twain depend on a sense of what is socially acceptable behavior rather than what is intrinsically right or moral.

Questions from the NR10

1. Chesterfield recommends to his son the rule "Do you as you would be done by" (paragraph 1). What kind of behavior does Chesterfield enjoin? How does his injunction differ from Jesus' injunction "Therefore all things whatsoever ye would that men should do to you, do ye even so unto them" (Matthew 7.12; see also Luke 6.31)?
2. Chesterfield does not recommend "abject and criminal flattery" of vices and crimes but rather "complaisant indulgence for people's weaknesses, and innocent, though ridiculous vanities" (paragraph 8). Make a short list of what you consider vices and crimes and another of what you consider weaknesses and vanities. Be prepared to defend your distinctions.
3. Rewrite Chesterfield's "Letter to His Son" for a modern reader.

Analytical Considerations

1. You may want to encourage a free response from the class to see how students' reactions differ: some students will be censorious of Chesterfield, others approving. I've played devil's advocate on both sides.
2. What does Chesterfield take for granted about women?
3. Ask students to supply, from their experience, applications of the golden rule that are self-serving and applications that are self-denying. Is it possible to discover a consistent pattern of differences between the two?

Suggested Writing Assignments

1. According to Willard Gaylin, in "What You See Is the Real You" (NR 676) in this section, our behavior defines our identity. Write an essay in which you conjecture how Chesterfield would respond to Gaylin.
2. Write a letter of advice to yourself from your father or your mother. Think carefully in advance about their assumptions. Can they take your understanding of and concurrence with their assumptions for granted? Or will they need to spell them out or argue for their views? Append a paragraph in which you explain your decisions and how they are reflected in the letter.

SAMUEL L. CLEMENS

Advice to Youth

The Norton Reader, p. 673; Shorter Edition, p. 363

Samuel L. Clemens—or Mark Twain—is nineteenth-century America's best (and best-known) comic author and satirist. "Advice to Youth," a lecture Clemens gave in 1882, was not published until 1923; we do not know the circumstances under which he gave it or who was in the audience. He says he was asked for something "suitable to youth . . . didactic, instructive, or . . . good advice" (paragraph 1). He then proceeds to mimic a conventional form of precepts for behavior delivered by age to youth. Those in the audience who expected comedy from him would probably have taken his "serious" beginning ironically—that is, as saying one thing and meaning another. Those who did not would have been startled by—or perhaps even missed— the comic turn he gives his first precept, "Always obey your parents" by adding "when they are present" (paragraph 2). The pattern of precept subverted by irony persists throughout the lecture. Eventually, we imagine, most of the audience would have apprehended Clemens's mode of speaking as ironic. Students should be able to identify his two modes, the ironic and the comic.

Irony is an unstable mode whose success presupposes ideal auditors (and readers)—in this instance, adults who would be amused by Clemens's satirizing the pompous advice age delivers to youth. Ironists contribute to its success by evoking an ideal audience. But irony can go wrong. Have students imagine a range of responses from the adults in Clemens's audience, from enjoyment to indignation. Then raise the question of children in the audience; in the nineteenth century they attended lectures. How might they have responded? How might their presence have complicated the adults' responses?

Satire can be for as well as against. However, in "Advice to Youth" we can identify what Clemens is satirizing more surely than we can identify what he is commending. Students who have read Jonathan Swift's "A Modest Proposal" (NR 848, SE 477), in "Politics and Government," should look again at paragraphs 30 to 31, where Swift lists "other expedients," that is, what he is for. Is it possible to make a similar list of what Clemens is for?

Questions from the NR10

1. Underline the various pieces of "serious" advice that Clemens offers and notice where and how he begins to turn each one upside down.
2. Samuel Clemens—that is, Mark Twain, already known as a comic author— delivered "Advice to Youth" as a lecture in 1882; it was not published until 1923. We do not know the circumstances under which he delivered it or to whom. Using evidence from the text, imagine both the circumstances and audience.
3. Rewrite "Advice to Youth" for a modern audience.

Analytical Considerations

1. Have students, as a class or in groups, imagine a range of responses from adults in Clemens's audience. What evidence in the text would have triggered these responses?
2. What is Clemens for? Ask students, as a class or in groups, to list or describe the values implicit in his lecture.

Suggested Writing Assignments

1. Imagine yourself an auditor offended by Clemens's talk and write a letter to its sponsors berating them for inviting him to give it. Or imagine yourself an adult amused by Clemens's talk and write a letter to its sponsors commending them for inviting him to give it. Or write both letters.
2. Take Polonius's precept-filled speech to his son Laertes (*Hamlet* 1.3) and use it as the skeleton of a talk in which you alternate irony and comedy in the manner of Clemens.
3. Invent a series of precepts for youth to deliver to age, and write a talk in which you alternate irony and comedy in the manner of Clemens.
4. Write a letter of advice to an adult invited to give a high-school commencement address about what kind of serious advice to give and how to give it without sounding pompous.

WILLARD GAYLIN

What You See Is the Real You

The Norton Reader, p. 676

Willard Gaylin announces that his intention is to rectify an error promulgated by psychoanalysis that the inner self is real, the outer self "an illusion or pretender" (paragraph 2). He then qualifies his intention: "The inside of the man represents another view, not a truer one" (paragraph 4). Gaylin is less concerned to deny the concept of an inner self than to show how it can be used to avoid making moral judgments. His essay is brisk and hortatory, hovering between deliberately simplified argument and advice. He writes rather short, simply constructed sentences organized in brief paragraphs and, by paragraph 5, addresses his audience directly, using imperatives and speaking to them as *you*.

Analytical Considerations

1. Gaylin illustrates two kinds of moral confusion that derive from the concept of an inner self: persons with good inner selves are to be excused when they behave badly and persons with less than good inner selves are to be blamed when they behave well. Ask students to locate and describe his examples of each. Are they convinced by them? Can they offer counterexamples?
2. Ask students to defend the concept of an inner self. Gaylin denies the existence of an inner self as part of an ethical argument, but in point of fact it is a useful concept that enables us to make a number of distinctions: the constancy and continuity of a self whose behavior changes, for example, or self-consciousness, the ability to watch our behavior as something apart from us.
3. Ask students to underline Gaylin's imperatives and *yous* to see how they convert argument to advice. What is the effect of rewriting these sentences as argument? Students often use *you* inappropriately in exposition, description, and argument, and this exercise will call attention to the ways in which addressing readers as *you* converts statements into admonitions.
4. Writing in 1977, Gaylin uses *man* as a generic (or gender-neutral) noun. Today many writers avoid it as a false generic, what Casey Miller and Kate Swift, in "Who's in Charge of the English Language" (NR 550, SE 289) in "Language and Communication," refer to as "exclusionary language" (paragraph 21). Ask students to underline Gaylin's uses of *man* and rewrite the sentences in which it occurs in gender-neutral or inclusionary language. You may want to have them do this rewriting in groups so that they can discuss alternative rewritings and their effects.

Suggested Writing Assignments

1. Write an essay in which you either argue for or against Gaylin's assertion, "You are for the most part what you seem to be, not what you would wish to be, nor, indeed, what you believe yourself to be" (paragraph 8).

2. Write an essay in which you describe your inner self and consider several instances in which the concept of an inner self has been useful, dangerous, or both.

JONATHAN RAUCH

In Defense of Prejudice

Norton Reader, p. 677; Shorter Edition, p. 365

Most students assume that prejudice is a bad thing. Rauch's essay does not attempt to resuscitate prejudice as an ethical good; rather, he examines the negative consequences of trying to eradicate prejudice by forbidding "hate speech" or by prosecuting racial bias, whether on campus, in politics, or in the workplace. In essence, Rauch argues that policing people's speech won't work; he makes the case for "intellectual pluralism, which permits the expression of various forms of bigotry" (paragraph 3). He believes that such pluralism will get the negative ideas and attitudes out in the open, where they can be discussed and countered. As you will want students to observe, Rauch's argument depends on close analysis of contemporary events, theoretical statements about the values of intellectual pluralism, and practical arguments about how best to achieve a just society.

Questions from the NR10

1. Rauch advances a controversial argument: that we should allow prejudice to be expressed rather than seek to repress or eradicate it. How, in the opening paragraphs, does he establish himself as a reasonable, even likable person whose views should be heard? Where else in the essay does he create this persona? Why is persona (or ethos) important in ethical argument?
2. What does Rauch mean by "intellectual pluralism"? Where does he come closest to giving a definition? How does he use examples to imply a definition?
3. In the third section of the essay (paragraphs 12–20), Rauch defines the position antithetical to his own as "purism." Why does he choose this term rather than another? What does it mean?
4. What are some counterarguments to Rauch's position? How many of these arguments does Rauch himself raise and refute? How effective is he at refuting them?
5. Rauch ends with quotations from Toni Morrison and Salman Rushdie. Why? What do their experiences as writers add to his argument?

Analytical Considerations

1. As a follow-up to Question 1, above, ask students to trace the places in Rauch's essay where he uses *I* or describes a personal experience. You might ask them what they know about him after the introduction (paragraphs 1–5) and what else they know about him by the end. Why, for

example, does he mention that he is a "homosexual" and a "dissident" only near the end of the essay?

2. As a follow-up to Questions 2 and 3, above, discuss the ways that binaries or opposing terms help a writer advance an argument. "Intellectual pluralism" versus "purism" is one binary Rauch uses. Are there others? What about enlightened versus authoritarian regimes (paragraphs 6–11)? Does Rauch introduce opposing terms for "multiculturalism" or "political correctness"?

Suggested Writing Assignments

1. If students formulate good counterarguments in response to Question 4, above, ask them to write a letter to the editor of *Harper's Magazine*, where this essay was published, to point out the flaws or omissions in Rauch's argument.

2. Use an incident of prejudice from your campus or community, along with Rauch's concept of "intellectual pluralism," to describe how you think it should be (or should have been) handled.

JAMES R. KINCAID

Purloined Letters

The Norton Reader, p. 686

Most academic institutions, including my own, have strong statements about academic integrity and against plagiarism. Yet, as Kincaid shows in this essay, the question of plagiarism is a difficult one—not only because academics often borrow the ideas of others but also because our views about originality and imitation have changed during the past century or two. If you have time before assigning this essay to raise the issue of plagiarism with your class, you might ask them for a definition or even circulate your college or university's official statement. After reading Kincaid's essay, you might ask how many instances in the essay represent real plagiarism, how many do not, and how many are ambiguous. *Why* cases are ambiguous is the most interesting question, and it will return you to the heart of Kincaid's analysis: the historical and theoretical discussion in sections 3 and 4 about originality, imitation, copyright law, and modern notions of individuality.

Questions from the NR10

1. What are the usual arguments against plagiarism? List as many as you can recall hearing. How many of these arguments does Kincaid use or discuss?

2. Kincaid begins by contrasting plagiarism in poetry and the "workaday swapping of stories" customary in journalism. Why is the first plagiarism, the second not? Later, Kincaid complicates our understanding of plagiarism with evidence from history, structuralism, and cyberspace. How do these three make it more difficult to identify plagiarism?

3. Near the end of the essay, Kincaid states, "The report that your fifth grader lifted from the encyclopedia . . . should not cause you much anguish." Why does Kincaid draw this conclusion? Write a brief response in which you either agree or disagree; in doing so, take into account Kincaid's points about plagiarism.

Analytical Considerations

1. What are the advantages of beginning an essay with a specific incident or example rather than a general introduction? Like Kincaid, many essayists begin with the concrete. Ask students to discuss Kincaid's use of the Sumner/Compton/Jones incident. Then ask them about the effect of adding the example of the student who plagiarized from Dorothy van Ghent (paragraph 5).
2. As a follow-up to Question 2, above, ask students to state their assumptions about writing poetry versus writing journalism. Discuss the way that fiction versus fact, or individuality versus general knowledge, influences our views of what constitutes plagiarism.
3. Where does Kincaid come closest to giving a definition of plagiarism? Why does it appear five paragraphs from the end of his essay?

Suggested Writing Assignments

1. Do further research on one of the incidents of plagiarism that Kincaid uses as illustration—for example, the Sumner/Compton/Jones case or the journalism of Ruth Shalit. Does Kincaid oversimplify? Are there other facts that might complicate the case?
2. Find your own institution's statement on plagiarism. How does it resemble Kincaid's definition? How is it different? Write a brief comparative essay, perhaps also speculating on why there is a difference.

MICHAEL LEVIN

The Case for Torture

The Norton Reader, p. 694; Shorter Edition, p. 374

Michael Levin is a professor of philosophy at City College of the City University of New York. He writes for nonprofessional readers as well as for professional philosophers; this essay originally appeared in the "My Turn" column of *Newsweek*. Levin is calculatedly aware that, in making a case for torture, he is making an unpopular, even shocking case: "It is generally assumed that torture is impermissible," he begins, "a throwback to a more brutal age" (paragraph 1). Although he clarifies the circumstances under which torture is permissible, his position that it is justified in extreme and in less extreme cases is controversial. The use of torture by regimes we condemn makes even more shocking his argument that we must, as he puts it, "choose to inflict pain as one way of preserving order" (paragraph 12).

This essay may profitably be read along with Paul Fussell's "Thank God for the Atom Bomb" (NR 735, SE 401) in this section. Fussell, like Levin, makes a controversial case. His essay is of course longer than Levin's: he lets readers hear the voices of those who disagree with him, even though he denies their counterarguments. Because his essay is more inclusive than Levin's, his case for the bombing of Hiroshima and Nagasaki is neither simple nor clear-cut. The genre of his essay is persuasion; he wants readers to understand his position even if they do not agree with it. Some students, as readers and as writers, will prefer Fussell's persuasive strategies.

Levin makes a case for torture like a debater, and like a debater, he is out to win. He illustrates his argument with hypothetical and clear-cut cases rather than complexly contextualized ones. For example, he does not consider whether or not we have found the right terrorist to torture or whether or not the bomb is really there. He brings up the counterarguments of those who disagree with him — as in a debate, they are his opponents — in order to rebut them rather than to acknowledge that they make his case less clear-cut, more hedged with uncertainty. His mode of writing is argument; he stakes out a position that we must agree or disagree with. Some students, as readers and as writers, will prefer such argumentative strategies.

Analytical Considerations

1. In paragraph 12 Levin poses as the alternative to "inflict[ing] pain as one way of preserving order" becoming paralyzed "in the face of evil." Ask students if this is a fair statement of alternatives. Can they produce fairer statements? Do fairer statements yield less clear-cut alternatives?

2. Have students look at Levin's hypothetical cases and ask them to invent hypothetical countercases. Does context complicate Levin's argument? What are the advantages and disadvantages of arguing from hypothetical and decontextualized cases?

3. You can use this essay as a springboard to ask students to consider what constitutes an ethical decision. Must it be absolute? Could a decision to torture and a decision not to torture, in the same instance, both be ethical? What are their criteria for ethical decisions?

4. You may want to ask students to consider what leads them to prefer either persuasion or argument, both as writers and as readers. Do they, as writers, self-consciously make choices as to which mode they use? Should they?

Suggested Writing Assignments

1. Write an essay in which you argue against torture with debater's strategies: using clear-cut hypothetical cases and rebutting rather than incorporating counterarguments.

2. Write an essay in which you make a persuasive case either for or against torture in a particular context, with the aim of having readers understand your position whether or not they agree with it.

3. Read Ursula LeGuin's story "Those Who Walk Away from Omelas"; it appears in her collection *The Wind's Four Quarters* and is frequently anthologized. Write an essay in which you consider how the context she creates complicates Levin's position that we must "choose to inflict pain as one way of preserving order" (paragraph 12).

TOM REGAN

The Case for Animal Rights

The Norton Reader, p. 696; Shorter Edition, p. 376

Tom Regan is a philosopher who writes about theoretical and applied ethics; this essay, contributed to a collection of essays edited by Peter Singer, *In Defense of Animals* (1985), is an abridgment of his book by the same name, *The Case for Animal Rights* (1983). Regan's contribution to the defense of animals, he believes, is "asking and answering deep, foundational moral questions about what morality is, how it should be understood and what is the best moral theory, all considered" (paragraph 6). He has strong feelings about animals, he claims, and he concludes this essay with some expression of them (paragraph 38).

The circumstances of publication may account for his emphasis on both argument and argumentative procedures, which he enunciates along with his case. They may also account for the density of his argument as he lays out four positions—indirect duty, contractarianism, cruelty-kindness, and utilitarianism—and argues against them before advancing his own rights case.

According to Regan, his rights case is rationally the soundest. It also eliminates complexity: the human use of animals as a resource is either right or wrong and, if wrong, no compromises (such as he describes in paragraphs 1–4 and paragraphs 35–36) are possible. But what if Regan had been unable to make a rationally sound case for animal rights? Would a flawed case have altered his experience of what he regards as the abuse of animals? (You will want to call attention to what he says in paragraph 37.) Regan's essay deserves reading in conjunction with experiential essays such as Barbara Huttmann's "A Crime of Compassion" (NR 420) and Sallie Tisdale's "We Do Abortions Here: A Nurse's Story" (NR 720, SE 391). His emphasis on argument and argumentative procedures and Huttmann's and Tisdale's emphasis on context raise important questions about the relations of principle to experience in ethics.

Questions from the NR10

1. Regan argues against four views that deny rights to animals: indirect duty, contractarianism, cruelty-kindness, and utilitarianism. Locate his account of each and explain his objections to it.
2. Regan then argues for what he calls a "rights view," which is, he claims, "rationally the most satisfactory moral theory" (paragraph 28). Explain both his view and his claim.
3. What are the advantages of arguing for views that conflict with one's own before arguing for one's own? What are the disadvantages?
4. Regan includes among his goals "the total dissolution of commercial animal agriculture" and "the total elimination of commercial and sport hunting and trapping" (paragraph 1). Do these goals include vegetarianism? If so, why does he not use the word "vegetarian"?

5. Write an essay in which you take a position on an issue about which you have strong feelings. Following Regan's example, focus on argument while both acknowledging and excluding your feelings.

Analytical Considerations

1. You may want to divide Questions 1 and 2, above, into five parts and have students work in groups on one part each. You may also want to identify students who have encountered these views in philosophy or ethics courses and assign them to different groups. At the end of this exercise, try asking the various groups to describe their experience of following and comprehending a philosophical argument.
2. What assertions does Regan make about political and social change? Do your students accept them? How important are they to his argument?
3. Carl Cohen, in "The Case for the Use of Animals in Biomedical Research" (NR 707) in this section, finds Regan's argument for a rights view flawed. After students grasp it, you may want to refer them to Cohen's argument against it.

Suggested Writing Assignments

1. Of the relation of this essay to his book *The Case for Animal Rights* (1983), Regan writes: "Most of the details of the supporting argument are missing. They are to be found in the book to which I alluded earlier" (paragraph 33). Follow, in his book, one of the four views he argues against in his essay or the view he argues for, with attention to its detail. Then write an essay in which you describe the detail he includes and evaluate the difference it makes to his argument.
2. Write an essay in which you imagine and describe, for your own life, the consequences of assenting to and acting on Regan's argument.
3. Look at the collection of essays edited by Peter Singer, *In Defense of Animals* (1985), and survey the other approaches to animal rights. Write an essay in which you choose one approach, describe it, and evaluate it in comparison with Regan's approach.
4. Read Sallie Tisdale's "We Do Abortions Here" (NR 720, SE 391) in this section. Regan alludes to "the terribly difficult question of the morality of abortion" (paragraph 16) and speaks of settling it. What does he mean by "settle"? Does Tisdale attempt to "settle" the question? Write an essay in which you discuss the relative merits and problems of their two approaches to difficult ethical questions.

CARL COHEN

The Case for the Use of Animals in Biomedical Research

The Norton Reader, p. 707

Carl Cohen's "The Case for the Use of Animals in Biomedical Research" is something of an oddity. Although it appeared in the *New England Journal of Medicine*, it is a philosophical argument rather than a scientific report, written by a philosopher rather than a medical researcher and by a single person rather than a team. Because Cohen does not report on or analyze data, as do John Henry Sloan et al. (Arthur L. Kellerman, Donald T. Reay, James A. Ferris, Thomas Koepsell, Frederick P. Rivara, Charles Rice, Laurel Gray, and James LoGerfo) in "Handgun Regulations, Crime, Assaults, and Homicide: A Tale of Two Cities" (NR 913, SE 521), also from the *New England Journal of Medicine*, he does not follow the form prescribed for scientific reports or present information in tables and figures. Nevertheless, like Sloan et al., he emphatically segments his argument, heads the segments with titles, and divides his conclusion into three parts: Substitution, Reduction, and Consistency (paragraphs 28–38).

Cohen also follows the *New England Journal of Medicine*'s system of annotation, which does not identify the authors of quotations in the text or refer to them by name. Consequently, stationing Cohen's essay in relation to Tom Regan's "The Case for Animal Rights" (NR 696, SE 376) requires careful reading of Cohen's notes. He rebuts (or attempts to rebut) two arguments against the use of animals in biomedical research, the rights argument (in Tom Regan's version) and the antispeciesist argument (in Peter Singer's version). Cohen, who published his article in 1986, cites Regan's 1983 book, *The Case for Animal Rights*, in note 1 (he does not cite the article in this section of *The Norton Reader*, which appeared in Peter Singer's *In Defense of Animals* [1985]), Singer's 1977 *Animal Liberation* in note 2, and a 1985 essay Singer wrote for the *New York Review of Books* in note 13. I use this piece of puzzle-solving to moralize upon my injunction to students writing nonscientific papers with quotations and documentation: never use quotations in your text without identifying, in the text, who said them, and never force readers to consult your notes in order to make sense of your text.

Questions from the NR10

1. Cohen limits his argument to the use of animals in biomedical research. What are the advantages of this limitation? What are the disadvantages?
2. Cohen defends speciesism; Tom Regan, in "The Case for Animal Rights" (NR 696, SE 376), condemns it. What are the issues at stake between them?
3. "Neither of these arguments is sound," Cohen opines. "The first relies on a mistaken understanding of rights; the second relies on a mistaken calculation of consequences" (paragraph 1). Find other examples of the language Cohen uses to dismiss arguments in opposition to his own. How do you respond to it? Is it the kind of language you would use in your own writing? Explain.
4. Write an essay in which you argue for or against speciesism. Be sure to define it. You may use Regan's and Cohen's arguments (with proper credit) in support of your own, but you need not.

Analytical Considerations

1. Cohen limits his argument to justifying the use of animals in biomedical research. You may want to ask students what other uses of animals his argument justifies and why they think he limited it to biomedical research.

2. Tom Regan, in "The Case for Animal Rights" (NR 696, SE 376), asserts: "Inherent value, then, belongs equally to those who are the experiencing subjects of a life" (paragraph 32). Ask students first to explore the full meaning of this assertion and, second, to consider the adequacy of Cohen's rebuttal.

3. Cohen, in paragraphs 37 to 38, extends Regan's (and Singer's) position and calls such extension a "reductio ad absurdum." Regan hedges on such an extension. Is it consistent with his argument? Ought he to have made it? Is it, as Cohen alleges, absurd?

4. Ask students to identify the no-holds-barred argumentative strategies of Cohen and Michael Levin, in "The Case for Torture" (NR 694, SE 374) in this section. You may want to begin by having them mark, in their texts, examples of what they take to be Cohen's and Levin's argumentative strategies. Levin dares us to confront unpleasant truths; Cohen, unpleasant truths and shoddy arguments. As readers, how do we respond to these strategies? As writers, how likely are we to use them? What other strategies are available?

Suggested Writing Assignments

1. Recast Cohen's arguments in a persuasive mode. Probably you will have to abandon the form of a scientific report as well; append a paragraph to your essay explaining the form you use and how you found it.

2. "Medical investigators are seldom insensitive to the distress their work may cause animal subjects," Cohen states (paragraph 273). What kind of evidence could rebut this statement? How much of it would you need? Do library research to find some, and write an essay in which you consider the function of experiential evidence in arguing with Cohen. If you can prove that medical investigators are sometimes or frequently insensitive, does Cohen's argument fail?

LEIGH TURNER

The Media and the Ethics of Cloning

The Norton Reader, p. 716; Shorter Edition, p. 387

Leigh Turner comments not so much on the cloning debate, at its peak late in 1997, as on the way it has been treated in the media. Although she seems to exonerate journalists and news commentators in the second paragraph by acknowledging the haste with which they are usually forced to write, she nonetheless blames them for falling into hyperbole, depending on sound bites, oversimplifying views, and so on. In her essay, originally a column in the *Chronicle of Higher Education* (September 26, 1997) and thus much like the Op-Ed form she criticizes, Turner tries to avoid such oversimplification; she does so not by offering a thorough analysis of the debate but by presenting a list of suggestions for improving the discussion (paragraphs 11–18). You might call students' attention to Turner's three-part structure, often a strategy used by writers and speakers who need to get their message heard.

Questions from the NR10

1. This essay begins with a journalistic "hook," a paragraph about the artist Andy Warhol and how his work anticipates some issues of cloning. For what purposes does Turner use Warhol? Does the reader need to have seen Andy Warhol's art to understand the argument Turner makes? (If you are unfamiliar with Warhol's work, you might want to look at some reproductions.)
2. Like several selections in "Op-Eds," this essay first lays out the problems, then proposes some solutions. What problems does Turner blame on the media? What solutions does Turner propose that address the media? Why are some of the solutions focused less on the media than on scientists and ethicists?
3. Take an issue of local or national relevance, and study how it is treated in the media. (You may want to limit your analysis to a group of newpapers or make it a comparison of newspaper and television coverage.) Which aspects of the media's coverage are good? Which are inadequate? What might be done to correct the problems?

Analytical Considerations

1. Ask students to outline or diagram Turner's essay: introduction with state-ment of the problem, analysis of the problem, suggestions for improving the debate. Why must Turner use this relatively simple structure for the column she is writing? What are its advantages and disadvantages?
2. How many of the issues about cloning does Turner manage to convey, despite her emphasis on the media? Ask students to list the issues and then add any she omitted.
3. Turner refers positively to Michael Walzer's and Michael Sandel's writing on assisted suicide (both in the NR, 417 and 415), as well as Leon Kass's on cloning (paragraph 16). Ask students to read one or all of the essays, and discuss why Turner approves of their writing.

Suggested Writing Assignments

1. What has happened to the debate about cloning? Do library research to find recent examples of articles and Op-Eds on cloning, and write a brief account of what the current issues are.
2. Read Michael Walzer's and Michael Sandel's writing on assisted suicide in the "Op-Eds" section (NR 417 and 415). Write an essay in which you explain why Turner approves of their approach and style of debate.

SALLIE TISDALE

We Do Abortions Here: A Nurse's Story

The Norton Reader, p. 720; Shorter Edition, p. 391

Like Barbara Huttmann's essay, "A Crime of Compassion," included in the "Op-Eds" section (NR 420), this essay reflects the intimacy and particularity of caring (as well as, of course, the gendering of the nursing profession). Tisdale and Huttmann stand together in their experiential approach and apart in their narrative development, which is linear in Huttmann's essay but associative and accumulative in Tisdale's. Tisdale moves incessantly back and forth in time and also, as she suggests, in scale: "I can sweep the horizon with both eyes, survey the scene in all its distance and size. Or I can put my eye to the lens [of a telescope] and focus on the small details, suddenly so close" (paragraph 4).

The five sections of Tisdale's essay are separated by typographical space rather than connected by prose transitions; within each section she moves back and forth in both time and space. Having students read Scott Russell Sanders's "Looking at Women" (NR 253, SE 132), in the section called "Human Nature," will introduce two different strategies of accumulation. Sanders gives each of his five sections a narrative focus, whereas Tisdale repeats within each section shifting perspectives on time and space. Neither essay follows the conventions of "academic" or "college" writing.

Although Tisdale does not use the term *situation ethics*, this essay may exemplify them. Tisdale plainly subscribes to their first principle: contextuality. She judges acts—insofar as she judges them—in context. She may or may not subscribe to their second principle, love, as a standard for judging her own and others' acts. Is it possible to read Tisdale's "We Do Abortions Here" as exemplifying both principles? The first can be demonstrated explicitly as well as implicitly; the second is problematic.

Questions from the NR10

1. Tisdale speaks of taking both broad views—"as if I am standing on a cliff with a telescope"—and narrow views—"I can put my eye to the lens and focus on small details" (paragraph 4). Choose one of the longer sections of this essay (such as, the second, third, or fourth) and mark the passages you would describe as taking broad views and the passages you would describe as taking narrow views. What is the effect of Tisdale's going back and forth between them? How does she manage transitions?

2. "We are too busy to chew over ethics" (paragraph 21), Tisdale observes. What does she mean by ethics? Does she engage with what you consider ethical issues in this essay? Explain.

3. Although Tisdale takes a pro-choice position, a pro-lifer could use parts of her essay against her. What parts? What are the advantages and disadvantages of including material that could be used in support of the opposition?

4. Write a pro-choice or pro-life essay of your own. Include material that could be used in support of the opposition. You may use Tisdale's essay (with proper credit), but you need not.

Analytical Considerations

1. Some people criticize situation ethics because they are relative rather than absolute. Do students think ethical principles must be absolute?
2. How might situation ethics have provided Tisdale with a framework for a different kind of essay, an analysis or an argument, instead of the associative and accumulative narrative that she wrote?
3. "I don't say 'pain' any more than I would say 'baby'" (paragraph 16), Tisdale observes. Where else in the essay are you aware of her using, as she puts it, "care with my language"? Why is language so important in discussing abortion?

Suggested Writing Assignments

1. In "The Case for Animal Rights" (NR 696, SE 376) in this section, Tom Regan makes a rights case for animals. Can the same case be made for fetuses? Write an essay answering this question.
2. Write an essay in which you have recourse to situation ethics implicitly, like Tisdale, or explicitly. Alternatively, write an essay critical of situation ethics.
3. Tisdale speaks of crisis pregnancy centers advertised in the Yellow Pages (paragraph 24). Can you locate one in the Yellow Pages of your own or a nearby city? Call them to see what they tell you. Write an account of the experience.
4. Tisdale's most recent book is *Talk Dirty to Me* (1994). Read parts of it and write an essay in which you discuss her recourse to situation ethics with respect to dirty talk.

STEPHEN JAY GOULD

The Terrifying Normalcy of AIDS

The Norton Reader, p. 727; Shorter Edition, p. 398

In this essay, Gould—a biologist, paleontologist, and historian of science—turns his attention to the AIDS "pandemic." Like Gould's regular column in *Natural History* magazine, "The Terrifying Normalcy of AIDS" was written for a lay audience; it appeared in the *New York Times Magazine* in April 1987. Gould characterizes AIDS as both normal and terrifying. He wants us to see it as occupying a middle position between just another disease for which "medicine will soon generate a cure" and "something so irregular that it must have been visited upon us to teach us a moral lesson" (paragraph 14).

Gould also wants to describe and criticize a particular American belief, that technology will solve all our problems. This belief he embodies in Disney's Epcot Center. His essay thus has a double focus: the power of nature (of which AIDS is part) and our false confidence in technological fixes.

Questions from the NR10

1. Gould uses current events, historical information, and scientific data to make his case. Identify examples of each.
2. What case does Gould make?
3. Why is this essay in the section called "Ethics" rather than in the section called "Science"?
4. Gould uses Disney's Epcot Center in Orlando, Florida, as a symbol of our belief in technology. Find another symbol of this belief and, in a brief essay, describe and interpret it.

Analytical Considerations

1. It is likely that at least some students will have been to Epcot Center. You may want to ask them, before they read "The Terrifying Normalcy of AIDS," to describe it—in discussion or in writing—so that all students can consider what aspects of American culture it can be made to embody. Students who have not been to Epcot Center may be asked, after a discussion of its uses, to locate in their own experience symbols that can be made to carry equivalent meanings.
2. Gould uses current events, historical information, and scientific data to make his case. You may want to ask students to mark examples of each. What are the advantages of including all three?
3. Gould divides "The Terrifying Normalcy of AIDS" into four sections by means of spacing: paragraphs 1–5, 6–9, 10–13, and 14–16. Ask students to consider whether these spatial divisions correspond to units of exposition and argument. You may also ask them, as a class, in groups, or individually, to construct titles for each section of Gould's essay.

Suggested Writing Assignments

1. "The Terrifying Normalcy of AIDS" appeared in 1987. Do library research to ascertain and report on the current state of what is known about the prevention and cure of AIDS. Write an essay in which you organize this information to support Gould's two-part assertion: "AIDS works by a *mechanism*—and we can discover it" (paragraph 16), to question it, or both.
2. Write an essay using different illustrative material—that is, something other than AIDS—to support Gould's assertion that "The message of Orlando—the inevitability of technological solutions—is wrong, and we need to understand why" (paragraph 10), to question it, or both.

KILDARE DOBBS

The Shatterer of Worlds

The Norton Reader, p. 730

"The Shatterer of Worlds" is a you-are-there essay in which Dobbs, a Canadian journalist, narrates the story of a Japanese girl, Emiko, who was in Hiroshima on August 5, 1945, the day an American B-29 bomber dropped the first atomic bomb. Dobbs periodically interrupts Emiko's story to narrate, briefly, the actions and responses of the American crew of the *Enola Gay*, the B-29 that dropped the bomb. Some students will undoubtedly have read John Hersey's *Hiroshima* (1946) or other accounts of the bombing; for other students, Dobbs's narrative will be the first. You might ask open-ended questions about it to engage as wide a range of student responses as possible. They will discern the kind of responses Dobbs hopes for and point to evidence for them.

Dobbs's alternating stories do more than provide two different perspectives on the same event: they juxtapose the physical and emotional pain of Emiko, her family, and other residents of Hiroshima with the detachment of the American crew. Dobbs's technique of juxtaposition or, as in film, cross-cutting, is designed to contrast powerfully the suffering and helpless victims with their unconcerned and amoral destroyers. At the end of his essay (paragraphs 39–41), he turns from stories to comment, but not, students should be asked to notice, comment *on* the stories. That he reserves for the very end, in which Emiko's scar becomes a "tiny metaphor" and "a faint but eloquent reminder of the scar on humanity's conscience" (paragraph 42). This metaphor evokes the moral judgments that have remained implicit rather than explicit throughout the essay.

Questions from the NR10

1. Dobbs moves between one narrative, Emiko's story, and another, the bombing mission of the *Enola Gay*; in film this technique is called cross-cutting. Where, do you suppose, did Dobbs get information for each narrative?
2. Consider the differences between the visible accumulation of information in Paul Fussell's "Thank God for the Atom Bomb" (NR 735, SE 401) that acknowledges sources (as in, for example, paragraphs 25 to 26) and Dobbs's you-are-there reconstruction. What are the advantages and disadvantages of each? Which one are you more likely to use as a college writer?
3. Dobbs waits until the final paragraph to make explicit the moral judgments that have been implicit throughout "The Shatterer of Worlds." Write an essay in which the narrative speaks for itself, without your intervention or interpretations, until the end.

Analytical Considerations

1. You-are-there narrative precludes footnotes; it aims to make readers think they are there. Dobbs was not. Where, other than from Emiko, do students think Dobbs got his information? Could Emiko have supplied all the Japanese details concerning the bombing of Hiroshima? Is Dobbs's you-are-there presentation more or less convincing than a presentation that documents sources and makes visible the assembling of details?

2. You may want to ask students to notice Dobbs's rather short, simply constructed sentences organized in brief and even in one-sentence paragraphs. Look at some of the one-sentence paragraphs and consider their effect. Why are they more appropriate to narrative than to argument?

Suggested Writing Assignments

1. Take an account of a contemporary or historical event in which sources are documented and the author's accumulation of details is visible, and turn it into a you-are-there narrative. Then add a paragraph explaining what you have added and what you have suppressed. (You may want to ask students to share sources, their own narratives, and their explanations in small groups.)

2. Read Paul Fussell's "Thank God for the Atom Bomb" (NR 735, SE 401) in this section and use the information he supplies either to revise Dobbs's juxtaposed narratives by keeping one and writing a substitute for the other or by writing substitutes for both. Decide before you begin to write what moral weight you want to assign to each narrative.

3. Kurt Vonnegut's *Slaughterhouse Five* is a fictionalized account of the fire-bombing of Dresden during World War II. Vonnegut was actually there, as a prisoner of war of the Germans. Choose a section of his novel and discuss his narrative strategies for combining real and imagined experience.

PAUL FUSSELL

Thank God for the Atom Bomb

The Norton Reader, p. 735; Shorter Edition, p. 401

"Thank God for the Atom Bomb" was originally published in the the the *New Republic* in August 1981. It became the title essay in Fussell's *Thank God for the Atom Bomb and Other Essays*, published in 1988, forty-three years after the bombings of Hiroshima and Nagasaki. Fussell speaks of writing on their forty-second anniversary, prompted, he says, "by the long debate about the ethics, if any, of that ghastly affair" (paragraph 1).

Fussell takes on a number of the debaters, mostly those questioning the necessity and the morality of the bombings. You will want students to look at his argumentative strategies, notably his *ad hominem* arguments (that is, "to the man"). He uses them two ways: in making his own case and in arguing against the cases of others.

In making his own case, Fussell begins by discussing the value of experience, "sheer, vulgar experience" (paragraph 1). He nevertheless embeds his experience in an argument, as, for example, Barbara Huttmann and Sallie Tisdale do not; see "A Crime of Compassion (NR 420) and "We Do Abortions Here" (NR 720, SE 391). In arguing against the cases of others, Fussell sharply and disparagingly contrasts their experience with his—even as he acknowledges the "offensive implications" of what he does (paragraph 9). Those wishing to read what his adversaries have to say will have to search beyond Fussell's essay; sometimes it contains the titles of books and periodicals, but never dates. (Depending on your interests, you might use this essay to consider the advantages and disadvantages of scholarly and popular conventions of annotation.)

Fussell's essay may profitably be discussed in conjunction with Michael Levin's "The Case for Torture" (NR 694, SE 374) in this section. Both Levin and Fussell deal with controversial instances and acknowledge that fact. But Levin deals with an hypothetical instance, whereas Fussell treats a messy and complex historical one; Levin presents himself as detached and magisterial, Fussell as engaged and sometimes irate.

Questions from the NR10

1. Note the places where Fussell includes personal experience in this essay. How much is his own, how much belongs to others? Why does he include both kinds?
2. Fussell dismisses with contempt those who disagree with him. Locate some examples. How do you respond to them? Would you use Fussell's strategies to dismiss those who disagree with you? Explain.
3. Mark some instances of Fussell's "voice." What kind of voice does he adopt? What kind of person does he present himself as?
4. Write an argumentative essay in which you take a strong position. Include your own experience and the experience of others if appropriate.

Analytical Considerations

1. You may want to focus a discussion of Fussell's use of sources by bringing photocopies of the debate between Joseph Alsop and David Joravsky in the *New York Review of Books* to class. This debate, "reduced to a collision between experience and theory, was conducted with a certain civilized respect for evidence," according to Fussell (paragraph 16). Does Fussell fairly summarize the debate? Why does he speak of it as *"reduced* to a collision between experience and theory"?
2. Fussell ends his essay with "The past, which as always did not know the future, acted in ways that ask to be imagined before they are condemned. Or even simplified" (paragraph 32). Ask students to explain what he means. Is his generalization true with respect to "Thank God for the Atom Bomb"?

Suggested Writing Assignments

1. Rewrite Fussell's essay using the argumentative strategies of Michael Levin in "The Case for Torture" (NR 694, SE 374).

2. August 1995 was the fiftieth anniversary of the bombing of Hiroshima and Nagasaki. As the Smithsonian Institution prepared to commemorate it with an exhibit at the National Air and Space Museum, controversy over the bombing was renewed. Write a narrative account of the controversy using the *New York Times* and the *Washington Post* as sources. (There are various ways of doing this project collaboratively.)

3. After completing the research in Suggested Writing Assignment 2, above, write an analysis of the issues involved in the controversy.

4. Write an essay in which you consider whether the issues surrounding the debate over the bombing have changed since the 1980s, when Fussell wrote "Thank God for the Atom Bomb."

PROSE FORMS: APOTHEGMS

The Norton Reader, p. 748

Who has not heard the expressions "God helps them that help themselves" or "Remember that time is money" or "Early to bed and early to rise, / Makes a man healthy, wealthy, and wise"? All come from Ben Franklin's *Poor Richard's Almanack*, all represent beliefs deeply engrained in the American psyche, and all are maxims or *apothegms*.

Apothegms represent, in the words of Sir James Mackintosh, "the condensed good sense of nations"; they convey the pithy, often witty observations of people about their own persistent conduct. Whether called "apothegms," "maxims," "proverbs," or "aphorisms," wisdom or good sense lies at the heart of these brief statements about human behavior. Unlike ordinary assertions of fact or opinion, which usually concern themselves with particular rather than universal experience, the apothegm means to assert a universal truth; it means to be complete and authoritative in its brevity and wit.

The examples in this section include traditional maxims, such as those Franklin collected in the eighteenth century for *Poor Richard's Almanack* or Duc François de La Rochefoucauld collected in the seventeenth century for his *Reflexions ou sentences et maximes morales*, or *Maxims*. We have also included two examples of countermaxims, apothegms that run contrary to conventional wisdom—what William Blake called *Proverbs of Hell* and what Ambrose Bierce included in his *Devil's Dictionary*. And, to give students a sense of this form as ongoing and relevant, we have selected a few of Mason Cooley's witty modern observations from *City Aphorisms*. These examples should give students a chance to think about the rhetorical power of a single sentence, to analyze the workings of brief, tightly crafted sentences, and to try writing their own modern-day apothegms.

Questions from the NR10

1. Many apothegms represent common sense or conventional wisdom—but stated in clever, unconventional form. Choose several examples that you think represent common sense, and explain why you find their form interesting or appealing.
2. Some apothegms represent unconventional wisdom or even advice contrary to common sense. Choose several examples of this sort, and explain what alternative truth they mean to articulate.
3. What makes an apothegm memorable? Choose one or two examples that you remember from your reading (or perhaps from childhood) and analyze the features that make it easily recollected.
4. Try writing several apothegms. Which features of this form are difficult? Which easy?
5. Choose an apothegm with which you agree, and write an essay explaining why it represents good advice. Alternatively, choose one with which you disagree, and write an essay in which you explain why it is incorrect or deceptive.

Analytical Considerations

1. Using the selections from Franklin and La Rochefoucauld, ask students which apothegms they have heard or read before, how they learned them, and why they think these apothegms have stayed current in the American (or Western) consciousness. What belief or truth do these apothegms represent? You might then ask why other apothegms have disappeared or become disused.

2. You may want to assign the apothegms in chronological rather than in the current alphabetical order. If you do, you might ask how and why the later writers, such as Blake and Bierce, take the form of the apothegm to invert or counter conventional wisdom. What advantages does a form associated with wisdom have for these countercultural writers?

3. Spend some time considering Ambrose Bierce's definitions, perhaps by looking up definitions in a conventional dictionary and comparing them with Bierce's, perhaps by analyzing his extended definitions (e.g., *cemetery*, *Christian*, *platitude*, *saint*, *valor*) as forms of cultural critique.

4. Analyze the forms of apothegms that students think are memorable. (They will have prepared answers for Question 3, above.) Point out such features as parallel structure ("Love well, whip well"), contrast ("Romance is tempetuous. Love is calm."), metaphorical language ("Let thy vices die before thee" or "An empty bag cannot stand upright"), irony ("God heals, and the doctor takes the fees"), and qualification ("Three may keep a secret, if two of them are dead"). Then ask students to try writing apothegms by using one or more of these features.

5. If you have read selections from the "Parables" section, ask students about the differences between these forms—the one that sums up truth in a brief statement, the other that tells a story to capture that truth.

Suggested Writing Assignments

1. Write two or three aphorisms, either in imitation of one of the writers in this section or as counterstatements to the apothegms of one writer.

2. Read one of the parables beginning on p. 1081 of *The Norton Reader*. Write an apothegm that, in your view, sums up the truth of the parable.

HISTORY

HENRY DAVID THOREAU

The Battle of the Ants

The Norton Reader, p. 762; Shorter Edition, p. 414

Taken from the chapter in *Walden* titled "Brute Neighbors," "The Battle of the Ants" is not so much history as natural history. Yet, because Thoreau alludes to historical battles and imitates the conventions of history writing, this brief account provides an opportunity for discussing what constitutes a historical event and how a historical style of writing gives status to some events—and not to others. The battle Thoreau describes would not normally be considered historical: it is, after all, only a struggle between two species of ants. But Thoreau's account leads us to ponder how the human struggles called "wars" become history—is it because historians record their maneuvers in detail, praise their leaders and soldiers, and treat their outcomes as decisive? Thoreau potentially subverts this traditional approach to history by suggesting that "history" is created by historians and that the events they present as "historical" attain this status in large part because we accept the conventions of their style.

Questions from NR10

1. Thoreau uses the Latin word *bellum* to describe the battle of the ants and follows it with a reference to the Myrmidons, the soldiers of Achilles in Homer's *Iliad*. Locate additional examples of this kind of allusion. How does it work?
2. Ordinarily we speak of accounts of natural events as "natural history" and accounts of human events as "history." How does Thoreau, in this selection, blur the distinction? To what effect?
3. Look up a description of the behavior of ants in a book by one of the entomologists Thoreau refers to or in another scientific text. Compare the scientist's style with Thoreau's. Take another event in nature and describe it twice, once in scientific and once in allusive language. Or, write an essay in which you describe and analyze the differences between the scientist's style and Thoreau's.

Analytical Considerations

1. In the long first paragraph Thoreau alludes to two well-known wars: the battles recorded in Homer's *Iliad* and the American Revolution, particularly the battles of Lexington and Concord (where the shot heard round the world was fired). What effect does Thoreau intend? By comparing the battle of the ants to classical Greek and American wars, he writes a form of mock heroic that both elevates the actions of the ants and paradoxically deflates the warlike actions of men.

2. This passage comes from a chapter in Thoreau's *Walden* titled "Brute Neighbors." How does the comparison alluded to in the first paragraph, between the fighting ants and human warriors, amplify the meaning of that title?

3. Why does Thoreau describe the wounds of the ants in such detail? You might think of his description as an example of natural history as well as an imitation of historical writing.

4. In the final paragraph Thoreau alludes to American and European entomologists, also called natural historians. Thoreau's style in this paragraph, however, is not that of a scientist but is a parody of the historian's. Why? (For a stylistic comparison, you might look at Alexander Petrunkevitch's "The Spider and the Wasp" in the section on "Nature and the Environment" (NR 630, SE 340).

5. What significance might there be in that Thoreau, at the end of this selection, dates the battle of the ants as occurring five years before the passage of Webster's Fugitive-Slave Bill? In Thoreau's mind, what kind of historical event seems to be genuinely significant?

Suggested Writing Assignments

1. Read an account of the battles of Lexington and Concord (where Thoreau lived); then write an essay analyzing the section of Thoreau's account that alludes to these battles, with attention to how Thoreau's fellow citizens might have responded to his allusions.

2. Look up a description of the behavior of ants in a book by one of the entomologists Thoreau refers to or in another scientific textbook. What are the conventions of scientific description? Why do you think scientists adopt them? Write an essay comparing the style of the scientist with Thoreau's.

BARBARA TUCHMAN

"This Is the End of the World": The Black Death

The Norton Reader, p. 765; Shorter Edition, p. 417

Barbara Tuchman's account of the Black Death, a chapter from her book *A Distant Mirror: The Calamitous Fourteenth Century* (1978), is a brilliant, justly renown re-creation of a famous historical event. Tuchman describes the movement of the disease from central Asia through Europe; creates statistical data to convey its enormous impact on European society; records human responses to the plague, from the horribly selfish to the literally saintly; and explores various medieval explanations for the cause and meaning of the plague. For many students, this essay will represent a classic—and the best— example of narrative history, for Tuchman is a master of its conventions and a skilled practitioner.

Questions from the NR10

1. Why does Tuchman begin with the account of the Genoese trading ships?
2. What ways does Tuchman find to group related facts together—in other words, what categories does she develop? Suggest other categories that Tuchman might have used in arranging her facts. What would she have gained or lost by using such categories?
3. Can you determine a basis for Tuchman's decision sometimes to quote a source, sometimes to recount it in her own words?
4. Write a brief account of a modern disaster, based on research from several sources.

Analytical Considerations

1. For many students, Tuchman's "'This Is the End of the World'" will seem more like "history" than the other selections in this section. Why? What features of her writing signal that this is history?
2. At some point in the discussion of Tuchman's chapter ask students what facts about the Black Death they remember best. Then consider why they remember them, what techniques in Tuchman's rendering make them memorable.
3. Tuchman begins with a date, October 1347, and initially proceeds in chronological order. At what point does chronology cease to organize the chapter? What other organization supplants it?
4. Ask students to summarize what each section of the essay does and how Tuchman moves from section to section.
5. In the final two sections (beginning "Ignorance of the cause" [paragraph 28] and "To the people at large" [paragraph 34]) Tuchman explores various explanations that medieval thinkers gave for the plague: the scientific and the religious. Ask students which they consider more authoritative—and why. Do contemporary thinkers—or some of them—still use religious explanations? Of the same sort as medieval thinkers?
6. Tuchman quotes an account left by Brother John Clyn of Kilkenny, Ireland, who kept a record of what happened lest "things which should be remembered perish with time and vanish from the memory of those who come after us" (paragraph 11). Discuss this statement as a motive for writing history: how important do students think it was and/or still is? Are there other motives for writing history as well?
7. Read Stephen Jay Gould's "The Terrifying Normalcy of AIDS" (NR 727, SE 398). In what ways is our reaction to this twentieth-century plague similar to the fourteenth-century response to the Black Death? In what ways is it different? You might approach these questions by asking students to consider the purposes that Tuchman and Gould have for writing and how these purposes influence their selection and presentation of material.

Suggested Writing Assignments

1. Has human nature changed since the Middle Ages? Do we still respond to disaster in the same ways? Write an essay in which you address these questions by using details from Tuchman's account and from a recent disaster you have witnessed and/or read about.

2. Tuchman gives us the medieval explanations for the spread of bubonic plague. Do research on the topic and write a modern explanation for its spread.

3. Consult one of the sources Tuchman cites at the end of her essay and analyze how Tuchman uses it. What does she quote? What does she paraphrase? What does she summarize? Write an essay in which you consider how she shapes her material.

4. Read another account of the Black Death in an encyclopedia or a history textbook. Compare that account with Tuchman's, trying to address this question: What does Tuchman hope to achieve in her account of this fourteenth-century event?

5. Write an essay in response to Analytical Consideration 6, above, using this and other essays in the "History" section as evidence.

Cherokee Memorials

The Norton Reader, p. 776; Shorter Edition, p. 428

The Cherokee Memorials of 1829 are a primary source for the history of the Cherokee Nation and the history of the United States' relations with the indigenous population of North America. Like all such documents, they require interpretation and, for interpretation, a context. We cannot but read the "Cherokee Memorials" ironically, certain that their eloquence failed to move the Congress of the United States. See the "Authors" section for the particulars of their context: the discovery of gold in Georgia, the role of President Andrew Jackson in removing the Cherokees, the names of the leaders of the Cherokee Council (the presumed authors of this document), and the aftermath of the Cherokee Memorials—the forced removal of 12,000 Cherokees in 1838–39 to what is now Oklahoma and the forced march along what is known as the "Trail of Tears" that killed one-third of them. What we cannot know—neither the document nor its context will tell us—is whether its Cherokee authors believed in their rhetoric or just adopted it as a persuasive strategy.

Analytical Considerations

1. Identify passages in which the Cherokee memorialists characterize themselves, their land, the Congress of the United States, and the history of their relations with the United States. Which can we assume represent their true sense of things, which seem suspect as rhetoric?

2. "By the will of our Father in Heaven, the Governor of the whole world, the red man of America has become small, and the white man great and renowned" (paragraph 2). Characterize this account of historical causation. Do you think the "Father in Heaven" they refer to is the Christian God?

3. The Cherokee memorialists are themselves interpreters of historical documents, that is, treaties. Explain the logic of their interpretation.
4. Imagine yourself a member of Congress reading the "Memorials" addressed to you. What might your response be?
5. Do you think the Cherokee rhetoric is dated? Imagine, for example, a similar petition written today. What passages would be eliminated or toned down? Why?

Suggested Writing Assignments

1. Write a request to someone for something. Make at least some statements you don't believe but think the person to whom the request is addressed will respond favorably to . Then provide a context: write a brief analysis of who the person is, what you decided to say, and why you thought it would work.
2. Do research on the Trail of Tears. Either describe how this context affects your interpretation of the "Cherokee Memorials" or, if you locate other Cherokee documents, choose one of them and interpret it.
3. The "Cherokee Memorials" refer to "a sweeping pestilence" (paragraph 2). Do research on this "pestilence" (or pestilences) and write an essay in which you compare it with the Black Death as described by Barbara Tuchman in "'This is the End of the World'" (NR 765, SE 417).

WALT WHITMAN

Death of Abraham Lincoln

The Norton Reader, p. 779

Whitman delivered this piece as a lecture several times—in 1879, 1880, and 1881, between fourteen and sixteen years after the assassination of Lincoln. He then included it in *Specimen Days* (1882), his collection of journal entries, articles, and other writings on the Civil War. In it he re-creates the scene of Lincoln's death with great immediacy: "probably the facts are yet very indefinite in most persons' minds" (paragraph 7), he observes. Whitman himself was not present at the performance of *Our American Cousin*, but his companion Peter Doyle was. According to Whitman, he re-created the event by reading "from my memoranda, written at the time, and revised frequently and finally since" (paragarph 7).

In this essay Whitman asserts the significance of Lincoln's death for the American imagination: Lincoln becomes the great American hero, as great as or even greater than any character in Homer. If you have assigned Whitman's account of the death of Lincoln in the section "Journals" (NR 92), you may want to compare the journal entry, written two days after the assassination, with this later, retrospective account.

Questions from the NR10

1. Whitman delivered this piece as a lecture. What features suggest a lecture? How might it have differed if he had composed it as an essay to be read rather than a lecture to be heard?
2. The events of the assassination lead Whitman to mention his perception of Lincoln's fondness for the theater. How does he make this observation serve a larger purpose?
3. At the end of this speech, Whitman speaks grandly of Lincoln's significance for far more than the citizens of the United States. As he sees it, what do all these people have in common that allows for Lincoln's more-than-national significance?
4. How does Whitman convey the sense of horror and confusion in the scene when Lincoln is shot? Using some of Whitman's techniques, write an account of a similar scene that produces a strong emotional effect.

Analytical Considerations

1. Note where Whitman shifts from the past to the present tense in the scene when Lincoln is shot. How long does he maintain the present tense? Plainly, he uses it for immediacy; how well does it work?
2. The lecture/essay divides into four parts: Whitman's first view of Lincoln in New York City, his overview of the Civil War, his account of the death of Lincoln, and his assessment of its significance. As a follow-up to Question 1 (above), ask several students to read aloud one passage from the lecture that they find dramatic. (For most, this passage will be from the third part.) Then ask how they imagine the other parts should be read.
3. Whitman refers to "real history's stage" (paragraph 9) and to "the stage of universal Time" (paragraph 16). Using students' responses to Question 2, above, discuss how Whitman uses the metaphor of history as a drama to re-create the events of April 14, 1865.
4. Whitman suggests that "the grand deaths of the race" (paragraph 18) are the foundation of nationality. Do you agree? Ask students to remember other "grand" American deaths they have lived through or heard about.

Suggested Writing Assignments

1. Write an essay comparing Whitman's account of the death of Lincoln written two days after the assassination, in the section "Journals" (NR 92), and his later account.
2. Write an essay comparing Whitman's account of the Civil War in paragraphs 5 to 7 with H. Bruce Franklin's analysis of the same war (in "From Realism to Virtual Reality: Images of America's Wars" [NR 786, SE 434]) in paragraphs 1 to 13. Why are these accounts different?
3. Whitman never calls the war the "Civil War." Write a brief account of what he does call it—and why.

H. BRUCE FRANKLIN

From Realism to Virtual Reality: Images of America's Wars

The Norton Reader, p. 786; Shorter Edition, p. 434

H. Bruce Franklin, a professor of literature, has written several books on war, including *War Stars: The Superweapon and the American Imagination* (1988). Students may be interested to know that he was fired from Stanford University, despite having tenure, for encouraging students to protest secret military testing on college campuses. (He now teaches at Rutgers University, Newark campus.) They may be asked whether they can guess his attitude toward war from this piece of scholarly writing.

Franklin uses images—photographs particularly, journalistic accounts more generally—to analyze changing attitudes toward American wars. As a pedagogical model, his essay is extremely useful for teaching close reading, not of words but of images. We suggest that for this essay you ask the class to work in small groups, both to analyze Franklin's argument and to find additional images of war that might provide the basis for their own essays—though these suggestions can be adapted for a large class or for individual students.

Questions from the NR10

1. Franklin tells a double story of technological advances in making war and making images. Trace each stage of both narratives. Explain, at each stage, how he links them.
2. Franklin includes seven illustrations in this essay. Explain his choice of each. Are there others he mentions that you wish he had included? Why? (Locating them might be a class project.)
3. Take one of the illustrations in this essay and write an essay in which you offer an alternative interpretation of it as a counterargument to Franklin's interpretation.
4. Franklin includes in his narrative literature (fiction, primarily, but also poetry), films, television, and comic books. How does he present the differences among them? Compare the powers he attributes to words and the powers he attributes to images.
5. Choose a recent United States war (or military action) and reconstruct your sense of it and how you acquired that sense. Locate some of the images you remember and write an essay comparing your memory of them with the images as you see them now. Or, if you had no sense of it, locate some of the important images of it and write an essay comparing how you think you would have seen them then and how you see them now.

Analytical Considerations

1. Divide students into groups, one for each war that Franklin analyzes: the Civil War, the two world wars, Vietnam, and the Gulf War. Ask each group to summarize the basic argument Franklin makes about images from that war.

2. Using the same groups, ask students to do their own analysis of one of the images reproduced in the text. (Students covering World War I and World War II will not find an image in the text; ask them either to analyze the text itself or to find one of the images Franklin discusses, perhaps by viewing a film.) Do they see the same things Franklin sees, or do they see different things?

3. Again in groups, ask students to find additional photographs or images from the same war (see Analytical Consideration 1, above), whether in books, magazines, or films. Ask them to consider whether these images confirm or contradict Franklin's account, and if they find contradictions, what modifications they would make in Franklin's argument.

4. Ask students if they have read Stephen Crane's *The Red Badge of Courage*, Herman Melville's *Billy Budd*, and Mark Twain's *A Connecticut Yankee in King Arthur's Court*. Consider Franklin's assessment of them in paragraphs 9 to 13; probably what he writes about *Billy Budd* is the most controversial.

5. Franklin coins the term *technowar* (paragraph 1); what does he mean by it? What recent wars (or military actions) are *technowars*? Discuss the concept of a *technowar*.

6. Compare what Franklin and Michael J. Arlen, in "The Tyranny of the Visual" (NR 1067) in the section called "Literature and the Arts," have to say about the power of images.

Suggested Writing Assignments

1. Find an image or photograph of war not discussed by Franklin and write your own analysis of the meanings it projects. If relevant, comment on whether your analysis confirms or contradicts his.

2. Write a counterargument to one of Franklin's analyses of a photograph, suggesting alternative interpretations of it.

3. Choose a recent image of a war not involving the United States and analyze it carefully to see if you think it reflects patterns or themes that Franklin discusses. If not, explain why.

4. Read the novel by Stephen Wright that Franklin discusses, *Meditations in Green* (paragraph 27), or look at the film *The Deer Hunter* that he discusses (paragraphs 29–32). Write an essay in which you consider what responses to the Vietnam War you think one or the other asks for and how it tries to evoke them.

HANNAH ARENDT

Denmark and the Jews

The Norton Reader, p. 802; Shorter Edition, p. 449

Perhaps the most important theme of Hannah Arendt's *Eichmann in Jerusalem: A Report on the Banality of Evil* (1963), from which this selection comes, is that of the ordinariness of evil. Adolf Eichmann regarded his role in the infamous Final Solution to the Jewish question as that of a functionary. At his trial in Jerusalem, he most regretted having been ill-used by superiors. According to Arendt, his inability to acknowledge personal blame is not unusual or abnormal, for evil apparently loses its character as evil when it is assimilated into the normal routines of living and working.

Arendt sets her account of the Danish reaction to the Nazi program of destruction against this background: she embeds history in argument. The Danes, she contends, provide the only case we know of in which the Nazis met open resistance to their treatment of the Jews. This point (and others in *Eichmann in Jerusalem*) have been criticized by some readers. Arendt fills her narrative with facts and statistics, which lend authority to her account. But her controversial interpretation does not concern what happened, but why. Whether or not one wholly accepts them, her views—about the Danes, about the ordinariness of evil—provide engaging points for discussion.

Analytical Considerations

1. What special force does Arendt's expression "the banality of evil" have?
2. "Denmark and the Jews" is partially narrative in organization. Does the narrative have a climax? Where does it occur?
3. Arendt spells out the meaning she gives her narrative: "One is tempted to recommend the story as required reading in political science for all students who wish to learn something about the enormous power potential inherent in non-violent action and in resistance to an opponent possessing vastly superior means of violence" (paragraph 2). What is the effect of being told the implications of the narrative before actually reading it?
4. Does Arendt regard her subject as primarily moral, ethical, or historical? What elements of "Denmark and the Jews" support your answer?
5. The tendency to think the Danes heroes seems an inevitable effect of this essay. Is there evidence that Arendt tries to temper this effect, to make us see them as something other or less than heroes? (This question should not imply seeing them as villains.)
6. Read this essay carefully for evidence of Arendt's bitterness about the history and fate of European Jews. What are her chief means of controlling this bitterness? Does her controlled bitterness make this essay more or less effective?

7. Evaluate the final paragraph of "Denmark and the Jews." Which statements are matters of fact? Which are matters of interpretation? How well does she prepare for these interpretations in preceding sections of this selection?
8. Why does Arendt describe the Danes as a nation or a group instead of focusing on individuals? In view of her purpose, is there a rhetorical advantage to describing them this way? For a sense of the difference focusing on individuals makes, see Amitav Ghosh, "The Ghosts of Mrs. Gandhi" (NR 806, SE 454).

Suggested Writing Assignments

1. If Nazis like Eichmann exhibit the ordinariness of evil, then the Danes exhibit the ordinariness of good. Drawing from your experience, observation, and reading, write an essay in which you support, refute, or qualify this assertion.
2. Write an essay comparing Arendt's ideas on resistance based on principled and non-violent action with Martin Luther King, Jr.'s in "Letter from Birmingham Jail" (NR 887, SE 503) and with Amitav Ghosh's in "The Ghosts of Mrs. Gandhi" (NR 806, SE 454).
3. Using "Denmark and the Jews" as a basis, construct a code of conduct for non-violent resistance to any unjust authority or unjust policy.
4. Write a historical narrative of some person or group who in some vital or violent controversy held to a principle and proved to be exceptional.

AMITAV GHOSH

The Ghosts of Mrs. Gandhi

The Norton Reader, p. 806; Shorter Edition, p. 454

Amitav Ghosh introduces himself early on in this essay: in 1984—when the violence against the Sikhs that he describes occurred—he was twenty-eight, had completed a doctorate at Oxford University two years earlier, and was teaching at Delhi University and trying to write a novel (paragraph 3). His degree was in anthropology, and he has since written and published a novel as well as several other books. He waited to write about the events of 1984 because, as he puts it, acts in opposition to violence are undramatic and hard to write about (paragraph 85); his essay was published in 1995. He was probably stimulated to write by religious and ethnic violence ("cleansing") elsewhere: it can hardly be accidental that he concludes his essay with a quotation from Dzevad Karahasan, a Bosnian writer who chronicled the siege of Sarajevo (paragraph 86).

Unlike Hannah Arendt (in "Denmark and the Jews" [NR 802, SE 449], who describes the Danes' opposition to violence collectively, Ghosh offers a series of vignettes: the woman on the bus; Mrs. Sen, Hari's mother; the Bawas's cook. Ghosh, as a presence, a participant even, is able to describe actions that would have gone unrecorded were it not for him. He had to do research, however, to inform himself about their context; see, for example his interview with Veena Das, a sociologist (paragraph 36). Arendt depended on records; the individuals she focuses on are prominent public figures such as Werner Best, the German SS commander in Denmark.

Questions from the NR10

1. Throughout this essay Ghosh interweaves personal history with Indian national history. Make an outline or flow chart that shows how this interweaving works.
2. Near the end of the essay Ghosh contends, "Writers don't join crowds" (paragraph 83), yet he meditates on the responsibility of the writer to intervene in political events. What position does he finally reach about the individual writer's relation to—and responsibility in—history?
3. If you have participated in a political or historical event of some importance, write about your experience, interweaving "personal" and "public" as Ghosh does. You may want to do some research about the event to learn more about the public record of its history.

Analytical Considerations

1. When the marchers, particularly the women among them, confronted the rioters, the rioters dispersed, "confused" (paragraph 77). Why?
2. Ghosh wonders if authors who write about violence fail "to find a form—or a style or a voice or a plot—that could accommodate both violence *and* the civilized, willed response to it" (paragraph 84). Ghosh's memoir accommodates civilized responses to violence; does it sufficiently accommodate violence?
3. When Ghosh joined the march to confront the rioters, they shouted, as he puts it, "hoary Gandhian staples of peace and brotherhood from half a century before" (paragraph 72). For another view of these "hoary Gandhian staples" see Martin Luther King, Jr.'s "Letter from Birmingham Jail" (NR 887, SE 503).

Suggested Writing Assignments

1. According to Ghosh, "repugnance" is the "commonest response to violence" (paragraph 85). Do you agree? Write an essay drawing upon your experience, observation, and reading to answer this question.
2. Ghosh, to his surprise, found his involvement in public life effective and meaningful. Are you involved in public life? Write an essay in which you consider your own involvement—or lack of involvement—in public life, drawing upon Ghosh's essay insofar as it suits your purposes.
3. Do research on the partition of India and Pakistan in 1947 and the violence accompanying it, and write an essay in which you assess Ghosh's belief that it "could never happen again" (paragraph 38). Is his response to that episode in Indian national history reasonable?

GEORGE WOODCOCK

The Tyranny of the Clock

The Norton Reader, p. 816

George Woodcock, a Canadian poet, essayist, and anarchist, argues that the clock, like the machine, has led to the mechanization of human life and to various negative consequences, including ruined health and shortened lives. The essay is obviously anticapitalist, treating the clock (sometimes too simply) as a tool of capitalist factory owners. Encourage students to consider and challenge Woodcock's ideas. His well-written, clearly presented ideas should provoke them into thinking about what life was like before the clock and how much their lives, under its influence, are governed by it.

Questions from the NR10

1. Woodcock begins by contrasting people who live according to "cyclical" time with those subject to "mechanical" time. What groups of people fall into each category? What does he imply by this contrast?
2. Using the information supplied by Woodcock, write a brief account of the development of clocks in the mode of what E. H. Carr, in "The Historian and His Facts" (NR 826), calls "scissors-and-paste" history (paragraph 18). What interpretations does Woodcock give this information? Does this information allow for other interpretations?
3. Both Woodcock and H. Bruce Franklin, in "From Realism to Virtual Reality: Images of America's Wars" (NR 786, SE 434), depict technical advances as inimical to human life. Write an essay in which you compare the nature of the cases they make and their effectiveness in making them.
4. Write a personal narrative about an experience that illustrates "the tyranny of the clock." Or, alternatively, write a personal narrative about an experience in which a clock or clocks contributed to your freedom.

Analytical Considerations

1. This essay works, at least in part, by comparison. Using the responses to Question 1, above, ask students to discuss how many paragraphs after the first two work by comparison and why this technique is effective.
2. In addition to comparison, this essay is also organized by chronology. Map out the key historical events or moments that Woodcock writes about and consider why he chooses them.
3. Woodcock enumerates the effects of clocks on human life in paragraph 7 and following. List, in the order he enumerates them, those effects. Why has he arranged these effects in this order?
4. Woodcock blames the clock for modern ills—including increased alcoholism, ruined health, hurried lives, and the general demoralization of the working class (paragraphs 10–11). Ask students if they think he attributes too much agency to the clock and oversimplifies modern history. Ask for counterexamples or other possible interpretations of the same phenomena.

Suggested Writing Assignments

1. Do research on the development of clocks, beginning with one detail mentioned in the essay. Write an expanded account of that detail and its effects, positive and negative.

2. In concluding his essay, Woodcock suggests that a truly "sane and free society" would not accept domination by the clock or any other man-made machine (paragraph 14). Do you agree that the clock represents a "tyranny" that a free society should resist? Write an argumentative essay in which you agree or disagree with Woodcock's position, using evidence from your experience, observation, and reading.

3. If we pay attention to the historian, as E. H. Carr, in "The Historian and His Facts" (NR 826), advises, what can we learn about Woodcock's allegiances and commitments? Do research on him and write a brief account of how his allegiances and commitments seem to influence his interpretation of the development of clocks.

FRANCES FITZGERALD

Rewriting American History

The Norton Reader, p. 820; Shorter Edition, p. 463

Frances FitzGerald is a talented journalist, popularly known for *Fire in the Lake*, an account of the Vietnam War. This essay, "Rewriting American History," is one of three parts of a long essay that appeared serially in the *New Yorker* in the winter of 1979 and was later included in her book *America Revised*. In this part, primarily, she compares American history textbooks of the 1950s and the 1970s. You will want to ask students if American history textbooks changed again in the 1980's and 1990's; see Question 2, below. If the students in your class vary in age, the discussion will be enriched by their recollections across decades.

Interesting in its own right, FitzGerald's comparison leads to something even more interesting: a general consideration of the nature of history as a discipline, which accounts for changes in history—in the sense of history as a text—and in our understanding of history—in the sense of history as historical events.

Questions from the NR10

1. What differences does FitzGerald find between the American history textbooks of the 1950s and those of the 1970s? In what ways—according to what she states or implies—have they been improved? Does she see any changes for the worse?

2. FitzGerald's *America Revised* was published in 1979, and textbooks, she argues, change rapidly (paragraph 15). Have American history textbooks changed since the late 1970s, and, if so, in what ways? What do you remember of the American history textbooks you used in school—and when

did you use them? What kind of American history textbooks are being used today? On your own or in a group, write a brief essay updating FitzGerald.

3. By "rewriting," FitzGerald does not mean changing the facts of American history. What is the relationship between the facts of history and history textbooks?

4. FitzGerald says that in the new texts "the word 'progress' has been re-placed by the word 'change'" (paragraph 8). Write an essay in which you consider the difference between these two words and the changes the replacement of one by the other reflects.

Analytical Considerations

1. Ask students to summarize FitzGerald's essay in a sentence or two; then ask several students to read their summaries aloud. From the similarities and differences, begin a discussion about the points most easily grasped, those less easily grasped, and why.

2. What is FitzGerald's understanding of "history"? Why does she think human beings need to create history?

3. FitzGerald relies mainly on the mode of comparison (and contrast) to show how American history has been "rewritten." By focusing on two para-graphs in her essay, perhaps the one beginning "Poor Columbus!" (para-graph 4) and the one beginning "The political diversity" (paragraph 10), ask students to discuss how comparison works.

4. Analyze any single section of "Rewriting American History" to show how FitzGerald defines by example. Possibilities include the section on the political diversity of textbooks today and the section on the physical appearance of textbooks today.

5. If we can't know what *really* happened, then why study history? Does FitzGerald's essay imply that history presents us with relative rather than absolute knowledge? If so, why do we study history?

6. Have students read Katha Pollitt's "Does a Literary Canon Matter?" (NR 1029, SE 584) in "Literature and the Arts." Can they locate the equiva-lents for American history of the conservative, liberal, and radical (or ultraradical) positions Pollitt describes for the literary canon? Fitzgerald should provide enough information; some students may know about the recent controversy concerning national guidelines for an American history curriculum.

Suggested Writing Assignments

1. Choose an event from American history with which you are familiar—either one that FitzGerald mentions or one that you know well. Write an essay in which you compare its presentation in three textbooks, each writ-ten during a different decade; be certain to select texts written for the same grade level.

2. Choose an event from American history with which you are familiar—either one that FitzGerald mentions or one that you know well. Write an essay in which you compare its presentation in three textbooks, each written during the 1990s; be certain to select texts written for the same grade level.

3. To what extent do history textbooks, or any other history books, present "truths"? Use your own ideas as well as ideas from other writers in this section to address this question.

4. The process of rewriting American history has taken away some of its romance and myth. Write an essay in which you consider whether that is good, bad, or both.

5. Read Frances FitzGerald's *America Revised* (1979), and write an essay in which you discuss one or more issues she lays out in the rest of her study. Does she take positions on them? On what kind of evidence? According to what principles?

6. Do research about the recent controversy concerning national guidelines for an American history curriculum, and write an essay about it. You may want to consider the extent to which FitzGerald, in 1979, laid out issues that are still debated today.

EDWARD HALLETT CARR

The Historian and His Facts

The Norton Reader, p. 826

Edward Hallett Carr's *What Is History?* (1961), a classic in the field of historiography, was originally delivered as the George Macaulay Trevelyan Lectures at Cambridge University in 1961. "The Historian and His Facts," Carr's first lecture, is also the first chapter of the volume; other chapters include "Society and the Individual," "History, Science, and Morality," "Causation in History," "History as Progress," and "The Widening Horizon." Forty years later, "The Historian and His Facts" would be more accessible had Carr revised his lectures for publication with an eye to, if not posterity, at least a wider audience: while the history faculty and students in attendance at his lecture would not have been fazed by his mention of many historians in passing, today readers may well be. The historians he mentions have been annotated; you may want to ask students to list them by century and to guess, by the amount of space Carr gives each, which are more important, which less important. How do they know, for example, that R. G. Collingwood (paragraphs 13–14) is more important than Dr. Kitson Clark (paragraph 5)? (The gingerbread vendor's being kicked to death by an angry mob is probably a historical fact more because of Carr's second mention of him than because of Clark's first.)

If, as Carr asserts, "nineteenth-century historians were generally indifferent to the philosophy of history" (paragraph 12), so too are twentieth-century historians: they would rather be doing research and writing history than theorizing about historiography, that is, the study of historical writing (as opposed to the study of history itself). Carr's philosophy of history is, in application, eminently pragmatic and commonsensical. It is, however, carefully articulated and its theoretical premises laid bare; for these reasons, *What Is History?* is a classic.

In addition, "The Historian and His Facts" illustrates the classical rhetoric of synthesis. With the kind permission of Charles Kay Smith (see his *Styles and Structures* [1974], especially chapter 13), here is a condensed version of Carr's analysis: Carr presents the nineteenth-century assumption that history is a series of self-evident inductions based on all available facts, as a thesis; the twentieth-century assumption that history has no objective facts but consists rather of interpretation, as an antithesis; and, rejecting both, the assertion that history is a tension or process of interaction between fact and interpretation, as a synthesis.

Questions from the NR10

1. Carr begins with a question, "What is history?", that he repeats several times during his essay to divide it into sections. Mark the sections, describe what Carr argues in each, and explain how each relates to the argument of the sections that precede and follow.
2. This essay began as a lecture. How do the repetitions of "What is history?" enhance oral comprehension?
3. Carr's answer to "What is history?" comes at the end of his essay in the form of a definition. Could he have offered this definition at the beginning of the essay? Why or why not?
4. How does Carr distinguish between "a mere fact about the past" and "a fact of history" (paragraph 5)?
5. Imagine yourself about to write a short historical essay on a recent local event. You may choose this semester's English class. Working on your own or in a group, list a number of facts (about the class) and mark those that will be mere facts, those that will be facts of history. What principles informed your decisions?
6. Read one of the historians represented in this section of *The Norton Reader* and discover what you can about him or her. Then write an analysis of how this historian, in Collingwood's terms, is concerned "neither with 'the past by itself' nor with 'the historian's thought about it by itself,' but with 'the two things in their mutual relations'" (paragraph 14).

Analytical Considerations

1. Locate the historians Carr mentions and list them by century; then assess which are the more important ones. (This exercise can be divided by centuries and assigned to different groups of students. It can also lead to the writing assignment suggested in Question 6, above.)
2. How does Carr define "history" in "The Historian and His Facts"? Is his definition compatible with that of Frances FitzGerald in "Rewriting American History" (NR 820, SE 463)?
3. If we can't know what *really* happened, then why study history? What, according to Carr, are the dangers of "the Collingwood view of history" (paragraph 19)? How does he confront them?
4. How does Carr develop and support his thesis, antithesis, and synthesis in "The Historian and His Facts"?
5. One distinguishing feature of Carr's essay is his use of metaphor. Ask students where and how he uses it: e.g., the fish market metaphor, theological

metaphors, biblical metaphors. What are the effects of his metaphorical language? What, if any, other historians in this section use metaphor?

6. Carr describes how, when he writes, reading and writing are simultaneous and inseparable (paragraph 21). For students they are probably sequential. Ask students to consider the virtues of Carr's method and the potential flaws of theirs.

Suggested Writing Assignments

1. Write an essay of definition for an important and disputed term, following the thesis-antithesis-synthesis pattern used by Carr in "The Historian and His Facts."
2. Write an essay about Frances FitzGerald's "Rewriting American History" (NR 820, SE 463) as a response to Carr.
3. Write an essay comparing FitzGerald's and Carr's senses of "history."
4. Respond to the question "What is history?" in an essay of your own.

GEORGE ORWELL

Shooting an Elephant

The Norton Reader, p. 842; Shorter Edition, p. 471

"Shooting an Elephant" is a classic example of an author using a personal experience to illuminate an institution or an abstraction: here, the experience of shooting an elephant and the British Raj (the imperial government of India and Burma), or colonialism itself. Orwell carefully and precisely renders setting, action, and character (himself) by developing his responses, feelings, and thoughts with novelistic density. He braids into the narrative the personal dimensions of the experience: "I often wondered whether any of the others grasped that I had done it solely to avoid looking a fool" (paragraph 14). Orwell, whom students are likely to know as the author of *Animal Farm* and *1984*, served in the British police force in Burma after leaving school. The experience heightened his political consciousness.

You may need to remind students that "Shooting an Elephant" is also an essay about how the expectations of others force us to play roles, to behave in ways that we do not choose and to behave as selves other than the selves we think we are, worse selves, as in this essay, and sometimes better selves as well. Orwell, though he does not use the term, is conscious of what we now refer to as the "social construction of reality." Yet, in "Shooting an Elephant," he both affirms and denies it: that is, he presents role-playing as educative. "I perceived in this moment," he writes, "that when the white man turns tyrant it is his own freedom that he destroys" (paragraph 7).

Questions from the NR10

1. Why did Orwell shoot the elephant? Account for the motives that led him to shoot. Then categorize them as, perhaps, personal motives, circumstantial motives, social motives, or political motives. Is it easy to assign his motives to categories? Why or why not?
2. In this essay the proportion of narrative to analysis is high. Mark which paragraphs contain which and note, in particular, how much analysis Orwell places in the middle of the essay. What are the advantages and disadvantages of having it there rather than at the beginning or the end of the essay?
3. Facts ordinarily do not speak for themselves. How does Orwell present his facts to make them speak in support of his analytic points? Look, for example, at the death of the elephant (paragraphs 11 to 13).
4. Write an essay in which you present a personal experience that illuminates a larger issue: schooling, or affirmative action, or homelessness, or law enforcement, or taxes, or some other local or national issue.

Analytical Considerations

1. Pose Question 1, above, again to demonstrate with reference to the text the dense rendering of Orwell's narrative and how it is done.
2. How does Orwell reconcile social construction and individual freedom?
3. Ask students to consider Orwell's role-playing (and their own) with reference to Willard Gaylin's "What You See Is the Real You" (NR 676) in "Ethics." How would Orwell respond to Gaylin?

Suggested Writing Assignments

1. Rewrite Orwell's "Shooting an Elephant" from the point of view of one of the Burmese.
2. Write an essay in which you consider at least two instances of your own serious (rather than trivial) role-playing, both of worse and of better selves. Is role-playing always educative?

JONATHAN SWIFT

A Modest Proposal

The Norton Reader, p. 848; Shorter Edition, p. 477

"A Modest Proposal" is often anthologized as a brilliant example of sustained irony. It is also shocking: you may want to ask students to read Samuel Clemens's "Advice to Youth" (NR 673, SE 363), in the "Ethics" section, to contrast the tameness of his irony with the savagery of Swift's. Swift violates one of our strongest and most universally held prohibitions, the prohibition against eating human flesh; Clemens merely upsets a prohibition against dishonoring fathers and mothers, a prohibition most of us upset frequently. Moreover, Swift disquietingly juxtaposes the reasonable voice of his putative author (or invented persona) and his horrifying proposals, horrifying to us as readers but apparently not horrifying to the proposer. The author's "modest proposal" can perhaps be entertained as logically consistent. But because it engages feeling and morality, it is indefensible. Students need to see that Swift's juxtaposition of reasonableness and horror is ironic: while the putative author of "A Modest Proposal" says one thing, Swift means another.

You can say something about Irish poverty in 1729, when Swift published "A Modest Proposal," and its historical causes. Irony over time is problematic. You will want to have students look at paragraphs 29 and 30, Swift's "other expedients," which will suggest some of the things Swift's audience knew that we no longer know. You may also want to remind them that, had Swift been anxious to prevent a literal reading of "A Modest Proposal," he could have included these expedients earlier; they are, after all, the remedies that a "reasonable" Swift would himself have proposed.

Questions from the NR10

1. Identify examples of the reasonable voice of Swift's authorial persona, such as the title of the essay itself.
2. Look, in particular, at instances in which Swift's authorial persona proposes shocking things. How does the style of the "Modest Proposal" affect its content?
3. Verbal irony consists of saying one thing and meaning another. At what point in this essay do you begin to suspect that Swift is using irony? What additional evidence of irony can you find?
4. Write a modest proposal of your own in the manner of Swift to remedy a real problem; that is, propose an outrageous remedy in a reasonable voice.

Analytical Considerations

1. Ask students to describe how Swift's putative author characterizes himself by his style. If style is the man, what kind of man are we listening to?
2. Although Swift's primary concerns are economic, issues of population control also run through "A Modest Proposal." What do the author's proposals indicate about his views of sexuality and reproduction? Can we infer Swift's proposals and his views of sexuality and reproduction from them? You may want to suggest ways in which time (and changing sexual and reproductive practices) destabilize Swift's irony with respect to population control more than with respect to economic policy.

Suggested Writing Assignments

1. Write an essay in which you consider your responses to "A Modest Proposal." Some readers have found Swift's irony too shocking, so strong as to detract from his really quite sensible proposals for reform. Does his literary form, for you, subvert his purposes or serve them? How and why?
2. Look up a brief proposal written by a contemporary of Swift, Daniel Defoe, in 1702, "The Shortest Way with the Dissenters," and also an account of its reception in a biography of Defoe. Write a brief essay on the risks of irony using this information.

KIM PHILLIPS-FEIN

Lotteryville, USA

The Norton Reader, p. 855

Chicago-based Kim Phillips-Fein provides a heavily factual, clear-eyed look at lotteries and their impact on the ghetto, in the context of American gambling throughout the past two centuries. Phillips-Fein's essay has a strong point of view; she has a social point to make. Even so, her essay is heavily data-driven. There is no sentimentality, no attempt at making those in power feel guilty. Instead Phillips-Fein builds her case on comparisons of gambling in the past with lotteries in more affluent areas of Illinois today and, chiefly, on close observation of how lotteries affect poor people's attitudes and behavior.

The lottery itself is not precisely the target of Phillips-Fein's essay, although it seems to be at first. Her larger purpose is to point to the lottery as a symptom of the inequitable distribution of income in present-day America and to its effects upon the poorest citizens.

Note that her viewpoint avoids the easy moralism that would condemn all gambling. She is not even against the concept of crime; she speaks somewhat fondly of the old-time numbers game, which returned a good deal of money to the ghetto itself, in the form of jobs, rents, and payoffs. Her real target is the state-run enterprise that sweeps up lottery money and takes it out of the poor neighborhood for good. Hers is strictly an economic argument, based on what is good or bad for the poor people of this particular part of Chicago.

Questions from the NR10

1. Phillips-Fein begins with the question, "What would you do if you won a million dollars?" Before reading her essay, answer for yourself. After reading, decide whether you more closely resemble the residents of Flossmoor or Posen, Illinois (paragraph 4), and why.
2. After describing how the lottery works and why people buy tickets, Phillips-Fein suggests better ways of using the lottery. What are they? What reasons does she give in support of her ideas?
3. In paragraph 18, Phillips-Fein introduces the concept of the "Total Social Lottery," derived from the British academic Barbara Goodwin. How serious is Phillips-Fein about instituting this sort of lottery? Does she mean it seriously, or is she introducing it ironically, as in Swift's "A Modest Proposal"?
4. Write a letter to the editor in which you agree or disagree with Phillips-Fein's essay, perhaps concentrating on one aspect or proposal and supplying new evidence for your viewpoint.

Analytical Considerations

1. Almost everyone has heard that lotteries are "a tax on the ignorant" (paragraph 10). Phillips takes that phrase and turns it around: "In fact, the lottery is a perfectly rational investment for a person facing a lifetime of drudgery and uncertainty" (paragraph 11). Ask students whether Phillips-Fein's speculative claim makes sense. Is buying one ticket okay? How about twenty? Is there a point at which buying lottery tickets becomes an irrational practice?
2. Is Phillips-Fein's essay a defense of poor lottery players? Imagine some consequences of heavy lottery gambling among the poor.
3. What is the rationale for placing this essay among the essays on politics and government? What seems to be Phillips-Fein's political stance on economic matters?

Suggested Writing Assignments

1. Write an essay telling what students in your college know about lottery playing among their parents' generation and among college-age students.

2. Describe lottery advertising in one particular locality, making an inventory of what the residents see: billboards, signs in stores, ads on television, and so on. Be as detailed as you can about the relationship between advertisements and their intended audience.
3. Write an essay in which you argue why the state should or should not prohibit gambling.

NICCOLÒ MACHIAVELLI

The Morals of the Prince

The Norton Reader, p. 863; Shorter Edition, p. 484

Niccolò Machiavelli, the Florentine whose political treatise *The Prince* was published in 1513, acquired in his time a scandalous reputation: he was "Old Nick" (or Satan), who held the diabolical doctrine that the end justifies the means. His reputation was largely established by the chapters on "The Morals of the Prince" reprinted here. Students should notice how Machiavelli is aware of making a different and controversial case, of writing about the *is*—"the way we really live"—rather than the *ought*—"the way we ought to live" (paragraph 1). Political treatises of Machiavelli's time were ordinarily utopian. Machiavelli's is not, and consequently, as he announces, he has something new to say. Today we might speak of his politics as *realpolitik*, a word derived from German that means a politics based on practical and material, rather than theoretical and ethical, considerations.

You may want to use "The Morals of the Prince" to exemplify shifting boundaries between idealism and realism, realism and cynicism: we can pretty much agree on their definitions, but when we come to apply them, what one person takes to be realistic, another person takes to be cynical. Nevertheless, Machiavelli appears to present his "realistic" argument with the intention of shocking readers. While it may be realistic to discuss the dangers of virtue in a world in which people are "a sad lot, and keep no faith with you" (paragraph 14), it is surely cynical to argue that the appearance of virtue is better than virtue itself. You can call attention to the antitheses in Machiavelli's argument: the qualities in a prince that elicit praise or blame (paragraph 2) and the chapter headings in which he opposes liberality to stinginess, cruelty to clemency, and love to fear. Part of his shock technique depends upon setting up binary oppositions and arguing for the conventionally pejorative term.

Questions from the NR10

1. This selection contains four sections of *The Prince*: "On the Reasons Why Men Are Praised or Blamed—Especially Princes"; "On Liberality and Stinginess"; "On Cruelty and Clemency: Whether It Is Better to Be Loved or Feared"; and "The Way Princes Should Keep Their Word." How, in each section, does Machiavelli contrast the ideal and the real, what he calls "the way we really live and the way we ought to live" (paragraph 1)? Mark some of the sentences in which he arrestingly expresses these contrasts.

2. Rewrite some of Machiavelli's advice to princes less forcibly and shockingly, and more palatably. For example, "Any man who tries to be good all the time is bound to come to ruin among the great number who are not good" (paragraph 1) might be rewritten as "Good men are often taken advantage of and harmed by men who are not good."
3. Describe Machiavelli's view of human nature. How do his views of government follow from it?
4. Machiavelli might be described as a sixteenth-century spin doctor teaching a ruler how to package himself. Adapt his advice to a current figure in national, state, or local politics and write about that figure in a brief essay.

Analytical Considerations

1. One feature of Machiavelli's style is his use of aphorisms, that is, terse formulations of truths and beliefs. You might ask students to gather a number of them and describe how Machiavelli uses them and to what effect or effects. See also the section called "Apothegms" (NR 748).
2. What are Machiavelli's customary sources of examples? How frequently does he use them? How extensively does he explain them? What do they indicate about his audience?
3. Man, in the Renaissance chain of being, stands between beasts and angels. You may want to have students look at paragraphs 14 and 15, in which Machiavelli proposes as models for imitation the fox and the lion. What do these metaphors contribute to his argument?

Suggested Writing Assignments

1. Do library research on the politics of Florence during Machiavelli's life (the way Florentines really lived) and write an essay in which you consider *The Prince* as a response to local conditions.
2. Write an essay defining "Machiavellian" by applying it to and illustrating it with examples from contemporary politics.
3. See Suggested Writing Assignments 2 and 3, below, for the "Declaration of Independence."

THOMAS JEFFERSON

Original Draft of the Declaration of Independence

The Norton Reader, p. 870

and

THOMAS JEFFERSON AND OTHERS

The Declaration of Independence

The Norton Reader, p. 874; Shorter Edition, p. 490

These two drafts of the "Declaration of Independence"—the first, Jefferson's preliminary draft, and the second, the final draft as printed—may provoke students into a fresh reading of a text whose familiarity dulls attention. The preliminary draft is a transcription of a copy in Jefferson's hand (in the Library of Congress), with illegible passages taken from a transcription made by John Adams and missing passages, presumably added later, taken from a copy Jefferson made for George Wythe (in the New York Public Library). We do not know how many drafts and revisions preceded it; we do know that Jefferson consulted with several people, among them Benjamin Franklin and John Adams. This preliminary draft was edited by members of the Second Continental Congress and probably, in large measure, by Jefferson himself.

Students should notice that the three-part structure of the preliminary and final drafts is the same: Jefferson enunciates a series of principles concerning human nature and the function of government, rehearses the offenses against them by George III, and proclaims the political connection between the American colonies and the king of Great Britain dissolved. The structure is derived from the syllogism: a major premise, a minor premise, and a conclusion. The logic is deductive: given the principles—which Jefferson calls "sacred and undeniable" in the preliminary draft, "self-evident" in the final draft—and given the facts, the conclusion follows ineluctably.

These two versions of the "Declaration of Independence" illustrate the final revision procedures of an experienced writer. With his argumentative structure and his particulars in place, Jefferson revises at the paragraph and sentence level. Chiefly he prunes and tightens: he recognizes that he has been somewhat overinclusive in his exemplification, somewhat clumsy in his sentences, and long-winded in using more words than he needs to say what he needs to say. While his language in the final draft is simpler and more direct, his sentence structure, especially with respect to repetition and balance, is more artful. In addition, the inconsistent spelling and punctuation of the preliminary draft have been regularized.

Questions from the NR10

1. The "Declaration of Independence" is an example of deductive argument: Jefferson sets up general principles, details particular instances, and then draws conclusions. Locate the three sections of the "Declaration" in both the original and final drafts. Describe a typical sentence in each section.
2. Locate the general principles (or "truths") that Jefferson sets up in the first section of both the original and final drafts. Mark the language he uses to describe them: for example, he calls them "sacred & undeniable" in the original draft, "self-evident" in the final draft. What kinds of authority does his language appeal to?
3. Stanton, in the "Declaration of Sentiments and Resolutions" (next essay), imitates both the argument and style of the "Declaration of Independence." Where does her declaration diverge from Jefferson's? And to what ends?
4. Write an essay explaining Jefferson's views on the nature of man, the function of government, and the relationship between morality and political life in the "Declaration of Independence." What assumptions are necessary to make these views, as he says in the final draft, "self-evident"?

Analytical Considerations

1. You may want to ask students to work on the first or second sections of the "Declaration of Independence" in the preliminary and final drafts, noting what has been pruned and conjecturing about the reasons for the omissions. This analysis can profitably be done in groups.
2. You may also want to ask them to "modernize" sentences in the final draft with pronounced repetition and balance by loosening both.

Suggested Writing Assignments

1. Jefferson died on July 4, 1826, exactly fifty years after the promulgation of the "Declaration of Independence." In ill health, declining an invitation to travel to Washington to participate in the fiftieth- anniversary celebrations, he wrote of the "Declaration":

> May it [the "Declaration"] be to the world what I believe it will be (to some parts sooner, to others later, but finally to all), the signal of arousing men to burst the chains under which monkish ignorance and superstition had persuaded them to bind themselves, and to assume the blessings and security of self-government. . . . All eyes are opened, or opening to the rights of man. The general spread of the light of science has already laid open to every view the palpable truth, that the mass of mankind has not been born with saddles on their backs, nor a favored few booted and spurred, ready to ride them legitimately by the grace of God.

Write an essay in which you trace the appearance of the ideas Jefferson singles out as important in this letter in the "Declaration of Independence." Does he give them due prominence there?
2. Write a letter to Jefferson from the perspective of today in which you assess the optimism of his letter of 1826. Or do the same in essay form.
3. Write a comparison of Jefferson's positions (in the "Declaration of Independence") and Niccolò Machiavelli's positions (in "The Morals of the Prince" [NR 863, SE 484]) concerning the nature of man, the function of government, and the relationship between morality and political life. What assumptions led them to diverge?
4. Are you a Jeffersonian or a Machiavellian? Explain.
5. Write an argument on a topic of your choice in which you use the three-part structure of a syllogism. Is it possible, for example, to recast the arguments of other essays in this section, such as George Orwell's "Shooting an Elephant" (NR 842, SE 471) or Martin Luther King, Jr.'s "Letter from Birmingham Jail" (NR 887, SE 503) in this mode?

ELIZABETH CADY STANTON

Declaration of Sentiments and Resolutions

The Norton Reader, p. 877; Shorter Edition, p. 494

The first women's rights convention was held at Seneca Falls, New York, July 19–20, 1848. It was called by Elizabeth Cady Stanton, Mary Ann McClintock, Lucretia Mott, and Martha C. Wright. The "Declaration of Sentiments and Resolutions"—or the "Seneca Falls Declaration," as it is often called—is usually attributed to Stanton; she read it at the convention, where, after some emendations, it was adopted. But, according to the *History of Woman Suffrage*, edited by Stanton, Susan B. Anthony, and Matilda Joslyn Gage (1881, reprinted 1969), the genesis of the "Declaration"—and perhaps its writing—was collective: Stanton, McClintock, Mott, and Wright decided "to adopt the historic document [i.e., the "Declaration of Independence"] with some slight changes such as substituting 'all men' for 'King George.'" Students will see how the "Declaration of Sentiments and Resolutions" recapitulates the three-part syllogistic structure of the "Declaration of Independence." They will also see how the language of the first and third sections of the "Declaration of Sentiments" is a paraphrase of the language of the first and third sections of the "Declaration of Independence." They will need to split three paragraphs of the second section of the "Declaration of Sentiments" to come up with the same number of offenses as appear in the second section of the "Declaration of Independence"—eighteen. The collaborators were determined to enumerate at least as many offenses in their declaration as the members of the Second Continental Congress had enumerated in theirs. As George III had been guilty of "absolute Tyranny," so were all men.

Analytical Considerations

1. The "Declaration of Sentiments and Resolutions" imitates the "Declaration of Independence" through quotation and paraphrase—that is, by changing its words. You may want to ask students to mark examples of each.
2. To what ends do Stanton et al. quote and paraphrase the "Declaration of Independence"?
3. How do their ends differ from those of parody, that is, quotation and paraphrase for comedy or ridicule? Louis Carroll's parodies are surefire examples: they are reprinted with originals in *Parodies*, ed. Dwight MacDonald (1960).

Suggested Writing Assignments

1. The "Declaration of Sentiments and Resolutions" concludes with the authors' (and signatories') anticipating "no small amount of misconception, misrepresentation, and ridicule" (paragraph 20). Consult the appendix to volume 4 of the *History of Woman Suffrage* (1881, reprinted 1969), which reprints some contemporary responses to the Seneca Falls Convention. Why was the Convention seen as ridiculous in the nineteenth century? Can it be seen as ridiculous today? Explain.

2. Frederick Douglass participated in the Seneca Falls Convention. Do library research on the role he played and write an essay discussing his role and why he felt betrayed afterward by the women he supported.
3. Do library research on one of the women who organized the Seneca Falls Convention: Mary Ann McClintock, Lucretia Mott, Elizabeth Cady Stanton, or Martha C. Wright. According to the *History of Woman Suffrage* (1881, reprinted 1969):

> While they had felt the insults incident to sex, in many ways, as every proud, thinking woman must, in the laws, religion, and literature of the world, and in the invidious and degrading sentiments and customs of all nations, yet they had not in their own experience endured the coarser forms of tyranny resulting from unjust laws or association with immoral and unscrupulous men, but they had souls large enough to feel the wrongs of others, without being scarified in their own flesh.

Write an essay in which you particularize these generalities with reference to the life of one of the organizers.

ABRAHAM LINCOLN

Second Inaugural Address

The Norton Reader, p. 879

Abraham Lincoln's "Second Inaugural Address" is a piece of ceremonial discourse formal in tone and diction, as required by the occasion. Like Martin Luther King, Jr., Lincoln assumes Christian belief even while pointing out that, although North and South "read the same Bible, and pray to the same God" (paragraph 3), neither has evidence of God's unqualified favor. Lincoln's strategy is to invite reconciliation with, not alienation of, the South while keeping up the resolve of the North in fighting for a just cause.

Analytical Considerations

1. You may want to remind students that Lincoln reviews four years of history in the course of this brief address. What events does he select, and what pattern does he see in them?
2. Lincoln uses three types of rhetorical appeal in this address: logical, emotional, and ethical. Ask students to identify examples of each. Which do they find most effective? Which do they think Lincoln's audience found most effective?
3. While Lincoln tries to speak to both North and South, students probably will not find him hypocritical or slippery. You may want to try arguing that he is, that his presentation of himself as honest and his purpose as single-minded is ethical posturing, in order to force close reading. How, finally, do we determine sincerity?

Suggested Writing Assignments

1. Write an essay in which you compare Lincoln's "Second Inaugural Address" with John F. Kennedy's inaugural address of 1961. Compare both rhetoric, content, and audience.
2. Do library research on the events immediately preceding Lincoln's second term as president and write an essay in which you consider his "Second Inaugural Address" as a response to them.

CARL BECKER

Democracy

The Norton Reader, p. 880; Shorter Edition, p. 496

This passage by Carl Becker appeared in a volume called *Modern Democracy*, published in 1941. The United States did not enter World War II until December 1941, after the Japanese attacked Pearl Harbor. But Becker— and his readers—would have been aware of the threat to European democracies by both Hitler's Germany and Stalin's Russia as a result of the German-Soviet Nonaggression Pact signed in 1939. Becker, choosing from a range of definitions of "democracy," elaborately stipulates the meaning he gives to the term.

Questions from the NR10

1. In this essay Becker carefully defines an abstract term with multiple meanings, *democracy*, using the following strategies: (1) he looks for extreme and paradoxical instances that most people would exclude; (2) he distinguishes between ideal instances "laid away in heaven" (paragraph 2) and real instances; (3) he settles for a common meaning derived "partly from the experience and partly from the aspirations of mankind" (paragraph 2); and (4) he looks at additional instances that provide a test for exclusion and inclusion. How, finally, does he define "democracy"?
2. Machiavelli, in "The Morals of the Prince" (NR 863, SE 484) also draws a contrast between the real and the ideal. What are the particulars of his contrast and Becker's? What is Machiavelli's sense of the relation between the real and the ideal? What is Becker's? What are the differences between them?
3. Guinier, in "The Tyranny of the Majority" (NR 884, SE 498), argues that "majority rule may be perceived as majority tyranny" (paragraph 10). How might Becker include the instances she describes in his definition?
4. Consult a standard desk dictionary for the definition of an abstract term with multiple meanings; you might consider terms such as *generosity, love, sophistication, tolerance, virtue*. Then write your own definition of the term following the strategy Becker uses to define democracy, supplying your own instances.

Analytical Considerations

1. Spend some time on Becker's discussion of definition in paragraph 1. You may want to bring in photocopies of the definitions of "democracy" in an unabridged dictionary or even the *Oxford English Dictionary*. Talk about how dictionaries are made and why, in the case of large abstractions like democracy, stipulative definitions are advisable. Consider this passage from Becker as an extended stipulative definition.

2. Look for evidence of contemporary events in this passage. Because definitions are abstractions from particulars, particulars shape definitions. Or, as Becker concludes, "This I take to be the meaning which history has impressed upon the term democracy as a form of government" (paragraph 3).

3. How would Lani Guinier, in "The Tyranny of the Majority" (NR 883, SE 498), criticize Becker's concept of "the common will," as in: "A democratic government has always meant one in which the citizens, or a sufficient number of them to represent more or less effectively the common will, freely act from time to time, and according to established forms . . . ."? Why does she find "the common will" problematic?

4. If you have given students the parallel writing assignments on Becker and White—Question 3 on E. B. White's "Democracy" (NR 883, SE 498) and Suggested Writing Assignment 2, below—compare the results. Is it possible to succeed in both modes of definition, metaphoric and stipulative? What constitutes success in each mode? What problems does each mode of definition pose?

Suggested Writing Assignments

1. It is possible, Becker indicates, to define actual democratic government as "government of the people, by the politicians, for whatever pressure groups can get their interests taken care of" (paragraph 2). To what extent do you agree with this definition of democratic government? Write an essay in which you express your views of the balance between ideal and actual institutions in this country now. Becker argued for a balance in 1941; would you argue for a tilt to the actual?

2. Using Becker's technique, write a definition of an abstract term; you might consider terms such as *speculation, obedience, fear, argument, charity*.

E. B. WHITE

Democracy

The Norton Reader, p. 882; Shorter Edition, p. 498

In this short essay E. B. White writes, on request (he explains the circumstances in the essay), about a well-worn topic. He makes it fresh by providing a series of examples that function as metaphors, technically as synecdoches, or figures of speech in which a part stands for the whole. He provides images and avoids abstractions. Presumably the War Board, which asked him to write about "The Meaning of Democracy" in 1943 (during World War II), expected a patriotic response. Is White's response patriotic, or is it flip? (Or are these alternatives a false opposition?) Ask students to be explicit about the grounds for their answers; encourage variety and disagreement.

Questions from the NR10

1. Consult a standard desk dictionary for the definition of *democracy*. Of the several meanings given, which one best encompasses White's definitions? What other meanings do his definitions engage?
2. Translate White's examples into nonmetaphorical language. For example, "It is the line that forms on the right" might be translated as "It has no special privileges." Can "It is the don't in don't shove" also be translated as "It has no special privileges"? Consider what is lost in translation or, more important, what is gained by metaphor.
3. Using White's technique, write a definition of an abstract term; you might consider terms such as *generosity, love, sophistication, tolerance, virtue*.

Analytical Considerations

1. White creates his definition with a series of examples. You may want to ask students if they can group them and if they can discern a principle that orders them? Or do they consider them random?
2. Ask students to consider the date of composition, 1943. Do they find any of White's examples dated? Can they suggest contemporary substitutes?
3. Ask students to consider an abstraction they might be asked to define in an examination in another course. Have them, probably in groups, construct answers in the manner of E. B. White and consider their professors' probable reactions. (You might dare them to try such an answer on an examination.)

Suggested Writing Assignments

1. Imagine, for yourself, someone without textual know-how who takes White's metaphors literally and finds White's essay silly. Write an explanation of several of White's metaphors. Can you explain them without giving a general explanation of how metaphor works?
2. Imagine yourself a member of the War Board who finds White's response unpatriotic and write him a letter explaining why the War Board declines to use it. Or imagine yourself a member of the War Board who finds White's response particularly useful and write him a letter thanking him for it. Or write both letters.

LANI GUINIER

The Tyranny of the Majority

The Norton Reader, p. 883; Shorter Edition, p. 498

Lani Guinier, a graduate of the Yale Law School and a professor at Harvard, was nominated by President Clinton to be Assistant Attorney General for Civil Rights early in 1993. Opponents of her nomination used five articles she published in law reviews (and later reprinted in *The Tyranny of the Majority* [1994]) to contest her nomination, which President Clinton withdrew. This essay, written for that volume, serves as part of its introduction. Opponents of her nomination characterized her views of representation as radical and subversive, and in a political climate in which the Supreme Court has declared parts of the Voting Rights Act unconstitutional, perhaps they are. Certainly her introduction to them calculatedly gives a different impression. Autobiographical material—her own experience, as a Brownie, of unfairness and her son Nikolas's principle of taking turns—suggests that the rightness of her proposals is apparent even to children. Nevertheless, her use of a Founding Father, James Madison, on the despotism of the people (paragraph 11), indicates that the issues of representation she considers are a perennial concern of political philosophers.

Analytical Considerations

1. Why, according to Guinier, did James Madison fear the tyranny of the majority? What are the usual remedies? Why does Guinier think they fail with respect to blacks?
2. Define Guinier's concept of a "Madisonian Majority"?
3. Guinier says that in her legal writing she "pursue[s] voting systems that might disaggregate The Majority so that it does not exercise political power unfairly or tyrannically" (paragraph 22). What does she mean by disaggregating the majority? How might this disaggregation be achieved? If your students do not bring up proportional representation, you will need to remind them of it, or explain it to them.

Suggested Writing Assignments

1. Have you ever encountered a situation in which what Guinier calls a "zero-sum solution" prevailed (paragraph 6)? And were you a member of the majority or the minority? Write about the situation with some reference to what Guinier calls a "positive-sum solution" (paragraph 5). Or imagine yourself in such a situation and write about it.

2. Read one of Guinier's law reviews articles reprinted in *The Tyranny of the Majority* and summarize its argument. Would you describe it as primarily argument or primarily persuasion? How convincing—or how persuasive— do you find it?

3. Read James Madison's *Federalist Paper* No. 10 on the rule of the majority and summarize his position. Does Guinier do it justice in the brief space she has?

4. Guinier was nominated to be Assistant Attorney General for Civil Rights early in 1993. Write a narrative account of the controversy over her nomination and its withdrawal using the *New York Times* and the *Washington Post* as sources. (Various way of dividing up this project collaboratively suggest themselves.)

MARTIN LUTHER KING, JR.

Letter from Birmingham Jail

The Norton Reader, p. 887; Shorter Edition, p. 503

Martin Luther King, Jr., was the most important figure in the American civil rights movement before his assassination in 1968, at the age of thirty-nine. He participated in the Montgomery, Alabama, bus boycott in 1955–1956 (see paragraph 35) and in the Birmingham, Alabama, demonstrations in 1963, where he was arrested along with many other demonstrators. He wrote "Letter from Birmingham Jail" in response to a published statement by eight Birmingham clergymen who supported the goals of the civil rights movement but criticized King for his "unwise and untimely" activism.

King uses Christian doctrine and Christian belief to make common cause with the white clergymen to whom he addresses his letter: see his reference to the Black Muslim movement and its repudiation of Christianity (paragraph 27). You can use his reference to Black Muslim bitterness and hatred to lead into a discussion of his nonviolent activism. Central to his justification of activism—"civil disobedience"—is his distinction between just and unjust laws (paragraphs 15–20). I should ask students to summarize his distinction and how he applies it.

Questions from the NR10

1. King addressed the "Letter from Birmingham Jail" to eight fellow clergymen (see note 1) who had written a statement criticizing his activities. Where and how, in the course of the "Letter," does he attempt to make common cause with them?

2. King was trained in oral composition, that is, in composing and delivering sermons. One device he uses as an aid to oral comprehension is prediction: he announces, in advance, the organization of what he is about to say. Locate examples of prediction in the "Letter."
3. Describe King's theory of nonviolent resistance.
4. Imagine an unjust law that, to you, would justify civil disobedience. Describe the law, the form your resistance would take, and the penalties you would expect to incur.

Analytical Considerations

1. You can ask students to explain the paradox of King's both urging obedience to the law, namely the 1954 Supreme Court decision outlawing segregation in public schools, and breaking it.
2. Do your students know about recent instances of civil disobedience other than those associated with the civil rights movement? You may have to explain resistance to the war in Vietnam, unless you have older students in your class. More recent instances would include resistance to the use of nuclear power, both peaceful and military.
3. King, who expresses his disappointment with whites who call themselves moderates, alternatively characterizes himself as a moderate and an extremist. Students can look at instances of both and the kinds of behavior to which he attaches these labels. Which characterization of King do they think was more accurate in 1963, which more accurate today?

Suggested Writing Assignments

1. If you can't see yourself engaging in civil disobedience, as in Question 4, above, imagine an unjust law and the form someone else's resistance to it would take, and then write a letter in which you try to convince this person to obey rather than to resist.
2. King calls into question, in the context of events in Birmingham, "the strangely irrational notion that there is something in the very flow of time that will inevitably cure all ills" (paragraph 26). Is this an "irrational notion"? Supply two or three other contexts in which the notion might figure and write an essay in which you agree or disagree with King.
3. Do library research on Mahatma Gandhi and his doctrine of nonviolent resistance. Then, on the basis of King's "Letter from Birmingham Jail," analyze similarities and differences between Gandhi's and King's ideas about and uses of nonviolent resistance.
4. Sort out, consulting King's text and the notes, the biblical figures King cites, the Church Fathers and earlier theologians, and the contemporary theologians and philosophers. Do library research on one of the contemporary theologians and philosophers and write a brief essay in which you consider why he was useful to King.

SCIENCE

JACOB BRONOWSKI

The Nature of Scientific Reasoning

The Norton Reader, p. 901; Shorter Edition, p. 517

Bronowski's "The Nature of Scientific Reasoning" is of a piece with his "The Reach of Imagination" (NR 233) in "Human Nature." In the latter essay he argues that scientific and poetic thinking are essentially the same in that both originate in the imagination. In this essay he extends his argument to their ends: Scientists and poets search for order, which "must be discovered and, in a deep sense . . . created" (paragraph 9). Central to Bronowski's purposes is disabusing readers of the notion that scientists mechanically accumulate inert facts; see, for example, Thomas S. Kuhn, "The Route to Normal Science" (NR 905), paragraphs 10 to 11. Bronowski provides multiple illustrations of scientific discovery ranging from Copernicus to Yukawa and makes them intelligible to nonscientists, that is, if they read them carefully. Students often don't; they skip explanations they expect to be hard to follow or drift away from the text. Making sure they understand Bronowski's examples can be a useful demonstration of active reading: what they have to do to make sense of them, what they have to bring to them, and what strategies, like imagery, are useful.

Questions from the NR10

1. Mark the generalizations Bronowski makes in the course of "The Nature of Scientific Reasoning" and their location; for example, "No scientific theory is a collection of facts" (paragraph 7). Where is the information that supports them?
2. Bronowski tells the well-known story of Newton and the apple (paragraphs 11 to 12). How many of his generalizations does it exemplify, and how?
3. "The scientist," Bronowski observes, "looks for order in the appearances of nature" (paragraph 9). Is this operation unique to scientists? Consider the operations of "knowers" in humanities and social-science disciplines such as history, literature, psychology, and sociology.
4. Bronowski sets up an adversary, a literary person who believes that scientists observe, collect, and record facts, and writes his essay as a refutation. Adapt his rhetorical strategy in an essay of your own: explain your beliefs about something by refuting the beliefs of someone who disagrees with them.

Analytical Considerations

1. You may have students list Bronowski's illustrations and references, perhaps in two columns labeled "science" and "literature." Which illustrations does he explain, which does he simply refer to? What do his illustrations and references suggest about his intended audience?

2. Ask students to list the dates for Bronowski's scientific illustrations. Bronowski turns more extensively to early modern than to modern science, and the example of Yukawa's calculations is less detailed than earlier examples. What does his choice of illustrations suggest about modern science? You may refer students to Thomas S. Kuhn's "The Route to Normal Science" (NR 905): in it Kuhn discusses how and when research reports ceased to be intelligible to laypersons (paragraph 17).

3. Bring to class a copy of a Renaissance drawing of a youth with outstretched arms—you can find one on p. 121 of *Leonardo on Painting*, ed. Martin Kemp (New Haven: Yale University Press, 1989)—and a copy of Blake's *Glad Day*, both of which Bronowski discusses in paragraph 5. Ask students if he gives enough detail for them to visualize these pictures, or is it necessary to see or to have seen them?

Suggested Writing Assignments

1. Write an essay in which you consider the science courses you have taken with respect to Bronowski's assertion "No scientific theory is a collection of facts" (paragraph 7). Were you taught science in such a way as to make Bronowski's assertion meaningful? Do you think you should have been?

2. Do library research on current debates over the teaching of science or conduct interviews with science faculty at your institution. What complaints are made about it, what remedies are suggested? Write an essay in which you discuss these debates. You may want to use Bronowski's essay to focus your own, but you need not.

3. "Science finds order and meaning in our experience" (paragraph 11). Can this statement be broadened to: "All fields of study find order and meaning in our experience"? Write an essay in which you consider a course or courses you have taken in another field of study. Use *I* in a way that seems appropriate to you. How much of your own experience will go into your essay, and how will you include it?

THOMAS S. KUHN

The Route to Normal Science

The Norton Reader, p. 905

Thomas S. Kuhn was a Ph.D. in physics turned historian and philosopher of science; "The Route to Normal Science" comes from his best-known work, *The Structure of Scientific Revolutions* (1962). His concept of a paradigm (or a research tradition) and a paradigm shift (or the end of one research tradition and the beginning of another) has been widely adopted, which is evidence of his influence. For example, we speak of changes in the teaching of writing— from emphasizing product (or the finished essay) to emphasizing process (or its production through multiple drafts)—as a paradigm shift.

You may begin class discussion of "The Route to Normal Science" by directing students to its first two paragraphs, in which Kuhn briefly and magisterially lays out the concepts that he will illustrate: normal science, the reporting of scientific achievements, the nature of a research tradition, and its relation to scientific practice. He naturally illustrates these concepts with examples drawn from science. You may be able to enlist knowledgeable students to explain current paradigms; they will probably not be able to explain discarded ones—which itself will illustrate their disappearance. To illustrate a current paradigm, you can look at Kuhn's distinction between a textbook and a research report: the references in John Henry Sloan et al.'s "Handgun Regulations, Crime, Assaults, and Homicide: A Tale of Two Cities" (NR 913, SE 521) point to the tradition these researchers built on and extended. So do the notes in Henry Wechsler et al., "Health and Behavioral Consequences of Binge Drinking in College" (NR 927). To illustrate a discarded paradigm (Kuhn features Newton's optics and Franklin's electricity), Isaac Asimov's "The Eureka Phenomenon" (NR 223, SE 123), Jacob Bronowski's "The Reach of Imagination" (NR 233)—both in "Human Nature"—will help.

Questions from the NR10

1. Mark the important terms in this selection from *The Structure of Scientific Revolutions* and Kuhn's definitions of them. How many does he illustrate as well as define? Why does he both define and illustrate?
2. What are prevailing paradigms in sciences other than those Kuhn discusses? You might consider biology, chemistry, psychology, and sociology. Are you aware of older paradigms in these sciences, or have they and the work based on them, as Kuhn says (paragraph 15), disappeared?
3. Without a paradigm, Kuhn writes, "all of the facts that could possibly pertain to the development of a given science are likely to seem equally relevant" (paragraph 10). What, according to Stephen Jay Gould in "Darwin's Middle Road" (NR 982, SE 558), was the paradigm that enabled Darwin to discriminate among his facts? How can he be said to have made a "scientific revolution"?

Analytical Considerations

1. You may want to look at Kuhn's discussion of paradigms in relation to gathering facts and establishing their relevance (paragraphs 10 and 11). Analogies with writing may be useful here: what gets included and excluded from an essay, when, and why?
2. Kuhn speaks of "the unfortunate simplification that tags an extended historical episode with a single and somewhat arbitrarily chosen name" (paragraph 9). Ask students for examples from history and literature and consider the various ways they function. Is simplification always "unfortunate"?

Suggested Writing Assignments

1. If you have encountered the term *paradigm* in another field of study, write an essay in which you describe what it refers to and how it is used and discuss whether it is used in Kuhn's sense.
2. Kuhn, in "The Route to Normal Science," mentions what happens to scientists who cling to discarded paradigms (paragraph 15). Elsewhere in *The Structure of Scientific Revolutions* he discusses several, including Louis

Agassiz, who held out against Darwin. Do library research on Agassiz or another holdout and write an essay about him or her using Kuhn's concept of a paradigm.

3. Kuhn's *The Structure of Scientific Revolutions*, published in 1962, engendered considerable debate that was essentially about definitions. Read his postscript to the second edition (1970) and describe the issues of definition he raises.

JOHN HENRY SLOAN ET AL.

Handgun Regulations, Crime, Assaults, and Homicide: A Tale of Two Cities

The Norton Reader, p. 913; Shorter Edition, p. 521

"Handgun Regulations, Crime, Assaults, and Homicide" is a scientific report written by a team of nine researchers, John Henry Sloan and eight others comprehended under "et al." (that is, *et alii*, or "and others"). They are listed in an order that represents their relative importance; multiple researchers (and multiple authors) are the rule in scientific research today. The report, published in the *New England Journal of Medicine*, is addressed to professional colleagues. It follows the form prescribed for scientific reports, with sections headed "Abstract," "Methods," "Results," "Discussion," and "References." Only the introductory section, between "Abstract" and "Methods," lacks a heading; in some scientific reports it is labeled "Background" or "Review of Literature." As a result of this prescribed form, scientists "consistently obscure the actual methods by which they obtain their results," as Isaac Asimov puts it in "The Eureka Phenomenon" (NR 223, SE 123), which appears in "Human Nature" (paragraph 81). Scientific information, whenever possible, is expressed mathematically: this report contains four tables and three figures. Scientific prose is generally agentless: Sloan et al. are largely invisible, though on occasion they refer to themselves as we, and so are the people who commit crimes. The title is long, exact, clumsy; the literary allusion in the subtitle, to Dickens's *A Tale of Two Cities*, is unusual for a scientific report.

Close reading of "Handgun Regulations, Crime, Assaults, and Homicide" will demonstrate how scientific reporting neglects to contextualize and explain, both of which experienced writers of other kinds of prose are careful to do. Consequently it demands unusually active reading. You may, to start, have students look closely at Table 1. What does it claim about comparability, and what are its anomalies? How (and where) do Sloan et al. take them into account? If this kind of attention seems useful to students, continue with Analytical Considerations 3 and 4. In addition, "Handgun Regulations, Crime, Assaults, and Homicide" is the most extensively annotated selection in *The Norton Reader*: it is even more extensively annotated than the other selection from the *New England Journal of Medicine*, Carl Cohen's "The Case for the Use of Animals in Biomedical Research" (NR 707), which appears in "Ethics." Virtually every sentence, in some sections, is followed by a reference number or numbers. You may want to explain the system; more important, you should explain that scientists, even more than other academic researchers, write to a specialized (rather than a lay) audience and locate their research with reference to other research. As Thomas S. Kuhn explains in "The Route to Normal Science" (NR 905), research is usually reported in "brief articles addressed only to professional colleagues, the men whose knowledge of a shared paradigm can be assumed and who prove to be the only ones able to read the papers addressed to them" (paragraph 16).

Questions from the NR10

1. Outline "Handgun Regulations, Crime, Assaults, and Homicide: A Tale of Two Cities" using the authors' section headings: abstract, introduction (unheaded), methods, results, discussion, and references. Explain how the authors fit their information and analysis into this structure.
2. Read Stephen Jay Gould's account of induction and prediction in "Darwin's Middle Road" (NR 982, SE 558). Is the structure of "Handgun Regulations" primarily inductive or primarily predictive? Do you think that the scientists involved worked inductively, predictively, or, as Gould claims Darwin did, shuttled between induction and prediction?
3. "Handgun Regulations, Crime, Assaults, and Homicide: A Tale of Two Cities" contains four tables and three figures. Locate the passages in which the information represented in the tables and figures appears. What kind of information is represented graphically and what are the advantages of such representation?
4. Sloan et al., aware that their research is relevant to the controversial issue of gun control, are cautious in their conclusion: "Although our findings should be corroborated in other settings, our results suggest that a more restrictive approach to handgun control may decrease national homicide rates" (paragraph 34). Use their research to argue for or against handgun regulation in an essay written to a general audience.

Analytical Considerations

1. Ask students to describe the differences between a table and a figure. What are the uses of each?
2. Look particularly at the examples of agentless prose in paragraph 7—for the suppression of researchers: "To date, no study"; for the suppression of people who commit crimes: "the rates of gun ownership are high but homicides are relatively uncommon." You may wish to ask students to locate additional examples of agentless prose in this report.
3. Tables 3 and 4 represent 1980–86; Figure 1 contains a line between 1983/84 and 1986. What is the reason for these variations, and where in the report are they explained?
4. The discussion section concludes with three limitations that "warrant comment" (paragraph 31). What are they? How do they qualify the results of Sloan et al.'s research? Why are Sloan et al. careful to include them?

Suggested Writing Assignments

1. Imagine yourself John Henry Sloan (or one of the eight other researchers). Write a personal account of this research on handgun control and your role in it.
2. Imagine yourself a journalist whose special area of reporting is science. You read "Handgun Regulations, Crime, Assaults, and Homicide" in the *New England Journal of Medicine* and decide the research is of general interest. Write a news story about it, or an editorial, or an Op-Ed piece, or all three.

HENRY WECHLSER, ANDREA DAVENPORT, GEORGE DOWDALL, BARBARA MOEYKENS, AND SONIA CASTILLO

Health and Behavioral Consequences of Binge Drinking in College: A National Survey of Students at 140 Campuses

The Norton Reader, p. 927

and

HENRY WECHLSER, CHARLES DEUTSCH, AND GEORGE DOWDALL

Too Many Colleges Are Still in Denial About Alcohol Abuse

The Norton Reader, p. 942

These two essays, based on the same study, form a natural pair. The first is the scientific paper, written for a specialized, technical audience of experts who read the *Journal of the American Medical Association*; the second is the opinion piece, written for the *Chronicle of Higher Education*, which attracts a wider audience, primarily of college administrators. As such, these two essays represent the scientific paper and its popularization. There is a clear primacy here: the scientific paper was published first; the popular piece is dependent upon it, and in fact much of the knowledge claimed in the *Chronicle* essay grows out of the scientific study. Without the grounding supplied by the scientific study, the opinion piece would carry a great deal less weight.

The thrust of *The Norton Reader's* questions on these essays is to get the students deeper into the knowledge base reported in the research. What seems to many students to be the scientific presentation of cold facts is instead a careful description of an experiment that grows out of plainly stated premises: that "binge" drinking is something that can be clearly defined, that students are accurate reporters of their experience, and that the survey questions reported in the article provide a useful way of getting at the phenomenon examined in the *Chronicle* essay.

The scientific article is particularly good at laying out all the questions asked and is exemplary at foregrounding its criteria for definitions. Students need to see how important this foregrounding is and how it is the very essence of scientific inquiry, since it presents the means by which information was gathered. This article, like all good scientific work, includes plenty of opinion, but this opinion is reasoned, explained, and most of all, carefully delineated for the readers to see and judge for themselves. The opinion piece, unlike the original article, moves far beyond the data to make its points.

Questions from the NR10 on "Health and Behavioral Consequences of Binge Drinking in College"

1. This article's conclusions depend on the wording of the questions asked. A central question is "Think back over the last two weeks. How many times have you had five or more drinks in a row?" What do you think "in a row" means? Do you think the question is precise or fuzzy? Why was it asked this way?
2. How do you and people you know define "binge drinking"? How close is your definition to the definition used by Wechsler et al.?
3. At 44 of the 140 colleges surveyed, more than 50 percent of the students were binge drinkers. Does that sound alarming? Accurate? What might some of those colleges be?
4. Paying particular attention to paragraphs 1–6, describe this article's paragraph style. How does it resemble the styles of Sloan et al., "Handgun Regulations, Crime, Assault, and Homicide" (NR 913, SE 521)?

Questions from the NR10 on "Too Many Colleges Are Still in Denial About Alcohol Abuse"

1. This article, written for college administrators, is a heavily revised version of the original study. Note the most important changes you see between the original study and this version. Are they changes in style? in audience? in format? in details? Which changes matter most to the overall impact of the essays?
2. What does the term "in denial" mean? Where does it come from? Do authorities on your campus act as if they are "in denial" about alcohol abuse?
3. Take the "weekend tour" the authors recommend on your own campus or a campus you know. Write up your results in a newspaper article.

Analytical Considerations

1. In their conclusion, the writers of the *Chronicle* essay switch from discussing their research to calling for change by directly addressing college administrators. The transition is handled deftly and subtly: note the invocation of "administrators" in paragraph 15, "college officials" in paragraph 19, and "campus authorities" in paragraph 20; by paragraphs 21 and 22 the authors are using imperatives and, finally, explicit second-person direct address in the last paragraph (paragraph 24).

2. Find parts of the *Chronicle* essay that are not supported by the data in the scientific study.
3. Ask students which article has more redundancy, and whether it seems to be intentional. Is a certain amount of redundancy helpful in some kinds of writing? Which types benefit from redundancy? Which types lose impact?

Suggested Writing Assignments

1. Interview a sample of people on your campus about their drinking habits, and write a piece aimed at authorities about whether they are in denial about drinking on their own campus.
2. Explain what would have to change at your college if college officials acted on the warnings in this article. How would campus life be different?
3. Write an essay explaining why college officials have every incentive to keep alcohol related problems covered up.
4. Write a description of a "problem" caused by drinking. Choose the problem from the list in Table 2 of the scientific article.
5. Dramatize one of the "secondary binge effects" in Table 4 of the scientific article by writing the dialogue that might occur between a drinker and someone affected by the drinking.

MELVIN KONNER

Why the Reckless Survive

The Norton Reader, p. 946; Shorter Edition, p. 535

Try asking students why "Why the Reckless Survive" is in the section called "Science" rather than in the section called "Human Nature." Melvin Konner poses questions about risk taking and, initially, attempts to answer them in the familiar language of behavioral science. Only later, more than halfway through the essay (paragraphs 23–24), when he brings in the physiological correlates of the risk-taking or sensation-seeking personality, does he attempt to answer them in the language of biological science. Students may need to be alerted to this shift from the psychological analysis they feel comfortable with to the less familiar biological and evolutionary analysis. Biology and behavior are linked, for Konner, by physical anthropology and, ultimately, by evolution and genetics. Clues to Konner's orientation appear early in the essay, when he suggests there may be "something inevitable—even something good" about taking chances (paragraph 3) and that risk taking is "a conundrum for an evolutionist" (paragraph 6). His final answer, that the risk taking that seems maladaptive now was adaptive in the dangerous environment of our ancestors, relies on Darwinian selection and a drive to reproduce.

Konner, who began as an anthropologist and then went to medical school, is stationed at the cutting edge of interdisciplinary research. As he wrote in an earlier work, *The Tangled Wing: Biological Constraints on the Human Spirit* (1982): "The encroachments of biology on behavioral science have come in two broad, separate areas: evolution and genetics on the one hand, anatomy and physiology on the other. These two areas have a natural link in the science of embryology, but the link—biochemical genetics—has only just begun to be explored." Unlike some sociobiologists, Konner is neither a determinist nor a conservative. "The result of the vastly long evolutionary balancing act," he writes in this essay, "is a most imperfect organism" (paragraph 39)—but one that we can improve, his writing demonstrates, by the exercise of intelligence and compassion.

Questions from the NR10

1. Mark the research and the researchers' disciplines that Konner relies on. How many kinds of studies does he bring together? What are they?
2. Konner is interested in the effects of biology on human behavior. Locate the evidence he draws from biology and explain his uses of it.
3. Konner introduces and concludes this essay with autobiographical material; he stations himself with respect to his subject. What does the autobiographical material contribute to this essay?
4. Write an essay in which you describe your own or someone else's irrational behavior and speculate about its causes.

Analytical Considerations

1. The psychological and biological research Konner cites is not footnoted. This section, "Science," illustrates degrees of popularization. At one end, Wechsler et al. write in the manner of a scientific report; also see John Henry Sloan et al., "Handgun Regulations, Crime, Assaults, and Homicide: A Tale of Two Cities" (NR 913, SE 521). At the other end, Konner, in "Why the Reckless Survive," and Stephen Jay Gould, in "Darwin's Middle Road" (NR 982, SE 558), include general references in the text. You can call students' attention to the advantages and disadvantages of each method; you may demonstrate them by assigning reports on the sources Konner and Gould use.
2. Sociobiology, which provides biological explanations of human behavior, is a controversial field of inquiry, especially insofar as it tends to determinism. How deterministic is Konner's account of risk-taking behavior?
3. Assign "Why the Reckless Survive" in conjunction with Evelyn Fox Keller's "Women in Science: A Social Analysis" (NR 989, SE 565). Why, as she puts it, has it become "fashionable" to view differences in intelligence as environmental rather than innate (paragraph 1)?
4. You can discuss current debates about Richard J. Herrnstein and Charles Murray's *The Bell Curve: Intelligence and Class Structure in American Life* (1994), perhaps by bringing in a review. Why has it become politically contentious with respect to both its science and its politics?

Suggested Writing Assignments

1. Imagine being told that some achievement, or some failing, or both were genetically programmed and beyond your control. Write an essay in which you describe the traits, the occasion of your discovery, and your response.
2. Read a section of Konner's *The Tangled Wing: Biological Constraints on the Human Spirit* (1982) and describe how psychological and biological explanations intersect.

ARTHUR C. CLARKE

The Light of Common Day

The Norton Reader, p. 955

This essay is an example of popular science, much like the essays by Edward O. Wilson, Rachel Carson, Richard Conniff, and a good many other writers in *The Norton Reader*. It is delivered in the confident voice of someone who has mastered the underlying science and is translating it for nonscientific readers. Like much popular science, it has its *wonders* and *curiosities*, though Clarke never uses those exact terms.

The science translator's art appears in the very first paragraph, where the solar spectrum is discussed not just as physics but in terms of piano octaves. Later Clarke will translate solar time of billions of years into the lifespan of a single human. This type of translation is only one way he makes the considerable complexities of his subject easier for his readers. (Scientific-minded students might well discover more complexities that Clarke has simplified.)

Some of the complexities this essay addresses stem from the limits of scientific knowledge. For instance, Clarke speaks of "a no man's land of radiation about which very little is known" (paragraph 10), revealing that science is as yet not clear about many aspects of his subject. And beyond the realms of sheer ignorance lie areas in which the numbers are so staggering that the untutored mind has trouble comprehending them. The temperature numbers he discusses are one example: Clarke writes of "blood-red dwarfs so cool that their surface temperature is a mere 4,000 degrees Fahrenheit; there are searing ghosts blazing at 100,000 degrees . . ." (paragraph 36). Another example is time, whether five or ten billion years. Clarke blandly acknowledges that "such figures are, of course, inconceivable" (paragraph 44).

If any students are knowledgeable about astronomy, a science that quite comfortably employs vast numbers, they can be asked how astronomers express themselves. Introducing concepts such as scientific notation, degrees of magnitude, and light years will make the rest of the students see how much translation Clarke has done.

Questions from the NR10

1. The organizing metaphors Clarke uses—music at the beginning, time at the end—frame his discussion of the spectrum. What does he gain by beginning and ending with these metaphors?
2. Rachel Carson referred to H. G. Wells in paragraph 12 of "Tides" (NR 598). Compare the way Clarke refers to Wells in paragraph 47.
3. What do you notice about Clarke's paragraphs? Describe their length, how they tend to open, and how they connect to other paragraphs. (It's useful to compare Clarke's to Cronon's [NR 651, SE 352]and Carson's [NR 598].)
4. What factual information did you learn from reading Clarke's essay? What attitudes toward light and the sun do you now have after reading Clarke's essay? Write a brief account of how your knowledge and attitude have changed.

Analytical Considerations

1. In the last part of his essay Clarke throws around some very large numbers: "whatever the vicissitudes of the next five or ten billion years" (paragraph 38), "A.D. 7,000 million" (paragraph 39), "Around the year 10,000 million" (paragraph 41), "by the year 15,000 million" (paragraph 42). Ask students for their reaction to such vast quantities. Does Clarke perhaps anticipate our discomfort and, in paragraph 45, try to put us at ease by calculating the life of the sun in human terms? Does it help?

2. Clarke is highly literary in his allusions, citing Wordsworth at the beginning and Shelley at the end. Both of these Romantic poets took light very seriously, as Clarke was no doubt aware. Is he having the last laugh by correcting Shelley in the final sentence? What seems to be going on? Is poetry wrong to speak of such matters?

3. Throughout this carefully crafted essay are some obvious signs of the impresario-like character of Clarke's narrator. Students can be asked to note the places where Clarke sounds like someone showing visitors around territory he finds quite familiar. (At the very least, students should note the opening of paragraph 6, "let us explore outward in each direction"; the "We see, then...." of paragraph 35; and the obvious stage direction in paragraph 42, "For now comes one of the most remarkable. . . .")

Suggested Writing Assignments

1. Write a brief description of something based on analogy, as Clarke does when describing the solar spectrum in terms of a piano octave.

2. Compare the ways Edward O. Wilson, in "Krakatau" (NR 975, SE 551), and Clarke explain the complexities of science for their mostly nonscientific readers. Pay particular attention to the places where they pause and sum up their material or directly address the reader (as in, "we see, then" in paragraph 35 of "The Light of Common Day").

HENRY PETROSKI

Little Things Can Mean a Lot

The Norton Reader, p. 962

Technology is applied science, science applied to the practical purposes of making our lives livable: it provides us food through mechanical improvements in raising it, transporting it, and packaging it and shelter through mechanical improvements in building, heating, and cooling. It also makes our lives comfortable: it provides us with Post-its. Available in the mid-1980s, they filled, as Petroski puts it, an "unperceived need" (paragraph 18). You may try dividing your students into those who remember a world without Post-its and those who do not, a world API (ante–Post-it) and PPI (post–Post-it). What are some other important technological markers in their lives? How have they shifted in the course of this century? Our grandparents and great-grandparents had the automobile, the airplane, and space flight; we have the Post-it. What will future generations have?

Petroski, describing the invention of masking tape, Scotch tape, and the Post-it, distinguishes between the individual entrepreneurship of technology and the team effort of science. How much "science" was involved in the invention of the Post-it? Technology, according to Thomas S. Kuhn, in "The Route to Normal Science" (NR 905), once "played a vital role in the emergence of new sciences" because craftspersons possessed facts "accessible to casual observation" (paragraph 10). Petroski, in "Little Things Can Mean a Lot," shows the continuing role of "casual observation" in technology. Modern science, however, has moved beyond casual observation to systematic observation by means of specialized instruments.

Analytical Considerations

1. Petroski writes a narrative: that is, he tells a story in chronological order. How does he make his generalizations stand out from the narrative flow? Begin by marking them.
2. Have the class generate a list of technological innovations made during their lifetimes. How many ways can they classify them? What principles are involved in each system of classification?

Suggested Writing Assignments

1. Imagine a world before some technological innovation, large or small, that you now take for granted. Write an essay about the before and after, with attention to the question of whether, like the Post-it, this innovation satisfied an "unperceived need."
2. Read, selectively, in Henry Petroski's *The Evolution of Useful Things* (1992) and compare a large-scale technological innovation with a small-scale one.
3. Petroski has written an entire volume on a single, small-scale technological innovation, *The Pencil* (1990). Describe the relation of technology to science, giving appropriate credit to Petroski, at several stages in the development of the pencil.

NEIL POSTMAN

Virtual Students, Digital Classroom

The Norton Reader, p. 968; Shorter Edition, p. 543

As a veteran educational commentator, Postman has often been in the vanguard of new advances in schooling, so it is unusual to see him sounding reluctant about the promise of technology. But the particular grounds of his complaint make perfect sense: there is a great deal of hype about computers in the classroom, and far too little common sense. Postman takes what he obviously considers to be a practical view of computers and worries that rapid technological adoptions will displace attention from more important questions.

One question for students is what they think the role of computers in the classroom will be in the future. If you break the question down, it gets more interesting. What will the role be in five years? Twenty years? Fifty years? Most will agree that computers will play an enormous role. Some other key questions are: who will control the rate of change? How can computers be introduced equally, so no students are penalized? How can we prepare now for a different future? Students will soon recognize that Postman raises traditional liberal arts values of an open mind and an informed citizenry. Does he provide ways of preserving these values in the face of the mechanization of computers?

Postman's other focus seems to be on willpower, on the motivations of the learner. Lively discussion can ensue when a class is asked who bears the responsibility for learning, the school or the student. Once students get beyond the usual valedictorian clichés (School is what you make it, etc.), they can use Postman's essay to interrogate educational theories and the technology that enthralls so many.

Questions from the NR10

1. Postman claims that "most of the population learns how to drive a car without school instruction" (paragraph 10). Is this true? How would one go about confirming this statement?
2. In paragraph 10, Postman says that "schools can provide . . . a serious form of technology education" and argues for "making technology itself an object of inquiry." Since this is exactly what Postman does as a writer and professor, is this argument an instance of self-interested special pleading? Why or why not?
3. Consult Postman's biography in the "Authors" section, then look through his essay for evidence of his professional expertise. What kinds of sources does he refer to? What is the range of his reading? Is he writing for a specific community of readers?
4. Write about computers in your own formal education, arguing from your own experiences whether Postman makes a good case or not.

Analytical Considerations

1. In paragraph 10, Postman says "using computers to process information . . . is a trivial thing to do." What is trivial about it? What meaning of "process" is Postman relying on? Are there other meanings of "process" that might make the task seem less trivial?
2. Postman is hard on technophiles, whose prophecies always have "a cheery gee-whiz tone" (paragraph 6). Students might recall some current or past overenthusiastic technophilic statements. Ask them if the technophiles' "cheery gee-whiz" tone is a by-product of an understandable enthusiasm or if it is evidence that they are out of touch with real life, as Postman seems to argue. (See the opening of paragraph 9: "These are serious matters, and they need to be discussed by those who know something about children from the planet Earth. . . .")

Suggested Writing Assignments

1. In an essay, describe another "Faustian bargain" (paragraph 8) society has made, in addition to the automobiles and television that Postman mentions. Potential subjects might include artificial birth control, missile technology, high-tech agriculture, and many others.

2. Use Postman's statement, "Schools are not now and have never been largely about getting information to children" (paragraph 9) as an epigraph for an essay that responds to this statement, drawing on your own knowledge. What in your own experience have schools "been largely about"?

3. Write about someone who is actually using the computer to make learning more effective. This can be a fellow student, a worker learning on the job, or someone learning a subject in his or her spare time. Think about whether this person's activities support or challenge Postman's contentions.

EDWARD O. WILSON

Krakatau

The Norton Reader, p. 975; Shorter Edition, p. 551

Famous for his pioneering work on ants, Wilson branched out into autobiography and, in his 1998 book *Consilience: The Unity of Knowledge*, to large-scale considerations of the role of science in explaining the nature of things. This essay is somewhere in between the highly scientific studies of the ant kingdom, which earned him his professional reputation, and the large philosophical speculations that have marked his most recent work. "Krakatau" is popularized science, an account of an exciting natural phenomenon and its highly unexpected yet quite natural results. It was not based on actual fieldwork or personal observation; instead it is a respected scientist's armchair summation of the work of others.

For those who believe science writing ought to portray "just the facts," "Krakatau" can serve as a useful corrective. Wilson uses the "facts" of the story—the volcanic explosion, the loss of habitat, and the eventual regeneration of plant and animal life—to make a point about the recuperative powers of nature. It is as if the shattered island served as a natural laboratory for humans to watch the forces of recovery at work. And clearly if no life had returned, Wilson would not be writing about it here. He is a naturalist, after all.

Wilson portrays the recovery after the explosion from the perspective of the natural scientist who is amazed at nothing, who confidently understands the forces at play. In this way, his essay contrasts strongly with Rachel Carson's "Tides" (NR 598), where the limits of human knowledge appear in the concluding poignant anecdote she relates. There are no poignant stories in Wilson's essay, no attempt at an empathetic understanding of the "creatures" under study, none of Carson's literary sense of what stands out to an observer. Instead there is the confident voice of a guide who knows everything, who has marshalled his data and now presents it to us seamlessly. Wilson's model is the university lecturer, and that is precisely what he has been for his entire career.

Questions from the NR10

1. How does Wilson organize his essay? Outline his main points.
2. What overall point does Wilson make? Does he make any points tacitly, without actually coming out and saying them?
3. What level of knowledge and understanding does Wilson anticipate from his readers? (For instance, he uses "barque" in paragraph 4, "tardigrades" in paragraph 14, and "flycatchers" in paragraph 18, all without explanation. He expects context to explain enough. Yet in paragraph 9 he explains both "aeolian" and "plankton," and in paragraph 14 he explains "phoresy.")
4. Wilson's details in "Krakatau" are based on reading, not actual field observation. Describe the different ways Wilson draws upon and gives credit to his sources.

Analytical Considerations

1. The division of scientific labor is an issue in this essay. Wilson has made use of the observations of many other researchers; his piece weaves them together seamlessly. In what sense is Wilson's essay like a student term paper, based as it is on a review of the literature and lacking any original observations?
2. What can an eminent scientist like Wilson bring to the observations of others? Clearly he doesn't have first-hand knowledge or field experience about everything in this essay. What kind of drawback is that? What are the gains?

Suggested Writing Assignments

1. Write some questions you would ask if you could interview Wilson about "Krakatau."
2. Take a real or fictional natural disaster and write a five-hundred-word description of the event, using the first five paragraphs of Wilson's essay as a model.
3. Write an essay comparing the approaches of Rachel Carson, in "Tides" (NR 598), and Wilson, paying particular attention to the principles they use to organize their information.

STEPHEN JAY GOULD

Darwin's Middle Road

The Norton Reader, p. 982; Shorter Edition, p. 558

Stephen Jay Gould is a biologist, a historian of science, and a superb popularizer; "Darwin's Middle Road," like others of his essays, was first published in the column he writes for *Natural History* magazine. In this essay he introduces Darwin's working toward a theory of natural selection by discussing two opposed views of scientific creativity: inductivism, or reliance on observation and the accumulation of data, and eurekaism, or reliance on predictive hunches and synthesis. Today, he observes, eurekaism is privileged; see, for example, Isaac Asimov's "The Eureka Phenomenon" (NR 223, SE 123) in "Human Nature." In Darwin's time, inductivism was privileged. There has been, to use Thomas S. Kuhn's nomenclature, a paradigm shift in accounting for scientific discovery; see "The Route to Normal Science" (NR 905).

Gould, by beginning with this general discussion, is better able to present the particulars of Darwin's achievement, and we are better able to follow not only the particulars of Darwin's achievement but also Gould's disentangling them from Darwin's own account of his achievement. Gould, arguing that Darwin shuttled between induction and prediction, puts one piece of evidence after another in place. The structure of Gould's essay, students should be asked to notice, is predictive (rather than inductive). But rhetorical structure need not reflect the method of discovery. Darwin's thinking and Gould's writing together may lead to a useful discussion of the writing process and the relation of rhetoric to thought. Like Darwin, we shuttle between induction and prediction when we think and frequently use our first and intermediate drafts to clarify what we are doing. Final drafts, however, usually require a predictive structure to prepare readers to follow our thinking.

Questions from the NR10

1. What, according to Gould, constituted Darwin's scientific research? How and why did he falsely depict it in his autobiography (paragraph 8)?
2. Rather than isolating scientific research from social and political experience, Darwin, Gould explains, was influenced by a social scientist, an economist, and a statistician (paragraph 20). Identify each one and explain what he contributed to Darwin's theory of natural selection.
3. Consider a recent experience of writing an essay. Did you, thinking and writing, shuttle between inductivism and prediction as Gould claims Darwin did? Describe your experience using Gould's analytic vocabulary.

Analytical Considerations

1. You may ask students to read one or more of the following essays: Isaac Asimov's "The Eureka Phenomenon" (NR 223, SE 123), Jacob Bronowski, "The Reach of Imagination" (NR 233), and Henry David Thoreau, "Observation" (NR 250), all in "Human Nature," and Jacob Bronowski's "The Nature of Scientific Reasoning" (NR 901, SE 517) and Thomas S. Kuhn's "The Route to Normal Science" (NR 905), both in this section. How does each, describing scientific discovery, present what Gould calls "inductivism" and "eurekaism"?
2. Society writes biology, at least in part, a science writer once claimed. How did society write Darwin's account of the operations of natural selection?
3. Ask students to describe their experience of thinking and writing as they produced a recent essay. Does Gould's account of inductivism and prediction clarify the experience for them? This task is best done in groups.

Suggested Writing Assignments

1. Write an essay about a eureka experience of your own. You may consider, in conjunction with it, Gould's conclusion to "Darwin's Middle Road": he refers to Louis Pasteur's remark that fortune favors the prepared mind.

2. Look at the prescribed form of scientific reporting—abstract, methods, results, discussion, and references—as exemplified by John Henry Sloan et al., "Handgun Regulations, Crime, Assault, and Homicide: A Tale of Two Cities" (NR 913, SE 521). Write an essay in which you consider the relation of its rhetoric to its thought: is its rhetoric primarily inductive or predictive?

EVELYN FOX KELLER

Women in Science: A Social Analysis

The Norton Reader, p. 989; Shorter Edition, p. 565

Evelyn Fox Keller, who earned a Ph.D. in physics, has held a variety of positions, including a joint appointment in Rhetoric, Women's Studies, and the History of Science at the University of California at Berkeley and, currently, an appointment in the Program in Science, Technology, and Society at the Massachusetts Institute of Technology; she has done what she says women in science often do, that is, redefine their field and remove themselves from the mainstream to the periphery of science. "Women in Science: A Social Analysis" surveys subjects she has written about elsewhere: the representation of women in science, child rearing, education, the practice of science, and its methods and goals. She includes autobiographical material, not only about her life but also about the genesis of her inquiry. Because she felt a need to assess her own experience and see if it could be generalized, differences between women's and men's minds—or the mythology of differences—seemed an important question.

Keller assumes that the situation of women in science is a problem, for men as well as for women. She proposes comprehensive, even revolutionary measures to alleviate it: less rigid gender stereotyping (which entails massive social reorganization) and encouraging and including women in science (which entails the substantial reorganization of scientific practice). Nevertheless, she underplays their revolutionary nature by proposing them persuasively, not as required by justice to women but rather as advantageous to men. Men as well as women, she argues, suffer from the mythology of different intelligences; moreover, scientific thinking at its best is probably androgynous, that is, incorporating both male and female qualities (paragraph 24).

Questions from the NR10

1. To what uses does Fox Keller put her own experience in "Women in Science: A Social Analysis"?
2. Fox Keller includes two tables. Where and how does she interpret them? Are other interpretations possible? Should the tables be updated? Why?
3. Write an essay in which you contextualize something in your own experience through statistical analysis. Some possibilities: grades, choice of major, choice of career, family composition, income, racial and/or ethnic origins, and gender.

Analytical Considerations

1. You may want to ask students to notice the carefully articulated structure of "Women in Science" and compare it with the structure of a scientific report; see John Henry Sloan et al., "Handgun Regulations, Crime, Assaults, and Homicide: A Tale of Two Cities" (NR 913, SE 521)." Are there resemblances?

2. You may also want students to notice how personal report figures in this essay; it is possible to adopt the structure of a scientific report without suppressing agents. Nevertheless, Keller does on occasion write agentless prose: see, for example, "Even though it has become fashionable to view such differences as environmental in origin, the temptation to seek . . ." (paragraph 1).

Suggested Writing Assignments

1. Write an essay describing elements of your experience of science that raise questions of gender and analyze them. You may want to consider your experience of science in comparison with your experience of another field of study. Is science more gender marked?

2. Keller says of her own experience as a graduate student that it was "extreme, but possibly illustrative" (paragraph 16). "Women in Science" summarizes it; "The Anomaly of a Woman in Physics," an autobiographical essay written for *Working It Out* (1977), describes it with particularity and feeling. Write an essay in which you consider the relation of "The Anomaly of a Woman in Physics" to "Women in Science."

3. Keller has written a biography of Nobel Prize winner Barbara McClintock, *A Feeling for the Organism* (1983). Read it and use material from it to amplify her remarks in "Women in Science" on the importance of "fertility and receptivity" to creative science.

LITERATURE AND THE ARTS

EUDORA WELTY

One Writer's Beginnings

The Norton Reader, p. 998; Shorter Edition, p. 573

Taken from her best-selling memoir by the same title, this essay turns to the world of Eudora Welty's childhood in Jackson, Mississippi, and offers an adult's reflections on formative early experience. "One Writer's Beginnings" is clearly a chapter from the autobiography of an artist and intellectual. Welty describes the books read to her and the books she read, notes the texts she admired and adored, and talks about reading as she experienced it—and as she hopes her readers will also experience it. Perhaps the most important aspect of "One Writer's Beginnings" comes near the end when Welty considers "voice." Her five-paragraph treatment of the subject, beginning with her mother's songs and records played on the Victrola, then retracing her own experience of reading and writing, provides a valuable opportunity to define and illustrate this difficult rhetorical concept.

Questions from the NR10

1. In the opening paragraphs of this essay Welty speaks of her "sensory education." What does she mean? What examples does she give?
2. Throughout this essay Welty lists the titles of books that she and her mother read. What is the effect of these lists? Have you read any of the books on them? Or books like them? How important were they to you?
3. Welty concludes her essay by talking of the writer's voice—of "testing it for truth" and "trust[ing] this voice" (paragraph 24). What meanings does she give the key words *truth* and *trust*?
4. Read John Holt's essay "How Teachers Make Children Hate Reading" (NR 436; SE 228). Write an essay of your own, entitled "How Children Learn to Love Reading," drawing your evidence from Welty's "One Writer's Beginnings" and your experience, observation, and reading.
5. Welty grew up before the advent of television. How does television affect a child's "sensory education"? Write an essay comparing modern children's sensory education with Welty's.

Analytical Considerations

1. Follow up on Question 2, above, by considering the following: why does Welty devote so much space to describing the books of her childhood? Are they the forces that most powerfully shaped her, or is she, through memory and words, also (re)shaping the self she presents in this autobiography of an artist?
2. Welty obviously loves books and loves to talk about them. Ask students what strategies she uses to communicate her responses to books—not just

adjectives, but metaphors, memories, anecdotes—and what strategies they most respond to.

3. Ask students why this selection has been titled "One Writer's Beginnings." Would they expect different "beginnings" from the autobiography of, say, a painter or politician or businessperson?

4. Welty writes, "Movement must be at the very heart of listening" (paragraph 23). This principle is also true for reading. Ask students to plot the movement of "One Writer's Beginnings" and then to consider what unifies the piece.

5. In what ways is Welty's essay a cultural document reflecting the world of the American South in the early decades of this century? You might begin discussing this question by asking students to note what is different about Welty's childhood from their own—or, perhaps, what details from Welty's childhood they have encountered in stories told by their parents or grandparents.

6. In paragraph 24 Welty offers a description of "voice" in a story or poem. After discussing it, ask students to characterize the voice they hear in "One Writer's Beginnings."

Suggested Writing Assignments

1. In describing her reading of classic tales from *Every Child's Story Book*, Eudora Welty notes: "I located myself in these pages and could go straight to the stories and pictures I loved" (paragraph 12). If you have had a similar experience with stories or books, write an essay about it. If your experience with books was quite different, that, too, will provide the subject of an essay.

2. Welty lists many of the children's tales she read and loved as she grew up. If you have read any of them, reread one and, in an analytical essay, suggest why it continues to appeal to children.

3. "Learning stamps you with its moments. Childhood's learning is made up of moments. It isn't steady. It's a pulse" (paragraph 16). Reflect on your own educational process, both formal and informal; then write an essay in response to Welty's observation about how learning occurs. You may find Alfred North Whitehead's essay, "The Rhythmic Claims of Freedom and Discipline" (NR 515), helpful.

VLADIMIR NABOKOV

Good Readers and Good Writers

The Norton Reader, p. 1004; Shorter Edition, p. 579

Although Nabokov is well known to teachers of literature and writing, his work may be unfamiliar to students. In preparation for this essay on reading and writing fiction, you may want them to read a short story by Nabokov, in order to consider connections among his fiction, his theory of fiction, and the writers he prefers.

More generally, you may want to ask students what they expect from fiction: why they read, what pleases them, what satisfies them at a story's end. Nabokov's views on what "good readers" ought to expect from fiction are likely to prove quite different from theirs; indeed, through the mock "quiz" he gives, Nabokov insists that action, emotional identification, and historical interest are not "good" motives for reading. The views of other essayists in this section—Eudora Welty, in "One Writer's Beginnings" (NR 998, SE 573), and Katha Pollitt, in "Does a Literary Canon Matter?" (NR 1029, SE 584)—will serve to counterpoise Nabokov's views.

Questions from the NR10

1. Make a list of the qualities that Nabokov believes "good readers" should have; then make a list of the qualities he believes "good writers" should have. Do they correspond? Why or why not?
2. Nabokov, as he points out in the conclusion to this essay (paragraphs 14–16), considers the writer from three points of view: as storyteller, as teacher, and as enchanter. He has not, however, organized his essay by these points of view. Where and how does he discuss each one? Why does he consider the last the most important?
3. Take Nabokov's quiz (paragraph 5). Write an essay in which you explain your "right" answers (as Nabokov sees "good readers") and defend your "wrong" ones.
4. How, for example, would Eudora Welty (see "One Writer's Beginnings" [NR 998, SE 573]) and Katha Pollitt (see "Does a Literary Canon Matter?" [NR 1029, SE 584]) do on Nabokov's quiz? Give what you think would be their answers and explain, using information from their essays, what you think their reasons would be.

Analytical Considerations

1. Why does Nabokov use a quotation from the French novelist Gustave Flaubert in the opening paragraph of his essay? Ask students what the quotation tells us about the style, tone, and persona of the writer.
2. Nabokov gives a "quiz" about "good readers" (paragraph 5) that he claims he once gave to students and that Question 2, above, asks students to take. Why does he give this quiz rather than present his ideas more directly? Does he, in a sense, coerce readers into choosing the "right" answers and shame them for choosing the "wrong" ones?
3. Nabokov distinguishes between "minor" and "major" authors in paragraph 4. Look at the metaphors he uses to describe the "major" (or "real") author.
4. Nabokov also distinguishes between two varieties of imagination in paragraphs 8 to 9. What are they? How are they related to his "good" and, by implication, his "bad" readers?
5. At the end of this essay Nabokov retells the story of the boy who cried wolf. In the standard version of this story, the boy is devoured when a real wolf finally comes along; it is a homily on the virtues of telling the truth. Why does Nabokov revise it? What new meanings does he want us to grasp?
6. The essay ends with an image of an artist who "build[s] his castle of cards," which turns into "a castle of beautiful steel and glass" (paragraph 16). Ask

students to analyze this image, the sense of the artist it conveys, and why Nabokov chose to end his essay with it.

Suggested Writing Assignments

1. Write an argument for or against Nabokov's suggestion that "the good reader is one who has imagination, memory, a dictionary, and some artistic sense" rather than an inclination toward "emotional identification, action, and the socio-economic or historical angle" (paragraph 5).
2. Read a story written by Nabokov and write an essay in which you consider the ways in which his fiction reflects the values expressed in "Good Readers and Good Writers."
3. Write your own essay on the topic "What Makes Good Writers."

DAGOBERTO GILB

Northeast Direct

The Norton Reader, p. 1009

Gilb's essay is an understated, sly commentary on fame and the perils of authorship, by a young novelist who unexpectedly gets to spy on someone reading his own book.

The authorial voice throughout this essay is worth spending time on. Students should be aware of how different Gilb is from other authors who speak of their own writing. Nabokov's confident voice is the prime example in this section of the book (NR 1004, SE 579), and a question below asks students to contrast Gilb, the young, hesitant writer starting out, with Nabokov, the proud, accomplished master.

One key element of Gilb's authorial voice is the particular verb tense he uses, the historical present, which appears consistently throughout the essay. Gilb, a novelist, has no hesitation in placing us there on the scene, inside his head, as he watches events occur. It's worth exploring what the historical present allows a writer to do, and what its limitations are as well. For instance, the historical present allows no room for retrospective reflection; the hesitant reflection Gilb provides all occurs in the present tense. Other elements of the authorial voice allow students to see that Gilb presents himself as a character lacking in confidence. They ought to ask why a published novelist should feel so hesitant, so dependent upon the approval of an unknown reader. (And perhaps one can connect Gilb's self-described behavior, his spying, with what some novelists do to get material for their stories.)

One clue to Gilb's modesty might have to do with the social distance between himself and his real-life reader on the train. Gilb no doubt means for us to notice that his reader is tall, blue-eyed, wearing the cap of an elite college, while he himself is instrusive, "breathing on his neck" (paragraph 8), wearing a bright yellow United Farm Workers T-shirt. Both reader and writer are wearing coded garments: one says "Brown University," the other is emblazoned with a union slogan in Spanish. These details are carefully placed; students ought to note that this is one section in which the novelist's skill appears most clearly.

For the aristocratic Nabokov, the writer is distant, the authoritative giver of meanings. The democratic-seeming Gilb snoops on his reader, hoping to find his own satisfaction through that of the man experiencing his book. Ultimately, though, Nabokov and Gilb do share one key attitude toward explanations: what they have to say is embodied in their books.

Analytical Considerations

1. Gilb's reactions bounce from exaggerated praise of his reader's astuteness (paragraph 11) to sympathetic rationalization over his falling asleep (paragraph 12) to doubts about his reader's laziness (paragraph 13). Note the precise phrases Gilb uses to sketch in his surmises about his reader. How seriously are we to take these judgments? What guides us as we decide how to respond?
2. When does Gilb deliberately break into incomplete sentences? Why do you think he does so? What have English teachers told you about sentence fragments?
3. What parts of this essay seem to reveal most clearly that Gilb is a novelist?

Suggested Writing Assignments

1. Write the two or three possible exchanges Gilb and his reader might have had in Penn Station had Gilb opened his mouth to speak.
2. We've all had moments when we showed our work to others; write what went through your mind as you watched someone else read or examine something you'd worked on.
3. Write a comparison of the way Gilb and Nabokov address their readers. What seem to be their characteristic attitudes toward literature? toward the act of reading?
4. Tell a story using only the historical present. You'll have to dramatize what's happening, and you'll need to keep your own mental reactions in the present as well, as Gilb does.

NORTHROP FRYE

The Motive for Metaphor

The Norton Reader, p. 1012

This essay, Frye explains, is part of a series of six talks for students and critics of literature. The title of each comes from a different poem (paragraph 19); "the motive for metaphor" occurs in a poem by Wallace Stevens that Frye quotes near the end of this essay, after he has developed a theory of poetic language and an apologia for literature. You can start with the poem: ask students about the relations between the self (Stevens's "you") and the world that he depicts in it. Or you can come to the poem after working through

Frye's theory of poetic language—either way works.

At the beginning of the essay Frye poses a number of resonant questions with respect to the value of literature, the identity of poets, and the differences between art and science. Ask students what uses they think literature has. Frye locates the roots of imagination in human desires and mental capacities. Students will grasp his distinction between the world they live in and the world they want to live in (paragraph 7). But they may not care to reconcile them in Frye's visionary, quasi-religious manner: religions, he observes, also "present us with visions of eternal and infinite heavens or paradises" (paragraph 18).

Questions from the NR10

1. At what point in this essay does Frye come to the meaning of his title? What is his conception of the motive for metaphor? Why does he wait to explain it?
2. Frye describes three kinds of English, or, rather, he describes one English and three uses to which we put it. What are they?
3. Frye describes metaphor, forcibly, as nonsense (paragraph 20). How, then, do we make sense of it?
4. Robert Frost, in "Education by Poetry: A Meditative Monologue" (NR 1021), wants "to make metaphor the whole of thinking" (paragraph 15). What kinds of argument are Frye and Frost making? How do their conceptions of metaphor figure in it? Write an essay comparing the claims each makes for metaphor.
5. Why, according to Frye, doesn't literature improve the way science does? What happens to old science? Read Thomas S. Kuhn, "The Route to Normal Science" (NR 905) and do additional research if necessary. Then write an essay in which you compare the fates of old literature and old science.

Analytical Considerations

1. How does Frye define three levels of the mind? How does each operate? Why does he take such pains to distinguish among them?
2. In paragraphs 5, 12, and 13 Frye presents his understanding of how science works. Compare his view with that of Jacob Bronowski in "The Nature of Scientific Reasoning" (NR 901, SE 517) or of Stephen Jay Gould in "Darwin's Middle Road" (NR 982, SE 558), both in "Science."
3. How does Frye distinguish between the arts and the sciences? Ask students what limitations they see in his distinctions. Ask them also about their own values. Students who plan to choose a "practical" major such as biology or engineering instead of a major such as art history or English (an "impractical" major?) will provide examples on the spot of how modern society acknowledges the importance of science and questions the value of art.
4. How does Frye distinguish between poetry and religion?
5. Frye poses the question "Is it possible that literature, especially poetry, is something that a scientific civilization like ours will eventually outgrow?" (paragraph 14). What answer does he expect us to give? Why?
6. Plot the design of this essay, accounting for its organization, development, and points of emphasis. The concluding paragraph merits special consideration.

Suggested Writing Assignments

1. Write an essay in which you compare Frye and Jacob Bronowski ("The Reach of Imagination" [NR 233]) on the function of the imagination.
2. Analogy, according to Frye, is "tricky to handle in description, because the differences are as important as the resemblances" (paragraph 20). Write a description of something in which you liken it to one or more other things. Then explain the points of resemblance that make the analogy (or analogies) work and the points of difference that must be ignored.
3. Choose an essay from this section in which metaphor is important—for example, Robert Frost's "Education by Poetry" (NR 1021) or Michael J. Arlen's "The Tyranny of the Visual" (NR 1067)—and using what you have learned from Frye, analyze its use of metaphor.
4. Frye observes, "We notice in passing that the creative and the neurotic minds have a lot in common" in dissatisfaction (paragraph 17). Write an essay in which you make something of his observation.

ROBERT FROST

Education by Poetry: A Meditative Monologue

The Norton Reader, p. 1021

Robert Frost's personal and rather quirky address to Amherst students in 1930 will acquaint students with one of twentieth-century America's most famous writers, whose poetry they probably have sampled but who looms as a literary figure rather than as a distinct personality. In "Education by Poetry" Frost reveals a lot about himself, not only by what he says but also by how he says it. The best way to approach the rhetoric of "Education by Poetry" would have been to hear Frost deliver it, because to a great extent the form as well as the content of this speech reflect Frost the man—at least the platform man. Since hearing him is no longer possible, you may want to have students read various parts of the speech as they think he might have delivered it.

Frost presents himself as a teacher—he did teach at Amherst College—and as a student. He has been to hear lectures on Virgil: see his praise of one that had "all the colors of an enthusiasm passed through an idea" (paragraph 11). Ask students what kinds of lectures they think he heard. He has been to hear a lecture by Niels Bohr: see his references to Heisenberg's, Einstein's, and Schrodinger's theories (paragraphs 16, 18, and 19). Ask students who have studied physics if Frost got them right; colleagues in physics say he did—but would be startled by his reduction of modern physics to metaphor. Students, Frost argues, should be able to discern metaphor in the world beyond poetry—in history, philosophy, psychology, and science. Indeed, he observes, "I have wanted in late years to go further and further in making metaphor the whole of thinking" (paragraph 14).

In "Education by Poetry," in a voice both humorous and cantankerous, Frost takes us on a circuitous route to make the point that poetry is essential to education because it teaches us to understand metaphor and, "unless you are at home in the metaphor, unless you have had your proper poetical education in the metaphor, you are not safe anywhere" (paragraph 21). This is a large claim; how much of its exaggeration is rhetorical? Frost also claims that poetry, by teaching metaphor, teaches belief—in self, love, country, God—and that belief is the only means of bringing something into being, of living creatively and responsively.

Questions from the NR10

1. In what ways does Frost's subtitle describe his essay? What terms would you use to describe it (for example, rambling, unified)? Define your terms with specific reference to Frost's essay.
2. Frost admires speech that has "range, something of overstatement, something of statement, and something of understatement." Does this spectrum appear in Frost's own speech? Show where and how.
3. What does Frost mean when he says "unless you have had your proper poetical education in the metaphor, you are not safe anywhere" (paragraph 21)? Mark some of the metaphors Frost examines in this essay. From what fields does he draw them? What does he say about each? How are they useful to him?
4. Northrop Frye, in "The Motive for Metaphor" (NR 1012), calls simile and metaphor "two crude, primitive, archaic forms of thought" (paragraph 20). Frost, however, wants to make "metaphor the whole of thinking" (paragraph 14). What kinds of argument are Frost and Frye making? How do their conceptions of metaphor figure in their arguments? Write an essay comparing the claims each makes for metaphor.
5. Choose two metaphors from an essay in *The Norton Reader* about a field other than literature and write an essay in which you consider the uses to which the author puts them, as well as their effectiveness.

Analytical Considerations

1. In this essay Frost first talks about riding a metaphor and knowing when it breaks down (paragraph 21) and then gives an example (paragraphs 24–34). In "The Motive for Metaphor" (NR 1012), Northrop Frye talks about analogy as tricky, "because the differences are as important as the resemblances" (paragraph 20). Put Frost's and Frye's passages together. Students should be able to see that they are talking about the same properties of metaphor, Frost metaphorically, Frye analytically.
2. Ask students to locate other places in this essay where Frost describes metaphor and to consider his understandings of it.
3. In perhaps a dozen places Frost digresses or becomes parenthetic. Are these digressions distractions or effective rhetorical devices that contribute to his purpose? What might a speech (which this originally was) demand or allow that an essay does not?
4. Ask students to determine if there is order or pattern in this essay. If so, what provides the thread of continuity? Is it Frost's personality? His theme? His imagery? Something else?

5. What does Frost mean when he says, "To learn to write is to learn to have ideas" (paragraph 39)? You may want to connect his statement with current ideas about writing as a mode of discovery.

Suggested Writing Assignments

1. The Latin poet Horace said that poetry should both delight and teach. Would Frost agree? Write an essay in which you answer this question by considering "Education by Poetry" and one or more of his poems.
2. Paul R. Gross and Norman Levitt, in *Higher Superstition: The Academic Left and Its Quarrels with Science* (1994), have attacked humanists who make claims about science without being adequately trained in it. Read their introductory chapter and write an essay in which you either extend their attack to Frost or defend him from it.
3. Write an essay in which you consider Frost's views on what he calls "the marking problem" (paragraph 7). Would you like to be graded by Frost?
4. Write an essay in response to Frost's declaration "We ask people to think, and we don't show them what thinking is" (paragraph 39). Draw examples from your experience and observation.

KATHA POLLITT

Does a Literary Canon Matter?

The Norton Reader, p. 1029; Shorter Edition, p. 584

Katha Pollitt's essay on the literary canon appeared in the *Nation*, of which she was an associate editor. She is a sharp, satirical writer who gives a debater's edge to her nuanced position. Her comment—"I found that I agreed with all sides in the debate at once" (paragraph 1)—is somewhat disingenuous; she also disagrees with all sides at once because she finds their positions too simple.

Pollitt expects her readers to know about the debate over the canon; students may not. However, in the course of this essay she describes three positions and names enough literary works—or "texts"—for students to identify what positions have informed their own literary education. Ask them what they read in school. Ask them what their teachers say are motives for reading. Ask them what their teachers call books—"literature" or "texts." Has their literary education reflected a conservative, liberal, or radical (even ultraradical) position on the canon?

Pollitt analyzes similarities as well as differences among the conservatives, liberals, and radicals: for example, they all believe that the books assigned in school are the only books students will ever read. At issue among them is "what books to cram down the resistant throats of a resentful captive populace of students" (paragraph 16). They may of course be right. Ask students about their extracurricular reading—their answers are likely to be depressing to readers. Ask them about their assigned reading.

Pollitt's position on the canon itself is closest to that of the liberals, as students are likely to discern. But, as she observes, "A liberal is not a very exciting thing to be" (paragraph 5). Her argumentative strategy enables her to present a more complex position than those advocated by other sides in the debate and to lend excitement to her liberal and inclusive views.

Questions from the NR10

1. Pollitt's strategy of argument is classification; she enunciates three positions on the literary canon. How many times does this three-part classification appear in her essay? Mark them.
2. What are the points of difference among the three positions? More important to Pollitt's own argument, what are their points of similarity?
3. What are the strengths and weaknesses of Pollitt's finding herself in partial agreement with all three positions? You may want to contrast her style of argument with Michael Levin's in "The Case for Torture" (NR 694, SE 374). Levin, like a debater, argues only his own position and puts down, entirely, the counterarguments of those who disagree with him. Is Pollitt's or Levin's approach more congenial to you?
4. Write a two-part or a three-part essay in which you argue the strengths and weaknesses of all positions.

Analytical Considerations

1. Conservatives, liberals, and radicals all believe, according to Pollitt, that "the chief end of reading is to produce a desirable kind of person and a desirable kind of society" (paragraph 14). What do students think of this argument? Do they themselves distinguish between medicinal reading and other reading?
2. In paragraph 12 Pollitt counters this simplistic account of reading (see Analytical Consideration 1, above) with a more elaborate one, which, she alleges, conservatives, liberals, and radicals suppress. To what extent does her account reflect students' experience? It may be useful to have students discuss this question in groups.
3. According to Pollitt, "if you read only twenty-five, or fifty, or a hundred books, you can't understand them" and "if you don't have an independent reading life . . . you won't like reading . . . them" (paragraph 11). Ask students to explain what Pollitt means. Even students who are readers are likely to need help in explaining how reading itself makes one a better reader.
4. While Pollitt disagrees with the radicals' argument that reading should enhance self-esteem, she sees virtue in it also. How are paragraphs 5 and 6 typical of her argumentative strategy?

Suggested Writing Assignments

1. Pollitt offers Randall Jarrell's list of "Important" and "Unimportant" books (paragraph 13). Make a short list of your own "Important" and "Unimportant" books and write an essay in which you explain your assignment of books to one category or another.

2. Look again at Pollitt's account of reading (paragraph 12). How many of the goals of reading that she mentions can be served by television adaptations of books? (You may want to reread Michael J. Arlen's "The Tyranny of the Visual" [NR 1067]). Write an essay in which you either take a position on television adaptations of literary works or stake out two opposing positions and explain your own by moderating between them.

3. The literature Pollitt considers in this essay is primarily fiction. Write an essay in which you explain the differences and similarities between her view of reading fiction and Vladimir Nabokov's (in "Good Readers and Good Writers" [NR 1004]) and use their views to help define your own.

ADRIENNE RICH

When We Dead Awaken: Writing as Re-Vision

The Norton Reader, p. 1036

Like Virginia Woolf's "In Search of a Room of One's Own," which follows, Adrienne Rich's essay takes up the problems and possibilities of the woman writer. Rich twice alludes to Woolf's essay in hers—once near the beginning (paragraphs 7–9) and again near the end (paragraph 22)—and if you prefer to work chronologically, you can begin by discussing Woolf's essay and then take up Rich's "re-vision" of Woolf's thought. Rich offers a much more personal consideration of the obstacles that confront women who wish to write.

In the course of this essay Rich tells us a great deal about her career as a poet—at least, about how it felt from the inside. From the outside it looked (and looks) different, for she has had a long, distinguished career as a writer. While she was an undergraduate, her first book of poetry, *A Change of World* (1951), was chosen by W. H. Auden for the Yale Younger Poet's Prize. She went on to write more than twenty books of poetry and prose and, in 1994, to win a MacArthur Award. You might ask students why the outward career, so obviously successful, might have felt different from the inside. Was the problem one of living in "traditional" women's roles—or is there something difficult about being in one's twenties and in the early stages of a career that is a problem for men as well as for women?

Questions from the NR10

1. Rich describes herself as hesitant to use her own experience as evidence and illustration in this essay: it would be "a lot easier and less dangerous to talk about other women writers" (paragraph 9). The dangers are personal— i.e., self-exposure and violating the privacy of others—and rhetorical— i.e., relying on evidence that readers may find limited, unconvincing, and self-serving. Locate instances of the first. Consider the second. What do you think are the advantages and disadvantages of Rich's using her own experience?

2. How does Rich work her own experience into a larger argument about

women writers—and all women—at a time when gender and gender roles are being called into question? Find particular instances for analysis.

3. How does Rich describe the experience of writing poetry? How does it follow that her life in the 1950s, as she describes it, was inimical to her writing?

4. Rich refers to "the influence that the myths and images of women have on all of us" (paragraph 11). There are also myths and images of men that influence us. Write an essay in which you consider one myth about either women or men, how it gets internalized, and how it affects the behavior of both women and men.

5. Write an essay on a larger issue in which you focus on your own experience as evidence and illustration.

Analytical Considerations

1. Why does Rich use the hyphen in "re-vision"?

2. The body of Rich's essay depends on quotations from her poetry—from her early years as a student ("Aunt Jennifer's Tigers," written in 1951) to the present ("Planetarium," written in 1971, the year she also wrote this essay). Perhaps in groups, ask students to analyze each poem that Rich quotes in terms of the argument she makes: what evidence does the poem provide—and in support of what point or points?

3. If you have assigned "In Search of a Room of One's Own" (NR 1048, SE 591) ask students how Rich both agrees with and alters Woolf's argument.

4. If you have assigned "In Search of a Room of One's Own," have students look at Rich's characterization of Woolf's tone in this essay: "I was astonished at the sense of effort, of pains taken, of dogged tentativeness. . . . And I recognized that tone. I had heard it often enough, in myself and in other women. It is the tone of a woman almost in touch with her anger, who is determined not to appear angry, who is *willing* herself to be calm, detached, and even charming in a roomful of men where things have been said which are attacks on her very integrity" (paragraph 7). How would they characterize Rich's tone? Is she angry? Is she in touch with her anger?

5. Rich ends this essay by speculating about "another story to be told"— that of masculine consciousness. What does she propose about the effect of women's "awakening" on men?

Suggested Writing Assignments

1. Rich wrote this essay in 1971. Write an essay in which you consider whether or not the situation has changed for the woman writer—or, alternatively, for women pursuing professional careers.

2. Compare what Virginia Woolf (in "In Search of a Room of One's Own" [NR 1048, SE 591]) and Adrienne Rich have to say about the problems and possibilities of the woman writer: on what do they agree? On what do they differ?

3. He: "Women take everything personally." She: "The personal is political." Write an essay in which you make a case for or against the personal. Use this essay of Rich's, her essay "Taking Women Students Seriously" (NR 482, SE 258) in "Education," and any other essays you find useful.

VIRGINIA WOOLF

In Search of a Room of One's Own

The Norton Reader, p. 1048; Shorter Edition, p. 591

This essay is from chapter 3 of Virginia Woolf's *A Room of One's Own*, a central document in twentieth-century feminist criticism. The work began in 1928 as lectures given to undergraduates at two of Cambridge University's women's colleges, Girton and Newnham. Woolf then developed her lectures into a text. "In Search of a Room of One's Own" presents Woolf at her characteristic best: impassioned, witty, learned, and insightful. The essay operates on the historical, imaginative, and personal levels simultaneously, for Woolf writes about the plight of women writers in history—emblematized by the fictitious Judith Shakespeare—which leads to an expression of her concern that women who want to write need to find the means and space to work without distractions.

Analytical Considerations

1. Ask students what they infer from Woolf's title, "A Room of One's Own." Does the essay confirm their inferences?
2. Why does Woolf choose to focus on the living conditions of women in England during the time of Queen Elizabeth? What rhetorical effect can she achieve by using the age of Shakespeare rather than, say, the age of Pope?
3. Explain what Woolf means when she says that "fiction is like a spider's web, attached ever so lightly perhaps, but still attached to life at all four corners" (paragraph 2). What other images might one use for fiction? Would they serve Woolf's purpose as well?
4. What, according to Woolf, is the image of womanhood gained from studying poetry and fiction written by men? Do you agree with her assessment?
5. What does Woolf mean by saying, "It is one of the great advantages of being a woman that one can pass even a very fine negress without wishing to make an Englishwoman of her" (paragraph 9)?
6. How does Woolf answer the question she poses: "what is the state of mind that is most propitious to the act of creation" (paragraph 10)?
7. Ask students to focus on the last seven sentences of paragraph 6 (about the bishop), and analyze what each sentence does. What is the total effect of the passage? How does Woolf use the bishop again? Does he become a metaphor in this essay?
8. Adrienne Rich (in "When We Dead Awaken: Writing as Re-Vision" [NR 1036]) says of Woolf's tone in this essay: "I was astonished at the sense of effort, of pains taken, of dogged tentativeness. . . . And I recognized that tone. I had heard it often enough, in myself and in other women. It is the tone of a woman almost in touch with her anger, who is determined not to appear angry, who is *willing* herself to be calm, detached, and even charming in a roomful of men where things have been said which are attacks on her very integrity" (paragraph 7). Ask students if they agree or disagree with Rich's characterization of Woolf's tone and her explanation of it.

9. This essay was once a lecture, shaped by the demands and conventions of spoken performance. After looking for textual clues that characterize the piece as a lecture, look at two other essays by Woolf in *The Norton Reader*—"My Father: Leslie Stephen" (NR 134, SE 59) and "The Death of the Moth" (NR 1138, SE 656)—both written for publication, not for oral delivery. Ask students how Woolf adapts her techniques and style to an audience of readers rather than listeners. Perhaps even direct the reading and discussion toward the preparation of an essay on this topic.
10. In what ways is "In Search of a Room of One's Own" a personal statement? In what ways it is a cultural document?

Suggested Writing Assignments

1. Write an essay in response to Woolf's description of "that very interesting and obscure masculine complex . . . ; that deep-seated desire, not so much that *she* shall be inferior as that *he* shall be superior" (paragraph 14).
2. *Unimpeded* is a key word in Woolf's essay. Discuss what the term represents in political, physical, and psychological terms for the artists—men, women, or both—whom Woolf discusses.
3. Write an essay in response to the question: do women today have a room of their own?

SUSAN SONTAG

A Century of Cinema

The Norton Reader, p. 1058; Shorter Edition, p. 601

Susan Sontag is a cultural and literary critic, a novelist, and a filmmaker: she has written and directed several films. She is also, obviously, a cinephile. Her essay, originally titled "The Death of Cinema," appeared in the *New York Times Magazine*; this slightly longer version of it, "A Century of Cinema," appeared in a journal called *Parnassus: Poetry in Review*. Sontag, assuming that readers of *Parnassus* would be better informed about European films than readers of the *Times*, added references that American students are likely to find obscure.

Nevertheless, her account of one hundred years of filmmaking is accessible as well as elegant. Questions included in the text ask students to locate themselves in relation to the one hundred years she surveys. Instructors will want to locate themselves as well. Probably some students will be taking or have taken a course in the history of film; ask them to talk about it. You may also suggest, as a topic for research, investigating when cinema became a serious subject of academic study.

Ask students, too, what attitudes they think are characteristic of people who use the terms *cinema*, *film*, and *movies*. Usually *cinema* signifies art, *movies* entertainment, and *film* falls somewhere in between. But, Sontag argues, in its beginnings film was entertainment "on a very high artistic level" (paragraph 7); now it no longer is. Where else do we find similar splits between art and entertainment? In literature, in music, in the visual arts? What is the cultural significance of these splits?

Questions from the NR10

1. In her essay Sontag summarizes one hundred years of film history, from 1895 to 1995. Diagram her periodization of this history. Locate her movie-going period (she was born in 1933) and yours on it. (If there are students of different ages in your class, you may want to include them as a group project.) Which of the older films Sontag mentions have you seen? If you have seen other films made before you began going to the movies, name some of them. How did you see them—in a film-studies course, for example, or on your own?
2. What is Sontag's definition of a "cinephile"? Are you one? Is Susan Allen Toth one? See her "Going to the Movies" (NR 1064).
3. Sontag has harsh things to say about contemporary films: they are "astonishingly witless," "bloated, derivative," "a brazen combinatory or re-combinatory art" (paragraph 1), reduced to "assaultive images, and the unprincipled manipulation of images (faster and faster cutting) to be more attention-grabbing" and, at the same time, "disincarnated, lightweight," and they don't "demand anyone's full attention" (paragraph 6). Write an essay using at least three contemporary films that you have seen in which you agree with, disagree with, or modify her charges.
4. Write an essay in which you compare what Sontag and Toth look for in film.

Analytical Considerations

1. What does Sontag mean when she writes that the "conditions of paying attention in a domestic space are radically disrespectful of film" (paragraph 5)? What are the differences between seeing a film in a theater and seeing it on television or video?
2. What, according to Sontag, are the characteristics of "cinema as industry" (paragraph 10)?
3. Ask students if they have seen any of the great movie houses of the 1930s? What are they like? (Pittsburgh's downtown movie house, for example, now houses the Pittsburgh Symphony Orchestra. You may need some pictures.) Contrast them with today's movie houses. What does each tell us about the place of movies in our culture?

Suggested Writing Assignments

1. Watch the same film in a theater and at home. Write an essay in which you consider differences in the film itself and in your experience of viewing it.
2. Watch for the first time one of the older films Sontag describes as a masterpiece and write an analysis of it. You need not formally compare it with a contemporary film but you should allude to some features of contemporary film as a way of defining features of the older film.
3. Michiko Kakutani, in "Portrait of the Artist as a Focus Group" (NR 408, SE 609) talks about "the sales imperative" (paragraph 5). Identify a new release that brings in a large amount of money in the first week it's shown,

view it, and write an essay in which you identify features that you think made it a success at the box office.

4. Do research on when film studies (or cinema studies) became a serious subject of academic study and write a paper on the founding of the discipline.

SUSAN ALLEN TOTH

Going to the Movies

The Norton Reader, p. 1064

In addition to writing books and regularly contributing to newspapers such as the *New York Times*, Toth teaches writing at Macalester College in Saint Paul, Minnesota. In this short essay she responds to various kinds of films not by analyzing the films but by describing the men with whom she sees them. Because the essay is neatly divided into four sections, it gives instructors an opportunity to show how "classification" and "division" work as rhetorical modes. It may be usefully contrasted with Susan Sontag's "A Century of Cinema" (NR 1058, SE 601) and Michael J. Arlen's "The Tyranny of the Visual" (NR 1067); both discuss film more analytically.

Questions from the NR10

1. Toth describes four kinds of movies by describing the men she sees them with: Aaron, Bob, Sam, and finally no man. Make a list of the adjectives or descriptive phrases she includes for each man. How do such descriptions convey, by implication, her attitudes toward the movies?
2. Which kind of movie does Toth like best—or does she like them all equally? How do you know?
3. Using Toth as a model, write an account of going to some event or participating in some activity by describing the person(s) you go with. Like Toth, convey your response to the event by means of your description of the person(s).

Analytical Considerations

1. Toth's simple arrangement allows for a discussion of the rhetorical techniques of "classification" and "division," and it also allows students to consider how the order in which parts are presented imply a sequence (often less important to more important). Use the students' responses to Questions 1 and 2, above, to discuss the structure of the essay and to ask whether the sequence from Aaron to Bob to Sam to herself alone implies an arrangement of increasing pleasure.
2. Ask students whether they think the men Toth describes are real, fictional, or composites. Does it make any difference in reading the essay? What advantages may Toth gain by associating men with movies?
3. Do the arts events that we attend reflect our values? Ask students what Toth thinks—and what they think.

Suggested Writing Assignments

1. View one of the movies Toth mentions and write an analytical account of it.
2. View one of the movies Toth lists in the last section and write a brief essay comparing your response with hers.
3. Write an essay in which you compare what Susan Sontag, in "A Century of Cinema" (NR 1058, SE 601), and Toth look for in film. Or, alternatively, write an essay in imitation of Toth's in which you describe going to the movies with Susan Sontag.
4. Write an essay about some literary or artistic subject that uses the rhetorical technique of "classification" or "division."

MICHAEL J. ARLEN

The Tyranny of the Visual

The Norton Reader, p. 1067

Arlen, born in London of Armenian parents, began his career with a memoir, *Exiles* (1970). He now writes regularly about television and the media for various newspapers and magazines, including the *New Yorker*. Because his essays often begin as reviews, they are dense with details from recent films, made-for-TV movies, or documentaries. "The Tyranny of the Visual" focuses on an adaptation of Nathaniel Hawthorne's *The Scarlet Letter* for television, but it includes a wide range of references to other movies, including *The Deer Hunter* (also discussed by H. Bruce Franklin in "From Realism to Virtual Reality: Images of America's Wars" in the section called "History" [NR 786, SE 434]).

Arlen, before analyzing the adaptation of *The Scarlet Letter*, describes "a new kind of aesthetic tyranny": visual manipulation, the "exploit[ation of] visual language" to control and bully the viewer (paragraphs 1 and 2).

Questions from the NR10

1. What associations do you have with the word *tyranny*? What does Arlen mean by "aesthetic tyranny" (paragraph 1)? Are visual media—as opposed to verbal media—tyrannical by their very nature?
2. List the visual media that Arlen discusses and the possible tyranny that each can exercise over viewers. Which visual medium in the most controlling?
3. Marshall McLuhan, a Canadian communications theorist, argued that "the medium is the message." Would Arlen agree? Do you? Why does redoing a Cezanne still-life or Chaplin's *City Lights* (paragraph 13) seem preposterous, while we take for granted the practice of redoing literary works?
4. Most of Arlen's essay focuses on public television's adaptation of *The Scarlet Letter*. Look at it or at some other television adaptation of a literary classic that you have read. Which of Arlen's points do you agree with? Which do you disagree with? What additional points do you want to make? Write an essay criticizing or defending the television adaptation of a classic.

Analytical Considerations

1. In paragraph 2, Arlen gives an account of "a visual non sequitur": a key found in the middle of a blacktop road at the beginning of the 1977 movie *Bobby Deerfield*. Before discussing this detail, ask students what they expect when they view an opening scene—or any scene—of a movie. Connect their responses to Arlen's point about "our traditional literary orientation" and about "visual bullying."

2. If you have read H. Bruce Franklin's "From Realism to Virtual Reality: Images of America's Wars" (NR 786, SE 434), you might ask if photographs also exercise a form of aesthetic tyranny. Then ask students whether Arlen's objections to the Russian-roulette sequences in *The Deer Hunter* (paragraphs 3–7) might be explained by connecting them to photographs of the Vietnam War rather than to movies. In other words, what might Franklin say about the Russian-roulette scenes that Arlen doesn't?

3. Why does Arlen minimize the threat of commercials in paragraph 8? Use his contrast between the straightforward playfulness of commercials and the arbitrary, self-referentiality of movies to understand what Arlen finds truly threatening.

4. Ask students if they have read or seen a TV adaptation of *The Scarlet Letter*. If someone has, ask for a summary of the plot; if not, be prepared to explain the gist of the story (partially given in footnote 1). Then ask why Arlen doesn't summarize the story the way he summarizes the opening scene of *Bobby Deerfield*. What does he assume about the cultural knowledge of his readers?

5. Arlen describes *The Scarlet Letter* as "an extraordinarily, profoundly *literary* work," by which he means it is brief, almost compressed, with little action, and "deliberately unrealistic" (paragraph 10). Why do these characteristics make it difficult—if not impossible—to adapt for television? How, according to Arlen, were these difficulties addressed in the film version?

6. Twenty-five consultants, according to Arlen, worked on the adaptation of *The Scarlet Letter*. What do you think they did?

7. You might assign Michiko Kakutani's "Portrait of the Artist as a Focus Group" (NR 408, SE 609) and ask students to consider whether public television is as guilty as commercial television of trying to please. Why or why not?

8. Does Arlen end this essay with the same concern for "the tyranny of the visual" with which he began it, or does he shift ground? Ask students to explain what Arlen means by the "visual vs. literary Capture the Flag contest" (paragraph 14) and whether this contest is related to his opening nine paragraphs.

Suggested Writing Assignments

1. Analyze the opening scene—or another key scene—of a recent film or TV movie and decide whether or not it represents "visual bullying." Write a brief essay describing the scene and explaining why or why not.

2. Look at one of the older movie versions Arlen mentions of a literary classic you have read: *A Midsummer Night's Dream*, *Moby Dick*, *Jane Eyre*, *Wuthering Heights*, *David Copperfield*. Write an essay in which you make a case for or against their likable foolishness and energy.

3. Write a personal essay describing some visual image that has exercised a "tyranny" over your imagination.

AARON COPLAND

How We Listen

The Norton Reader, p. 1074; Shorter Edition, p. 611

Aaron Copland, an American composer, writes a cogent analysis of the listening process in "How We Listen." Because he wishes to inform and instruct, he takes pains to be clear. He first splits listening into its component parts (or "planes") through classification; he characterizes this splitting as mechanical but useful in providing clarity (paragraph 1). He then proceeds to analyze each part, and, finally, he reintegrates the three. The structure of his essay, his use of example and analogy, and the simplicity of his language lead readers to understand that they listen to music in multiple ways at the same time. His essay provides a model of how an expert can communicate ideas in a form accessible to a lay audience.

Analytical Considerations

1. Ask students to mark Copland's categories in "How We Listen." Are they mutually exclusive and clearly explained?
2. Copland's categories—or "planes"—are hierarchical and arranged in ascending progression. Why? How does he assign value to each?
3. Consider Copland's judgments. How, for example, is Beethoven "greater" than Ravel (paragraph 6)? And Tchaikovsky "easier to 'understand' than Beethoven" (paragraph 11)? What criteria does Copland use?
4. How does Copland use analogy? Ask students to mark his analogies and consider how they work and how effective they are. This exercise may be done in groups.
5. Copland extends his categories, by analogy, to theatergoing. Can they also be extended to viewing art, reading literature, and reading essays?
6. How do we take Copland's references to "simple-minded souls," one "timid lady" (paragraph 9), and "the man in the street" (paragraph 18)? Do we identify with or distance ourselves from them? How, then, do these labels function as rhetorical devices?

Suggested Writing Assignments

1. Write a rhetorical analysis of "How We Listen," detailing the means by which Copland succeeds or fails in discussing a difficult topic.
2. Apply the categories of listening discussed in Copland's essay to a piece of his own music. Consider a piece that has a theme.
3. According to Copland, "A subjective and objective attitude is implied in both creating and listening to music"; see his explanation in paragraph 25. Write an essay analyzing subjective and objective elements in his three categories of listening.

PROSE FORMS: PARABLES

The Norton Reader, p. 1079

The parable and fable are didactic forms, ideal for conveying moral or religious truth, ideal for communicating advice for living by means of story and storytelling. Parables usually have human characters; fables usually achieve their special effect with birds, mammals, or insects. In writing a parable or fable, a modern writer will continually verge on straight prose narrative but also will, by means of narrative, preserve the essayist's essential commitment to the definition and description of ideas in relation to experience.

Two of the selections in this section, the New Testament parables of Jesus and the Zen parables, represent classic examples of religious teaching using the parable form. Two others, Plato's "The Allegory of the Cave" and Aesop's fable of "The Frogs Desiring a King," show how writers in the western tradition have long used the form to explain and illustrate philosophical truth. The final two selections, Jonathan Swift's "The Spider and the Bee" and Mark Twain's "The War Prayer," give examples of literary fables and parables that intervene in contemporary issues and debates and, by means of a story, make an implicit argument about an appropriate course of human action.

Questions from the NR10

1. Many parables end with a moral explicitly stated—as in the conclusion to Aesop's fable, "Let well enough alone!" Which parables in this section include such morals? Which do not? Why might some writers choose not to conclude with an explicit statement of the "moral"?
2. For those parables that do not include morals, write your own version of a moral or maxim that might be dedcued from the narrative. Is it possible to deduce more than one moral?
3. Write a parable that, while using a narrative form, has a moral or maxim embedded within it.

Analytical Considerations

1. Some fables, like Aesop's, end with a moral. Some parables, like those Jesus told to his disciples, have morals embedded within them. Others, like Plato's allegory and the Zen parables, do not end with explicit morals. Ask students to read the morals they have written for such parables (see Question 2, above), and perhaps write them on the blackboard. Most likely, they will vary in focus and even in meaning. Discuss why this variation occurs: what is it about interpreting a complex parable that makes it difficult to sum up in a single sentence?
2. In pairs or small groups, ask students to read the parables they have written for Question 3, above, but without including the moral. Then ask the group to write down the moral they derive. Use these morals to help the writer think about where revision might be needed, as well as to discuss how and why some details in a story may lead readers astray.

Suggested Writing Assignments

1. Take one of the ancient parables and write a personal essay in which you use your experience to demonstrate the truth of the parable.
2. Choose one of the modern, literary parables, and instead of a story, write a formal argument in which you advance a thesis and present evidence for a view similar to that expressed by the writer.
3. Write a fable of your own that tells a story about "animals" but implicitly comments on human behavior.
4. Write a parable that tells a story and embeds a moral or maxim within it.

PHILOSOPHY AND RELIGION

LANGSTON HUGHES

Salvation

The Norton Reader, p. 1094; Shorter Edition, p. 616

"Salvation" reveals in full measure Langston Hughes's gifts as a storyteller: economy and precision of language, a keen ear for dialogue, a sharp eye for descriptive detail, a detached ironic voice, and a capacity for seriousness with humor. Hughes's re-creation of a revival meeting in rural America around 1914 or 1915 is an engaging cultural document. It's possible to see it both as an expose of the sometimes dishonest theatrics of a manipulative preacher in front of a gullible flock of souls and as an account of the efforts of a community of believers to induce a reluctant inquirer to share their experience. It is also an account of an experience with considerable symbolic importance in Hughes's memory; as such it might be considered a rite-of-passage narrative.

Questions from the NR10

1. Hughes describes how he lost his faith in Jesus at the age of twelve. How did the grownups in his life contribute to the experience?
2. Hughes expected to "see" Jesus. How did he understand the word *see*? How did he need to understand it?
3. Hughes was twelve ("going on thirteen") when the event he describes in first-person narration took place. How careful is he to restrict himself to the point of view of a twelve-year-old child? How does he insure that we, as readers, understand things that the narrator does not?
4. Write a first-person narrative in which you describe a failure—yours or someone else's—to live up to the expectations of parents or other authority figures.
5. Write an essay in which you compare the use of first-person narration in this essay, in Edward Rivera's "First Communion" (NR 1096, SE 618), and in Mordecai Rosenfeld's "Genesis, Chapter 22—A Respectful Dissent" (NR 1109, SE 631).

Analytical Considerations

1. How do we know that "Salvation" was written by an adult? You will want students to notice the strategies Hughes uses to record the experience of a twelve-year-old and adult reflections on it.
2. The discussion evoked by Analytical Consideration 1, above, can be extended to a discussion of autobiography as both a record of and a reflection on personal experience with cultural resonance.
3. A rite of passage is a ritual associated with a crisis or a change of status. What are some of the ways the revival meeting changed Langston Hughes?

4. What is the tone of Hughes's first sentence? Of his second sentence? What is the effect of paragraph 12, which consists of one four-word sentence?
5. Ask students to analyze Hughes's techniques as a narrator. Is his narrative effective? Why or why not?
6. Compare Hughes's ability to recapture childhood experience with that of one or more of the following authors whose narratives appear in the section called "Personal Report": Maya Angelou, in "Graduation" (NR 1, SE 1) and Wallace Stegner, in "The Town Dump" (NR 20).

Suggested Writing Assignments

1. Write an essay on the ways in which "Salvation" re-creates a particular time and place. Why, for example, are some characters named but no specific location cited?
2. Write a personal essay in which you recount feeling pressured into doing something you would have preferred to have avoided. Try to convey, as Hughes does, both your feelings at the time and your present attitude toward the experience.
3. Write your own rite-of-passage narrative.

EDWARD RIVERA

First Communion

The Norton Reader, p. 1096; Shorter Edition, p. 618

Born in Puerto Rico, Rivera moved to New York's Spanish Harlem while in elementary school. He recounted his growing up in his 1982 autobiographical memoir, *Family Installments*. This chapter is a comic recounting of his first communion, a rite of passage for him and his family.

Rivera contextualizes his religious memories, reminding us that profound spiritual events and feelings take place in the midst of social, economic, and political turmoil. Here the background to his first communion is the grinding poverty of a welfare family, the nuns' rigidity, the neighborhood changing from Irish and Italian to Puerto Rican, the rivalries between public and parochial school kids, the personal relations between Rivera and his classmates, and even the quest for Puerto Rican independence, as Maestro Padilla's organ playing reminds us. In contrast to traditional narratives of spiritual development, this vivid story of a comic failure presents a lived religion enforced by family, teachers, and church officials while menaced by peers, society, and an eight-year-old's lack of confidence.

Questions from the NR10

1. One theme of this narrative is the conflict between Puerto Ricans and "others" who represent authority. Point out instances where this conflict operates. Does this theme dominate the entire essay? Why or why not?

2. Chart the behavorial conflicts within the young Rivera, who sometimes acts like an impulsive eight-year-old and sometimes acts by the standards of his parochial school.
3. Describe an experience in which you or someone else was unable to live up to the expectations of parents or authority figures.

Analytical Considerations

1. How do we know that "First Communion" was written by an adult? You will want students to notice the strategies Rivera uses to record the experience of an eight-year-old and adult reflections on it.
2. Have students compare Rivera's "First Communion" with Langston Hughes's "Salvation" (NR 1094, SE 616), also in this section, as rite-of-passage narratives. Does Edward Rivera show his first communion changing him as much as Hughes shows the revival meeting changing him? How might the difference in their ages contribute? How about the fact that Hughes's "Salvation" is a stand-alone narrative, while "First Communion" is a chapter in an autobiography?
3. Both Rivera and Eudora Welty, in "Clamorous to Learn" (NR 423) mention *deportment*. Ask students if the word has any resonance for them. Some will never have heard it, while others are likely to have had it engraved on their consciousness. Ask them if they know the word *conduct*. Then ask them the significance of different schools naming these concepts differently.
4. Are there any signs in the depiction of Rivera as an eight-year-old that he will grow up to be an English professor and a writer?

Suggested Writing Assignments

1. Write about two different cultures coming into conflict through the eyes of a younger person. The cultures can be ethnic, as in Rivera's essay, or religious, generational, or geographic.
2. Rivera describes both a community and a family occasion. Write your own account of a community or family event that went wrong. Be sure to give your version a narrator who was also a participant.

MORDECAI ROSENFELD

Genesis, Chapter 22—A Respectful Dissent

The Norton Reader, p. 1109; Shorter Edition, p. 631

Mordecai Rosenfeld is an attorney who writes a monthly column for the *New York Law Journal*. Two collections of his columns have been published: *The Lament of the Single Practitioner* (1988) and *A Backhanded View of the Law* (1992). Ordinarily he uses these columns to comment on legal proceedings, often current ones, as in this essay, which was prompted by a brief notice in the *New York Times* of a Supreme Court justice's refusal to stay the jail sentence of Texas parents named Port who had been held in contempt of court for refusing to give evidence when their son was tried for murder. Often Rosenfeld works in material from his childhood to illustrate his points.

Students should note that Rosenfeld holds off on the details of the Port case until the end of this essay. Instead he starts with chapter 22 of Genesis or, rather, with his own unconventional reading of the sacrifice of Isaac: that God was disappointed in Abraham's willingness to sacrifice his son.

Rosenfeld describes his young self as "indifferent" to religion (paragraph 3). If there was a rite of passage that led to this indifference, or a family crisis when it became manifest (as it apparently was by the time he was nine), they are not the subjects of this essay. The contentions he describes concern religious observances: attending services, listening to the radio, studying Hebrew, keeping kosher. In each instance his parents apparently recognized that their son was his own person.

Questions from the NR10

1. In his essay Rosenfeld combines an autobiographical narrative with an argument about a Supreme Court decision. How are the two combined? Which one do you think predominates?
2. What is the usual interpretation of the story of the sacrifice of Isaac? What is Rosenfeld's interpretation?
3. Isaac, according to Rosenfeld, "was his own person and not Abraham's to give" (paragraph 2). What does it mean to be one's own person? Was the young Rosenfeld his own person? the young Langston Hughes, in "Salvation" (NR 1094, SE 616)? the young Edward Rivera, in "First Communion" (NR 1096, SE 618)? In what sense, if any, can children be their own persons?
4. Write an essay in which you compare the use of first-person narration in this essay, in Langston Hughes's "Salvation," and in Edward Rivera's "First Communion."

Analytical Considerations

1. Most discussions of the sacrifice of Isaac, you may need to point out to students, focus on Abraham, not Isaac. See, for example, Jean Paul Sartre's "Existentialism" (NR 1168, SE 666), paragraphs 6 to 8; Sartre also alludes to the famous discussion of the "anguish" of Abraham in the Danish philosopher Søren Kierkegaard's *Fear and Trembling* (1941).
2. Langston Hughes, in "Salvation" (NR 1094, SE, 616), and Edward Rivera, in "First Communion" (NR 1096, SE 618), both record the experience of their young selves and their adult reflections on it. Does Rosenfeld? Have students specify some of the differences in their narratives.
3. There are several arguments implicit in Rosenfeld's essay. What are they? Are there arguments implicit in Hughes's and Rivera's essays?
4. Are there any signs in this essay that the young Rosenfeld will grow up to become an attorney?
5. Explaining how he came to write his column in the *New York Law Journal* (in the introduction to *The Lament of the Single Practitioner*), Rosenfeld tells how, at a seminar sponsored by the journal, he noticed the audience

becoming drowsy and decided to "wing it with a lighter touch." What are the components of his "lighter touch"? What elements of his experience does he downplay to maintain it?

Suggested Writing Assignments

1. Restricting yourself to evidence from Langston Hughes' "Salvation" (NR 1094, SE 616), Edward Rivera's "First Communion" (NR 1096, SE 618), and Mordecai Rosenfeld's "Genesis, chapter 22—A Respectful Dissent," write an essay in which you analyze the differences between evangelical Protestantism, Roman Catholicism, and Judaism. Try not to bring in other information and opinions.
2. Take a brief notice of something from a newspaper and develop some sort of autobiographical narrative or argument from it.
3. Read Genesis, Chapter 22, and offer your own interpretation of the sacrifice of Isaac. You may take other interpretations into account if you wish.
4. Do research on the religious observances of Orthodox Jews. Write an essay in which you consider the restrictions that make them stand apart from secular society in America.

JAMES THURBER

The Owl Who Was God

The Norton Reader, p. 1111

Thurber was a master of the brief humorous piece, shorter than an essay but longer than a joke. Like Aesop's fables, Thurber's are animal stories with single-sentence morals; see Aesop's "The Frogs Desiring a King" (NR 1081), with its moral, "Let well enough alone!" But, unlike Aesop's, his morals are turned upside down (or inside out), and his humor always flirts with the subversive. In this fable, for example, his moral plays off Abraham Lincoln's remark: "It is true that you may fool all the people some of the time; you can even fool some of the people all the time; but you can't fool all of the people all the time."

Analytical Considerations

1. Tone is all-important to Thurber's fables. Ask students to consider his knowing narrative voice. What are its characteristics? Where have they heard it before? What makes it effective?
2. Does the silliness of Thurber's fable imply a serious message? Or is his variation on Lincoln's remark one more joke?

Suggested Writing Assignments

1. Invent a three- or four-paragraph animal fable of your own, leading up either to a well-known saying or to a variation on one. Try to achieve the same knowing tone as Thurber.

2. Write an essay explaining why the Thurber fable either does or does not belong in this chapter on philosophy and religion.

3. Read some additional Thurber fables; they are collected, with his line drawings, in *Fables for Our Time* (1940) and *Further Fables for Our Time* (1956). Write an essay about at least three of his fables in which you analyze his strategies; you may also wish to consider what his drawings contribute.

LOUIS MENAND

The Gods Are Anxious

The Norton Reader, p. 1112

Louis Menand is both a professor of English and what might be called a public intellectual: he teaches at the Graduate School and University Center of the City University of New York and is a contributing editor of the *New York Review of Books*. He writes about and reviews books on culture, film, literature, and politics for a number of periodicals. This brief essay, reflections on a genetic discovery reported in the journal *Science* and on the front page of the *New York Times*, appeared in the *New Yorker*.

Irony makes Menand's essay both witty and serious—and students are likely to need help understanding it. Menand deploys his irony in elegantly modulated sentences. For example, he calls "gene-based explanations of personality" "immensely clarifying contributions to thought" and then invents a wildly reductive account of how a gene for anxiety causes people to live in New York (paragraph 2). The silliness of the account exerts pressure back on and undercuts his suave formulation, "immensely clarifying contributions to thought." Following an equally reductive account of how the same gene causes people to become cabdrivers, he observes, tersely and enigmatically, "The animus seeks its animal" (paragraph 3). His observation requires some unpacking.

Menand extends his reflections on gene-based explanations of behavior, which he terms "the new polytheism" (paragraph 5), to larger considerations about determinism. Students will have to understand the parallels he draws, first, between the old polytheisms of multiple gods and the new polytheisms of culture and genes, and second, between the old religious monotheisms and the new secular monotheisms—Freudian, Marxist, and economic—that he alludes to but does not name (paragraph 5). All determinisms, he concludes, can be both dreams and nightmares; they are most attractive when they relieve us of "the burden of responsibility" (paragraph 8).

Analytical Considerations

1. Ask students to locate examples of Menand's ironic locutions in this essay and to explain how they work.

2. In "Why the Reckless Survive" (NR 946, SE 535), "Science," Melvin Konner, an anthropologist and medical researcher, takes what he calls "genetic predispositions" seriously; these include a predisposition to bungee-jumping. Assign Konner's essay in conjunction with Menand's to discuss

differences between genetic predispositions and genetic determinism. Does Konner provide the "little of both" that Menand says most of us want to believe in (paragraph 7)?

Suggested Writing Assignments

1. Locate the articles in *Science* and the *New York Times* that provoked Menand's essay. Is the genetic polytheism Menand finds in them implicit or explicit? Write an essay in which you compare how the discovery of a shorter gene in anxious people is handled in the scientific report, the journalistic report, and Menand's essay.
2. Write an essay explaining why Menand's essay either does or does not belong in this chapter on philosophy and religion.
3. "Most people," according to Menand, "are likely to want to believe in a little of both—to think that people are pretty much the way they are, and also that reading aloud from 'The Book of Virtues' can make them a bit better—but these are very different belief systems." Do you agree or disagree? Make your case with examples from your experience, observation, and reading.
4. Find a news item that will support ironic reflection and try your hand at a brief essay of the sort Menand has written.

ROBERT GRAVES

Mythology

The Norton Reader, p. 1114

Graves was seriously wounded in World War I, wrote a powerful memoir of his experience, *Good-bye to All That* (1929), and then turned to writing poetry. He had a lifelong interest in myth, even claiming that his own poetry could not have been written without the inspiration of a "White Goddess." Late in life he was asked to edit two popular collections: the two-volume Penguin books paperback *The Greek Myths* (1955) and the *Larousse Encyclopedia of Mythology* (1959), both aimed at the general reader. This essay is the introduction to the second. Graves approached myths not as a scholar but as a collector, a writer who used them for inspiration. He was particularly attracted to Greek and Roman mythology, and he made his home in Spain's Balearic Islands, in the midst of the Mediterranean world that was the locus of many of the myths about which he wrote.

Thinkers about myths in this century, such as the Swiss psychologist Carl Gustav Jung and the French social anthropologist Claude Lévi-Strauss, have elaborated various theories about them: Jung regarded them as connected to universals of human consciousness, while Lévi-Strauss thought of them as having a grammar or sign system of their own. Graves regarded them rather more simply as "a dramatic shorthand record of such matters as invasions, migrations, dynastic changes, admission of foreign cults, and social reforms" (paragraph 13). He also regarded them as material to be used, particularly by writers, for, as he concludes this essay, "myths are seldom simple, and never irresponsible" (paragraph 16).

Analytical Considerations

1. Graves introduces his discussion of myths by laying out two functions for them. To what extent does he organize this essay by these categories?
2. The first and last sentences of this essay are examples of Graves's ability to turn a memorable phrase. Ask students to pick out three more such phrases and to note particularly what purpose they serve. (Often these striking statements are summarizing sentences, introducing or concluding detailed listings of particular myths drawn from different traditions.)
3. According to Graves, standard European mythologies omit Judeo-Christian beliefs while including myths from Persia, Babylonia, Egypt, and Greece, among others (paragraph 1). Is it ethnocentric to call some religious beliefs and not others myths, in effect, to draw a line around Judeo-Christian beliefs and exclude them?
4. Contrast the way Graves uses the word myth with Betty Rollin's use of the same term, in "Motherhood: Who Needs It?" (NR 354, SE 203) in "Cultural Critique."

Suggested Writing Assignments

1. Write an essay on contemporary understandings of myth after collecting evidence from people you know. Ask them for their definition of *myth* and specific examples. Do their myths answer questions about origins and justify existing social systems?
2. Ask people you know how they differentiate their religious beliefs from myth and write an essay on contemporary understandings of myth and religion.
3. Cast yourself as a narrator unfamiliar with North American life and write an essay describing three myths that seem to animate people in this decade. (Jessica Mitford, in "Behind the Formaldehyde Curtain" [NR 328, SE 180] in "Cultural Critique," does something on this order. She describes American funeral practices as if they were embodiments of odd myths and makes the ordinary seem strange and somewhat preposterous.)

MARTHA NUSSBAUM

The Idea of World Citizenship in Greek and Roman Antiquity

The Norton Reader, p. 1118

Martha Nussbaum is an academic trained in classics, philosophy, and law. Recently she has begun to write cultural criticism; in *Cultivating Humanity: A Classical Defense of Reform in Liberal Education* (1997), from which this essay is taken, she turns her considerable erudition to contemporary debates about liberal education and the curriculum. While some argue that multiculturalism is a newfangled form of political correctness, Nussbaum argues that it has its roots in classical antiquity and persists in the legacy of Stoicism.

Nussbaum introduces this essay by setting up two oppositions, one, the natural and normal versus the parochial and habitual, the other, nature versus convention (paragraphs 3–4); she concludes it with a third, multiculturalism as it leads to the affirmation of human identity versus multiculturalism as it leads to the affirmation of minority identities. Her focus in most of the essay, however, is a history of the idea of multiculturalism and multicultural inquiry from classical antiquity to the present. Her challenge: to be clear, engaging, and accurate without becoming bogged down with minutiae and qualifications. Instructors are likely to think she succeeds; students may or may not. It's worth pointing out to them that biography—her sketches of Diogenes and Marcus Aurelius—is one strategy she employs to present ideas in relation to each other.

This essay, compared with others in *The Norton Reader*, is rather heavily annotated and offers an opportunity to discuss the multiple functions of footnotes. Ask students to mark Nussbaum's footnotes (as opposed to the editors' footnotes). Which cite references? Which are explanatory? What kind of statement do her notes make about the range of her reading? How do they buttress her authority? You may wish to bring to class copies of Nussbaum's article in the *Journal of Political Philosophy* cited in note 5 (NR 1119)—or just its notes—to contrast annotation for general readers with that for specialized readers.

Analytical Considerations

1. Look at the biographical sketches of Diogenes the Cynic and Marcus Aurelius. How many of Nussbaum's points about multicultural inquiry does each embody?
2. Contrast the education of the Athenians and the Spartans, as Nussbaum presents them. What might be their contemporary analogues?
3. Citizens of the world are, according to Nussbaum, "philosophical exiles from our own ways of life" (paragraph 15). What are some examples of this exile in her essay? What examples can be drawn from the contemporary world?
4. In the course of this essay Nussbaum quotes Rabindranath Tagore, Kwame Anthony Appiah (both in paragraph 2), and the African National Congress (paragraph 38). Why?
5. Nussbaum acknowledges the force of the local and particular with respect to language and literature. How? Do you agree with her argument?
6. "The task of world citizenship requires the would-be world citizen to become a sensitive and empathic interpreter. Education at all ages should cultivate the capacity for such interpreting" (paragraph 30). Ask students if and how their education has developed this capacity.

Suggested Writing Assignments

1. Choose a custom that some people take to be natural and normal and write an essay in which you argue that it is parochial and habitual. Or, alternatively, choose a custom that some people take to be parochial and habitual and argue that it is natural and normal.
2. Write an essay in which you characterize your own education or a segment of it (elementary, secondary, or postsecondary) as Athenian or Spartan.

Do you agree with Nussbaum's claim that an Athenian education is superior to a Spartan one?

3. Take one or more instances, in school or elsewhere, when you behaved as an empathic interpreter of someone else. Write an essay in which you analyze how you behaved as one and the ease or difficulty of the task.

4. "To understand is to forgive"—so goes the adage. Write an essay in which you consider whether empathic interpretation is always a virtue.

PAUL TILLICH

The Riddle of Inequality

The Norton Reader, p. 1132; Shorter Edition, p. 647

Tillich was one of Protestantism's towering intellects, a theologian and preacher who first made his mark in Germany and then, after fleeing Hitler, at New York's Union Theological Seminary. This essay takes the form of a sermon: a biblical text (a saying of Jesus) at the beginning, an extended examination of its meaning (both in the Bible and in people's lives), a look at the difficult questions it raises, an attempt at resolving these questions, and a concluding amen.

Throughout the sermon-essay Tillich moves deliberately. His sermon style has no room for flights of fancy or complex, showy rhetoric. It is a sober examination of a troubling issue of faith, and Tillich assumes his audience is ready to explore with him Jesus's seemingly offensive acceptance of inequality.

The shape of class discussion is likely to be determined by students' familiarity with sermons. Students who have listened to a number of them may be able to recollect some and help instructors identify their characteristic organization and style; otherwise instructors will have to point them out. It is important to emphasize that sermons' rhetorical conventions are rooted in oral delivery: strong structural elements leading to some sort of resolution, along with emphatic statements and extended development. (Prose written to be read can be more fluid, dense, and allusive.) A good discussion of Tillich can result when at least some students are able to compare sermons they've heard with Tillich's.

Analytical Considerations

1. Tillich claims that inequality is "the greatest and perhaps most painful riddle of life" (paragraph 1). Ask students if they thought so before they read this piece; then ask if they have changed their opinion in any way now that they have read it.

2. Students need to look carefully at paragraph 18, in which Tillich alludes to the transmutation of souls: "can we trespass the boundaries of the Christian tradition," he inquires. Once students are sure they know what Tillich is talking about, they will be able to understand why he refers to this doctrine so obliquely and how it functions in his argument.

3. Many readers will think that the key to Tillich's resolution of the questions his text raises is paragraph 20, in which he offers not a simple statement but rather a sweeping conclusion: "There is an ultimate unity of all beings, rooted in the divine life from which they come and to which they go." Why doesn't he feel the need to explain or argue for this statement?

Suggested Writing Assignments

1. Tillich writes movingly of losing things such as childish innocence and youthful enthusiasm in order to gain maturity and wisdom. Have you had to give them up as well—or do you expect to have to give them up? Using your experience, observation, and reading, write an essay in which you discuss one or more particular instances of giving up in order to gain.

2. Tillich describes how different students approach college: "to buy their entrance ticket into the upper middle classes" or "driven by the desire for knowledge" (paragraph 6). Which motives does Tillich approve of? Is he too simplistic, too sweeping in setting out his alternatives? Write an essay with reference to Tillich in which you agree, disagree, or work out your own resolution of these alternatives.

VIRGINIA WOOLF

The Death of the Moth

The Norton Reader, p. 1138; Shorter Edition, p. 656

This essay, one of Virginia Woolf's best-known works of nonfiction, combines narration and description in the service of definition. Woolf writes with feeling but not sentiment, offering her reader a carefully realized observation before speculating about its meaning.

Woolf plays the role of observer and reporter in this essay. What begins as idle curiosity becomes conscious speculation, but no explicit conclusions are drawn. Although she points to possible meaning immanent in the death throes of the moth, she does not overshadow the event itself with analysis. Her technique here might be contrasted with that of other essayists who draw out their meanings more directly; students might be asked to think about how writers' choices interact with discourse conventions to create a range of possibilities in the essay form.

Questions from the NR10

1. Trace the sequence in which Woolf comes to identify with the moth. How does she make her identification explicit? How is it implicit in the language she uses describe the moth?
2. Choose one of the descriptions of a small living creature or creatures in Annie Dillard's "Sight into Insight" (NR 1140) and compare it with Woolf's description of the moth. Does a similar identification take place in Dillard's essay? If so, how; if not, why not?
3. Henry David Thoreau, in "The Battle of the Ants" (NR 762, SE 414), also humanizes small living creatures. How do his strategies differ from Woolf's?
4. Write two descriptions of the same living creature, one using Woolf's strategies, the other using Thoreau's. Or, alternatively, write an essay in which you analyze the differences between them.

Analytical Considerations

1. Ask students what aspects of "The Death of the Moth" they remember best—and why? Imagery will likely be relevant to their responses. If so, have students select several images and describe the primary appeal of each (visual, aural, tactile). Then ask them to determine how each image functions within the essay.
2. Does Woolf provide a thesis statement? Does she have a central point she wishes to make? Or is her essay a speculative exercise, more important for the act of reflecting than for making a point?
3. You may want students to describe the persona Woolf creates in this essay and how she creates it. Call attention to her use of the third person ("one") in much of the essay and her shift to the first person in the last paragraphs. What effects do these pronouns and their sequence create?
4. How and to what effect does Woolf use a kind of triple focus—the world "out there," the moth, and the narrator—in this essay?
5. What is the relationship between the life and death of the moth and the life and death of human beings in "The Death of the Moth"? Does Woolf offer any conclusions about death in this piece?

Suggested Writing Assignments

1. If the death of an animal has moved you to speculate on significant questions concerning life and death, write an essay describing and analyzing the experience.
2. With ironic understatement, Woolf writes: "The insignificant little creature now knew death" (paragraph 5). Yet this little creature was not insignificant. Write an essay explaining why.
3. Observe an insect and describe it from two points of view—one objective and one subjective, as a scientist might describe it and as a poet or a novelist might describe it.

ANNIE DILLARD

Sight into Insight

The Norton Reader, p. 1140

Dillard is known for personal essays about nature and religious experience. "Sight into Insight," which appeared first in 1974 as a magazine essay, was then included in her most famous book, *Pilgrim at Tinker Creek* (1974). Attending to everyday matters at Tinker Creek, she is, without traveling, a pilgrim who awaits illuminations that reveal the timeless and universal.

Dillard accumulates examples and renders them in detail with a showiness and panache that may put students off. You may want to consider a single paragraph or assign single paragraphs to groups of students to consider; paragraphs 3, 4, 5, 6, 11, 12, 19, 27, and 36 will serve the purpose.

Each of this essay's six sections begins with sight. Section two ends with insight, section three with blindness, section four with untutored infant sight, and sections five and six with insight. All the passages describing insight warrant close reading. Dillard claims that the effort to achieve insight "marks the literature of saints and monks of every order east and west, under every rule and no rule, discalced and shod" (paragraph 34). Evelyn Underhill, in *The Essentials of Mysticism* (1911), schematizes the stages of mystic experience as reported by mystics themselves across religions and cultures: they go from an intense and enlarged perception of the natural world to a perception of realities above and beyond it to union with divine presences. The first two stages are present in this essay. Students are likely to need help in understanding and characterizing Dillard's descriptions of insight; contrasting them with her descriptions of sight will help.

Dillard also describes insight as unedited and unlearned (see section four), unverbalized (see section five), and unwilled (see sections five and six). Sight, she implies, is edited and learned, verbalized, and willed. These distinctions afford another way of contrasting her descriptions of sight and insight.

One of Dillard's masters is Thoreau. She quotes him directly (in paragraph 33), and his doctrines and strategies can be found throughout this essay, especially in her terse, apothegmatic general statements. Thoreau is represented in *The Norton Reader* by selections from his journal (NR 90), by "Observation" (NR 250), and by "The Battle of the Ants" (NR 762, SE 414).

Questions from the NR10

1. Dillard works by accumulation: she heaps up examples. Sometimes, not always, they are accompanied by a terse, apothegmatic general statement, such as "nature is very much a now-you-see-it, now-you-don't affair" (paragraph 3). Locate other examples of these accumulations; mark the general

statements that accompany them. What uses do these accumulations serve? In what kinds of writing are they appropriate, in what kinds inappropriate?

2. How does the kind of seeing Dillard describes at the end of her essay differ from the kind of seeing she describes at the beginning? How does material that appears in the sections on sight help her describe insight?

3. Take one of Dillard's terse, apothegmatic general statements and write your own accumulation of examples for it.

4. Dillard says, "I see what I expect" (paragraph 8). Write a description of something familiar, paying attention to how you "edit" your seeing. Then write a parallel description of it as if you were seeing it "unedited," as Dillard tried to see "color-patches" like the newly sighted (paragraph 27).

Analytical Considerations

1. How can Dillard's descriptive prose be justified or condemned? How does she bind a series of descriptive statements together? How does she make us see?

2. Contrast two of Dillard's individual pieces of description, one of sight and one of insight. What are the components of each?

3. Identify doctrines and strategies in a selection by Thoreau (see NR 90, 250, 762; SE 414) that also appear in this essay by Dillard.

4. Compare Dillard's descriptions of the world of the newly sighted with Edward Hoagland's description of the world he saw when he regained his sight, in "Brightness Visible" (NR 1151). What difference does it make to their descriptions that Dillard gained her knowledge from reading Marius Von Senden's *Space and Sight*, while Hoagland gained his from experience.

Suggested Writing Assignments

1. Write an essay in which you compare Dillard's account of sight and insight with William Wordsworth's account in "Ode: Intimations of Immortality from Recollections of Early Childhood."

2. Dillard takes some ordinary creek water and places it in a white china bowl to look for small creatures. Do the same with some rainwater, creek, pond, or puddle water and report what you see, first in a plain, factual style and then with elaboration in Dillard's fashion.

3. Read Gilbert Highet's "The Mystery of Zen" (NR 1159, SE 658). Write an essay in which you compare Highet's reflections on the instruction in archery he describes with Dillard's reflections on giving up in order to see in section six of this essay (paragraphs 34–36). What are the similarities between them?

EDWARD HOAGLAND

Brightness Visible

The Norton Reader, p. 1151

Edward Hoagland is a prolific essayist. "Brightness Visible" first appeared in *Harper's Magazine*; his most recent collection of essays is *Tiggers and Ice* (1999).

The fluid organization of Hoagland's essay may well irritate students accustomed to looking for topic sentences and paraphrasable content when they read. This essay's organization affords a useful contrast to the coherent organization and the careful presentation of appropriate evidence characteristic of "academic" or "college" writing. Hoagland's essay does develop in the sense that by its end readers can look back and apprehend the connections he makes between nature and God. But the journey requires navigating his associative leaps and exuberant digressions. (A writing assignment that asks students to proceed by leaps and digressions is likely to engage them and will help to make them conscious of the connections they are expected to provide in ordinary college writing.)

One strategy for teaching "Brightness Visible" is to have students write about the opening section before and after reading the rest. After their first reading ask them to make some predictions about the rest of the essay; after their second reading ask them to assess their correct and incorrect predictions. Hoagland of course does more in the opening section than indicate his themes, God and nature; he also introduces himself, partly through a biographical account of regaining his sight (and seeing again the natural world that figures so largely in the rest of the essay) and partly through establishing the idiosyncratic voice that creates his persona. By the end of this essay students should have a clear sense of Hoagland and what his presence contributes to it.

In the long central section Hoagland attends to his themes: God—that is, nature's God—and nature, his creation. Have students focus on Hoagland's brisk characterizations of the God of the Old Testament and the God of the New Testament and his statements about his preferences. Is there shock value in them? What would happen if students tried making similar statements—at home, to their friends, in church? Then turn to nature, God's creation. What are Hoagland's views about the environment? How important are they to this essay? Would this essay have fit equally well in the section called "Nature and the Environment"?

Questions from the NR10

1. Hoagland's essay, fluid in organization, seems to move by association. Spaces indicate three sections: a short introductory section (paragraphs 1–6), a long middle section (paragraphs 7–22), and a short concluding section (paragraphs 23–25). What themes does Hoagland introduce in the first section? How many of them does he continue in the second section? What themes does he add? Where do his emphases fall? How many of his themes does he pull together in the third section?

2. Hoagland has strong views about the Bible. What are the parts he approves of? What are the parts he disapproves of?

3. Hoagland describes his religion as "American transcendentalism" (paragraph 15) and "[t]ranscendentalism" (paragraph 22). Explain, with reference to this essay, what he means by *transcendentalism*.

4. In this essay we can hear a strong, individualized voice. Choose several passages and write an essay showing how, in them, Hoagland creates a persona through tone, diction, and other features of his prose.

5. Sight is important to Hoagland and also to Annie Dillard, in "Sight into Insight" (NR 1140). Write an essay in which you compare the kinds of sight each describes and the uses to which each puts them.

Analytical Considerations

1. In the first section of "Brightness Visible" Hoagland talks about regaining his sight and what the world looks like when seen anew. What kinds of things does he describe?
2. Compare Hoagland's descriptions of seeing anew with Annie Dillard's descriptions of the world of the newly sighted in "Sight into Insight" (NR 1140). What difference does it make to their descriptions that Hoagland gained his knowledge from experience, while Dillard gained hers from reading Marius Von Senden's *Space and Sight*?
3. Have students look at some of Hoagland's opinions about God: for example, "he [the Old Testament God] did not have much appeal for me as a boy, though the Old Testament stories we heard in church . . . were riveting" (paragraph 10); "Jesus spoke for a God whose teachings I could better swallow" (paragraph 11); "[m]y own bias is against a monotheism so people-centered, and thus the Old Testament God who most appeals to me is least 'Hebrew'" (paragraph 13). Does Hoagland offer detail to explain and support these opinions? Where?
4. Where, in the central section of "Brightness Visible," does Hoagland make connections between nature and nature's God? What are they? How are these connections important to Hoagland's description of his religion as "American Transcendentalism" (paragraph 14) and "[t]ranscendentalism" (paragraph 22).
5. Hoagland often quotes various translations of a single passage from the Bible. Take one of these instances and look closely at it. What, if anything, does he gain from these multiple quotations?

Suggested Writing Assignments

1. Write an essay on a topic of your choosing that proceeds by leaps and digressions.
2. Annie Dillard, in "Sight and Insight" (NR 1140), cultivates mystical insight; Hoagland doesn't. Write an essay in which you discuss this difference between them and speculate on the reasons for it.
3. "No stretch of grief or the imagination, no precedent in science or logic," Hoagland writes, "can get a handle on this catastrophe—half of Creation extinguished in a single life span" (paragraph 16). Do research on the extinction of species and write a paper that extends and, if possible, documents Hoagland's remark.

GILBERT HIGHET

The Mystery of Zen

The Norton Reader, p. 1159; Shorter Edition, p. 658

In "The Mystery of Zen," Gilbert Highet, a well-regarded teacher and author of *The Art of Teaching* (1950), writes about a German philosopher, Eugen Herrigel, who studied archery under a Zen master for six years. Highet is at least as concerned with the method by which Herrigel learned as with the content of what he learned from his lengthy course. At a deeper and more abstract level, the essay confronts the difficulties of describing a dimension of human existence that, Highet concludes, cannot be analyzed but must be lived to be understood (paragraph 12).

In this essay Highet depends heavily upon a single source, Herrigel's *Zen in the Art of Archery* (1953). He credits it explicitly in his own text. He does not quote directly from it; presumably he summarizes and paraphrases. He does not provide footnotes. Most important, he brings to it clearly defined interests of his own that guarantee he will rearrange Herrigel's account and reshape it to his own purposes, that virtually guarantee he will not plagiarize. These features of Highet's essay are worth discussing with students, who in their writing often find themselves relying on a single source and uncertain about what does and what does not constitute plagiarism.

Questions from the NR10

1. In his essay Highet depends heavily on Eugen Herrigel's *Zen in the Art of Archery*. What does Highet himself bring to the essay? Mark passages in which he makes his own contributions and summarize them.
2. "Zen teachers," Highet observes, "seem to deny the power of language and thought altogether" (paragraph 18). How, then, does Highet manage to write about Zen?
3. Highet says Zen is "a religion rather than a philosophy" (paragraph 22). How has he led up to this conclusion? What definition of religion and philosophy does it imply?
4. In his essay Highet turns to criticism of Zen only at the end, while Jean-Paul Sartre, in "Existentialism" (NR 1168, SE 666), defends existentialism as he explains it. Consider the differences these two approaches make in the content, organization, and tone of the two essays. What might Highet's essay be like if he defended Zen throughout, Sartre's if he turned to criticism of existentialism only at the end?
5. Write an essay in which you describe learning to perform a physical action. Pay particular attention to what you learned through language, what through doing.

Analytical Considerations

1. Consider Highet's contrast between philosophical and Zen meditation (paragraph 15). Is Zen meditation a goal you would pursue?
2. Highet's discussion of mystical writers (paragraph 18) is worth considering in detail, for he dwells upon the insufficiency of language "to describe experiences which are too abstruse for words." In what situations and in what ways does language fail them? Why do they "fall back on imagery and analogy"?
3. Would Annie Dillard be a likely candidate for Zen meditation? Use her essay "Sight into Insight" (NR 1140) as evidence.

Suggested Writing Assignments

1. Highet refers to D. T. Suzuki's *Introduction to Zen Buddhism* as an authoritative text. Locate a passage in which Suzuki describes from the "inside"

something Highet describes from the "outside" and write an essay comparing their strategies. You may wish to consider which description works better for you and why.

2. Highet confuses *The Magnificent Seven*, an American film, with the Japanese film from which it was adapted, *The Seven Samurai*, but he remembers the scene in which the elderly samurai selects his comrades (paragraph 16). View *The Seven Samurai* with particular attention to this scene and write an essay in which you consider the differences between Kurosawa's cinematic representation and Highet's linguistic representation of swordplay.

3. Write an essay comparing *The Seven Samurai* with *The Magnificent Seven*. Consider, in particular, how compatible the Japanese film is with an American western and what notable changes were made in the American version.

4. Write an essay in which you, like Highet, depend heavily upon a single source and credit it in the text. Be sure, again like Highet, to bring your own interests to your source and to reshape it to your own purposes.

JEAN-PAUL SARTRE

Existentialism

The Norton Reader, p. 1168; Shorter Edition, p. 666

One of the most famous twentieth-century philosophers, Sartre developed his philosophy of existentialism in the 1940s; this essay is one of his attempts to define it and to refute charges made against it. Sartre enumerates these charges in the course of the essay: existentialism is a counsel of despair; it deprives humans of a standard of conduct; it is too inward-looking. (It was also regarded as a serious threat to religion; as Sartre claims in paragraph 31, existentialism is "nothing else than an attempt to draw all the consequences of a coherent atheistic position.")

The essay's opening is the most difficult part; once past the first few paragraphs, Sartre keeps matters simple and provides drawn-out examples to make his points. But his opening benefits from close analysis, which the questions below attempt to provide.

Sartre tries to distinguish his philosophy from Christianity on the one hand and Marxism on the other. He shares a great deal with both. Growing up in prewar France and attending parochial schools gave him early exposure to Roman Catholicism. And from the 1930s on he was a committed socialist, frequently aligning himself with the Communist party agenda, a kind of fellow traveler though not a member. He is careful to point out, though, that his political activism stems from his existentialism, not the other way around.

Questions from the NR10

1. "Existence precedes essence": this concept is central to Sartre's existential philosophy. What does he mean by it?
2. Sartre develops his essay by definition: existentialism, he says, enables us to understand the "actual content" of three terms: *anguish, forlornness,* and *despair* (paragraph 4). What are Sartre's definitions of these three terms? How does he distinguish among them?
3. Throughout this essay Sartre defends existentialism against criticism as he explains it, in contrast, for example, to Gilbert Highet, who, in "The Mystery of Zen" (NR 1159, SE 658), turns to criticism only at the end. Consider the differences these two approaches make in the content, organization, and tone of these two essays. What might Sartre's essay be like if he turned to criticism of existentialism only at the end, Highet's if he defended Zen throughout?
4. Sartre says "when we say that a man is responsible for himself, we do not only mean that he is responsible for his own individuality, but that he is responsible for all men" (paragraph 1). Write an essay explaining how, in the framework of existentialist beliefs, this paradoxical statement is true.

Analytical Considerations

1. The essay opens with large, sweeping statements. A look at the opening and closing of paragraph 1 reveals not a developed argument but a series of provocations. Mark them. Why do you think Sartre adopts this rhetorical strategy? What does he gain? What does he risk?
2. Sartre draws analogies among the patriarch Abraham, a madwoman, and himself (paragraphs 6–9). What dilemma do they share? How does each resolve it?
3. According to Sartre, "No general ethics can show you what is to be done. . ." (paragraph 20). What examples does he provide? What examples can you provide? What counter examples? Are they sufficient to call his generalization into question?

Suggested Writing Assignments

1. Write a paragraph in which you define "existentialism" without using Sartre's language.
2. Examine the term *existentialism* in at least two dictionaries and two encyclopedias. Write an essay on the commonly accepted meaning of the word. If you find differences in nuance or of substance among the entries, be sure to consider them. Also consider whether the entries appear to fit Sartre's own conception of existentialism.

SAMPLE SYLLABI

Great Ideas and Enduring Questions: Sample Syllabus

Each of the six units outlined below introduces a question central to human experience that has provoked response from writers and thinkers over many centuries. Each unit is designed to last two weeks. The first week concentrates on readings that can serve to sharpen critical thinking skills through discussion and writing. The second week allows time for conducting workshops on the students' essays and discussing additional essays that reflect on the central question of the unit. To supplement the content of any unit, instructors can invite students to bring in newspaper or magazine articles or other readings that put the central question in a contemporary light.

Identity: What Does It Mean to Be Human?

First week: Readings and draft of a writing assignment.

> John Donne, "No Man Is an Island"
> Stephen Jay Gould, "Our Allotted Lifetimes"
> Elisabeth Kübler-Ross, "On the Fear of Death"
> Sven Birkerts, "Homo Virtualis"

Assignment: Draft of a writing assignment suggested in the *Guide*.

Second week: Writing workshop, plus additional readings on the concept of identity within a special group. Alternatively, this unit might focus on "identity" in terms of ethnicity, gender, or sexual orientation.

> Zora Neale Hurston, "How It Feels to Be Colored Me"
> James Baldwin, "Stranger in the Village"
> Herb Goldberg, "In Harness: The Male Condition"
> Anna Quindlen, "Between the Sexes, A Great Divide"
> Andrew Sullivan, "What Is a Homosexual?"

Assignment: Writing workshop or peer review, followed by revision of draft. Alternative writing assignment, if desired, on identity and belonging.

Learning and Language: What Is the Purpose of Education?

First week: Readings and draft of a writing assignment.

> Frederick Douglass, "Learning to Read"
> William J. Scheick, "Books Oft Have Such a Charm"
> John Holt, "How Teachers Make Children Hate Reading"
> Richard Rodriguez, "Aria"

Benjamin R. Barber, "America Skips School"
Adrienne Rich, "Taking Women Students Seriously"

Assignment: Draft of writing assignment suggested in the *Guide*, especially Holt (p. 114), Douglass (p. 111), Scheick (p. 112), or Barber 1 (p. 118).

Second week: Writing workshop, plus additional assignments on language usage, if desired.

George Orwell, "Politics and the English Language"
Casey Miller and Kate Swift, "Who's in Charge of the English
    Language?"

Additional assignment: Analysis of a political "paid announcement" or newspaper editorial.

Memory, Imagination, and Expression: Why and How Do We Interpret Experience?

First week: Readings and draft of a writing assignment.

Northrop Frye, "The Motive for Metaphor"
N. Scott Momaday, "The Way to Rainy Mountain"
E. B. White, "Once More to the Lake"
Maya Angelou, "Graduation"

Assignment: Draft of a writing assignment suggested in the *Guide*, especially Momaday 2 (p. 45), White 1 (p. 18), or Angelou 1 (p. 2).

Second week: Writing workshop plus additional readings. Instructors may also wish to consider other nonverbal ways of interpreting experience using these essays.

H. Bruce Franklin, "From Realism to Virtual Reality: Images of
    America's Wars" (photography)
Aaron Copland, "How We Listen" (music)
Susan Allen Toth, "Going to the Movies" (film)
Susan Sontag, "A Century of Cinema" (film)

Assignment: Writing workshop or peer review, followed by revision of draft.

Nature and Technology: How Should We Live In Our Environment?

First week: Readings and draft of a writing assignment.

Margaret Atwood, "True North"
Noel Perrin: "Forever Virgin: The American View of America"

William Cronon, "The Trouble with Wilderness"
Chief Seattle, "Letter to President Pierce, 1855"
Terry Tempest Williams, "The Clan of One-Breasted Women"
E. B. White, "Progress and Change"

Assignment: Draft an essay for or against the existence of progress, using environmental issues as evidence. Alternatively, write a personal essay that describes an ideal or appropriate relation between human beings and the environment.

Second week: Writing workshops and additional readings.

Robert Finch, "Very Like a Whale"
Edward Abbey, "The Serpents of Paradise"
Richard Conniff, "Spineless Wonders: Leapers"

Assignment: Writing workshop or peer review, followed by revision of draft. An additional assignment could be a personal essay responding to nature and the natural world.

Freedom, Power, and Justice: What Is the Individual's Relationship to Government?

First week: Readings and draft of a writing assignment.

Niccolò Machiavelli, "The Morals of the Prince"
George Orwell, "Shooting an Elephant"
Martin Luther King, Jr., "Letter from Birmingham Jail"
Abraham Lincoln, "Second Inaugural Address"
Thomas Jefferson and Others, "Original Draft of the Declaration
    of Independence"
Elizabeth Cady Stanton, "Declaration of Sentiments and
    Resolutions"

Assignment: An assignment suggested in the *Guide*, especially Machiavelli 2 (p. 219), Orwell 1 (p. 215), King 1 and 3 (p. 229), and Stanton 3 (p. 223).

Second week: Writing workshop, plus additional readings. One topic for group discussion might be the politics of revision in the two versions of the "Declaration of Independence." An alternative topic might be the issue of justice for minority groups, as discussed by the following writers:

Lani Guinier, "The Tyranny of the Majority"
Kim Phillips-Feins, "Lotteryville, USA"

Assignment: Workshop on assignment from the first week, with an additional assignment on Jefferson or on the Guinier or Phillips-Fein essays.

Truth and Belief: How Do We Know Right from Wrong?

First week: Readings and draft of a writing assignment.

> Hannah Arendt, "Denmark and the Jews"
> Barbara Huttman, "A Crime of Compassion"
> Sallie Tisdale, "We Do Abortions Here: A Nurse's Story"
> Kildare Dobbs, "The Shatterer of Worlds"
> Paul Fussell, "Thank God for the Atom Bomb"
> Michael Sandel, "Last Rights"
> Michael Walzer, "Feed the Face"

Assignment: Draft of a writing assignment suggested in the *Guide*, especially Arendt 4 (p. 206), Tisdale 2 and 3 (p. 189), or one of the writing assignments for "Op-Eds."

Second week: Writing workshops, plus additional readings on myth, parable, and fable as means of conveying moral or ethical teachings.

> Plato, "The Allegory of the Cave"
> Zen Parables ("Muddy Road," "A Parable," "Learning to Be Silent")
> Jesus, "Parables of the Kingdom"

Assignment: Workshop on assignment from the first week, with perhaps an additional assignment to write (or rewrite) a parable that conveys a modern-day moral lesson.

Writing Across the Curriculum: Sample Syllabus

The second half of *The Norton Reader* is readily adaptable to a writing-across-the-curriculum course, whether one that emphasizes writing to learn or one that focuses on the rhetorical conventions of academic discourse. Instructors might simply choose five or six sections of the *Reader* and use a sampling of essays to construct a syllabus for such a course. We have outlined seven possible units corresponding to sections of the *Reader* but have integrated selections from other sections of the *Reader* into each unit so that multiple connections will emerge.

The seven units below are each designed to last for two weeks. If an instructor feels the pace is too fast or wishes to give additional reading or writing assignments, any unit could be expanded to three weeks—and, of course, an instructor might choose to use only four or five units.

The first week concentrates on readings that show conventions of critical thinking and writing in the discipline and that might serve, in some ways, as models for the students' own writing. The second week allows time for conducting workshops on the students' essays and for discussing additional essays that reflect on the nature and concerns of the discipline. The content of any unit might be supplemented with articles written by professors at one's own college or university, with visits from such professors to discuss their own work, or with newspaper and magazine articles that address similar issues as they are addressed to a general audience.

Education

First week: Education from the teacher's point of view.

> John Holt, "How Teachers Make Children Hate Reading"
> William G. Perry, Jr. "Examsmanship and the Liberal Arts: A Study in Educational Epistemology"
> Wayne C. Booth, "Boring from Within: The Art of the Freshman Essay"
> Adrienne Rich, "Taking Women Students Seriously"

Assignment: See suggestions in the *Guide* for the essays listed above.

Second week: Education from the learner's point of view.

> Frederick Douglass, "Learning to Read"
> William J. Scheick, "Books Oft Have Such a Charm"
> Eudora Welty, "One Writer's Beginnings"
> Maya Angelou, "Graduation"
> Maxine Hong Kingston, "Tongue-Tied"
> Richard Rodriguez, "Aria"

Assignment: A personal essay about an educational experience or one of the writing assignments suggested in the *Guide* for the above essays, especially Douglass 3 (p. 111), Welty 1 and 3 (p. 110), Angelou 2 (p. 2), Kingston 1 (p. 134), or Rodriguez 4 (p. 135).

Environmental Studies

First week: Readings and draft of a writing assignment.

> Robert Finch, "Very Like a Whale" (nature writing)
> Richard Conniff, "Spineless Wonders: Leapers" (nature writing)
> Alexander Petrunkevitch, "The Spider and the Wasp" (natural history)
> Edward Abbey, "The Serpents of Paradise" (environmental advocacy)
> Chief Seattle, "Letter to President Pierce, 1855" (environmental
> advocacy)
> Terry Tempest Williams, "The Clan of One-Breasted Women"
> (environmental advocacy)

Assignment: Draft either an essay about something in nature, whether an animal, plant, or place, or write an argument about an environmental issue, based on suggestions from the *Guide* for these essays.

Second week: Writing workshops and readings about contemporary environmental issues.

> Joseph Wood Krutch, "The Most Dangerous Predator" (preserving
> Baja)
> Noel Perrin, "Forever Virgin: The American View of America"
> (reflections on American attitudes)
> William Cronon, "The Trouble with Wilderness"
> (reflections on American attitudes)

Assignment: Writing workshop or peer review, followed by revision of draft. Because this unit is especially rich and diverse in its forms, it could be divided into two units, one on nature writing, another on environmental issues. Students might then try writing one essay of each kind.

Science

First week: Readings and draft of a writing assignment.

> John Henry Sloan et al., "Handgun Regulations, Crime, Assaults, and
> Homicide: A Tale of Two Cities" (scientific report in its standard
> form)
> Henry Wechsler, Andrea Davenport, George Dowdall, Barbara Moeykens,
> and Sonia Castillo "Health and Behavioral Consequences of
> Binge Drinking in College: A National Survey of Students at
> 140 Campuses" (scientific report in its standard form)

Melvin Konner, "Why the Reckless Survive" (social science drawing on
   scientific research)
Alexander Petrunkevitch, "The Spider and the Wasp" from "Nature
   and the Environment" (scientific observation of nature)

Assignment: Draft of a writing assignment suggested in the *Guide*, especially
those for Sloan et al. (p. 235), Petrunkevitch (p. 165), or Konner (p. 238).
Alternatively, ask students to conduct a survey of drinking habits on campus
(of the sort that Wechsler et al. did) and write up their findings in the form of
a scientific report.

Second week: Writing workshops, plus additional readings on technology or on
the nature of scientific thinking.

Neil Postman, "Virtual Students, Digital Classroom" (on computers)
Henry Petroski, "Little Things Can Mean a Lot" (on the Post-it)
Jacob Bronowski, "The Nature of Scientific Reasoning"
Thomas S. Kuhn, "The Route to Normal Science"
Stephen Jay Gould, "Darwin's Middle Road"

Assignment: Writing workshop or peer review, followed by revision of draft.
Alternatively, students might (1) write an account of the invention of some useful
object (as Petroski does) or (2) do additional readings and a writing assignment on
the nature of science and scientific thinking, as derived from the essays and from
the *Guide* entries for Bronowski, Kuhn, Gould, or Keller.

History

First week: Readings and draft of a writing assignment.

Barbara Tuchman, "'This Is the End of the World': The Black Death"
   (classic history)
Amitav Ghosh, "The Ghosts of Mrs. Gandhi" (public and personal
   history)
Hannah Arendt, "Denmark and the Jews" (history and moral
   philosophy)
Cherokee Memorials (historical document)
Walt Whitman, "Death of Abraham Lincoln" (historical document)

Assignment: Draft of a writing assignment suggested in the *Guide*, especially
those combining the students' personal experiences or knowledge of history with
official, public history—as in Ghosh's account.

Second week: Writing workshops, plus additional readings on the nature and
practice of writing history.

Frances FitzGerald, "Rewriting American History"
Edward Hallett Carr, "The Historian and His Facts"
Henry David Thoreau, "The Battle of the Ants"

Assignment: Writing workshop or peer review, followed by revision of draft. Use the readings for this week to help students reflect on the history assignments they are writing. Additional writing assignments on the nature of historical writing could be taken from the *Guide* entries for Thoreau 1 (p. 198), FitzGerald 1 (p. 210), or Carr 1 and 3 (p. 213).

Philosophy and Ethics

First week: Readings and draft of a writing assignment.

> Plato, "The Allegory of the Cave" (philosophical text)
> Martha Nussbaum, "The Idea of World Citizenship in Greek and
>   Roman Antiquity" (modern uses of classical philosophy)
> Gilbert Highet, "The Mystery of Zen" (philosophical discussion)
> Zen Parables (religious document)
> Paul Tillich, "The Riddle of Inequality" (philosophical discussion)
> Jean-Paul Sartre, "Existentialism" (philosophical text)

Assignment: Draft an essay that explores one of the above philosophies in greater depth. See writing assignment suggestions in the *Guide*, especially Plato 1 and 3 (p. 267), Sartre 1 and 2 (p. 286), or Tillich 1 and 2 (p. 278).

Second week: Writing workshops, plus additional readings. Because the philosophical positions presented above are so complex, instructors may wish to devote additional discussion to each. Alternatively, one might concentrate on ethical questions such as those raised by the following essays, all but one of which are from "Ethics":

> Kildare Dobbs, "The Shatterer of Worlds" (on the atomic bomb)
> Paul Fussell, "Thank God for the Atom Bomb" (on the atomic bomb)
> Barbara Huttman, "A Crime of Compassion" (euthanasia)
> Sallie Tisdale, "We Do Abortions Here: A Nurse's Story"
> Michael Levin, "The Case for Torture"

Assignment: Writing workshop or peer review, followed by revision of draft. Students who have chosen to write on the same issue might work together in small groups to test and refine their arguments.

Literature

First week: Readings on literature and draft of a writing assignment.

> Vladimir Nabokov, "Good Readers and Good Writers"
> Dagoberto Gilb, "Northeast Direct"
> Virginia Woolf, "What the Novelist Gives Us"
> Eudora Welty, "One Writer's Beginnings"
> Northrop Frye, "The Motive for Metaphor"
> Robert Frost, "Education by Poetry: A Meditative Monologue"

Supplementary reading: A short story by Nabokov, Welty, or Woolf or a poem by Frost.

Assignment: Draft of an assignment suggested in the *Guide*, especially Nabokov 2 and 3 (p. 251).

Second week: Writing workshop, plus additional readings in other arts. Instructors may wish to divide the readings listed above into two segments, one on fiction, the other on poetry; or they may wish to consider a second art form, such as movies or music.

> Susan Allen Toth, "Going to the Movies"
> Susan Sontag, "A Century of Cinema"
> H. Bruce Franklin, "From Realism to Virtual Reality: Images of
>   America's Wars" (war photography)
> Aaron Copland, "How We Listen" (music)

Assignment: Writing workshop or peer review, followed by revision of draft. For an assignment on film, see the questions in the *Reader* for Toth and Sontag, as well as the writing suggestions in the *Guide*, especially Toth 2 (p. 262) and Sontag 1 (p. 261).

Politics and Government

First week: Readings and writing assignment (draft).

> Niccolò Machiavelli, "The Morals of the Prince" (political treatise)
> Martin Luther King, Jr., "Letter from Birmingham Jail" (political
>   treatise)
> Jonathan Swift, "A Modest Proposal" (parody of political treatise)
> George Orwell, "Shooting an Elephant" (personal essay on
>   colonialism)
> Jamaica Kincaid, "The Ugly Tourist" (personal essay on colonialism)

Assignment: A writing assignment suggested in the *Guide*, especially Machiavelli 1 to 3 (p. 219), Orwell 1 (p. 215), or King 2 (p. 229).

Second week: Writing workshops, plus additional readings on American politics.

> Thomas Jefferson, "Original Draft of the Declaration of
>   Independence"
> Thomas Jefferson and Others, "The Declaration of Independence"
> Elizabeth Cady Stanton, "Declaration of Sentiments and Resolutions"
> Abraham Lincoln, "Second Inaugural Address"

Assignment: Workshop on assignment from the first week, with perhaps an additional assignment on Jefferson, Stanton, or Lincoln, as suggested in the *Guide*. Alternatively, this unit might focus on the "Declaration of Independence," its draft forms, and its influence on later documents such as Stanton's.

Race, Class, and Gender: Sample Syllabus

The Tenth Edition of *The Norton Reader* lends itself particularly well to extended classroom explorations of race, class, and gender. Many essays that directly address these issues are grouped together in separate sections (such as the end of "Cultural Critique," pp. 349–68, on gender, and 375–401, on race). But since essays in all parts of the book deal with race, class, and gender, we have outlined five possible two-week units. Instructors can assign any number of these units, since the selections do not overlap. Thus in a one-semester course an instructor may wish to assign the two-week unit "Race: A Variety of Perspectives," and the two-week unit "Gender: Women's and Men's Perspectives." A deeper examination of these issues is possible by assigning the additional two-week units on race and on gender.

We present these units as suggestions. If an instructor feels the pace is too fast or wishes to give additional reading or writing assignments, any of the five units could be expanded to three weeks. And the reading selections given in the five units do not exhaust all of *The Norton Reader*'s rich collection of essays touching on race, class, or gender. Instructors can make use of many additional essays from other parts of the book and may also want to assign other essays and reading selections from current books, newspapers, or periodicals.

In each of the five units, the first week serves to introduce the issue and includes an essay assignment. The second week allows time for workshops, for further drafts of the first week's essay, and for additional reading and writing assignments.

Race: The African American Experience

First week: Readings and draft of a writing assignment.

> Martin Luther King, Jr., "Letter from Birmingham Jail" (struggle for equal rights)
> Maya Angelou, "Graduation" (struggle for equal rights)
> James Baldwin, "Stranger in the Village" (confronting racism)
> Gloria Naylor, "Mommy, What Does 'Nigger' Mean?" (confronting racism)

Assignment: Describe whether you think these writers' dependence on their personal experience strengthens or weakens their case for racial equality. What does a writer gain from using his or her own experience? What are the potential losses or limitations?

Second week: Writing workshops and additional drafts of week one's writing assignment, along with essays that add complexity to the first week's readings.

> Zora Neale Hurston, "How It Feels to Be Colored Me"
> Henry Louis Gates, Jr., "In the Kitchen"
> June Jordan, "For My American Family: A Belated Tribute to a Legacy of Gifted Intelligence and Guts"

Assignment: Writing workshop or peer review, followed by revision of draft. All three of the second week's essays employ personal experience; however, in each case the arguments in favor of equality take a backseat to celebrations of the special qualities of life in the African American community. (It is useful to have students trace the arguments in favor of equality that are implicit in each essay.)

Race: A Variety of Perspectives

First week: Readings and draft of a writing assignment.

> Shelby Steele, "The Recoloring of Campus Life" (racial divisions on campus)
> Richard Rodriguez, "Aria" (the costs of success)
> Chief Seattle, "Letter to President Pierce, 1855" (Native Americans in search of dignity)
> Judith Ortiz Cofer, "More Room" (Latino concerns)
> Marianna De Marco Torgovnick, "On Being White, Female, and Born in Bensonhurst" (white consciousness of difference)

Assignment: Draft an essay about "making it" in American society and what has to be left behind. Use examples from your own experience, the week's readings, and perspectives of people you know about.

Second week: Writing workshops and additional drafts of week one's writing assignment, along with essays that add complexity to the first week's readings.

> Edward Rivera, "First Communion"
> Brent Staples, "Black Men and Public Space"
> Debra Dickerson, "Who Shot Johnny?"

Assignment: Writing workshop or peer review, followed by revision of draft. These additional essays are about failing to "make it" in acceptable ways. Rivera cannot receive his First Communion, while Staples cannot remain inconspicuous, no matter how hard he tries. The essays, in very different ways, raise questions about exactly what "making it" means.

Class

First week: Readings and draft of a writing assignment.

> Lars Eighner, "On Dumpster Diving" (homelessness)
> George Orwell, "Shooting an Elephant" (expectations about class)
> Niccolò Machiavelli, "The Morals of the Prince" (training for aristocrats)
> Kim Phillips-Fein, "Lotteryville, USA" (economic basis of gambling)

Assignment: Draft an essay on how these authors react to others who aren't of the same standing in society. What is their opinion of people who are higher or lower on the social ladder? How much do they identify with people who are at the same level they themselves are?

Second week: Writing workshops and additional drafts of week one's writing assignment, along with essays that add complexity to the first week's readings.

Jonathan Swift, "A Modest Proposal"

Assignment: Writing workshop or peer review, followed by revision of draft. The second week's readings stand in stark contrast to each other (and to the first week's readings as well). Students need to see that Swift, two centuries ago, rejects the meliorist solutions proposed by moderates and instead reacts with barely suppressed rage. (Some students need to be shown that Swift's "solution" is not merely ghoulishly clever but represents a moment of genuine despair about the possibility that any simple "project" can improve the lot of the poor.)

Gender: Women's and Men's Perspectives

First week: Readings and draft of a writing assignment.

Anna Quindlen, "Between the Sexes, A Great Divide" (journalistic observation)
Dorothy Allison, "Gun Crazy" (equal rights with weapons)
Paul Theroux, "Being a Man" (male perspective)
Scott Russell Sanders, "Looking at Women" (male perspective)
John McMurtry, "Kill 'Em! Crush 'Em! Eat 'Em Raw!" (sports and maleness)
Alice Walker, "Beauty: When the Other Dancer Is the Self" (self-esteem)

Assignment: Draft an essay about whether people consider the differences in men's and women's attitudes inherent in human nature or the product of society. Base your essay on the beliefs of those you know and of these writers.

Second week: Writing workshops and additional drafts of week one's writing assignment, along with essays that add complexity to the first week's readings.

Herb Goldberg, "In Harness: The Male Condition"
Betty Rollin, "Motherhood: Who Needs It?"
Gloria Anzaldúa, "How to Tame a Wild Tongue"

Assignment: Writing workshop or peer review, followed by revision of draft. These three essays can serve as test cases for the writing assignment students have been drafting. Discussion of Goldberg, Rollin, and Anzaldúa will help sharpen the drafts and allow students to evaluate the nature of the evidence they are using.

Gender: Women, Language, and Schooling

First week: Readings on literature and writing assignment (draft).

> Adrienne Rich, "Taking Women Students Seriously" (school)
> Dorothy Gies McGuigan, "To Be a Woman and a Scholar" (school)
> Casey Miller and Kate Swift, "Who's in Charge of the English
>   Language?" (language)
> Deborah Tannen, "Conversational Styles" (language)

Assignment: Using your own experience and the works you have read, describe the particular difficulties women have faced in schools. Then speculate on what it will take to overcome these obstacles, however large or small they seem in the present.

Second week: Writing workshop or peer review, followed by revision of draft.

> Maxine Hong Kingston, "Tongue-Tied" (training for women)
> Lord Chesterfield, "Letter to His Son" (training for men)

This follow-up lends itself particularly well to anecdotal evidence from class members about parental advice, warnings, and examples. Such testimony may not have much impact singly, but can be overwhelming when taken as an indication of broad cultural values transmitted from generation to generation.

An alternative is to have class members recall clichés and common sayings that embody male/female stereotypes.

Persuasion and Argument: Sample Syllabus

The Norton Reader lends itself to a course emphasizing persuasion and argument by including many essays that illustrate a range of argumentative strategies and *personae*. The sections "Ethics," "Politics and Government," and "Nature and the Environment" are the most concentrated sources of persuasive and argumentative essays: in the Regular Edition, "Ethics" has eight, "Politics and Government" seven, and "Nature and the Environment" six, while in the Shorter Edition "Ethics" has five, "Politics and Government" five, and "Nature and the Environment" three. In addition, a new section in the Regular Edition (though not in the Shorter Edition), "Op-Eds," has six. Appended to the end of this syllabus are the argumentative and persuasive essays in the Regular Edition listed by section; those that also appear in the Shorter Edition are asterisked.

At the same time *The Norton Reader* includes other kinds of essays that provide material for persuasive and argumentative essays and suggests assignments using them. Typical assignments for persuasive and argumentative essays, in both the *Reader* and the *Guide*, ask students to take a position and support it by drawing on their experience, observation, and reading.

This syllabus is set up for a fourteen-week semester. It contains five units of two weeks each and a four-week unit on a longer paper with attention to library research and documentation. It assigns students five papers in two drafts: a paper analyzing an essay, a personal report, two persuasive/argumentative essays, and a longer persuasive/argumentative paper using library research. It also assigns them a third draft of one of the persuasive/argumentative essays and, at the end of the course, in first draft only, an analysis of their experience in writing persuasion and argument. Any of these units can be repeated using additional essays; any of them can be dropped.

Class discussion should focus on purpose, evidence, *personae*, and audience, both in the essays assigned from *The Norton Reader* and in students' own writing. Both editions of *The Norton Reader* offer a rich variety of all these.

First week: Reading assignment: Read the following selections in the "Op-Eds" section.

> *Molly Ivins, "Get a Knife, Get a Dog, but Get Rid of Guns"
> Brent Staples, "Why Colleges Shower Their Students with A's"
> *Michiko Kakutani, "Portrait of the Artist as a Focus Group" (in
>   "Literature and the Arts" in the Shorter Edition)
> Michael J. Sandel, "Last Rights"
> Michael Walzer, "Feed the Face"

In-class: Analyze, for several of these selections, the author's purpose and evidence, the kind of persona the author creates, how, and for what audience. How effective is the author's evidence and persona?

Writing assignment (draft): Draft an essay about one of the selections in the "Op-Eds" section not discussed in class. Analyze what the author's evidence is, how it is deployed, what kind of persona the author creates, how, and for what audience. How effective do you find the author's evidence and persona? Append a paragraph in which you consider whether you, as a student, could adopt a similar persona or, if not, what kind of persona would be suitable to the audiences you will be addressing as a writer in college.

Second week: Reading assignment.

> *Michael Levin, "The Case for Torture" ("Ethics")
> Katha Pollitt, "Does a Literary Canon Matter?" ("Literature and the Arts")

In-class: Discuss evidence and *personae* in the Levin and Pollitt essays.

Writing assignment (revision): Divide into groups for peer review of drafts; revised drafts to be handed in at the next class.

Third week: Reading assignment.

> *Scott Russell Sanders, "Under the Influence" ("People, Places")
> *Andrew Sullivan, "What Is a Homosexual?" ("Human Nature")
> Barbara Huttman, "A Crime of Compassion" ("Op-Eds")
> Sallie Tisdale, "We Do Abortions Here: A Nurse's Story" ("Ethics")

In-class: Discuss several of these essays as narrative or exposition, and consider how they provide material that could be used in arguing a controversial issue.

Writing assignment (draft): Draft a personal essay based on an experience or experiences that will provide material to be used in arguing a controversial issue.

Fourth week: Reading assignment.

> *Maya Angelou, "Graduation" ("Personal Report")
> *Lars Eighner, "On Dumpster Diving" ("Personal Report")
> David Guterson, "Enclosed. Encyclopedic. Endured: The Mall of America" ("People, Places")
> Sven Birkerts, "Homo Virtualis" ("Human Nature")
> *Jessica Mitford, "Behind the Formaldehyde Curtain" ("Cultural Critique")

In-class: Discuss how one or more of these essays could be used as evidence in taking a position or in arguing for a change or changes.

Writing assignment (revision): Divide into groups for peer review of drafts; revised drafts to be handed in at the next class.

Fifth week: Reading assignment.

> *"Cherokee Memorials" ("History")
> *Lani Guinier, "The Tyranny of the Majority" ("Politics and Government")
> *Martin Luther King, Jr., "Letter from Birmingham Jail" ("Politics and Government")

In-class: Discuss evidence and *personae* in the "Cherokee Memorials" and the Guinier and King essays.

Writing assignment (draft): Draft a persuasive or argumentative essay that uses as evidence experience, observation, and reading of one of the essays above or any other essay in *The Norton Reader*.

Sixth week: Reading assignment.

> *Tom Regan, "The Case for Animal Rights" ("Ethics")
> *Carl Cohen, "The Case for the Use of Animals in Biochemical Research" ("Ethics")

In-class: Discuss the principles and values that underlie the disagreement between Regan and Cohen.

Writing assignment (revision): Divide into groups for peer review of drafts; revised drafts to be handed in at the next class.

Seventh week: Reading assignment.

> Thomas Jefferson, "Original Draft of the Declaration of Independence" ("Politics and Government")
> *Thomas Jefferson and Others, "The Declaration of Independence" ("Politics and Government")
> *Elizabeth Cady Stanton, "Declaration of Sentiments and Resolutions" ("Politics and Government")

In-class: Discuss syllogistic argument: a major premise, a minor premise, and a conclusion.

Writing assignment (draft): Draft an essay on animal rights or some other controversial topic that highlights the major premises (or principles and values) about which you and your opponents cannot agree.

Eighth week: Reading assignment.

> Sloan et al., "Handgun Regulations, Crime, Assaults, and Homicide: A Tale of Two Cities" ("Science")
> Wechsler et al., "Health and Behavioral Consequences of Binge Drinking: A National Survey of Students at 140 Campuses" ("Science")

Wechsler et al., "Too Many Colleges Are Still in Denial about Alcohol Abuse" ("Science")

In-class: Discuss the conventions of reporting scientific research and the rhetoric of Wechsler et al. as they report their research in the *New England Journal of Medicine* and argue from it in *The Chronicle of Higher Education*.

Writing assignment (revision): Divide into groups for peer review of drafts; revised drafts to be handed in at the next class.

Ninth week: Reading assignment: Read through the essays in either "Nature and the Environment" or "Ethics" or "Politics and Government," and begin library research in preparation for writing a persuasive or argumentative essay on an issue that appears in one of them.

In-class: Introduction to print and electronic resources in the library.

Writing assignment (draft): Brainstorm, make notes, list, free write—whatever works best to get you started—about what you know and what you need to know, where you are in your research, where you are going, and where you think you will come out.

Tenth week: Reading assignment: Continue library research.

Writing assignment (draft): Divide into groups for peer review of brainstorming, etc. Begin to draft a persuasive or argumentative essay that incorporates library research.

Eleventh week: In-class: Discuss the purposes of bibliography and notes, and review their form.

Writing assignment (draft): Divide into groups for peer review of drafts.

Twelfth week: Writing assignment: Divide into groups for peer review of bibliography and notes; final draft of essay that incorporates library research due.

Thirteenth week: Reading assignment: Read persuasive and argumentative essays in either "Cultural Critique" or "Education."

*Anthony Burgess, "Is America Falling Apart?" ("Cultural Critique")
*Betty Rollin, "Motherhood: Who Needs It?" ("Cultural Critique")
*Brent Staples, "Black Men and Public Space" ("Cultural Critique")
Benjamin R. Barber, "America Skips School" ("Education")
Caroline Bird, "College Is a Waste of Time and Money" ("Education")
*Adrienne Rich, "Taking Women Students Seriously" ("Education")

Writing assignment (draft): Draft an essay in which you review the papers you wrote this semester and analyze your strengths and difficulties in writing persuasion and argument.

Fourteenth week: Writing assignment (draft). Divide into groups, share drafts, and report to class the issues concerning persuasion and argument that emerged in the groups.

Assignment (revision): Revise one of your earlier papers from this course and hand it in; append a paragraph in which you describe what you aimed for in your revision.

Essays Exemplifying Persuasion and Argument (by section)

Human Nature

> *Stephen Jay Gould, "Our Allotted Lifetimes"

Cultural Critique

> *Anthony Burgess, "Is America Falling Apart?"
> *Betty Rollin, "Motherhood: Who Needs It?"
> *Brent Staples, "Black Men and Public Space"

Op-Eds

> *Molly Ivins, "Get a Knife, Get a Dog, but Get Rid of Guns" (in "Cultural Critique")
> Brent Staples, "Why Colleges Shower Their Students with A's"
> *Michiko Kakutani, "Portrait of the Artist as a Focus Group" (in "Literature and the Arts")
> Russell Baker, "American Fat"
> Michael J. Sandel, "Last Rights"
> Michael Walzer, "Feed the Face"

Education

> Benjamin R. Barber, "America Skips School"
> Caroline Bird, "College Is a Waste of Time and Money"
> *Adrienne Rich, "Taking Women Students Seriously"

Nature and the Environment

> *Carl Sagan, "The Abstractions of Beasts"
> *Chief Seattle, "Letter to President Pierce, 1855"
> Noel Perrin, "Forever Virgin: The American View of America"
> *William Cronon, "The Trouble with Wilderness"
> Joseph Wood Krutch, "The Most Dangerous Predator"
> *Terry Tempest Williams, "The Clan of One-Breasted Women"

Ethics

> Lord Chesterfield, "Letter to His Son"
> *Jonathan Rauch, "In Defense of Prejudice"
> James R. Kincaid, "Purloined Letters"
> *Michael Levin, "The Case for Torture"

*Tom Regan, "The Case for Animal Rights"
Carl Cohen, "The Case for the Use of Animals in Biochemical
    Research"
*Stephen Jay Gould, "The Terrifying Normalcy of AIDS"
*Paul Fussell, "Thank God for the Atom Bomb"

History

*Cherokee Memorials
*Hannah Arendt, "Denmark and the Jews"
Edward Hallett Carr, "The Historian and His Facts"

Politics and Government

*Jonathan Swift, "A Modest Proposal"
Thomas Jefferson, "Original Draft of the Declaration of
    Independence"
*Thomas Jefferson and Others, "The Declaration of Independence"
*Elizabeth Cady Stanton, "Declaration of Sentiments and
    Resolutions"
Abraham Lincoln, "Second Inaugural Address"
*Lani Guinier, "The Tyranny of the Majority"
*Martin Luther King, Jr., "Letter from Birmingham Jail"

Science

Henry Wechsler et al., "Too Many Colleges Are Still in Denial about
    Alcohol Abuse"
*Stephen Jay Gould, "Darwin's Middle Road"

Literature and the Arts

*Katha Pollitt, "Does a Literary Canon Matter?"

Philosophy and Religion

*Paul Tillich, "The Riddle of Inequality"

In Process: A Collaborative Approach to Reading and Writing: Sample Syllabus

Contributed by Dawn Rodrigues, Massachusetts College of Liberal Arts

The breadth of selections in *The Norton Reader* makes it easily adaptable to a collaborative approach to reading and writing. The units below are designed to last for two to three weeks each. If an instructor feels the pace is too fast or wishes to give additional reading or writing assignments, any unit can be simplified or expanded. The first week of each unit concentrates on reading the essays, finding a topic, and keeping an informal learning log; the second and third weeks focus on writing drafts and conducting workshops on the students' work.

I recommend that students keep a learning log, a three-ring notebook in which they record their in-class writing and homework writing exercises; a folder for all of their completed papers, including rough drafts; and a writing portfolio of their best work. At the end of the semester, the portfolio might include an expository essay, a documented research paper, a piece of the student's own choosing (a journal entry, a collage of brief free writings, or another essay or research-based paper), and a cover letter in which the student explains and reflects on the contents of the portfolio.

Paper 1: Autobiographical Essay

First week: Readings and learning log assignment.

> Zora Neale Hurston, "How It Feels to Be Colored Me"
> Nancy Mairs, "On Being a Cripple"
> Alice Walker, "Beauty: When the Other Dancer Is the Self"
> Henry Louis Gates, Jr., "In the Kitchen"
> Langston Hughes, "Salvation"
> Edward Rivera, "First Communion"

Learning log assignment: For each reading, select one of the two questions below:

1. Write about a personal memory triggered by the reading assignment.
2. Write about how your experiences are similar to or different from those described in the selection you read.

After students have responded in their learning logs to all of the essays, they should draft an autobiographical essay of their own.

Second week: Additional autobiographical essays, writing workshops, and second drafts.

> Scott Russell Sanders, "Looking at Women"
> Debra Dickerson, "Who Shot Johnny?"
> Frederick Douglas, "Learning to Read"
> William Scheick, "Books Oft Have Such a Charm"

Assignment: Write an autobiographical essay, using one or more of the selections you have read as inspiration for the essay. If none of the essays you have read provides that inspiration, you can choose another text—from a book you have read, from the feature section of the newspaper, or from another source—and use that as the basis for your essay.

Third week: Writing workshop or peer review, followed by revision of draft.

Paper 2: Synthesis Essay

This assignment calls for an argumentative essay in which students choose a single issue of interest to them, synthesize the viewpoints of several readings, find at least two additional readings from other sources, and then take a stand on the issue.

First week: Readings and learning log. For groups of argumentative essays, see "Persuasion and Argument: Sample Syllabus," pp. 304–309.

Learning log assignment: For each reading, do the following:

1. Summarize the main points of the selection.
2. Write a personal response or reaction to the selection.

Second week: Additional, outside readings chosen by students on an issue that both interests them and is connected to the assigned readings. Students draft analytical essays in which they synthesize different points of view and argue the position they think is most convincing.

Assignment: Find two selections from *The Norton Reader* or from other sources that relate to an issue in one of last week's assigned essays. Draft an essay in which you synthesize the argument of each essay, state your opinion on the issue, and try to persuade readers to think as you do or to take action along the lines of your opinion..

Third week: Writing workshops and revisions.

Paper 3: Synthesis of Group-Selected Readings

This assignment calls for students to write a paper with several classmates, synthesizing several readings from the *Reader*. The group can produce one traditional paper, or if they choose, they can produce a collection of individual pieces along with a summary of the group's consensus on an issue or their continuing dissensus. The paper can be revised as desired by students who wish to use it in their portfolios.

Each group proposes its own collection of readings and its own work plan. Each group presents its work to the class in the form of skits, panel discussions, or readings. In any case, the group's presentation should be more than simply turning in a completed paper.

First week: Selecting a subject area and getting into groups. The subject areas might be drawn from the following sections of the *Reader*:

Cultural Critique
Education
Language and Communication
Nature and the Environment
Politics and Government
Science
Literature and the Arts
Philosophy and Religion

Assignment: After selecting a subject area, get together with a group of students interested in pursuing the same general issue or topic. You should not formulate your specific paper topic until you have all read several essays. In your groups, you should:

1. Develop a list of readings relevant to your topic.
2. Determine how you would like to share readings (for example, by writing log entries and sharing them with one another or by assigning different group members the task of leading group discussion on a specific essay).
3. Turn in your plan so that the instructor will have a record of what you will be reading.

Second week: Group discussion on how to draft the essay, followed by actual draft.

Assignment: Devise a plan for drafting your group's essay. You might ask each person to do one section; you might all write drafts on the issue and then combine parts from each into one whole; or you might assemble around one computer and start drafting with one person typing while the others talk.

After you decide how to collaborate, decide how to share your responses to the readings. You might have each person write down one or two points that he or she thought interesting; or you might talk for a while, then write down your personal response to the discussion. You could then read one another's responses. Don't start working on your draft, however, until you come up with a working plan.

Third week: Groups revise their draft in their groups before turning in their final work.

Paper 4: Individual Papers Based on Another Group's Readings

Working with a group, students write individual papers based on the readings chosen by one of the other groups in the previous unit and in response to that group's final paper or papers. Students also write a summary and response for at least two additional essays related to the readings for this assignment.

Paper 5: Individualized Research Paper

The final research paper should grow out of students' personal interests in issues addressed during the term, either raised during class discussion or by one of the readings.

First week: Readings and learning log assignments. For suggested thematic groupings, see the sample syllabi in this *Guide* for "Great Ideas and Enduring Questions," pp. 291–94; "Writing Across the Curriculum," pp. 295–99; and "Race, Class, and Gender," pp. 300–303.

Assignment: Choose four new readings from *The Norton Reader* or from outside sources on a topic you would like to pursue in a research paper. Write learning log entries for each selection and try to arrive at a question you would like to pursue further. Then, find two additional outside sources on that question and write learning log entries for them.

Second week: Additional readings and draft of essay.

Assignment: Once you arrive at a question you wish to pursue, consult three to five additional sources. Draft an essay, using MLA style to document all sources you have consulted.

Third week: Writing workshop or peer review, followed by revision of draft.

NOTES

NOTES

NOTES

NOTES

NOTES

NOTES

NOTES

NOTES

NOTES

NOTES